STANDING AGAINST
THE WHIRLWIND

RELIGION IN AMERICA SERIES

Harry S. Stout, General Editor

THE FRANK S. AND ELIZABETH D. BREWER PRIZE ESSAY
FOR THE AMERICAN SOCIETY OF CHURCH HISTORY FOR 1993

STANDING AGAINST THE WHIRLWIND

Evangelical Episcopalians in Nineteenth-Century America

Diana Hochstedt Butler

New York   Oxford
OXFORD UNIVERSITY PRESS
1995

Oxford University Press

Oxford   New York
Athens   Auckland   Bangkok   Delhi   Bombay
Calcutta   Cape Town   Dar es Salaam   Delhi
Florence   Hong Kong   Istanbul   Karachi
Kuala Lumpur   Madras   Madrid   Melbourne
Mexico City   Nairobi   Paris   Singapore
Taipei   Tokyo   Toronto

and associated companies in
Berlin   Ibadan

Published by Oxford University Press, Inc.
198 Madison Avenue, New York, New York 10016

Oxford is a registered trademark of Oxford University Press

Library of Congress Cataloging-in-Publication Data

Butler, Diana Hochstedt, 1959–
Standing against the whirlwind : evangelical Episcopalians in
nineteenth-century America / Diana Hochstedt Butler.
p.   cm. -- (Religion in America series)
Revision of thesis (doctoral)--Duke University.
"The Frank S. and Elizabeth D. Brewer prize essay of the American
Society of Church History for 1993."
Includes biographical references and index.
ISBN 0-19-508542-6
1. Evangelicalism–Episcopal Church–History–19th century.
2. Episcopal Church–History–19th century.   3. Interdenominational
cooperation–United States–History–19th century.   I. Title.
II. Series: Religion in America series (Oxford University Press)
BX5925.B84   1995
283'.73–dc20   93-34323

1 3 5 7 9 8 6 4 2

Printed in the United States of America
on acid-free paper

For my parents,
J. Robert and Marcia Hochstedt,
who gave me two gifts: a love of learning
and the freedom to find my own faith

Preface

While a graduate student at Duke University in Durham, North Carolina, I attended an Episcopal church convulsed by controversy. Instead of brawling over inclusive language liturgies, women's ordination, or homosexual unions, these particular Episcopalians waged war over evangelical religion. Once a sleepy "country club" parish, they had called a new minister from a large, well-known, Evangelical Episcopal congregation in Pittsburgh. Within weeks of his arrival, the church split into pro- and antievangelical factions. The war for the soul of the parish had begun.

The proevangelical group argued that evangelical religion enriched the Episcopal Church through youth ministry, Bible preaching, and evangelistic outreach. The antievangelical faction identified evangelical religion with Jim Bakker and Jimmy Swaggart and accused its proponents of enthusiasm and hypocrisy. At the height of parish tension, I painstakingly tried to explain to one woman that she misunderstood the nature of evangelicalism. Historically, evangelical religion had long found a place within the Episcopal Church. She protested violently, "Oh no, it hasn't. We've always stood against those Baptists and Methodists! Just show me one history of the Episcopal Church which has anything good to say about evangelicals." Unable to resist a challenge, I scurried to the library to find a book defending my position. From my own study of nineteenth-century American religion, I knew the Episcopal Church once comprised a large Evangelical party. Much to my surprise, I found very little written about Evangelical Episcopalians – and what existed was often biased, negative, misleading, or simply wrong.

To some people, the term *Evangelical Episcopalian* seems odd if not downright oxymoronic. *Evangelical* connotes being born again, dramatic conversion testimonies, unambiguous morality, soul-winning television preachers, pulpit-centered Bible preaching, conservative theology, and, more often than not, conservative politics. *Episcopal* conjures up images of infants in christening gowns, decorous liturgy, sherry on the church lawn, trendy prelates, short homilies followed by ancient eucharistic prayers, and liberal views on theological, social, and political issues. In spite of such apparent contradictions, in recent years Evangelical Episcopalianism reemerged as a tradition within the Episcopal Church.

In the 1970s and 1980s, a new burst of evangelical enthusiasm made its way into America's mainstream Protestant denominations – including, to the surprise of many, the Episcopal Church. In the last two decades, charismatic and evangelical renewal organizations have proliferated, and recently "renewed" parishes have multiplied in size. A new Evangelical Episcopal seminary has enjoyed "remarkable success" in both student enrollment and financial contributions.[1] These developments occurred at a time when the Episcopal Church suffered one of the most dramatic membership declines in its history. In spite of its having brought new people into the church, not all Episcopalians have welcomed evangelical enthusiasm. Many have severely criticized such renewal movements. "There is an attempt," wrote one Episcopal theologian worried about contemporary evangelical encroachments, "to bring to this country a brand of English Evangelicalism which has never really found much acceptance here before."[2]

American Episcopalians do recognize a tradition of evangelical Anglicanism in their sister communion, the Church of England, but they persist in believing that evangelicalism is alien to their church. George Carey, an overt Anglican Evangelical, now archbishop of Canterbury, seems to epitomize this fundamental difference between the two churches. In contrast to British Anglicanism, American Episcopalianism recognizes little or no heritage of evangelical religion. Such beliefs illustrate an inexcusable case of historical blindness. In the nineteenth century, the American Episcopal Church (then called the Protestant Episcopal Church) contained a sizable Evangelical party deeply indebted and closely related to both Anglican and early American interdenominational evangelicalism. Throughout the church's first century of existence, evangelical religion contributed to the shape of Episcopal piety, theology, and mission.

I could not prove all this in the midst of the Durham church controversy. From my own research in primary materials, I knew of a long heritage of Evangelical Episcopalianism. In 1988, however, nobody believed me. After eighteen months of ecclesiastical warfare, the Evangelical Episcopal rector capitulated and retreated from Durham to find a new ministry. Defeated and confused, many of his supporters left the parish as well—a number left the Episcopal Church altogether. I changed parishes but remained an Episcopalian. Still bewildered by this unpleasant experience, I decided to write the book I could not find in the library—a history of the Evangelical party in the Episcopal Church.

To explore the vicissitudes, successes, and tribulations of nineteenth-century Evangelical Episcopalianism, I have chosen to look at the life and ministry of one of the party's great leaders, Charles Pettit McIlvaine, the second bishop of Ohio. Born in 1799, McIlvaine served the Episcopal Church for fifty-three years, from the early days of the Ohio frontier through the Civil War to the growth of urban America. He was an extremely complex person: a powerful and dynamic preacher, a capable theologian, a forceful and authoritarian bishop, an obdurate controversialist, a sentimental husband and father. He was deeply emotional, meditative and pious, and rigorously logical and committed to, above all else, what he believed to be truth. "Gentle, kindly and affectionate in his private intercourse," remarked one of his friends, "where truth and principle were concerned he was unyielding as a rock."[3] A man of intense activity, he also suffered from a lifelong struggle with nervousness, anxiety, and depression, which forced him to rest periodically from his duties by traveling to Europe.[4] He inspired great loyalty and devotion among those who admired and agreed with him. He was a formidable opponent to those with whom he disagreed.

Nearly everyone in the nineteenth century agreed on one thing, regarding McIlvaine, however: he stood above all others as the leader of the Episcopal Church's Evangelical party. Alfred Lee, a fellow bishop, wrote:

> Among the men thus honored by God to revive his work in this branch of his Church—a radiant constellation, whose record is in heaven—no name shines with greater lustre than that of Charles Pettit McIlvaine. No one was more widely known. No one did more to overcome unfriendly prejudices, command universal respect, and conciliate favor from those without his own Communion.[5]

Although Lee's affection was unbounded, McIlvaine's critics were equally impressed by the bishop's influence. Writing in 1890, William Wilberforce Newton recalled his "commanding social influence" and spoke of bishops Hobart and McIlvaine as having "guarded different sides of the citadel of the church."[6] "Amongst all evangelical enthusiasts," admitted one of his most hostile critics, "especially ladies, Bishop McIlvaine was a hero, a sort of apostolic divinity . . . though most violent and bitterly evangelical, with his high talents and fine elocution, was something superhuman."[7] He counted among his friends many of the great evangelical leaders of the day: Phillip Schaff, Charles Hodge, Henry Ward Beecher, Henry Boynton Smith, the Earl of Shaftesbury, Charles Simeon, Edward Bickersteth, J. B. and Charles Sumner, and Daniel Wilson. He was politically well connected as well; Salmon P. Chase, Abraham Lincoln, Jefferson Davis, the British royal family, and a number of military leaders were his personal friends. In his forty years as bishop of Ohio, his diocese grew from 17 to 106 clergy, 116 parishes, 9,745 communicants, and a missionary budget of over $200,000.[8] He published over seventy works in his lifetime. When he died in 1873, he was honored by the archbishop of Canterbury with a funeral service held at Westminster Abbey. In the nineteenth century, when someone wanted to know the thoughts, beliefs, or activities of American Evangelical Episcopalians, they asked Charles Pettit McIlvaine.

This study, however, is not a biography of Charles McIlvaine.[9] It tells the story of a party that McIlvaine led. At the height of its influence in the 1840s and 1850s, Evangelicals made up slightly less than half of the House of Bishops, approximately a third of the clergy, and an indeterminate number of laypeople.[10] In the mid-1830s, McIlvaine urged Evangelical Episcopalians to "stand" against "the whirlwind" of American revivalism and forge an orderly, decorous, church-oriented evangelicalism that would provide stability and promote the gospel in a rapidly changing world. As one of the chief architects of the Evangelical Episcopal vision, McIlvaine's career serves as a sort of window through which to view evangelical religion in the Episcopal Church.[11]

In the nineteenth century, the Episcopal Church was dominated by two great parties—the Evangelicals and the High Churchmen. Each vied for control of the church and offered competing versions of Episcopalianism. Each had a distinct agenda for the church, and their conflict centered on a very important issue for antebellum Americans: How could one be saved? The High Church party, drawing its inspiration from seventeenth-century Anglicanism, emphasized the role of the church and sacraments to prepare the soul for salvation. In the early years of the nineteenth century, Bishop John Henry Hobart of New York led a luminous revival of High Church theology. His personal power and charisma commended an alternative, liturgical Protestantism to revival-weary antebellum Americans. In contrast, Evangelicals believed salvation came through a born-again experience in which one would turn away from sins and follow Jesus' call to service, moral purity, and "heart-felt" spirituality. Influenced by the eighteenth-century Great Awakening and Evangelical Revival, these Episcopalians created an orderly, liturgical evangelicalism which, they believed, combined the best of both Anglicanism and evangelical religion. Often at odds, High Churchmen and Evangelicals envisioned two different identities for the Episcopal Church.[12]

The story of Evangelical Episcopalians has been largely lost to both the Episcopal Church and American religious history. It is a story of a group of evangelicals committed to a liturgical church with aristocratic-type polity who tried to make their church appeal to antiformalist, democratic Americans while, at the same time, they retained the doctrines and piety of evangelical religion. It is the story of a fight for denominational identity. They brought to that fight great strength, canny strategies, deep spirituality, and overwhelming devotion. After a century of battle, and having won a few victories, they eventually lost. Their story, however, is worth telling. By standing against the whirlwinds of their age, they still tell much about continuities and change in nineteenth-century American religion and the history of the Episcopal Church.

I have long awaited the opportunity to thank the many friends and colleagues who contributed to this project. My greatest debt is to George Marsden, who not only taught me the research skills and interpretive questions of American religious history but also gave me a vision for the art of history in all its creativity, narrative power, and grace. As teacher and friend, his insightful guidance in both my life and vocation is warmly appreciated.

The committee members who guided this work in its dissertation incarnation deserve much praise. Robert Bruce Mullin helped shape the original idea, never failed to interject High Church opinions, and served as an unofficial second advisor during George Marsden's sabbatical year. Russell Richey saved me from a multitude of mistakes regarding Methodism; Ted Campbell kept reminding me of British perspectives; and Grant Wacker always asked provocative questions. A critical yet congenial committee, they willingly lent their scholarly expertise to make this a better book.

I want to thank those who attend the summer meetings of the Institute for the Study of American Evangelicals—especially George Marsden, Grant Wacker, Mark Noll, Nathan Hatch, Harry Stout, Edith Blumhofer, Randall Balmer, Michael Hamilton, and, although not herself a historian, Lucie Marsden, all of whom served as informal influences on this work. A sort of academic family, these scholars and friends have given me more than they know in terms of support, advice, friendship, and encouragement. They model the grace of the gospel better than most of the evangelicals we commonly study. In trying to express thanks for these gifts, my sense of gratitude far outstrips my descriptive power.

Others contributed suggestions by reading the whole or parts: Allen Guelzo, Kathryn Long, Jonathan Wilson, Michelle Woodhouse, Buck Butler, Todd Granger, and Timothy Kimbrough. Special thanks to Nancy Favor Phinney, David Mills, and Rebecca Adams for editorial comments. Steve Baker, a promising and capable student, handled many tedious, last-minute computer tasks.

The personnel in the interlibrary loan department at Perkins Library, Duke University, deserve special mention. Their patience and persistence—especially that of Linda Purnell—secured a large number of rare materials for my use. In addition, I wish to thank Jamie Peelle and the late Thomas Greenslade at the Olin Library, Kenyon College, Gambier, Ohio; Garner Raney, the Maryland Diocesan Archives, Episcopal Diocesan House, Baltimore, Maryland; Ellen Slack, Pennsylvania Historical Society, Philadelphia, Pennsylvania; and Donald Shepherd, Ohio Diocesan Archives, Cleveland, Ohio. All these people demonstrated a high commitment to scholarship. Without them, I would have no story to tell.

During various stages of this project, I was supported financially by the Graduate School of Duke University; the Institute for the Study of American Evangelicals in Wheaton, Illinois; the Louisville Institute for the Study of Protestantism and American Culture at Louisville, Kentucky; and my current academic home, Westmont College in Santa Barbara, California.

I will never forget being awakened at 6:30 A.M. by a phone call from Stephen Stein of Indiana University telling me that this work had won the Brewer Prize of the American Society of Church History! This is a great honor, and I thank the prize committee and the society for their gracious award.

Finally, to Chip and Carol Nix: here is the book I promised long ago. Although we have traveled many difficult miles since Durham, I always appreciate the love you show me and the good news that you both embody.

D.H.B.

Santa Barbara, California
June 1993

Notes

1. David E. Sumner, *The Episcopal Church's History, 1945–1985* (Wilton, Conn., 1987), 103–104. See also his chapter on renewal movements, 120–130.
2. Urban T. Holmes, "Education for Liturgy: An Unfinished Symphony in Four Movements," in *Worship Points the Way: A Celebration of the Life and Work of Massey Hamilton Shepherd, Jr.*, ed. Malcolm C. Burson (New York, 1981), 138.
3. Alfred Lee, *In Memoriam. Charles Pettit McIlvaine* (Cleveland, 1873), 18.
4. Mark H. Hall, "Bishop McIlvaine: The Reluctant Frontiersman," *Historical Magazine of the Protestant Episcopal Church* 44 (1975): 81–96, identified this "mental disease" as a fundamental flaw in McIlvaine's personality stemming from his theological Calvinism. This does not seem entirely correct to me. McIlvaine suffered, as did many other men and women of his class and time, from what appears to be some sort of anxious depression. It

was extremely common for such sufferers to travel to Europe for rest. This, along with McIlvaine's preoccupation with death (which is also identified as mentally unbalanced), was a common part of the nineteenth-century world. For the melancholy aspect of antebellum evangelicalism, see Lewis O. Saum, *The Popular Mood of Pre-Civil War America* (Westport, Conn., 1980).

5. Lee, *In Memoriam*, 11.

6. William Wilberforce Newton, *Dr. Muhlenberg* (Boston and New York, 1890), 233–234.

7. Clarence E. Walworth, *The Oxford Movement in America* (New York, 1895; reprint, New York, 1974), 165.

8. This is a substantial number of communicants given the rigorous requirements McIlvaine placed on confirmation in his diocese.

9. Although my work is the closest thing to one that exists. There is one very good nineteenth-century biography of McIlvaine: William Carus, ed., *Memorials of the Rt. Rev. Charles Pettit McIlvaine, D.D., D.C.L.* (New York, 1882). Carus is an excellent source of now-lost material and a goldmine for anyone interested in the relationship between nineteenth-century American and British evangelicalism. From the point of view of an American religious historian, however, Carus's book is limited by its Anglican Evangelical perspective. The only modern source is a short dissertation by Loran Dale Pugh, "Bishop Charles Pettit McIlvaine: The Faithful Evangel" (Ph.D. diss., Duke University, 1985).

10. Writing in 1856, Presbyterian minister Robert Baird identified half of the Episcopal Church's bishops and two-thirds of its clergymen as Evangelicals. Even taking into account Baird's proevangelical agenda, his number for the bishops is about right. While other nineteenth-century sources repeat the percentage of clergy, the figure is probably too high. Nearly all nineteenth-century sources, while not particular about numbers, comment on the influence, strength, size, and vitality of the Evangelical party–particularly in the 1830s, 1840s, and 1850s. Robert Baird, *Religion in America; or an Account of the Origin. Relation to the State, and Present Condition of the Evangelical Churches in the United States* (New York, 1856), 444–445. Baird generally defined evangelical as those who held to the theology of the Protestant reformation, emphasized experiential religion and preaching, participated in voluntary societies, and practiced evangelical piety.

11. The choice of McIlvaine as a "window" into the Evangelical Episcopal world created three interpretative biases: (a) this is largely a study of the northern and western expression of the party; (b) this is a study of clerics and bishops; and (c) because it is a study of a fight over church identity, there is a lack of Evangelical Episcopal women in these pages. The omission of women does not mean Episcopal women were not attracted to evangelical religion. They were. Women were active, as were upper-class nineteenth-century women generally, in voluntary societies, mission work, Sunday school teaching, revivals, and prayer meetings–all intrinsic parts of the evangelical program in the Episcopal Church. Women's names appear in abundance on lists of church patrons and financial contributors. Because the church barred them from formal ministry, their status limited their participation in the institutional debates over church identity. Since this study focuses on church conflict, it does not include the public voices of women because they were not permitted to take part in this clerical discourse. Evangelical clerics needed women to carry out their program. They made up most of the church membership, accounted for the largest number of conversions, and did most of the work on a lay level. Without Evangelical women, the Evangelical clergy would not have succeeded. Despite their activism and support, these women were not allowed an official role in shaping the Evangelical program; they did, however, shape Evangelical Episcopalianism on informal levels. Evidence exists that women took the public arguments quite seriously. There is also a notable lack of research on

evangelical women in the Episcopal Church. Mary Sudman Donovan's *A Different Call: Women's Ministries in the Episcopal Church, 1850–1920* (Wilton, Conn., 1986) concentrates on Anglo-Catholic and Broad Church women following the historiographic bias of Episcopal studies generally. The newer *Episcopal Women: Gender, Spirituality and Commitment in an American Mainline Denomination*, ed. Catherine M. Prelinger, (New York and Oxford, 1992), deals primarily with the twentieth century. I was aware of this lack as I researched this book and have attempted to integrate findings on evangelical women within the text and notes. For a fuller discussion of these biases, see Diana Hochstedt Butler, "Standing Against the Whirlwind: The Evangelical Party in the 19th Century Protestant Episcopal Church" (Ph.D. diss., Duke University, 1991).

12. The High Church tradition has fared a bit better than Evangelicalism in historical studies. But even with it, the most significant study of the High Church party is very recent: Robert Bruce Mullin's *Episcopal Vision/American Reality: High Church Theology and Social Thought in Evangelical America* (New Haven and London, 1986).

A note on terminology: I recognize the importance of inclusive language, but, quite frankly, could think of no "inclusive" terms to replace *High Churchman* and *churchmanship* that retain their simplicity or meaning. *Evangelical* does not share this linguistic problem. Occasionally, I have inserted something like High Church *partisans* or *colleagues* to encourage the reader to remember that women were also part of the High Church movement. By and large, however, I retain the nineteenth-century usage of the party label. *Churchmanship* should be considered inclusive throughout the text because it includes women's views and opinions. Emily McIlvaine, the wife of Bishop Charles McIlvaine, for example, was vocally Evangelical in her churchmanship. *Church-style* or *churchpersonship* does not seem to capture the nineteenth-century sense of the term. In addition, the word *evangelical* is rendered with a capital *E* to denote the Evangelical party in the Episcopal Church. With a small *e*, it refers to either the evangelical religion as a whole or distinctive aspects of its theology as practice. For example, Charles McIlvaine was both an *Evangelical*–that is a member of a church party–and an *evangelical*–a certain kind of pietistic Protestant.

Contents

STANDING AGAINST
THE WHIRLWIND

"The restless, insubordinate and innovating spirit of the times . . . these bitter things are some of the fruits already reaped, for which multitudes of sober-minded Christians, of all names, are in great mourning, lamenting after times that with many have passed away—times in order and peace, of government and soberness—anxiously casting about for some remedy, or at least some refuge, till this storm be overpast. . . . They that sow the wind must reap the whirlwind.

These institutions, Episcopal and Liturgical, based upon articles of faith so evangelical . . . are the only ones that bid fair to stand unmutilated . . . (by) the tastes of the day. . . . By all means let us stand."

Charles Pettit McIlvaine, 1836
*Present Condition and Chief Want
of the Church*

1

From Enthusiasm to Identity:
An Evangelical Revolution
in the Episcopal Church,
1740–1820

On October 30, 1739, revivalist George Whitefield returned to America. Previously an Anglican missionary to Georgia, he had determined to revisit the colonies "to preach the Gospel in every province in America."[1] Not everyone anticipated his return eagerly; young Whitefield's reputation as a controversial preacher preceded him. For years, he had agitated within the Church of England, preaching the necessity of being "born again"—one must feel one's sins, repent, believe in Jesus Christ, and experience a new birth for salvation; only those so reborn were true Christians. He attacked formalism, spiritual deadness, and salvation by works—all aspects of his church. Multitudes received this message with enthusiasm and popularly acclaimed the messenger. Not everyone in England agreed with him, but anyone interested in religion knew of him. Whitefield's return to America was no inauspicious event; it was a triumphal entry.

While many colonial American church leaders hailed the Rev. Whitefield, others proceeded to vilify him. Within a matter of months, Anglican ministers in Philadelphia, Charleston, New York, and Boston refused him access to their pulpits, closed their churches to his meetings, and wrote bitter attacks criticizing him and his message. Whitefield must have felt betrayed: these ministers were not members of some competing denomination; they were his brothers in Church of England orders. No single American group rejected him with more anger and invective than his fellow clergy. Recalled Whitefield of one clergyman's attack: "Had some infernal spirit, been sent to draw my picture, I think it scarcely possible that he could have painted me in more horrid colours."[2]

Whitefield was referring to the Rev. Alexander Garden, the Anglican commissary in South Carolina.[3] One of Whitefield's most vocal critics, Garden publicly denounced Whitefield's message. The revivalists, he argued, "begin at *Regeneration or the New-Birth . . . that they are the Children of God*: that is, *regenerate or born again*," and "that in this *Act* or Work of *Regeneration, we are wholly* and *absolutely passive*." No act of moral or religious duty, no sacrament, and no obedience to religious ritual could encourage or instill salvation. Garden argued that this was

3

not the doctrine of the Church of England. "My brethren," he warned, "the Work of *Regeneration* is not the Work of a *Moment*, a sudden *instantaneous* Work . . . but a *gradual* and *co-operative* Work of the *Holy Spirit,* joining in with our *Understandings*, and leading us on by *Reason and Persuasion*, from one Degree to another, of Faith, good Dispositions, Act and Habits of Piety."[4] Garden's theology followed the traditions of Restoration Anglicanism and echoed the dominant position of the Church of England at the time. Drawing from seventeenth-century Anglican divines, particularly George Bull and Jeremy Taylor, Anglicans in colonial America argued that, on account of Christ, God accepted human faith and spiritual endeavors before justification. Through both faith and good works, men and women cooperated with God's grace in salvation. As a result of this theology, Anglican moralists depreciated the Reformation doctrine of justification by faith alone and emphasized human participation in salvation[5] – and it was this point on which Whitefield attacked Anglican theology, by self-consciously preaching the Reformation doctrine of justification by faith alone.

To many Anglican clergy, Whitefield's message of personal salvation appeared both un-Anglican and enthusiastic – to them, *enthusiasm* smacked of Puritanism, and Puritanism reminded Anglican clergy of their seventeenth-century persecution:

> Look back to the *Oliverian* Days, what Ruin and Desolation *such Pretenders* brought upon the Kingdom! How did they swarm throughout the Nation! A *Parliament;* – even an *Army* all Saints, Preachers, spiritual and regenerate Men! And yet alas, how were they *divided* and *subdivided* by the *Spirit* into 1000 Sects, Sorts and Divisions, 'till nothing but *Confusion* as a Cloud covered the whole Face of the Land.[6]

The case was clear: for Anglican ministers, Whitefield's experiential new birth meant enthusiasm, and enthusiasm led to social disruption, radical politics, and sectarianism.[7] In spite of Whitefield's impeccable Church of England credentials, most Anglican colonial leaders found his brand of religious revivalism alien to the Anglican tradition.[8]

But Alexander Garden and his eighteenth-century colleagues did not have the last word on Anglican enthusiasm in America. By the early nineteenth century, Enlightenment Anglicanism was losing intellectual dominance in the newly democratic country.[9] On a national level, revivalist evangelical religion was fast becoming a sort of religious establishment. During the early years of the republic, new evangelical leaders arose in the young Protestant Episcopal Church. They wanted to establish an evangelical identity for the new church which would be, as they believed, more biblical than Restoration Anglicanism and would appeal to the new republic's citizens.

The need to be born again, as Whitefield had preached a few decades earlier, formed the very center of Evangelical Episcopal identity: *"If any man be in Christ,"* proclaimed the Rev. Charles Pettit McIlvaine, *"he is a new creature.* The new birth – regeneration, *spiritual* regeneration – [lay] at the basis of all saving religion in the heart."[10] This *new birth*, a spiritual experience, changed the mind and heart by conversion: the old sin nature passed away, and the individual became a new creature in Jesus Christ. No human agency, moral effort, or religious rite could effect this change—it was wholly and completely a gift of God, given in grace and known experientially by the believer. McIlvaine argued that this was—and always had been—the doctrine of the Church of England and the Episcopal Church. Other Episcopal clergymen agreed. "There is but one way of salvation," stated Bishop Gregory T. Bedell: "It is through the atonement of our Lord Jesus Christ, and through faith in his name. Men must repent, believe, accept Christ as Saviour. Doing this they would be saved; not to do it was to be eternally damned."[11] Theology professor William Sparrow agreed: "The everlasting cry of the Evangelical orthodox [is] 'ye must be born again.' "[12]

Although some Episcopalians, such as Bishop John Henry Hobart of New York, echoed Garden's reservations about the sectarian and antichurch tendencies of evangelical religion, in less than seventy years nothing short of a revolution had occurred in the leadership of the Protestant Episcopal Church. During the eighteenth century, only a few Anglican clergymen preached an evangelical gospel; in the nineteenth century, a number of influential Episcopal bishops and clergymen preached a gospel of experiential faith not unlike other American evangelical ministers. What caused such a change? In the difficult years following the Revolutionary War, the older Anglican moralist and rationalist tradition was eclipsed by two new, often-contending parties: Evangelical and High Church Episcopalianism. Each claimed that it was the truest expression of American Anglicanism. Each claimed their own party distinctives to be the identity of the new Protestant Episcopal Church. Each was guided by youthful, visionary leadership. For the next fifty years, conflict in the Episcopal Church would revolve around these competing visions and the attempt of leaders from both sides to capture the soul of the church.

In many ways, the growth of evangelical religion in the Episcopal Church was part of its Americanization. Evangelical religion had always had a history within the Anglican and Episcopal churches in America, usually as a lay movement. After the American Revolution, however, it attracted powerful and visionary young leaders, who institutionalized a religious movement and created an evangelical identity for the Episcopal Church. They envisioned the *forms* and *rituals* of a liturgical, theologically rich, Protestant church enlivened by the *spirit* of American evangelicalism. They understood their church as "strictly Protestant and strictly Evangelical."[13] Based on their interpretation of Protestant and Evangelical, they created a church identity that would appeal to the citizens of the new republic: an orderly, and yet still democratic, vision of Evangelical Episcopalianism.

Evangelical Religion and the Episcopal Church

In spite of the disdain of colonial Anglican leaders like Alexander Garden for "enthusiasm," evangelical religion infiltrated American Anglicanism from the First Great Awakening in the 1740s onward. As the established church in a number of colonies during the first awakening, Anglican leaders felt that evangelical religion undermined social order, Anglican theology, and morality; with only few exceptions, then, the clergy rejected evangelicalism. Anglican laypeople, however, often embraced revivalist religion and retained their church ties while attending Methodist meetings; thus, the laity advanced the cause of evangelicalism within colonial Anglicanism.

In the eighteenth century, there were three interconnected aspects of Anglican evangelical renewal: the Whitefieldian revival, the Methodist movement, and the settled evangelical Anglican clergy. Initially, their boundaries were vague: many Anglicans moved freely among all three, and support for one part of the revival implied support for the whole. Methodist missionaries, Whitefieldian itinerants, and evangelical Anglican clergy worked together for the spiritual renewal of colonial Anglicanism. However, when the popular Methodist movement became a separate church and after many of Whitefield's followers joined Presbyterian, Baptist, or Congregational churches, much of the evangelical laity left Anglicanism for other churches. So it was the third group, the settled Anglican clergy, by far the smallest, who laid the foundation for the nineteenth-century church's evangelical wing.[14]

Although historians have generally pictured Anglican churches as shelters from the Great Awakening, some parishes did split over Whitefield's preaching.[15] There is also rough geographic correspondence between the strength of the Church of England and the development of revivalism. For instance, Anglicanism was very strong in Delaware, Maryland, and Virginia, the Delmarva peninsula, the area one historian has called the "garden of American Methodism."[16] Laymen and -women listened anxiously to the message of revivalist preachers, although sometimes little more than out of curiosity. The spiritual rigor of the Methodists attracted many who flocked to their meetings, however. Genteel Anglican women, such as Virginia aristocrats Mary Randolph Meade and Frances Tasker Carter, were especially attracted to the evangelical message, and after they experienced new birth, they promoted the evangelical religion.[17] In Philadelphia, a group of prorevival laymen and -women broke from Christ Church in 1760 and founded St. Paul's Church after Whitefield's associate, the Rev. William McClenachan, was forbidden access to their pulpit. St. Paul's evangelical laity did not merely invite revivalist McClenachan to preach but called him as their first rector.[18] Then, when Whitefield returned to Philadelphia in 1763, he was also invited to preach at St. Paul's, and, after a twenty-three year absence, in the other two Anglican churches as well. After McClenachan resigned in 1765, St. Paul's lay leaders called the Rev. William Romaine, the well-known English Evangelical leader, to be their rector, but Romaine's commitment to his London parish prevented him from accepting their offer. By the 1760s, through the influence of Whitefield's preaching and Methodism, revival religion was making headway among Anglican laity despite strong resistance from the clergy.

Although they were not large in number, some settled Anglican clergymen embraced the revival. In addition to McClenachan, clergy in Virginia, South Carolina, and Georgia allowed Whitefield to preach in their churches—and often agreed with him. Devereux Jarratt, minister of Bath parish in Virginia, preached revival and openly admired both Whitefield and John Wesley.[19] In the Chesapeake Bay area, Anglican clergymen Hugh Neill, Samuel Magaw, and Sydenham Thorne promoted evangelical piety (both Neill and Magaw later served as rectors at

Philadelphia's St. Paul's). In New Jersey, missionary Uzal Ogden of the Society for the Propagation of the Gospel (SPG) favored evangelical preaching and administered the sacraments at Methodist meetings. English Methodist missionary Joseph Pilmore and Maryland-born Methodist exhorter William Duke both considered themselves faithful members of the Church of England and remained Anglicans (both secured Episcopal orders) after the American Methodists formed their own church, and William Percy, a chaplain of the Lady Selina Huntingdon, served Georgia and South Carolina parishes, preaching evangelical religion before and during the Revolution. It is important to remember that the Methodist missionaries were still members of the Church of England when they preached the lively piety of the revival.

Most of the settled Anglican clergymen and a number of SPG missionaries in America rejected the enthusiasm of the Great Awakening, however; with some notable exceptions, the majority of them were opposed to evangelical religion. One historian has argued that these "ministers immunized their congregations against the evangelical virus, and thus limited the Awakening's influence."[20] Because of the resistance of Anglican leaders, the Church of England in America was never engulfed by the Great Awakening. The growth of Methodism, however, certainly shows that Anglican laity were never completely "immunized" and that, for many, evangelicalism was a significant force. In spite of clerical hostility, by the 1760s evangelical religion was making slow inroads into some Anglican churches through the laity, particularly in the middle and southern colonies.[21]

Immediately following the Revolution, most Americans associated Anglicanism with Toryism and the Church of England had lost its credibility. Those who remained in the church represented Anglicanism's various theological traditions: rationalism, evangelicalism, and High Church. The patriot William White, whose theology was an admixture of rationalism and Broad Church polity, forged a compromise with the High Church of Samuel Seabury and established a governmental basis for a new American church. In the meantime, evangelical clergy and laymen, such as Joseph Pilmore, Samuel Magaw, Francis Scott Key, and John Jay, actively contributed to forming the new institution. In winter 1787, William White and John Wesley attempted to meet and discuss the future of Methodism within the new church. The meeting never occurred, but the attempt shows that White was interested in keeping the revival movement within the church.[22] Thus in the formation of the church, Episcopalians of every theological opinion—rationalist, evangelical, and High Church—cooperated. The compromises among these leaders gave the church a unified national structure but, by the end of the eighteenth century, left the church in theological confusion.[23]

Problems Facing the American Episcopal Church

In the years following 1776, Anglican churches in America were clearly in crisis. Anglicanism had been the established church in most of the colonies and was associated with loyalty to colonial governors and the crown. During the Revolution, the association with the establishment created a number of problems for members of the Church of England. First was the problem of loyalty: Could Anglicans support the American effort against England? Second was the problem of church organization and bishops: Once the tie with England was broken and access to bishops was cut off, how could the church ordain ministers and perpetuate itself? Third was the problem of identity: How could a hierarchically ordered church survive in the new, democratic republic? During and after the war, the colonists' historic suspicion of prelates intensified and the idea of English episcopacy was treasonous; American Christians who favored an episcopally ordered church were in trouble. During the Revolution almost all the Anglican churches closed their doors. These questions were pointed: How could they retain the Anglican episcopacy without a connection to the Church of England?[24]

The first problem, that of loyalty, proved painful for Anglicans. The clergy were required to swear an oath of allegiance to the monarch's supremacy, and American clergy were under the direct jurisdiction of the bishop of London. Oaths to a king were no doubt difficult for Anglican clergy to break, and many Anglican clergymen remained loyal to England. The clergy tended to be split fairly evenly on the question, but the majority of the laity sided with the Revolutionaries. Laity, while under no oath of allegiance, nevertheless participated weekly in prayers for the ruler and the royal family. Some churches eliminated these prayers while others closed completely to avoid the problem. Anglicans, therefore, were divided over the Revolution. David Holmes has noted that "although Anglicanism supplied more loyalists during the Revolution than any other denomination in the colonies, the majority of all Anglicans were patriots."[25] In the colonies where Anglicanism was numerically strongest, Anglicans tended to be patriots; in the colonies where Anglicanism was weak, Anglicans tended to be loyalists. As a result, in Virginia and the rest of the south, Anglicanism and the American cause went hand in hand. In the north, particularly in New England with its longstanding Congregational establishment, many Anglicans sided with England. Although Anglicanism was not exactly synonymous with Toryism, the fact that the Church of England was the national church of the enemy created problems of conscience for many American Anglicans and created the popular perception that Anglican churches were Tory churches.[26]

The second, and in many ways more vexing, problem was that of bishops. The idea of "no bishop, no king" had a long history in the American colonies from the seventeenth century onward. New England Puritans viewed their history as an escape from the tyranny of bishops and associated prelacy with religious repression. To the south, Virginia Anglicans had little more use for residential bishops than the New England Puritans. Having developed a system of lay control of churches through vestries, independent-minded Virginians were loath to surrender local control to some far-removed bishop. The Church of England's neglect created a lay-oriented American Anglicanism. In the 1760s and 1770s, when the long-proposed American bishop became a real possibility, both Anglican and dissenting church members resisted.[27]

In the years following the Revolution, American Anglicans were concerned about the structure of an Episcopal church and the role of bishops within that structure. Episcopalians faced a perplexing problem of church government. Most of the states reorganized their churches around a plan of confederation proposed by William White, in which traditional terminology for bishops was avoided and replaced by "overseer," "president," and "superior order." These overseers would share authority with clergy and lay delegates in a convention. While White and others carefully navigated the currents of anti-Episcopal sentiment, however, a group of Connecticut clergy attempted to secure the consecration of Samuel Seabury as bishop for their diocese. Having failed in England, Scottish Nonjuring bishops consecreated Seabury in 1784. As a result, the struggling Episcopal churches now had two possible models for the episcopacy: one developing along democratic lines, as proposed by White, and another along traditional and hier-archical lines, as demonstrated by Seabury.[28]

With careful negotiation, the two parties barely avoided schism. The new Protestant Episcopal Church adopted the idea of *spiritual bishops* with spiritual—but not temporal—authority; they could confirm, ordain, and perform pastoral duties, but they were to have no state duties or functions. In England, the monarch, powerful clergymen, and lords chose bishops; in the new American church, the clergy and laity elected bishops. As Frederick Mills aptly pointed out, this concept of "mitre without sceptre" was "an ecclesiastical revolution . . . [that] would conform to the ideology of the American Revolution."[29]

By 1789, the formal structure of the Protestant Episcopal Church had become Americanized, but solving its structural issues did not solve the church's prob-lems. Virginia, for example, had the largest number of Anglicans before the war, but they were often deists, moralists, or liberal rationalists. After the radical extremes of the French Revolution, these liberal theological options became increasingly less popular.[30] William Meade, future bishop of Virginia, noted that after the war, the Episcopal Church "came under reproach and hate among rival denominations, and with aspiring politicians, so that her lands were sold, and her temples for the most part deserted; and all men, the General Convention of the Church, regarded her as extinct."[31] The questions remained: Could the new Episcopal Church attract members? Could it function as an American church in an American environment? The practical problem remained: Could the most monar-chical, most English, and least evangelical of all America's Protestant churches survive in the new, democratic republic?

The third problem, that of the identity of the Protestant Episcopal Church, was raised by the disestablishment of religion: in America, there would be no nationally privileged churches. Anglican churches would have to compete directly for both members and public influence with churches they regarded as sectarian. Could the Episcopal Church appeal to the American people? The prejudice against the Anglican episcopacy and the suspicion that Anglicanism was unpatriotic were still great. Episcopalians had to make up for their losses during the Revolu-tion, and they had to learn how to function as one denomination among many. The young leaders of the Protestant Episcopal Church had a huge task before them.[32]

The Antebellum Generation

Alexander Garden's prediction that enthusiasm would lead to the creation of "1000 Sects, Sorts and Divisions, 'till nothing but Confusion as a Cloud covered the whole Face of the Land" seemed realized in the early American republic. By 1820, America had become a popular religious free-for-all – what one historian has called the "antebellum spiritual hothouse."[33] A new revival, commonly called the second Great Awakening, began in the last years of the eighteenth century and spread throughout the states and the frontier in the early years of the nineteenth century. Revivalistic fervor covered the nation until nearly all parts of the new country and all churches were influenced by it.[34]

The second Great Awakening continued many of the practices that Americans had seen in the first Awakening: mass outdoor meetings with extemporaneous preaching and prayer, itinerant preachers, visible and physical manifestations of the gifts of the Holy Spirit, use of the print media to spread the revival, and development of an evangelical network in America and England to promote the revival. Even the camp meeting, usually considered a revivalist innovation of the second Awakening, was an adaptation of an eighteenth-century tradition.[35]

In some ways, the differences between the first and second awakenings were minimal;[36] the biggest change was their historical setting. The first Great Awakening had taken place during a relatively stable period of American history: the colonies were part of an empire, were growing, and were materially prosperous.[37] The second Great Awakening followed a period of national crisis: the American Revolution was over. Settlement pushed toward the west. The former colonists were establishing their own country, and democracy was yet little more than a hopeful political experiment. Threatening that experiment was the increased radicalism of the French Revolution. Politically, Democrats and Federalists vied to become the dominant national party; each offered a different view of the scope, rights, and responsibilities of citizens in a democracy.[38]

During the revivals of the early nineteenth century, Americans were consumed by excitement over their experiment, and enthusiasm for democracy affected all areas of American life and culture, including the church. The democratic ethos placed individual Americans on the center stage of history, and churches adapted their message to fit the changing times.[39] Evangelical revivalism took on a new vigor and intensity, and evangelical churches, especially the Baptists and Methodists, grew rapidly. Americans responded enthusiastically. By the mid-nineteenth century, evangelical Protestantism, in its various denominational guises, had become America's mainstream religious tradition.[40]

While American religion was changing, the Episcopal Church was changing as well. A new generation of Episcopal church leaders was coming to the fore, and many of these men had been born after the Revolution and thus never knew the Episcopal Church as the established state church. As children, the church they knew was unsure of its direction, and the dominant theological tradition was moralistic and rationalistic Anglicanism. Although the intellectual glories of Enlightenment Anglicanism had carried the church through the Revolution, in evangelical America it was clearly out of step. Deism had become an enemy of liberty and democracy, and one of the most prominent—and theologically liberal—Anglican churches, King's Chapel in Boston, became Unitarian. Although an orthodox form of Anglican rationalism continued as part of the church's tradition in the nineteenth century, after William White, few capable leaders arose to rearticulate it within new political and social contexts. Instead, the intellectual and organizational vitality of the Episcopal Church fell to two contending parties: High Churchmen and Evangelicals. The new generation of leadership was symbolized by the consecrations in 1811 of two Episcopal bishops: John Henry Hobart of New York and Alexander Viets Griswold of the Eastern Diocese (all of New England except Connecticut). Hobart was the leading High Churchman in antebellum Episcopalianism, and Griswold was an early Evangelical leader. As the older Anglican intellectual tradition receded in a sea of American evangelicalism, the two remaining Anglican traditions vied to dominate the church's identity.[41] The High Church party was distinguished by its distance from American evangelicalism, the Evangelical party by its willingness to cooperate with other evangelicals.

Thus the Evangelicals were presented with an opportunity in the early republic to assert leadership in the new institution and to establish their tradition as the identity of the Protestant Episcopal Church. There was one major problem, however: once the American Methodists split off in 1784, it was not exactly clear how to organizationally maintain the evangelical religion within the church. The American Methodist schism angered some revivalist Anglicans and prompted them to reject a separate Methodist church and remain within the Episcopal Church. The result: Evangelical Episcopalians distanced themselves from Methodism and became more institutionally committed. The charge that had been leveled back in the 1740s—that enthusiasm would lead to schism—had been realized by their Methodist coreligionists. Thus, there arose a need for a kind of revivalism that would proclaim a Methodist-like message but, at the same time, retain Anglican church order and the church's creedal statement, the Thirty-nine Articles. The loss of the Methodists, therefore, resulted in the growth of a church party committed to both revivalist religion and historic Anglicanism.[42]

It is clear as well that some class issues fed the development of evangelicalism within the Episcopal Church. The members of the new Methodist Church were drawn largely from middle and working classes; Episcopalians tended to be from higher classes, and the new evangelical leadership in the Episcopal Church was resolutely upperclass. The clergy tended to be from wealthy, elite New England and Middle Atlantic families with records of military service and political involvement. This contrasts sharply to leadership even within their own church: most High Church clergy tended to come from the middle class.[43] Evangelical Episcopalianism, therefore, with its orderly vision, seems to have been a way for elite early Americans to be evangelicals without the taint of "enthusiasm" that would have come from associating with Methodists and Baptists. Not coincidentally, Evangelical Episcopalians most often associated with Presbyterians, a church that shared some of their concern for orderly evangelicalism and most closely resembled it in social class. Far from empowering the poor and outcast in society, Evangelical Episcopalianism offered religion of the heart to the rich and influential. Because of this, Evangelical Episcopalianism tended to be dominated by powerful, well-educated, socially conservative, white male leaders.[44]

The reaction against Methodism—its emergence as a separate denomination and its social location—was only one source of evangelical religion in the Episcopal Church. Another source was an independent tradition of evangelical religion that was developing within the Episcopal Church itself. In the north in particular, young Episcopalians, influenced by their associations with evangelical Presbyterians and Congregationalists at Yale and Princeton, began to preach a gospel that was both revivalistic and Episcopalian.[45] Not just a scattered minority, nor a "fringe" group within the church, these young men, who later became powerful Episcopal clergymen and bishops, began to promote an evangelical gospel as the identifying mark of the new Protestant Episcopal Church.

In the first years of the nineteenth century, evangelicalism began to be felt as a presence in the church. The movement's geographic center was the middle Atlantic states—particularly Washington, D.C.—but it was widespread, and evangelical churches were prominent in several High Church dioceses. Virginia's decaying church was revitalized by the recruitment of evangelical ministers from the north whose religion was a "resolute, austere, orthodox, and scholarly form of American Anglicanism, tinctured with Calvinism, Methodism, and Puritanism."[46] In the years before 1820, Boston and Rhode Island were centers of evangelical activity under the leadership of Alexander Viets Griswold. Even in New York, the stronghold of High Church theology, evangelical religion had some articulate spokesmen and practitioners. Evangelical laymen, such as lifelong Episcopalian William Jay, freely criticized Bishop Hobart's antievangelical principles, and several New York City parishes, most notably St. George's, were openly evangelical. Elizabeth Channing Moore, communicant at Hobart's own Trinity Church, participated in weekly home meetings for women that promoted evangelical piety.[47]

Even though Griswold's 1811 consecration symbolized the emergence of evangelical religion in the Episcopal Church, for years the diocese of Maryland was convulsed by a particularly bitter contest between church factions. Since the end of the eighteenth century, Maryland's Episcopal clergy were divided into two rival camps: the Formalists (or the High Church party) and the Evangelicals. Wrote Episcopal rector George Dashiell in 1814:

> It is well known, to every person conversant in the affairs of the Protestant Episcopal Church in Maryland, that for twelve or fifteen years past there have existed in it two distinct parties, whose opposition to each other has been open and undisguised. The one party has been denominated Formalists, who have advocated . . . an undeviating adherence to all prescribed forms and ceremonies. . . . The other party was called Evangelical; who, though they loved the Liturgy and ceremonies of the Church, exercised a discretionary power of occasionally or generally omitting some parts of the prescribed service. . . . They also thought and preached that all human institutions, Liturgies, Confirmations, Ceremonies, &c. are nothing when compared to the grand essential doctrines of

the Gospel—the fall of man, the atonement by Jesus Christ, the new birth and the perfect sanctification of the soul by the spirit of God.[48]

The Formalists, as George Dashiell observed, were committed to perpetuating the *forms* of Anglican religion. Following the High Church tradition, they believed liturgies, rites, and sacraments prepared men and women for salvation and formed Christian character. They stressed the uniqueness of the Episcopal Church against other Protestant churches. They promoted sober piety and rational devotion. They decried "over-righteousness" and opposed excessive zeal in religion. In the late eighteenth and early nineteenth centuries, Maryland's Formalists, led by the Rev. J. G. J. Bend, rector of Baltimore's powerful St. Paul's parish, preached on the dangers of enthusiasm. The Rev. James Kemp, rector of, first, Great Choptank parish and, later, St. Paul's, gained fame from his battles with "enthusiasts" on Maryland's Eastern Shore and joined Bend in an antievangelical crusade.[49]

The Evangelicals believed that "excessive zeal does not appear to be our besetting sin." For them, the Episcopal Church could be compared to the lukewarm Laodician church of the Book of Revelation: the church was satiated with "that Laodician spirit which, under a thousand forms, would eat out the vitals of godliness."[50] Form without spirit had choked lively piety; formalism was antithetical to evangelicalism. For Evangelicals this was the crux of the conflict: the forms of Episcopalianism were only good as long as they promoted the *spirit* of true Christianity. Episcopal forms, according to them, had to be enlivened by an inward and spiritual experience of new birth. High Churchmen believed that Episcopal forms, in and of themselves, promoted piety and Christian living. Nothing could be further from the Evangelical idea of true religion.

"The power of godliness," Bishop Charles McIlvaine of Ohio would later declare, "is *the substance, or reality* of godliness, as distinguished from all its forms. . . . [It is] that inward and spiritual grace which is the life and being of all genuine piety before God. Its only abiding place is the heart." Such grace comes, he argued, only through "a new and inward birth" in which God would give power for personal transformation, becoming a "new creature." McIlvaine argued that some Episcopalians act as if "*the more form, the more godliness.*" This he rejected explicitly. Episcopal forms, he maintained, should be "highly valued for their proper uses, affectionately cherished, faithfully observed, [and] jealously guarded." They should not be "lifted into a false importance, and made to hinder instead of helping truth."[51]

> Like the moon's cold disk, as lately seen, eclipsing instead of reflecting the sunlight. Like the garments of our bodies, they may be good to protect the health they can not impart, or evil to deform the simplicity they can not adorn. . . . Like the veil of cloister life, they may purposely hide in mystery what God has revealed to be plainly seen of all men—the beautiful, open face of Gospel truth.[52]

Formalism, the elevation of forms above inward reality, would always result in the "denial of the power of godliness."[53]

For the rest of the nineteenth century, Evangelicals and High Churchmen battled over this point. Evangelicals subordinated the forms of the Episcopal

Church to the spirit of the gospel: without the spirit and power of the gospel, the church would be a hollow form. What was needed, they believed, was not closer attention to the distinct forms of Anglicanism, but a new birth, "a radical and thorough change of heart."[54] A new heart, a new inner being, a new spirit—to the Evangelicals this was true Christianity.

In the early years of the Maryland diocese, the evangelical clergy looked to George Dashiell as their leader. Ordained in 1791 by Bishop White, Dashiell spent several years as rector of a number of churches on the Delmarva peninsula where he sponsored prayer meetings and conducted revivals promoting "real and spiritual religion."[55] Dashiell's opponents complained to Bishop Claggett that his prayer meetings would "produce Enthusiasm and foment schisms"[56] and furthered the spirit of "Methodistical riot."[57] In spite of such criticism, Dashiell was called to Baltimore's St. Peter's church in 1804. Bend was furious with Dashiell's appointment, charging that "Mr. Dashiell's church is no more Episcopal than a Methodist conventicle."[58] Dashiell's innovations scandalized High Churchmen: singing unauthorized hymns, allowing extemporaneous prayer, omitting parts of the liturgy, and permitting a female evangelist to preach in St. Peter's pulpit. As a result, Baltimore's two most powerful parishes became centers of rival party factions.

In 1811, an ailing Bishop Claggett appealed to his convention for an assistant bishop, who would become the next bishop. Maryland's evangelicals protested. Not fond of Bishop Claggett's formalism, they wanted to elect one of their own— George Dashiell—but they did not yet have enough votes for their own candidate. Claggett backed James Kemp, the opponent of evangelical religion, as his assistant and thus guaranteed an antievangelical succession for Maryland's episcopacy. Kemp himself threatened that "I will never, as long as I live, yield obedience to Dashiell in any capacity."[59] After three years of public ecclesiastical warfare, the evangelicals lost, and in 1814, James Kemp was elected assistant bishop of Maryland.[60]

Dashiell and some of his followers did not lose gracefully. Although they formally protested the legality of the election, their protest failed. Within a few months, charges of immorality were brought against Dashiell. Convinced that he was being persecuted for his part in the anti-Kemp campaign, Dashiell defied the authority of the ecclesiastical court and renounced his connection with the Episcopal Church. He organized his own church, the Evangelical Episcopal Church, and sought to take his parish into the new denomination. St. Peter's vestry resisted leaving the Episcopal Church, and, eventually, only three of Maryland's clergy followed Dashiell.[61]

The schism embarrassed and infuriated the Evangelicals. Since the Methodist schism, High Churchmen argued that evangelical religion's natural tendency was sectarian; the forms of the Episcopal Church worked to check enthusiasm, and without allegiance to those forms, Evangelicals would always abandon the church. The Dashiell controversy confirmed this view, and for years thereafter, whenever the Evangelicals attempted to form an association or start a program, High Church ministers would reiterate this argument.[62] In turn, the Evangelicals grumbled about the treatment of their party following Dashiell's departure.[63] The Dashiell schism left a legacy of embarrassment, invective, and continuing party warfare in Maryland's divided Episcopal Church.

Most of Maryland's evangelical clergy, however, stayed with the church. Unlike Dashiell, who believed "there remained no hope of stemming the torrent of Formalism and unsound doctrine," they believed that formalism would be proved empty and evangelical religion would prevail.[64] Like Dashiell, they recognized that the church comprised two distinct parties with two distinct ideas of Christian life. The Formalists, they maintained, had corrupted the evangelical core of the Episcopal Church by multiplying forms and turning away from Reformation theology. The Evangelicals argued that the Episcopal Church was, at its core, an evangelical church.

The new generation of evangelical leaders believed that the salvation of men and women occurred through atonement and the experience of new birth. This message was true Christianity, and the central doctrines of the Episcopal Church expressed it in her articles, liturgy, and homilies. By preaching this gospel, one with so much appeal for early Americans, the Evangelicals revived decaying Episcopal churches and promoted their church to other Americans.

Bishop Griswold sadly noted that the "exclusive claims" of the Episcopal "no bishop, no church" were "abundantly fraught with *excluding* energy." To him, "old school" Episcopalians (whom he identified with High Churchmen) were more effective in keeping people out of the church with their "defence of the distinctive principles of the Protestant Episcopal Church, to the too great neglect of the essential doctrines of Christ." Believing that High Church Episcopalians had actually cut themselves off from the "Church Catholic" (the rest of evangelical Protestants), Griswold adopted evangelical measures (prayer groups and evening meetings) and preached on the Bible and "true piety and renovation of heart."[65]

The Evangelical vision downplayed the exclusive claims made by the High Church party and emphasized unity with other Protestants who embraced evangelicalism. At the same time, Evangelical Episcopalians were required, by virtue of their denominational association, to defend the Anglican episcopacy, which was repulsive to other American evangelicals. So they abandoned the theological traditions of Restoration Anglicanism and argued for a warm and personal experience of Jesus. They maintained that the Episcopal Church, though supremely important, was not as important as true Christianity. By eliminating exclusivist rhetoric, preaching an evangelical gospel, and emphasizing the oneness of all true Christians, Evangelical Episcopal leaders brought their church into the mainstream of nineteenth-century American Protestantism. Their program was successful, but it was fraught with difficulties. Sometimes the Evangelical clergymen of the Episcopal Church so resembled other American evangelicals it was difficult to tell them apart. Sometimes, their commitment to church order and the episcopacy made them vigorous critics of American religion. They were both welcomed and held in suspicion by other American Protestants for their views. Finally, their evangelical vision for the church met its greatest challenge from within their own ranks when it came under attack by their Episcopal colleagues who were influenced by a new incarnation of High Church theology in the 1840s, the Oxford Movement.

Nevertheless, these new leaders brought together evangelicalism and Episcopalianism and adapted the Episcopal Church to the temper of the early republic:

they developed a combined evangelical and Episcopal vision that was not exclusive, but open toward all who believed in Jesus Christ. This combination was neither moralistic nor rationalistic, but pietistic, devotional, and experiential. In addition, they insisted on maintaining the historic order of the Anglican Church. Eventually, however, the tensions between Episcopal order and evangelical religion tore at the Evangelical party, as it was threatened on one side by enthusiastic, non-Episcopal American evangelicalism and on the other side by High Church Episcopal exclusiveness. Thinking that they stood against both extremes, members of the Evangelical party in the Episcopal Church lost their way.

The rest of this story will examine these ironic tensions by looking at the Evangelical party through the life and thought of Charles Pettit McIlvaine. McIlvaine, one of the chief architects of the evangelical vision for half a century, was its leading spokesman. In the year following his death, the Evangelical party in the Protestant Episcopal Church suffered a small schism, and some of his Evangelical colleagues left the church altogether and formed the Reformed Episcopal Church. Most Evangelicals, however, stayed within the Protestant Episcopal Church. In the final decades of the nineteenth century, new issues arose and McIlvaine's form of evangelicalism was eventually rejected in favor of Protestant liberalism. By 1900, there were very few people left in the Protestant Episcopal Church to carry on the Evangelical Episcopal vision. But that lay in the future. In 1820, Charles McIlvaine had arrived in the diocese of Maryland and began his career at Christ Church, Georgetown. By that time, Evangelicals and High Churchmen had begun their long argument over the nature and identity of the Episcopal Church. Charles Pettit McIlvaine would always be near the center of that argument.

Notes

1. From the *Pennsylania Gazette*, 570 (November 22, 1739), 3. Quoted in Stuart C. Henry, *George Whitefield: Wayfaring Witness* (New York and Nashville, 1957), 51.

2. George Whitefield, *Journals* (Edinburgh, 1960), 442. For the controversies surrounding Whitefield's 1740 preaching tour, see John F. Woolverton, *Colonial Anglicanism in North America, 1607–1776* (Detroit, 1984), 189–195; Joseph Tracy, *The Great Awakening* (Boston, 1842; reprint, Edinburgh, 1976); Arnold Dallimore, *George Whitefield: The Life and Times of the Great Evangelist of the Eighteenth-Century Revival* (Edinburgh, 1970), I: 479–562; and Harry S. Stout, *The Divine Dramatist: George Whitefield and the Rise of Modern Evangelicalism* (Grand Rapids, Mich., 1991), 87–132.

3. In the colonial period, commissaries took care of the administrative work of the Church of England in America because there were no resident bishops.

4. Alexander Garden, *Regeneration, and the Testimony of the Spirit. Being the Substance of Two Sermons . . . Occasioned by Some Erroneous Notions of Certain Men Who Call Themselves Methodists* (Charleston, S.C., 1740), cited in Alan Heimert and Perry Miller, *The Great Awakening Documents Illustrating the Crisis and Its Consequences* (Indianapolis, 1967), 50–51, 56.

5. For the theological changes in Anglicanism in general in the seventeenth century, see G. R. Cragg, *From Puritanism to the Age of Reason, 1660–1700* (Cambridge, 1950), and for

Anglican moralism specifically, see C. FitzSimmons Allison, *The Rise of Moralism* (Wilton, Conn., 1966).

6. Garden, *Regeneration and Testimony*, 61.

7. For summaries by Episcopal historians on the negative reception of Anglican clergy to the first Great Awakening, see William W. Manross, *A History of the American Episcopal Church* (New York, 1935), 63–64, and S. D. McConnell, *History of the American Episcopal Church From the Planting of the Colonies to the End of the Civil War* (New York, 1899), 136–146. The most comprehensive, though biased, treatment of the Anglican leadership's dislike of revivalism is Gerald J. Goodwin, "The Anglican Reaction to the Great Awakening," *Historical Magazine of the Protestant Episcopal Church* 35 (1966): 343–371.

8. Anglican moralism was also the mainstream tradition in England, where moralists and evangelicals were also deeply embroiled in controversy. For the divisiveness of the revival on the Church of England, see L. E. Elliot-Binns, *The Early Evangelicals: A Religious and Social Study* (London, 1953), 183–195. Although many Church of England leaders disliked Whitefield and the revival, a number of clergymen–separately but at nearly the same time–experienced a spiritual rebirth and began to preach an evangelical gospel. These leaders formed networks of cooperation through which they advanced the revival. And although Anglican evangelical leaders worked with both Whitefield and Wesley, they eventually formed a third revival party and distanced themselves from both Methodist and Whitefieldian revivalism. Among the best works on the development of a separate Anglican Evangelical tradition are Kenneth Hylson-Smith, *Evangelicals in the Church of England, 1734–1984* (Edinburgh, 1989); Elliot-Binns, *Early Evangelicals*; G. R. Balleine, *A History of the Evangelical Party in the Church of England* (London, 1908); Wesley D. Balda, "Ecclesiastics and Enthusiasts: The Evangelical Emergence in England, 1760–1800," *Historical Magazine of the Protestant Episcopal Church* 49 (1980): 221–231, and idem, " 'Simeon's Protestant Papists: A Sampling of Moderate Evangelicalism Within the Church of England, 1839–1865," *Fides et Historia* 11 (1983): 55–67; and Alexander C. Zabriskie, "Rise and Major Characteristics of the Anglican Evangelical Movement," in *Anglican Evangelicalism*, ed. Alexander C. Zabriskie (Philadelphia, 1943).

9. This tradition never completely faded from the American scene, however. For Enlightenment Anglicanism in the early republic, see Robert Bruce Mullin, ed., *Moneygripe's Apprentice: The Personal Narrative of Samuel Seabury III* (New Haven and London, 1989).

10. Charles P. McIlvaine, *Spiritual Regeneration with Reference to Present Times: A Charge Delivered to the Clergy of the Diocese of Ohio.* (New York, 1851), 4.

11. Quoted in E. Clowes Chorley, *Men and Movements in the American Episcopal Church* (New York, 1946), 63. Chorley's is the best study of the Evangelical party of the Episcopal Church. Nineteenth-century Evangelical bishops include Alexander Viets Griswold, Eastern Diocese; Richard Channing Moore, Virginia; Philander Chase, Ohio and Illinois; William Meade, Virginia; Charles P. McIlvaine, Ohio; Alfred Lee, Delaware; John Johns, Virginia; Manton Eastburn, Massachusetts; Benjamin B. Smith, Kentucky; Gregory T. Bedell, Ohio; J. P. K. Henshaw, Rhode Island; Alonzo Potter, Pennsylvania; Henry Washington Lee, Iowa; and Thomas Vail, Kansas. Among the best-known Evangelical clergy were Gregory T. Bedell, Sr., Heman Dyer, John Alonzo Clark, Stephen Higginson Tyng, Sr. and Jr., Benjamin Clarke Cutler, John S. Stone, and Benjamin Allen. Geographically, Evangelicals were strongest in Virginia and the south (excluding North Carolina), the Washington D.C. area, Philadelphia, Delaware, Massachusetts and the rest of New England (excluding Connecticut), Kentucky, Ohio, Iowa, and Kansas. As to the growing strength of the party, at the General Convention of 1820, Bishop McIlvaine said that of thirty-six clerical deputies, six were Evangelicals. In 1832, the parties were fairly balanced,

and in 1841, Stephen Tyng estimated that two-thirds of the clerical deputies were Evangelicals. Even though these numbers come from Evangelicals themselves, many nineteenth-century observers commented on the growth in size of the Evangelical party between 1820 and 1840 in particular. For this summary, see Chorley, *Men and Movements*, 51. Although Tyng's number was probably exaggerated, it was repeated in several nineteenth-century sources, including Baird's *Religion in America*.

12. Cornelius Walker, *The Life and Correspondence of Rev. William Sparrow, D.D.* (Philadelphia, 1876), 80.

13. Charles P. McIlvaine, *The Inaugural Address Delivered at the Opening of Huron College, Canada West on the 2nd of December, 1863* (London, 1864), 6.

14. These "divisions" corresponded to the ones existing in the Evangelical Revival in England. See Zabriskie, "Rise and Major Characteristics," 3–38. Although each becomes a separate entity by the latter years of the eighteenth century, in the early years of the Evangelical Revival, it was by no means clear that they were separate movements. As described by Luther Gerlach and Virginia Hine in *People, Power, Change: Movements of Social Transformation* (Indianapolis, 1970), it is a common pattern for a religious movement to have several centers of leadership with flexible boundaries. During the first Great Awakening, leaders and laity moved freely back and forth between the three Anglican renewal movements without perceiving any substantial difference among the groups. For example, on the Delmarva peninsula, the settled Anglican ministers Hugh Neill and Samuel Magaw served communion for Methodist meetings and openly sympathized with Whitefield. The term *Methodist* was used indiscriminately in the early years of the Evangelical Revival to describe anyone who embraced the evangelical message. Only as clear differences emerged on theological and organizational issues did the term begin to apply solely to the followers of John Wesley.

15. Woolverton, *Colonial Anglicanism*, 196.

16. For Wesley's relationship to Anglicanism, see Frank Baker, *John Wesley and the Church of England* (Nashville and New York, 1970). On the development of Methodism, along with some reference to Evangelical Anglicanism, in Delaware, Maryland, and Virginia, see William Henry Williams, *The Garden of American Methodism: The Delmarva Peninsula, 1769–1820* (Wilmington, Del., 1984).

17. Much more work needs to be done on the reception of evangelical religion among women and on the theological and spiritual implications of evangelical piety and its impact on both American religion as a whole and individual denominations. For Anglican evangelical women, see the brief bits in ibid., 100–101, and Woolverton, *Colonial Anglicanism*, 197–198. For full-scale studies on evangelical religion, gentility, gender, and Anglicanism, see Donald Mathews, *Religion in the Old South* (Chicago, 1977), and Richard Eugene Rankin, "Evangelical Awakening and Episcopal Revival: Cultural Change and the Development of Genteel Piety Among North Carolina Episcopalians, 1800–1869" (Ph.D. diss., University of North Carolina at Chapel Hill, 1989), recently published as *Ambivalent Churchmen and Episcopal Churchwoman: The Religion of the Episcopal Elite in North Carolina, 1800–1860* (Columbia, S.C., 1993).

18. For the beginnings of St. Paul's and McClenachan's rectorship, see Norris Stanley Barratt, *Outline of the History of Old St. Paul's Church, Philadelphia, Pennsylvania* (Lancaster, Pa., 1917), 28–54, 66–78.

19. Jarratt is frequently described as the forerunner of the Evangelical party in the Protestant Episcopal Church. See his autobiography: Devereux Jarratt, *The Life of the Reverend Devereux Jarratt* (Baltimore, 1806). Chorley, *Men and Movements*, 1–25, is a summary of the Evangelical historiography of Jarratt's ministry and influence on the beginnings of the Episcopal Church. For a newer view, see David L. Holmes, "Devereux

Jarratt, A Letter and a Reevaluation," *Historical Magazine of the Protestant Episcopal Church* 47 (1978): 37–49. Rhys Isaac's *The Transformation of Virginia, 1740–1790* (Chapel Hill, N.C., 1982) mentions Jarratt as an example of Methodist evangelicalism, but neglects Jarratt's criticism of the Methodists on their polity and lack of commitment to Anglican forms.

20. Goodwin, "Anglican Reaction," 344.

21. Frederick V. Mills, Sr., makes this point to support a different thesis in his *Bishops by Ballot: An Eighteenth Century Ecclesiastical Revolution* (New York, 1978). He argues that the Great Awakening did affect certain colonial Anglican churches by encouraging "the idea that the laity had a right to judge a minister's orthodoxy and performance" (77), thus undermining the idea of bishops by divine right. Not even American Anglicans were immune to this Awakening influence. In Mills's account, evangelical sentiment, Low and Broad Church Episcopal polity, the political realities of vestry-controlled churches, and moderate deism all combined to produce a climate in which hierarchical bishops could no longer be acceptable. Americans devised a system through which they elected their bishops, and thus Americanized their church. Although Mills does not make a very big point of it, it is clear from his study that in the areas that prorevival sentiment was strongest, the sentiment against a monarchial episcopate was also strongest. Conversely, in strongly antirevival Connecticut, the strongest opinion existed for a traditional, English-style bishop. A favorable attitude toward evangelical religion was not the only factor playing into the rejection of a traditional episcopate, but Mills's work points out that it was at least one factor. For the development of evangelical religion in the Anglican Church after 1760, see Nelson R. Burr, "Methodism and Its Separation from the Church," in *The Anglican Church in New Jersey*, ed. Nelson R. Burr (Philadelphia, 1954), 311–335. Burr argues that Methodism was more acceptable to Anglican clergy because it was a reform movement within the church, whereas Whitefield was seen to have tendencies away from the church. Burr may draw the distinctions between Whitefield and Wesley too cleanly, but his basic point – that by the 1760s more evangelical religion was to be found within the Anglican Church (at least in New Jersey) than previously – is sound.

22. For the proposed meeting, see Mills, *Bishops by Ballot*, 252–256.

23. See Robert Walton Prichard, "Theological Consensus in the Episcopal Church, 1801–1873" (Ph.D. diss., Emory University, 1983), especially 2–13.

24. Frederick V. Mills, Sr., "The Protestant Episcopal Churches in the United States, 1783–1789: Suspended Animation or Remarkable Recovery?" *Historical Magazine of the Protestant Episcopal Church* 46 (1977): 151–170, gives a good summary of the problems that faced Episcopalians during and after the war. In 1776, the Methodists were still members of the Church of England, and insofar as they obeyed their bishops and showed allegiance to the king, they were suspect. John Wesley himself urged American Methodists not to rebel against the British government.

25. David L. Holmes, "The Episcopal Church in the American Revolution," *Historical Magazine of the Protestant Episcopal Church* 47 (1978): 265.

26. Anglican churches were targets for popular attack against the British. See *ibid.*, 274–278.

27. On the history of English attempts to settle an American episcopate, see Arthur Lyon Cross, *The Anglican Episcopate and the American Colonies* (Cambridge, Mass., 1902). Carl Bridenbaugh's *Mitre and Sceptre: Transatlantic Faiths, Ideas, Personalities and Politics, 1689–1775* (New York, 1962), discusses the fears and opposition of dissenters toward an American bishop. Mills, *Bishops by Ballot*, is a study of the Anglican reaction – mostly negative – to an American bishop. See also Woolverton, *Colonial Anglicanism*, 220–233.

28. The full story of this is told in Mills, *Bishops by Ballot*, and in Clara O. Loveland, *The Critical Years: The Reconstitution of the Anglican Church in the United States of America, 1780–1789* (Greenwich, Conn., 1956). For White's proposal, see William White, *The Case of the Episcopal Churches in the United States Considered* (n.p., 1782).

29. Mills, *Bishops by Ballot*, 306–307. Mills argues that although White compromised with Seabury in a few places, White's conception, a "low-church" Americanized episcopacy, won. John F. Woolverton in his article, "Philadelphia's William White: Episcopalian Distinctiveness and Accommodation in the Post-Revolutionary Period," *Historical Magazine of the Protestant Episcopal Church* 43 (1974): 279–296, argues that White's case was not a product of White's Americanization of the English episcopacy. Rather, White's church and governmental theories were an outgrowth of his "liberal, anti-Calvinist, Lockean Whig" views, and he was much more interested in muffling Loyalist sentiment than Americanizing the episcopacy. These two views—Mills's theory of Americanization and Woolverton's theory of White's traditional English thought—are not irreconcilable. White might not have been self-conscious in his attempt to Americanize the church. Nevertheless, the English Whig thought in which he imbibed certainly fit with the temper of Revolutionary times, and American thought became characterized by the very traditions to which White was most indebted. Even though White's intellectual tradition was English, it was also the tradition that became most "American." Thus, White, intentionally or not, did propose a scheme that "Americanized" the English episcopacy.

30. In the first years following the Revolution, enlightened Anglicanism formed the basis of religious beliefs for many early American intellectuals, as well as for political and social leaders. After the French Revolution, however, evangelical religion began to replace the more liberal forms of Enlightenment-influenced Protestantism in the United States, with the exception of the Unitarians, who flourished in New England.

31. William Meade, *Reasons for Loving the Episcopal Church* (New York, 1854), 12.

32. For the identity crisis of the Protestant Episcopal Church as it related to its High Church party, see Mullin, *Episcopal Vision/American Reality*. For a sociological analysis of the change from state church to denomination, see William H. Swatos, Jr., *Into Denominationalism: The Anglican Metamorphosis* (Storrs, Conn., 1979).

33. Jon Butler, *Awash in a Sea of Faith: Christianizing the American People* (Cambridge, Mass., 1990).

34. For good summaries of the religious movements of the early republic, see Sydney Ahlstrom, *A Religious History of the American People* (New Haven and London, 1972): Part IV, "The Golden Days of Democratic Evangelicalism," 415–509, and George M. Marsden, *Religion and American Culture* (San Diego and New York, 1990), 47–93. Helpful monographs on the second Great Awakening and American revivalism include the following: Nathan Hatch, *The Democratization of American Christianity* (New Haven and London, 1989); Richard Carwardine, *Transatlantic Revivalism: Popular Evangelicalism in Britain and America, 1790–1865* (Westport, Conn., 1978); Timothy Smith, *Revivalism and Social Reform in Mid-Nineteenth Century America* (Nashville, 1957); Whitney Cross, *The Burned-over District: The Social and Intellectual History of Enthusiastic Religion in Western New York, 1800–1850* (Ithaca, N.Y., 1950); Paul E. Johnson, *A Shopkeeper's Millennium: Society and Revivals in Rochester, New York, 1815–1837* (New York, 1978); Alice Felt Tyler, *Freedom's Ferment: Phases of American Social History from the Colonial Period to the Outbreak of the Civil War* (New York, 1962); Perry Miller, *The Life of the Mind in America from the Revolution to the Civil War* (New York, 1965). In addition, Butler, *Awash in a Sea of Faith*, chapters 7–9, is helpful in understanding the diversity of antebellum religion.

35. See Leigh Eric Schmidt, *Holy Fairs: Scottish Communions and American Revivals in the Early Modern Period* (Princeton, 1989), especially 59–68.

36. On the artificial nature of the category *first Great Awakening*, see Jon Butler, "Enthusiasm Described and Decried: The Great Awakening as Interpretative Fiction," *Journal of American History* 69 (1982): 305–325. Although I am using these terms as they are commonly used by American religious historians, I believe there is a continuing revival tradition from the early colonial period onward. It is somewhat artificial to divide these revivals into first, second, and so forth, but these terms help place the revivals chronologically.

37. Patricia U. Bonomi, *Under the Cope of Heaven: Religion, Society, and Politics in Colonial America* (Oxford and New York, 1986), is particularly strong in establishing colonial prosperity as the setting for the Great Awakening.

38. For the standard history of the period, see A. M. Schlesinger, Jr., *Age of Jackson* (Boston, 1945).

39. For the effect of democracy on American Christianity, see Nathan Hatch, "Sola Scriptura and Novus Ordo Seclorum," in *The Bible in America: Essays in Cultural History*, ed. Mark Noll and Nathan Hatch (Oxford, 1983), and idem, "Evangelicalism as a Democratic Movement," in *Evangelicalism in Modern America*, ed. George M. Marsden (Grand Rapids, Mich., 1984). These two essays are expanded and revised in Hatch, *Democratization of Christianity*. To emphasize the relationship between evangelicalism and democracy in the early Republic is not to say that the two were previously unconnected. Recent historiography credits the first Great Awakening with influencing the growth of democratic ideals. Several works have developed the theme of the relationship of evangelicalism and the American Revolution, starting with Alan Heimert's groundbreaking *Religion and the American Mind from the Great Awakening to the Revolution* (Cambridge, Mass., 1966). Although a number of historians have taken exception to parts of Heimert's thesis, the connection he established—that of evangelicalism and patriotism—has remained an intrinsic part of historical work on this period. See also Nathan Hatch, *The Sacred Cause of Liberty: Republican Thought and the Millennium in Revolutionary New England* (New Haven and London, 1977); Harry S. Stout, *The New England Soul: Preaching and Religious Culture in Colonial New England* (Oxford, 1986); Bonomi, *Under the Cope*; and Isaac, *Transformation of Virginia*. This view is challenged by Butler, *Awash in a Sea of Faith*, 194–224.

40. A similar phenomenon occurred in England as well. See David W. Bebbington, *Evangelicalism in Modern Britain* (London, 1989), 105ff.

41. Robert W. Prichard, *A History of the Protestant Episcopal Church* (Wilton, Conn., 1991), 105–123, argues that the liberal Anglican tradition was discredited by the French and Haitian revolutions. He says the mainstream church tradition became *rational orthodoxy*, which rejected radical forms of Anglican liberalism and combined trinitarian orthodoxy, public morality, and education. The High Church and Evangelical parties fought over this broad vision—each group sought to make their own interpretation of this centrist position the dominant position in the Protestant Episcopal Church.

42. A similar dynamic was at work in late eighteenth-century England. Balda, "Ecclesiastics and Enthusiasts," has argued that Anglican Evangelicalism emerged between the "mutually exclusive tenets of churchmanship and enthusiastic methodism" (p. 231). For the tensions between evangelicalism and church order, see C. E. H. Smyth, *Simeon and Church Order: A Study of the Origins of the Evangelical Revival in the 18th Century* (Cambridge, 1940).

43. I am indebted to Robert Bruce Mullin for pointing this out. It is an observation from his research on the High Church party.

44. That does not mean, however, that women were not attracted to Evangelical Episcopalianism. Evangelical Episcopalians had more flexible views toward women in leadership than did High Church Episcopalians. Women were active, as were upperclass women generally, in voluntary societies and missions, and they had secondary leadership in

revivals and prayer meetings. On the social conservatism of Evangelical Episcopalians and their voting patterns, see Robert P. Formisano, *The Birth of Mass Political Parties: Michigan, 1827–1861* (Princeton, 1971), 154–158, 314–317. Evangelical Episcopalians were usually Whigs and later Republicans. Other Episcopalians were usually Democrats.

45. For example, among the early Evangelical clergy and bishops who were influenced by northern Evangelicalism, William Meade, John Johns, and Charles P. McIlvaine studied at Princeton. Stephen Tyng, Sr., attended Harvard College, but spent the year 1811 at Phillips' Academy at Andover where the new Andover Seminary exercised "a permanent blessing" on him (Charles Rockland Tyng, *Record of the Life and Work of the Rev. Stephen Higginson Tyng* [New York, 1890], 27). John P. K. Henshaw's father was a professor at Middlebury College; young Henshaw attended Harvard and had a conversion experience while serving as a resident graduate in Cambridge. Alexander Viets Griswold attended Yale; Gregory Bedell graduated from Columbia; Benjamin Allen studied privately with a Presbyterian minister in Berlin, New York, and then at the Theological Seminary of the Associate Reformed Church in New York; Reuel Keith studied at Middlebury College and Andover Seminary; Thomas M. Smith, Daniel R. Goodwin, and John S. Stone were also from Andover. James Milnor graduated from the University of Pennsylvania. Of all these northern schools, only Columbia and the University of Pennsylvania were historically Anglican; the rest are associated with revivalist Presbyterianism or Congregationalism. It appears that very few early evangelicals were educated in the south (not, at least, until the establishment of the Virginia Seminary at Alexandria) or by other Episcopalians. The men who would become the leaders of the Evangelical party in the Episcopal Church were mostly northerners who were educated in the north. In addition, none were Methodist by background—most had always been Episcopalians; a few were converts from Congregationalism and Presbyterianism; and there was one former Quaker among them.

46. For the influence of northern evangelicalism on Virginia Episcopalianism, see David L. Holmes, "The Decline and Revival of the Church of Virginia," in *Up from Independence: The Episcopal Church in Virginia*, ed. Brewster S. Ford et al. (Orange, Va., 1967), 94–97.

47. Among Channing Moore's descendents were three priests and two evangelical bishops—Richard Channing Moore of Virginia and Gregory T. Bedell of Ohio.

48. George Dashiell, *An Address to the Protestant Episcopal Church in Maryland* (N.p., but internal evidence places the date at 1814), 1. The standard histories of the Episcopal Church date the denomination's party divisions from 1811 when John Henry Hobart, a High Churchman, and Alexander Viets Griswold, an Evangelical, became bishops. Party tensions were acute in Maryland, however, from at least as early as 1803 when the evangelical vestry of St. Peter's refused to accept a diocesan publication promoting a High Church view of the episcopacy. For more on Maryland's divided clergy, see Francis L. Hawks, *Contributions to the Ecclesiastical History of the United States of America*, Vol. 2, *The Rise and Progress of the Protestant Episcopal Church in Maryland* (New York, 1836). For a well-researched study of the divisions produced by evangelical revivalism in the first years of nineteenth-century Maryland, see Terry Bilhartz, *Urban Religion and the Second Great Awakening: Church and Society in Early National Baltimore* (Rutherford, N.J., 1986); on Episcopalians in particular, see pages 48–51, 126–129.

49. For more on Bend, see William B. Sprague, *Annals of the American Pulpit* (New York, 1857), V: 353–355. Bend's sermons have not been published. The archives of the diocese of Maryland has over 500 handwritten Bend manuscripts; a few of these sermons deal with the topic of enthusiasm. Of particular interest are his "Visitation Sermon" of April 11, 1799, which attacks "the wild theories of enthusiasm," and "Over-righteousness" from August 29, 1791, which attacks excessive zeal in religion and praises moderation. Bend died

in 1812 (before the controversy in Maryland reached its zenith) and was succeeded by Kemp at St. Paul's. For Kemp's battle against enthusiasm, see "The Parochial Report of the Great Choptank Parish," *Journal of a Convention of the Protestant Episcopal Church in the State of Maryland* (Baltimore, 1807), 11–14.

50. Preceding quotes from "On Meetings for Prayer," *Washington Theological Repertory* 1 (May 1820): 301.

51. All quotes this paragraph from Charles McIlvaine, *The Form and the Power of Godliness: A Sermon Preached at the Opening Services of the New St. Ann's on the Heights, Brooklyn, New York on Wednesday, October 20, 1869* (New York, 1869), 10, 17.

52. Ibid., 17–18.

53. Ibid., 21.

54. "Religion and the Affections," *Washington Theological Repertory* 1 (January, 1820): 163.

55. Dashiell's definition of evangelical religion as "real and spiritual" comes from George Dashiell to the Rev. William M. Stone, April 8, 1808, in the Ethan Allen Collection, Maryland Diocesan Archives, Episcopal Diocesan House, Baltimore. [Hereafter cited as EA, MD Dio. Arch.]

56. Rev. John Kemley to Bishop Claggett, February 21, 1805, in EA, MD Dio. Arch.

57. Rev. Archibald Walker to Claggett, September 9, 1808, in ibid.

58. J. G. J. Bend to William Duke, September 3, 1810, in ibid.

59. James Kemp to Rev. Joseph Jackson, May 1, 1813, in ibid.

60. The story of the political and ecclesiastical maneuvers is told by Nelson W. Rightmyer, "The Episcopate of Bishop Kemp of Maryland," *Historical Magazine of the Protestant Episcopal Church* 28 (1959): 66–84.

61. The last days of Dashiell in the Episcopal Church are recorded in *Journal of a Convention of the Protestant Episcopal Church of Maryland, Held in Annapolis, June, 1816* (n.p., 1816). Dashiell attempted to secure the episcopacy for the schismatic church through Bishop Provoost and then through the Moravians, but he failed. Dashiell then claimed the right to ordain his own clergy: see George Dashiell, *An Ordination Sermon Delivered on the 30th of April 1821 in St. John's Church, Baltimore* (Baltimore, 1821).

62. For example, see Rev. J.A.T. Kilgour to Bishop Kemp, July 25, 1822, in EA, MD Dio. Arch. Kilgour argues that a theological seminary in Washington would surely result in "a singular incorporation . . . under the appellation of the 'Evangelical Church' "–a notion he considered incompatible with the Episcopal Church.

63. Reported by Rev. William H. Wilmer to Bishop Kemp, May 3, 1821, in EA, MD Dio. Arch.

64. Dashiell, *Address to the Church*, 13.

65. All quotes this paragraph from John Seeley Stone, *Memoir of the Life of the Rt. Rev. Alexander Viets Griswold, D.D., Bishop for the Protestant Episcopal Church in the Eastern Diocese* (Philadelphia, 1844), 119–122.

2

The Evangelical Mission: The Spirit of True Christianity, 1820–1831

At fourteen, Charles Pettit McIlvaine matriculated at Princeton College. As the son of a military man, lawyer, and United States senator, and grandson of the governor of Pennsylvania, McIlvaine prepared for a career fit for such an illustrious family and received training as a republican gentleman at Princeton.[1] His parents, Joseph and Maria McIlvaine, did not hold strong religious views. They attended an Episcopal church but remained unbaptized and did not join the church. His two older brothers, both Princeton graduates, achieved success in law and business. The parents expected their third son to follow the family tradition of public service, and Charles gave no indication that he would choose a clerical career.

Shortly after his entrance, an evangelical revival engulfed Princeton. "Every religious service," recalled the president of the college, "both on secular days and on the Sabbath, was attended with a solemnity that was very impressive. . . . There were very few individuals in the college who were not deeply impressed with a sense of the importance of spiritual and eternal things. . . . For a time it seemed as if the whole of our charge was pressing into the kingdom of God."[2] Moved by the events around him, Charles McIlvaine converted to Christianity. "It was powerful and pervading and fruitful," he remembered years later, "the conversion of young men to God. . . . In that precious season of the power of God, my religious life began. I had *heard* before; I began then to *know*."[3] The newly converted McIlvaine returned to his Episcopal parish, St. Mary's in Burlington, New Jersey, presented himself for baptism, and received the Lord's Supper for the first time.[4]

Like a number of other young men who converted during the great Princeton revival of 1815,[5] Charles Pettit McIlvaine felt called of God to the ministry. While still a student, he practiced preaching and conducted Bible classes. With his friends Charles Hodge and John Johns he began an interdenominational Sunday school in Princeton. In 1816, he graduated from Princeton as first honor graduate and returned to Burlington to read theology for holy orders under Dr. Charles Wharton, the minister of St. Mary's.[6]

The standard curriculum for Episcopal ministerial candidates had been drawn up by William White, who was then serving the church as presiding bishop. The list reflected the theological tradition of the colonial church and comprised seventeenth- and eighteenth-century Anglican works. White's authors repre-

24

sented the various traditions of post-Restoration Anglicanism: Carolines, latitudinarians, rationalists, moralists, and Nonjurors. Except for Richard Hooker, White included no figure from the English Reformation, and, in line with his almost fanatical dislike of Calvinism, he included only anti-Calvinistic works.[7] This standard list, reflecting White's Anglican rationalism (which Wharton shared), formed the core of the Episcopal theological curriculum for both Evangelicals and High Churchmen. Thus, McIlvaine's formal theological reading contained no works considered standard for American evangelicals; he studied no Reformation theology, no classic devotional works, and no Puritan or Pietist writings. He learned that Anglican tradition was, above all else, reasonable.

This course caused a conflict for enthusiastically evangelical McIlvaine. He approached his former Princeton professor and spiritual mentor, Archibald Alexander, and asked if he should leave the Episcopal Church and become a Presbyterian. After all, McIlvaine had been converted in a Presbyterian revival at a Presbyterian college. The only evangelicals he knew were Presbyterians. In 1816, the Episcopal church did not appear particularly hospitable to the newly awakened young man.[8] Alexander urged McIlvaine to remain an Episcopalian and to work to convert others in the Episcopal Church to the evangelical faith. Despite the nonevangelical nature of his formal theological course, McIlvaine's evangelical convictions not only persisted, but grew in depth and intensity. Alexander had given him a vision: to be both evangelical and Episcopal. Returning the Episcopal Church to its evangelical heritage became the mission of his life. Charles McIlvaine had been called.

His personal sense of this divine calling empowered McIlvaine's ministry. In 1820, he was ordained a deacon and called to his first pastorate at Christ Church, Georgetown, in Washington, D.C. He became a priest in 1823. His friend William Carus later recalled how often McIlvaine spoke of his ordination and with what reverence and seriousness.[9] Indeed, McIlvaine considered his vocation the highest, and most solemn, of all earthly callings. To him, the ministry meant more than simply a pastoral office, baptizing, marrying, and comforting the sick and dying. He viewed it as a prophetic office of the "*man of God*" who preached truth and acted on it. "Now the minister of the Gospel," he proclaimed, "as God's messenger, is the prophet of the Christian dispensation." Such men, he believed, were "personally, individually, directly, chosen and anointed of God for his work."[10] McIlvaine considered the text John 15:16–"I have ordained you that you should go and bring forth fruit, and that your fruit should remain"–as the very definition of ordination. *God* had called him for a particular ministry; McIlvaine had not chosen a clerical call. " '*I have ordained you*,' " he explained [referring to God] "means, *to me you are to give an account*."

> Your day of ordination and your day of judgement are most intimately connected. The vows and the duties here to be bound upon you, will be bound in heaven; and whether you heed them or not, fulfill them or not, they will meet you and confront you in the day when you shall give account of your stewardship.[11]

McIlvaine frequently compared the work of the ministry to the work of farming. "God giveth the increase," he stated; "man doeth the work." In an illustration pregnant with meaning for antebellum Americans, he said, "We are but the *field-hands*." His ordination marked his slavery to God. Ministry, therefore, became the Master's work from which there could be no rest: God has "ordained that the world shall have no spiritual light but by reflection from his Church, and his Church no power of reflection but by the agency of her ministry." Not only did the burden of the Church rest on the shoulders of the clergy, but so did the well-being of the world: "Thus shall we understand how, by a fundamental law of the whole moral and spiritual government of God, the advancement and the very existence of religion in the world have been rendered dependent upon the ministry of the Gospel."[12] This was a solemn calling. McIlvaine believed that the spread of righteousness depended on faithful, evangelical ministers carrying out God's work in the Episcopal Church. This was his mission: to be a prophet of evangelical truth. To fulfill this calling, he drove himself relentlessly. His life centered on being a minister and eventually a bishop. Everything else—family, happiness, health—came second to serving God.

If a sense of divine calling empowered McIlvaine's ministry, it also created great tension in his life. During the course of his entire ministry, he suffered from recurring anxiety attacks and nervous collapse. Perhaps not surprisingly, his first collapse occurred right before he began his ministerial training. It was a necessary corollary to the responsibility of the ministry, McIlvaine later stated, that ministers "feel the legitimate effect of such views in bowing them down in the dust for their unworthiness and insufficiency."[13] His favorite hymn, "Just as I Am," "contains my religion, my theology, my hope. . . . When I am gone, I wish to be remembered in association with that hymn."[14] The words express the personal inadequacy McIlvaine felt through his life:

> Just as I am
> Without one plea
> But that Thy blood was shed for me
> And that Thou bid'st me come to Thee
> O Lamb of God, I come.

Other stanzas describe internal conflicts, doubts, fears, blindness, and wretchedness. The sinner recognizes his infinite distance from God, bridged only by a gracious Savior who reaches out to the hopeless. "I have no other plea," mused McIlvaine; "I can come in no other way . . . above the sense of my deep unworthiness, to a full embracing of Thy promises."[15]

These words represent more than pious rhetoric; McIlvaine's deep fears of inability and failure dogged him for decades. A tension in his own worldview created extreme stress: human beings were completely unworthy of grace, yet God had placed the responsibility for the spread of the gospel in human hands. We cannot work, McIlvaine believed, yet we must. Although the theological category of grace and the Reformation doctrine of justification by faith alone provided intellectual comfort for this dilemma, McIlvaine struggled with the conflict his whole life. His belief in his fundamental unworthiness and inadequacy tore at his overwhelming sense of duty to reform the Episcopal Church. Death terrified him.

His diary reflects his constant anguish that he had not done the Lord's work and would be judged accordingly.

He first experienced this fear shortly after his call to the ministry while at Princeton.

> All I knew was that something, some power, some darkness, some unutterable *dread* was upon me and before me. . . . The dread increased. It seemed a *horror* of darkness. . . . I knelt, and in broken sentences prayed. . . . In a few moments it was all gone; but I was drenched with perspiration, my limbs shook, my nerves were thoroughly shaken, and all the next day the physical effect was upon me. For thirty-six hours my nerves did not recover.[16]

He periodically experienced episodes of anxiety and terror that he attributed to Satan, but we may wonder whether he suffered from a psychological disorder. Family correspondence indicates that his father did not fully approve of his career choice and often took it upon himself to caution his son against pride. Whatever the case, his condition grew out of his conversion and his ministerial vocation. The mantle of prophet did not rest easily on Charles McIlvaine: outwardly, he appeared to be a successful clergyman and church leader; inwardly, he suffered great melancholy.[17]

McIlvaine's personal struggles point out certain characteristics of the internal, spiritual dimensions of evangelical religion. These include a deep awareness of personal sin, the necessity of being born again, and an evangelical activism that burned itself out in service for God. McIlvaine may have felt these things more intensely than some evangelicals, but most shared them to some degree.

In general, Protestant evangelicals viewed evangelical religion as both a theology and a spiritual disposition, which required mental assent to certain Protestant doctrines and heartfelt transformation of the inner self. Evangelicals preached that believers should experience Protestant theology through the power of the Holy Spirit. As such, evangelical religion was the soul of the church: as a soul enlivens a body, so the experiential faith of evangelicalism enlivens the church. Without the soul, the body dies; without the spiritual reality of evangelical religion, the church is only a lifeless form.[18] Evangelical Episcopalians shared these beliefs about the importance of experiential religion with other evangelical Protestants.[19] Not exclusively the possession of one denomination, the spirit of true Christianity existed wherever God had transformed human hearts.

The Evangelical Episcopalians, however, faced a special dilemma by maintaining these views. As the most formal of America's Protestant churches, Episcopal traditions threatened to obscure the spirit of evangelical religion. In the face of this constant threat, the Evangelicals urged fellow Episcopalians to experience the personal, inward, and spiritual reality of Christ's salvation. They argued that this experiential religion reflected the essence of both Episcopal and true Christian faith.

Evangelicals set as their goal knowing their salvation through an experience of Jesus Christ. To promote this experience, they used various means: prayer meetings, preaching, Bible classes, and revivalism. Once men and women felt assured of salvation, the Evangelical ministers urged them to discipline their lives and practice their faith in the world by witnessing for and building up the kingdom of God on earth. To achieve this task, they willingly cooperated with other Protestants in various voluntary societies. Evangelical Episcopalians believed that a transformed person could transform the world and that holy living would bring forth a holy society. To this end they invested all their energies, and they sincerely believed that formalism would not win the day in the Episcopal Church.

As a result of Dashiell's schism, the center of the Evangelical party shifted from Baltimore to Washington. When one of Washington's largest parishes, Christ Church in Georgetown, lost its evangelical rector, Charles Pettit McIlvaine arrived to replenish the ranks.

Evangelical Core

In 1820, the newly ordained McIlvaine began his ministry in the heavily evangelical area around Washington. Within a year, his abilities as an evangelical minister were widely known, and he received a call from St. Paul's, Philadelphia's redoubtable evangelical parish, to be their pastor.[20] McIlvaine turned down St. Paul's, preferring instead to bring his young bride, Emily Coxe McIlvaine, to Washington and fulfill his duties as the newly elected chaplain to the United States Senate. With high hopes, a sense of mission, a confirmed call, a growing reputation, a new wife, and a prestigious position, McIlvaine started his career. Few young men could imagine such a beginning.

McIlvaine found Washington a congenial environment for his views; the early 1820s were heady days for Evangelical Episcopalians in the nation's capitol. "At this time," reported clergyman Ethan Allen, "there were no differences in the District. The clergy acted together and were alike interested in the church of the District."[21] McIlvaine, Stephen Tyng, William Hawley, John Johns, Ethan Allen, William Wilmer, William Meade, and Oliver Norris were all clergyman in and around the nation's capitol, but at this date, these evangelicals hardly compromised a church "party." They were friends and coworkers united by a common vision: teaching evangelical doctrines of the gospel, "the power and practice of godliness," and uniting them with the form of the Episcopal Church.[22] Deadened by formalism, the church lacked zeal. But McIlvaine and his friends believed they could revive the church. With high expectations, they preached the doctrines of the Protestant Reformation and exhorted Episcopalians to be born again.

In the 1820s, the Washington Evangelicals began two projects to spread evangelical religion: the Education Society to train young men for the ministry, and a journal, the *Washington Theological Repertory*, as a platform for their beliefs. The projects were interconnected: McIlvaine, for example, served as a director of the society and an editor for the journal. Their evangelical program was clear. They preached classical Reformation doctrines, insisted on the experience of new birth, and believed that every saved person must live a holy and transformed life.

The Mind of the Reformation

The *Washington Theological Repertory*, founded in 1819, was the first sustained publication venture of the Evangelical party. It articulated the central principles of evangelical belief, which stood at the core of the party's identity throughout the nineteenth century. "The principles," stated the editors in the first issue, "upon which [the magazine] will be conducted, are those of the Bible, as illustrated in the Articles, Liturgy, and Homilies of the Protestant Episcopal Church. . . . Their chief object will be to inculcate sound theological knowledge and to delineate and recommend pure and vital religion." The Bible and the creedal formulations of the English Reformation formed the intellectual foundation of the Evangelical worldview. Accordingly, "the indispensable prerequisites for admission into Heaven" included intellectual assent to the following doctrines: (a) God is perfect; (b) human beings fell from "original rectitude"; (c) fallen humanity is sinful by nature; (d) the atonement and mediation of Jesus Christ overcomes sin; (e) divine grace can change the sinful hearts of men and women; (f) all those who experience grace are called to live a life conformed to the gospel.[23]

After presenting this basic outline of Christian theology, the editors proceeded to defend one point in detail: the complete sinfulness of humanity. Human depravity was the cornerstone of Evangelical theology. Without a recognition of the absolute need for salvation, the rest of the evangelical system became untenable. "Our Lord Jesus Christ came to save the lost," wrote Charles McIlvaine. "Have you been led so to see your sinfulness as to see that by it you are lost, except you flee to him for salvation? . . . Till a man knows himself as a sinner, how little will he ever learn of the Saviour."[24] Evangelical theology began by proclaiming the devastating extent of sin: the hopelessness of humans to escape this devastation was the "fundamental article of Christianity."[25] The Evangelicals defined sin as "the corruption of man, inherent in his nature, derived or propagated to us all by our first parents, by which we are overwhelmed by depraved desires, averse from good, inclined to evil, full of distrust, contempt and hatred of God; and cannot do nor even think of any thing good of ourselves."[26]

This strong commitment to the doctrine of total depravity brought the Evangelicals under attack. High Church clergy accused them of holding a Calvinist theory of predestination—regarded by many American clergymen as outside the Anglican tradition.[27] The *Repertory*'s editors met this accusation head-on. "If by Calvinism," they protested, "be meant the doctrines of original sin, sanctification by the Holy Spirit and justification by the sole merits of our Lord Jesus Christ, we plead guilty to the charge." They argued that such "Calvinist" doctrines were completely Anglican, and they appealed for their "defense to the articles and liturgy of our church." They clinched their argument by declaring the label of Calvinist as erroneous. What High Churchmen called Calvinism, explained the Evangelicals, was really "the common doctrine of all the reformed churches. . . . That which is now ignorantly called Calvinism is interwoven with the very rudiments of Christianity." Thus they claimed that they were "neither Calvinists nor Arminians"—only that in their belief of these doctrines they were committed to "the very language of the Bible itself."[28]

The *Repertory*'s response did not placate the High Churchmen, and the charge of Calvinism surfaced again. A few months after the *Repertory*'s editorial, Bishop Kemp became furious with the Evangelical clergy over the Education Society's plan to start a seminary in Maryland to compete with the High Church–leaning General Theological Seminary in New York. Seen as an attack on church unity, the proposal exacerbated party divisions. The Education Society's proposed seminary intended to teach and train Evangelical clergy for the Episcopal Church. The Rev. J. A. T. Kilgour wrote to Kemp complaining of the plan: "I cannot imagine a factory for making ministers harmonizes with our ideas of religion."[29] Kilgour was right. Kemp issued a scathing pastoral letter denouncing both the seminary and Washington's Evangelical clergy. "The general character of the Theology of the District," he charged, "was well known and unquestionably varied on some points from the clearly received doctrines of the church . . . and strenuous efforts had been made to give the doctrines of the church a Calvinistic cast."[30]

Incensed and bewildered by the attack, McIlvaine, Hawley, and Stephen Tyng responded to the bishop.[31] Kemp charged them with two things: they mutilated the liturgy, and their "Calvinism" varied from the doctrines of the Protestant Episcopal Church. McIlvaine, Hawley, and Tyng refuted the charges of liturgical innovation and argued that their practices fell within the canons of the church. Suppose we were Calvinists, they also argued. "What is the theology of the Lambeth Articles? Calvinistic of the very highest description." "Who wrote those articles?" they asked. "Whitgift, Bancroft, Cranmer and Ridley." Did these great Anglican reformers depart from Episcopal doctrine? No, they argued, of course not. "Such a theology," they pointed out, "the Clergy of the District are accused of maintaining. You . . . have not the least warrant, from the history of the Church, or the opinions of its best divines, to insinuate that our sentiments are at variance with the doctrines of our Church."[32]

Having disposed of the charges of departing from Episcopal theology, Hawley, McIlvaine, and Tyng moved to the main point: "Are we Calvinists?" As in the *Repertory* editorial, they insisted that it depended on one's definition of Calvinism. If by Calvinism one meant "the most distinguishing and peculiar of those doctrines which usually are embraced in the creeds of Calvinists, we have no right to such an appellation. The doctrines of *particular redemption and uncondi-tional reprobation*, no Episcopal Minister in the District maintains."[33] Hawley, McIlvaine, and Tyng thus rejected double predestination as un-Anglican.[34] But, on other points of Calvinism, they admitted to being Calvinists, even, as they argued, as many other Anglican divines may be called Calvinists. Charging them with Calvinism, however, was a smokescreen; it was the evangelical religion that actually galled the High Churchmen. They denounced heartfelt religion – "whatever is strict in doctrine and fervent in spirit" – by whatever name worked. "Calvinism" was now as unpopular as "Methodism" had been a few years earlier, when High Churchmen accused the Evangelicals of being "Methodistical"![35]

The discussion as to whether or not Evangelical Episcopalians were Calvinists can be confusing because of the varying ways people used the term. Kemp used Calvinist to designate those who believed in total depravity, a doctrine the Evangelicals clearly held. In the context of early American theological debates,

Calvinism generally meant God's election of persons versus human free will. Evangelical Episcopalians self-consciously placed themselves outside this debate. Drawing from the Thirty-nine Articles and Anglican theology, they believed in "ecclesiastical election." God, they argued, had elected individuals because he had elected the whole church. This, they believed, was not tied to any particular view of divine foreknowledge or free will.[36] The Calvinist-Arminian debate on free will that raged among their Reformed neighbors did not belong to the Evangelical Episcopal theological world; they were comfortable with the languages of both election and free will. McIlvaine attributed this spirit of neutrality in a Reformed quarrel to his belief that "the Articles of the English Church chiefly derive their origin from Lutheran Formularies,"[37] which he perceived placed less emphasis on the theology of predestination.

In addition to the theological rationale, some Evangelical avoidance of the conflict between predestination and free will sprang from their own history. In the 1740s and again in the 1770s, arguments over the issue between Wesley and Whitefield and their respective followers had fractured the English Evangelical revival. By the late eighteenth century, rent by Calvinist-Arminian dissention, a significant number of Evangelicals eagerly dismissed the old dispute. In 1784, when young Charles Simeon, leader of the Anglican Evangelical party (often noted for its supposed Calvinism), visited an aged John Wesley, the two men discussed the Calvinist-Arminian quarrel and concluded that they agreed on the most important issues of theology. Declared Simeon: "This is all my Calvinism. This is my election, my justification by faith, my final perseverance: It is, in substance, all that I hold, and as I hold it: and therefore, if you please, instead of searching out terms and phrases to be a ground of contention between us, we will cordially unite in those things wherein we agree."[38] Simeon was McIlvaine's hero. He read and admired no one more. He self-consciously modeled himself after the great Anglican Evangelical—a fact Simeon's Anglican colleagues recognized; they gave McIlvaine Simeon's cassock upon his death.[39] Simeon's conciliatory attitudes tremendously affected Evangelical thought in general, and McIlvaine in particular, regarding theological disputes. The Evangelicals concluded that their strength lay in unity on a few Protestant essentials; beyond those points, Evangelical Episcopalians, with other evangelicals at least, allowed for some theological latitude. Unity ranked above the finer points of either Calvinist or Arminian theology.

In America, Evangelical Episcopalians enjoyed closer relationships with Congregationalists and Presbyterians than they did with Methodists. Consequently, Evangelical Episcopal sympathies leaned (although they almost always tried to stay officially neutral) toward Calvinism, a direction their High Church colleagues clearly recognized. They viewed themselves as heirs of the Anglican Reformation, not of Calvin. Election was a biblical concept and part of Anglican formularies, but they attempted to hold the doctrine in tension with an equally biblical doctrine of free will. This *moderate Calvinism* resembled the position developed by their evangelical colleagues in the Church of England.[40] Yet in democratic America, *Calvinism* had taken on extremely objectionable connotations. Thus, Evangelical Episcopalians willingly aligned themselves with Calvinist colleagues but refused to identify their own theology as Calvinistic. They were Calvinists only as far as the English Reformers had been Calvinists, and this was a point of some debate.

For the Evangelicals, Anglican Reformation theology was the scaffolding that supported the experience of being born again. Without a correct doctrine of depravity, "how can we expect to partake of that illumination, that resurrection, and that glorious liberty?" A rightly informed theology affected the inner being, pointed to the need for God, and provided a way to escape from sin. "Our plan is," stated the *Repertory*'s editors, "to humble the sinner, and to exalt the Saviour; to show him the utmost depth of his depravity, as the best and the only means of inducing him to fly for refuge to the Lord Jesus Christ."[41]

The Heart of the Matter

Like other evangelicals, Evangelical Episcopalians believed individuals needed to experience "a change of heart by Divine Grace," to be born again.[42] Without a self-conscious turn away from sin toward God, men and women died with no hope of heaven. McIlvaine asked:

> Where will you be, what your home and portion, some thousands of ages hence? How solemn the certain truth, that in Heaven or Hell your portion must be! Will it be yours to awake to "the resurrection of life everlasting," or be summoned to "the resurrection of damnation"?. . . . There is but one promise in all the Bible which applies to you, and that is, that if you will turn unto the Lord, he will have mercy upon you.[43]

Conversion was the center of a Christian's spiritual life.[44] Depending on the experience of conversion, an individual existed in one of three spiritual states: saved, unsaved, or nominal Christian. The saved have repented of their sins and turned to God; the unsaved have rejected (or not yet had an opportunity to respond to) God's grace. Nominal Christians think they are Christians (through baptism or church attendance), but they lack ardor for Christ and are often hostile to vital, heartfelt religion.[45] Both the unsaved and the nominal need to experience new birth. Though conversion, anyone—rich or poor, educated or uneducated, white or black, male or female—entered into the presence of God and was saved.[46] Conversion was the doorway to eternal life. To gain entrance, sinners must repent of their sins, acknowledge their inability to save themselves, believe that Jesus died for them, and turn to God. Being born again involved a self-conscious change from a life of self-centered sinfulness to a life of God-centered trust.[47]

Conversion changed the inner being, and a new understanding of God transformed the sinner. "I had *heard* before," wrote McIlvaine about his own conversion; "I began then to *know*."[48] The new birth, experienced through conversion, issued forth an inner knowledge of God's transforming love and power. Conversion did more than rescue a sinner from future damnation; it revolutionized everyday life.

Although as Episcopalians, the Evangelicals were bound to a liturgical service with a set form, they did not consider forms in and of themselves to be spiritually beneficial. Forms became bad when they degenerated into formalism and hid the essence of true Christianity. The form of the liturgy could be good, however, when it led the believer into the experience of sinfulness and the need for conversion. But Evangelicals considered formalism to be a deadly enemy: pious-looking forms could disguise the sinners' need for grace to even themselves. Religious formalism relaxed the sinners' inward sensibilities by placating spiritual need. Therefore, people who actually needed to be converted found comfort by participating in forms that smothered the promptings of the Holy Spirit. Formalism caused lukewarmness, the state of being a nominal Christian. Form enabled people to think they could achieve salvation without actually experiencing God inwardly. It supplied false comfort, dulled the sense of sin, and stifled the ability to sense the inner workings of the Holy Spirit. In short, the formalism resulting from forms was evil and constrained sinners from experiencing the power of the gospel.

Evangelical Episcopalian views on forms were somewhat ambiguous throughout the nineteenth century. Depending on the situation (and the person speaking), sometimes the form was neutral, other times it was good—just not the ultimate good of true religion. Although some Evangelicals vacillated between these views, as a whole, Evangelical Episcopalians did not completely reject the use of Episcopal forms. They only rejected High Church formalism. They sought to instill the forms of the Episcopal Church with the spirit of true Christianity. They envisioned liturgy invigorated by individuals filled with personal, experiential knowledge of God's saving grace.[49]

Experiential knowledge of God implied that converted believers experienced a transformation in all areas of life. The most noticeable changes involved outward behaviors. Temperance, modesty, and moderation guided Christian behavior and included strict prohibitions against drinking, dancing, gambling, and breaking the Sabbath. Converted believers frowned on worldly amusements as a waste of God's time and as a sign of wrongly directed spirit. Evangelical Episcopalians vigorously promoted personal morality as a sign of a transformed life. Many Episcopalians, such as the latitudinarian William White, joined with the Evangelicals in promoting moral taboos and moderation in public behavior.[50] Both parties of the Episcopal Church shared religious taboos, often considered a hallmark of evangelical religion. While Evangelicals viewed abstinence, morality, and moderation as important signs of inward change and personal holiness, they recognized there could also be a different kind of formalism—little more than religious performance or proscribed duties. The question became how to differentiate between human-based morality and true Christianity.

The answer lay with the affections—the faculty of inner being centered in the heart.[51] The affections differed from the mind, which was the seat of rational ability. Infidels and fallen angels possessed intelligence and rationality. Therefore, God must judge the creatures of earth not on intelligence (or even moral ability), but on the direction of the heart. If one's heart is directed toward God, then one is saved. Holy affections, therefore, were the only sure indication of one's spiritual state. The Evangelicals balanced the practice of personal holiness—external moral behavior—by their belief in "the absolute necessity of feeling the power and influence of the spirit of God upon our hearts." Piety, virtue and holiness must arise out of transformed affections. "To be born again of the Spirit," wrote the editors of the *Washington Theological Repertory*, "requires such a change of the heart and affections, that in all cases where the change is real, it will be known and felt."[52]

The Evangelical Episcopalians believed that religious feelings—even extreme feelings—were a normal part of spiritual life: "Is it reasonable," they argued, "that a man should be charged with fanaticism, because the momentous truths of the Gospel of Christ, instead of being regarded with stoical indifference, strike with resistless force upon his mind, and excite in his bosom the liveliest emotions of admiration, wonder, love and gratitude?" New spiritual vision opened up a new world to see and experience, a realm of truth that only the "deepest emotions of the soul" could contemplate. Visions of God the creator, of the Trinity, and of Christ's resurrection could only be discerned in fullness through the affections— spiritual vistas unveiled by God through the transformation of the "eyes" of the heart in conversion. For the real Christian, the heart is "penetrated, softened and deeply affected" by the great mysteries of the gospel. This is the Christianity of the New Testament, differing radically "from that heartless and barren system of formality, with which so many rest contented."[53] True spirituality, a realm once invisible to an unregenerate person, became visible to the born again who have been given eyes to see.

Evangelicals did not neglect the mind, for proper theological doctrine explained the inner workings of men and women, but the human heart was their chief concern. They aligned themselves with Calvinist doctrines of depravity and grace because those doctrines pointed to the true wickedness of the heart; they emphasized conversion because only a radical transforming experience delivered the heart from its evil inclinations; they believed that true Christianity was the faith that sprang from a new heart—one inclined toward God. "The doctrine of the bible," Evangelical Episcopalians proclaimed, "is, that those who have truly embraced the gospel, have been born from above—have been the subjects of a radical and thorough change of heart."[54]

Evangelical Method: The Means to a Changed Heart

How to achieve a changed heart was a matter of controversy among nineteenth-century American Protestants. In the eighteenth century, Calvinist revivalists such as Jonathan Edwards believed that God sent revivals; the only effective means of promoting conversions was prayer.[55] Even in the eighteenth century, however, some evangelicals began to use a number of additional means—itinerant preaching, extended services, and class meetings—to elicit conversions to Christianity.

Early republican revivals heightened emotional fervor, and the revivalists increasingly embraced Arminian theology.[56] In the early nineteenth century, the use of additional means expanded and eighteenth-century practices were revised. The traditional sacramental meetings of the Presbyterians, for example, developed into the revivalist camp meeting.[57] Charles Finney gained fame employing these controversial revival practices. Finney, a lawyer turned Presbyterian revivalist, opposed formalism as vigorously as the Evangelical Episcopalians did, and he promoted the same sort of lively faith.[58] However, he went further with his use of means than ministers had previously, and he expanded existing revival practices. His "new measures" included protracted meetings, anxious or mourner's benches, emotional singing, inquirer's meetings, and prayer meetings. Although some of these techniques had been used before, Finney vigorously promoted them and combined them with his Arminian theology, creating a new pattern of American revivalism.[59] This pattern, in concert with the extreme emotionalism it encouraged, formed the basis for understanding salvation for many antebellum Protestants.[60] Not all used Finney's innovations, but his controversial campaigns and fiery style set the tone for much of nineteenth-century America's revivalism.[61]

In the ensuing controversies over revivalism, many American theologians rejected Finney's anxious bench style.[62] Opting for a more church-oriented approach to Christian salvation, these conservative theologians rejected the need for a conversion experience, the use of means, and the extreme emotionalism of the new measures. Among these critics were Old School Presbyterians, Lutherans, the Mercersberg German Reformed, and High Church Episcopalians.[63] New School Presbyterians, some Congregationalists, Baptists, Methodists, and some sectarian groups accepted most, and often all, of the new revival measures.[64] This lineup of pro- and antirevival factions has led historians to posit a dichotomy in antebellum American religion between evangelicals and confessionalists.[65]

Evangelical Episcopalians do not fit easily into either category. They represent a moderate, third response to America's revival culture.[66] Like other evangelicals, they accepted revivalism as an effective means of spreading true Christianity: since the 1760s, they had promoted revivals, and in the early nineteenth century, they borrowed the new revivalism and modified it. They preferred to see themselves as the revival heirs of Jonathan Edwards rather than Charles Finney, however. Revivals, they maintained, were primarily an act of God's grace. The means to promote them were extremely limited: prayer, preaching, the Episcopal liturgy, and Lenten observation. Evangelical Episcopalians conducted revivals, but they conducted them in a somewhat different, more restrained, and generally less emotional form than was current in some segments of American culture at the time. They prided themselves on the decorum of their revivals. Evangelical Episcopalians adopted such means as prayer meetings and preaching, but avoided other measures which they believed created unhealthy excesses and fanaticism.

In addition to prayer meetings and preaching, Evangelical Episcopalians experimented with Bible classes, Sunday schools, and inquiry meetings as means to extract conversions. Bible classes held particular appeal for women. Benjamin Allen, rector of St. Paul's in Philadelphia, reported great success with Bible classes for women. During the classes, young women read the litany together, studied the Scripture, listened to lectures, asked questions, and expressed their opinions about the text (usually in the form of written meditations). In the 1820s, Allen was so impressed by the serious and spiritual character of the young women in his Bible classes, he wanted to start a Christian institute for women that would teach the Bible, history, and Christian evidences. Many of his female students experienced salvation, and they started a missionary society to promote women's Bible classes in other Episcopal churches. Charles McIlvaine's Bible classes at St. Ann's in

Brooklyn were also successful in eliciting conversions. In the first year alone, seventy-one members of his Bible class at St. Ann's became born again.[67]

Liturgical and Extemporaneous Prayer

Evangelical Episcopalians conducted informal, mid-week gatherings for prayer and worship. In the eighteenth-century revival, midweek meetings accommodated the crowds of men and women who came to church, and prorevival Episcopalians, such as Devereux Jarratt in Virginia, approved of their use to promote lively religion. "We see no good reason," wrote the editors of the *Washington Theological Repertory*, "why those who fear God, and desire to save their souls, may not meet together once a week, to 'exhort one another to love and to good works', without incurring the imputation of enthusiasm and over-righteous zeal."[68] According to the Evangelicals, these meetings were a "valuable means of grace" in the promotion of vital piety.[69] Evangelical prayer meetings included a short form of liturgy, lecture, hymn-singing, Scripture reading, and extemporaneous prayer–the latter being the activity that proved most controversial to other Episcopalians. While High Church Episcopalians might allow for additional meetings that followed the forms of the liturgy, they objected to meetings that permitted extemporaneous prayer, believing it a sure course to Methodism and fanaticism. According to the High Churchmen, Evangelical prayer meetings were unruly and deviated from the liturgy. Such irregularity would undoubtedly lead people away from the church.

In spite of the controversy, Evangelical Episcopalians continued to hold prayer meetings and vigorously defended the practice. In the years before 1820, Bishop Griswold led a stunning and long-lived revival in Bristol, Rhode Island, by conducting prayer meetings in parishioner's homes.[70] Throughout his ministry, he promoted the use of "social prayer" for conversion and for Christian growth. He encouraged lay leadership and lay exhoration of such meetings as part of the biblical pattern of ministry. In addition, he defended extemporaneous prayer on the basis that *"social prayer* is generally more profitable and edifying than *hearing prayer".*[71] Prayer meetings, according to Griswold, allowed for greater lay participation and made the people not only "hearers" but "doers" of God's word. Since in early America, the liturgy was almost exclusively read by clergy, with minimal lay participation, prayer meetings widened the attractiveness and appeal of the Episcopal Church to laymen and -women in a democratic culture.[72]

In addition to broadening participation in the church, extemporaneous prayer attracted some clergy for the sense of freedom and spiritual power they derived from it. During this period, for example, the Rev. Gregory Bedell, who early in his ministry had opposed extemporaneous prayer, became convinced of its power to change hearts. On August 18, 1819, Bedell visited a sick and depressed woman, who wanted to speak of the state of her soul; Bedell talked with her and then offered an extemporaneous prayer. She was deeply moved and asked him to pray with her again, and

> it was during this second prayer that the very remarkable change in her took place. . . . We stood watching her emaciated continence, so full of pain, anxiety,

and misery, suddenly it became radiant with happiness, and lighted up with seraphic smiles. She struggled to suppress her transporting emotions until the prayer was finished, when, after a short pause, she broke the silence, and thrilled everyone present with exclaiming rapturously, "Thank God! how happy I am; let me arise and praise God for what he has done for my soul."[73]

For Bedell, this woman's conversion provided a remarkable example of the power of extemporaneous prayer. He began to hold regular, weekly prayer meetings in his own home. Stephen Tyng, McIlvaine, and other ministers similarly employed social prayer meetings and defended the practice of extemporaneous prayer.

Evangelical Episcopalians were convinced that extemporaneous prayer touched and moved the affections in ways that formal prayer sometimes could not. Therefore, they insisted on using it and argued against considering it "irregular." They claimed that the Episcopal canons provided for weekday services, as long as they read the liturgy and delivered a lecture or sermon. After meeting these conditions, they freely added a time of extemporaneous prayer without violating any Episcopal standards. Evangelical Episcopal prayer meetings always combined liturgy, teaching, and extemporaneous prayers.

Because of these liturgical "restrictions," Evangelical Episcopal prayer services were known for their decorum, but "violent shrieks of agony and obstreperous shouts of joy" were not unheard of. Emotional excesses sometimes occurred as a result of "the work of grace on the heart," so evangelicals were willing to accept them if they were not taken to the extreme.[74] God might radically move the affections, and when this occurred naturally, Evangelical Episcopalians did not object. They did oppose any method that purposefully sought to stir such emotions without the corresponding work of God's grace.

Although they modified prayer meetings to fit their tradition by including a short liturgy, Evangelical Episcopalians accepted the common practice of other American evangelicals: using additional, and sometimes emotional, meetings of teaching and extemporaneous prayer to promote vital religion.

Extemporaneous Preaching

Departing from the formalism of the eighteenth-century written Anglican sermons, nineteenth-century Evangelicals valued and practiced extemporaneous preaching. They insisted on freedom and spontaneity in both prayer and preaching. Since the days of Whitefield and the Great Awakening, American revivalist religion featured emotive, extemporaneous oratory. This style became widely accepted in the new republic and was used not only by evangelical ministers but also by politicians and other orators. The American public was fascinated by exciting and capable rhetoricians. As a young rector in Georgetown, McIlvaine "was anxious . . . to acquire the ability to speak extempore."[75] He watched politicians and practiced his sermons by memorizing texts. Within a few years, he could speak without memorization or prepared notes. He became known as a great preacher. One observer wrote:

The character of Mr. McIlvaine's preaching attracted greater interest and made a deeper impression, because such was not the prevailing style of the sermon in the

Episcopal Church at the time of his entrance upon the ministry. With some noble exceptions, the tone of the pulpit was dry, frigid and legal. Scholarly men delivered moral essays, or discoursed upon ecclesiastical order and similar topics; but there was little of life or fervor and the cardinal truths of the gospel were but faintly and feebly presented.[76]

Extemporaneous preaching was a valuable skill: a minister could speak when called on in any circumstance. Its practicality and popularity appealed to Evangelical Episcopalians. They were always willing to adapt their style to the prevailing culture in order to promote their message.

Stephen Tyng, McIlvaine's friend and fellow minister in Georgetown, became convinced that extemporaneous preaching was one of the minister's greatest tools. He cultivated this skill—not always successfully. One Sunday, when "a very conspicuous number of distinguished men" were attending his parish, Tyng attempted to preach without a manuscript. He became badly frightened, yet "I stumbled on," he recalled, "until, in entire confusion of mind and feeling, I was obliged to stop, and I left the pulpit with excessive mortification." His wife, the daughter of Bishop Griswold, reminded him, "You remember that father said, 'Extemporaneous preaching would always be crude and unconnected.' "[77] Undaunted, young Tyng kept trying. Years later, the great preacher Henry Ward Beecher said of Tyng: "He is the one man that I am afraid of. When he speaks first I do not care to follow him."[78]

Extemporaneous preaching appealed to the Evangelicals, in part, because of its simplicity. "No man," declared Tyng to a group of ministerial candidates, "begins to tell me in the midst of a fire that there is a vast amount of combustible material in great danger of ignition around my habitation; no, he cries, 'Fire! fire!' And there is direct sense in that."[79] "Your grand instrument of power," Tyng urged, "is the simplicity of the message of truth."

> Go tell what Jesus has done and suffered. Tell what Jesus has felt and said and promised. Proclaim the fullness of His divine deliverance. Testify of the glory of His complete righteousness. Open simply and distinctly to view the fountain of His atoning, all-cleansing blood. Waste not your time in earnest and unceasing exhortation, but simply, plainly, faithfully, proclaim the truth.[80]

Quite simply, the Evangelical message matched the rhetorical style of extemporaneous preaching. Nineteenth-century Evangelicals recognized this strength and made preaching an intrinsic part of their Episcopal ministry.

Evangelical Episcopalians believed that ministers should not merely perform certain rites and liturgies, but proclaim new life in Christ. Preaching, therefore, was at the center of their vision of the Christian ministry. "The influence of the gospel ministry," stated Tyng, "is not that of visible ceremony, of official duty, but it is the influence of proclaimed truth."[81] As much as they valued liturgy, preaching was held up as supremely important. "How far your ministry," McIlvaine advised young clergymen, "will be that of a faithful 'steward of the mysteries of God' will depend on how far it shall be the faithful preaching of Jesus Christ."[82] They elevated preaching—particularly extemporaneous preaching—above the liturgy. "Our Saviour's command to preach the Gospel to all," wrote Bishop Griswold, "is not to be restricted to those who have Prayer-Books, and will perform the service."[83] "Go preach the gospel," not "go celebrate the eucharist," was the constant call of nineteenth-century Evangelicals.

Revivalism and a Theology of Revival

Since its founding in the 1780s, isolated revivals had occurred in the Protestant Episcopal Church, but in the early years of the nineteenth century, their number and frequency increased. Between 1812 and 1820, Bishop Griswold led his Bristol, Rhode Island, parish in a series of revivals. At about the same time, the Rev. Richard Channing Moore revived St. Stephen's Church in New York City with prayer meetings, Bible classes, clerical associations, and preaching. Moore vigorously opposed Finney-style revivalism, but he believed that Evangelical ministers should promote vital religion—that which excited the affections.[84] When Moore was elected bishop of Virginia, he encouraged Evangelical revivalism throughout his diocese with spectacular results.[85]

In the early 1820s, the Washington Evangelicals conducted revivals in all their parishes, and the *Washington Theological Repertory* regularly reported on revivals in both the Episcopal Church and other communions. In his early years at the parish in Georgetown, McIlvaine set apart a congregational day of prayer and fasting with "a special view towards the revival of religion among us."[86] During his five years at Christ Church, McIlvaine was a popular preacher, well liked particularly for his zeal and piety.[87] In 1825, he left Georgetown and accepted the prestigious appointment as chaplain to the military academy at West Point.[88]

When McIlvaine arrived at West Point, no faculty or cadets there publicly professed faith. The only communicants at the academy were three wives of faculty members. His sermons made quite an impression, as Gen. Crafts Wright remembered years later: "On the first Sunday of Dr. McIlvaine's preaching at West Point the cadets went to chapel, as usual, some with books to read, and others hoping to sleep, but none expecting to take any interest in the sermon. Had a bugle been sounded in the chapel they could not have been more astonished. Books were dropped, sleep was forgotten, attention was riveted."[89] McIlvaine continued to pray, preach, and teach, but even his preaching did not result in a single conversion in that first year. The second year, however, proved quite different. Cadet Leonidas Polk came to him after having read a tract on the evidences of Christianity. Convicted of his sins, Polk desired forgiveness from Christ. McIlvaine counseled him and prayed with him for salvation.

McIlvaine knew that the news of Polk's conversion would spread throughout the academy, so he advised the young cadet to make a public profession of his new faith quickly. Recalled McIlvaine:

> The next day when the confession in the service came, I could hear his movement to get space to kneel, and then his deep tone of response, as if he were trembling with new emotion; and then it seemed as if an impression of solemnity pervaded the congregation. It was a new sight, that single kneeling cadet. Such a thing had not been supposed to be possible.[90]

Polk's example prompted many young men to consult Chaplain McIlvaine. With spiritual fervor rising, he "found it necessary to have meetings for them twice or thrice a week" in his house for instruction, worship, and prayer. Polk, along with a fellow converted cadet, was baptized forty days after his first confession. No adult baptism had ever been performed in the academy's chapel, and the service led to more conversions.[91] Although he tried to limit publicity, word soon leaked out of a revival at West Point, and McIlvaine became a nationally known preacher and revivalist.[92]

Not all Episcopalians approved of an Episcopal chaplain conducting revivals. From his parish in New York, James Milnor reported to McIlvaine that "the enemies of truth are busy in spreading here the grossest misrepresentations of the character of the revival." McIlvaine faced charges of turning "the military academy into a theological seminary, and aiming to make young men soldiers in the Church militant."[93] That Milnor heard grumbling in New York probably did not surprise McIlvaine; in spite of Milnor's presence at St. George's, no Episcopal diocese was more completely run by the High Church party than that of New York. High Church Episcopalians vigorously criticized revivalism as disorderly and irrational, and they charged the Evangelical revivalists with "innovation." They maintained that their own conception of church and ministry was primitive and apostolic, and thus in line with the practice of the early church. Revivalist religion, they argued, was not biblical. Only Episcopal church order could combat the evils of revivalistic innovations.[94]

In spite of his reputation as a revivalist, even Charles McIlvaine was worried about fanaticism at West Point—anxieties he shared with his friend James Milnor. Some aberrations occurred, and some of the charges leveled in New York were not without basis. As a result, McIlvaine wondered what distinguished true revivals from mere "extravagances." Revivals, he came to believe, must produce both conversions and holy living. Many so-called revivals were little more than excitement. In genuine revival, the converted will demonstrate the fruit of the Holy Spirit. A few years later, McIlvaine advised a congregation in Ohio:

> If professing Christians have been led to more prayer and love, more diligence in all duty, and a more circumspect walk and conversation; if those who entertain the hope that they have lately given themselves to Christ, and found reconciliation, are careful to maintain good works, and manifest the genuine evidence of conversion in humility and meekness, in brotherly kindness and charity [then] . . . it is the work of the Spirit.[95]

Efforts to kindle excitement—for McIlvaine excitement must not be worked up by the revivalist, but must arise from the effect of the Spirit working in the inner person—and "endeavors to produce animal feeling" will mark a false revival. All these things must be avoided. In a genuine revival, McIlvaine believed that "all things be done decently and in order" and that "quietness and soberness" should pervade the atmosphere.[96]

Only a few means to promote revivalism existed, and they must minimize the possibility of fanaticism: preaching, prayer (both private and communal), and Bible study. Multiple meetings were an important part of a revival, but ministers should limit them. Whenever possible, ministers should lead meetings, but they may also choose "those whose Christian character is established" to lead these additional gatherings.[97] Inquiry meetings should be used with discretion. They should not encourage excitement; rather, these meetings should be a time when those interested in salvation may ask the minister (or other mature Christians) questions about the Christian faith.

McIlvaine emphasized caution and order when conducting revivals. Appalled by excesses of emotionalism, he warned that counterfeit revivals were "forgeries of Satan." A false revival was more dangerous than no revival at all: "The fever may look and act exceedingly like healthy religion – but it will either mount at last to wild derangement, or pass off and leave the subjects more perfectly prostrate and helpless than ever."[98] False revivalism, McIlvaine argued, was a new, and insidious, kind of formalism: participants would believe they had been saved by acting their part in a revival, but actually they would be as far from the transforming effects of true Christianity as ever. Revival techniques had become a new sort of "evangelical liturgy." Without the spirit of God, they could be as dangerous as any other kind of formalist religion.

To prevent the spread of false religion, a genuine revival must be guided by a discerning and educated clergyman. The surest check against both innovation and excess was that of the minister and other mature leaders who must carefully follow all the rules of the denomination. "Old modes of doing things," recognized McIlvaine, "are apt to seem worn out . . . to minds under new excitement." But those very things have been established by "the ordinances of the gospel, and the wisdom of all ages has been content with" them. Novelty, for McIlvaine, should "consist in newness of life, in an unwonted spirit of prayer, and faith, and love, rather than in new devices and novel modes."[99] He believed that old forms could be filled with new life and urged that the Episcopal liturgy be used more frequently during revivals than at other times: "Never does a Church need a liturgy, a form of prayer for public worship, more than in a revival of religion. It serves as a help to all that is of the Holy Ghost, as a check against that disposition to extravagance and novelty by which so many revivals have been deformed."[100]

McIlvaine's position on revivalism was neither a full-scale rejection (as was that of High Church Episcopalians) nor a wholesale acceptance of Finneyite revivalism. He argued that revivals were necessary and vital to the church, but that they should be limited to a few and be under the direct control of the minister. Revivals were of two sorts: true and counterfeit. The chief marks of a true revival were decorum and the participants' commitment to church order; counterfeit revivals may resemble real revivals, but they would lead to excesses, disharmony, and disorder. True revivals promoted true Christianity and unified Christians in the love of God; false revivals obliterated true religion, inoculated people against vital piety, and caused schism. By articulating this position, McIlvaine was in the company of other American Protestants who accepted revivalism within proscribed limits.[101] These moderates both practiced revival religion within the context of their traditional Protestantism and criticized the more extreme and sectarian forms of revivalism.

McIlvaine eventually lost his position at West Point as a result of the revival.[102] As a response to the unnamed excesses of the West Point revival, he developed a guarded form of revivalism – one heavily dependent on trained leadership. During his long career, he would conduct many more revivals, but none would be quite like the controversial West Point affair. Although he was criticized by the New York City Episcopal establishment, the publicity earned him friends among revivalistic Episcopalians. Several churches issued him calls to become rector. One, St. Paul's, in Rochester, New York, had been rocked by Charles Finney's revivals. The St. Paul's invitation issued forth a storm of controversy. McIlvaine's High Church enemies, particularly Henry Onderdonk, used the West Point revival as ammunition against his appointment to St. Paul's[103] and McIlvaine eventually declined the offer. Instead, he accepted a call from St. Ann's Church in Brooklyn, New York, to fight for evangelical truth in the middle of the Episcopal Church's most High Church diocese.[104]

Episcopal Spiritual Experience: Confirmation as Public Profession of Conversion

During his years at St. Ann's, McIlvaine faced the question of how to incorporate revivalistic religion into the weekly life of his parish. How could the forms and rites of the Episcopal Church be used to promote true religion? In addition to prayer, preaching, and revivalism, Evangelical Episcopalians developed a uniquely Episcopal approach to eliciting a born-again experience. They used confirmation as a time of spiritual preparation and admitted only those confirmands who testified to being reborn into the church's membership.

In early Christianity, when adult baptism was the norm, baptism and confirmation formed a single initiation rite; later, when infant baptism became standard practice, the one rite was separated into two. Infant baptism was the initiation, and confirmation, (usually administered to children and adolescents) became a time to catechize and reaffirm the baptismal vows. Only those confirmed could partake of the Lord's Supper. The English Reformers retained both rites, and confirmation became a time for baptized persons to give some sort of knowledgeable assent to the Christian faith.[105] American Episcopalians, Evangelical and High Church, treated the service with great seriousness and urged confirmands to devote themselves to God and to embrace the spiritual benefits of Christian life found through renewing work of the Holy Spirit and the sacrament of the Lord's Supper.[106]

Evangelical Episcopalians viewed infant baptism in terms of covenant theology and confirmation as an ideal time for the baptized to personally appropriate their baptismal covenant. In confirmation, one was required to publicly profess a personal faith in Christ. Since they did not believe that every baptized person would necessarily be saved, confirmation supplied them with a liturgical rite congruent with their idea of evangelism. To them, personal profession included intellectual assent to certain doctrines and testified to inward, spiritual change. The Episcopal Church's official qualifications for confirmation were few: knowledge of the Apostles' Creed, the Lord's Prayer, the Ten Commandments, and the catechism. But the Evangelicals added spiritual qualifications to the rite, which emphasized their belief in the need to be born again. "Knowledge is a small part," wrote McIlvaine, "of the qualifications required for Confirmation. There is a *preparation of the heart*, as well as *the answer of the tongue*."[107]

To assist confirmands at St. Ann's, McIlvaine prepared a series of meditation questions that emphasized Evangelical beliefs and separated his views from those of High Churchmen. For example, he asked the candidate to examine his or her heart. Is it, he inquired, "the fountain of sin, so that in you naturally dwells no good thing?" "Are your affections set upon God and upon holiness?" He implored the candidate to renounce all human "religious efforts," duties, works, and feelings in hope of salvation. "Have you fled to [Christ] and committed your soul to him as all your refuge and righteousness?"[108] Although his questions follow the sense of the confirmation rite in the Book of Common Prayer, they nevertheless reflect the distinct evangelical concerns for sin and the total reliance on grace (and not, in any way, the church) for salvation, holy living, and spirituality.

"The single paramount, indispensable qualification," wrote Stephen Tyng, "for this ordinance, is a *converted heart*."[109] The High Churchmen believed that spiritual disposition was important as well, but they also believed that confirmation would add grace for salvation. In short, confirmation would help the baptized person be a better Christian. In contrast, Evangelicals did not believe that all baptized persons were already Christians, so confirmation, therefore, added no grace to salvation. To the Evangelicals, one must already be converted before being confirmed. Confirmation was a public sign and profession of the internal work of grace. For them, it functioned much as adult baptism did for Baptists. Because of these beliefs about confirmation, Evangelical clergymen and bishops used the rite to urge baptized laypeople to examine their spiritual state and, if they found themselves distant from God, to repent and be born again. The rite, therefore, served as an evangelistic tool for those who had been baptized but had not yet experienced grace. Evangelical bishops, such as McIlvaine would later become, frequently warned clergy that no Episcopalian should be confirmed who could not testify to an *experience* of grace.[110] Only such an experience admitted one into the full privileges of the Christian life and the Episcopal Church. "On no occasion," boasted one prominent Ohio clergyman, "have any been admitted to the Table of the Lord, without giving sound 'spiritual evidence' . . . that they were '*born again*,'–that they knew, by a personal experience, what it is to become '*new creatures* in Christ Jesus.' "[111]

The Evangelical Goal: Kingdom of God on Earth

During his five years at St. Ann's, 1827 to 1832, McIlvaine joined in many of the great Christian causes consuming American Protestants. Evangelical Episcopalian religion was not simply an internal spiritual change; it was an activist stance against the evil of the world. New York was a strategic center in this crusade against Satan's forces: the American Bible Society, the American Tract Society, seamen's societies, temperance societies, and numerous moral reform groups all had headquarters there.

In the early years of the nineteenth century, Christians formed a remarkable number of such voluntary societies to further the work of their churches and spread the kingdom of God. They were formed for many purposes–everything from church building to missions to education to social reform. The voluntary principle—that of joining together to promote the cause of religion—was alive and well in the early years of the Episcopal Church, also. High Church Bishop Hobart was involved in founding several societies, including the Protestant Episcopal Theological Education Society (1806) and the New York Bible and Common Prayer Book Society (1809).[112] Evangelicals started societies for the education of ministers and for the distribution of prayer books and Anglican sermons. In spite of their unanimity on the voluntary principle, Evangelicals and High Churchmen argued about the extent of voluntary participation with other Protestants. Both parties agreed that it was right to organize societies to further Episcopal religion, but only the Evangelicals believed that they could cooperate with other Protestants to advance a general Christian good. Evangelicals, therefore, participated in mixed societies: that is, voluntary societies whose membership was drawn from a number of denominations. High Churchmen argued that such participation would undercut the exclusive claims of the Episcopal Church; Evangelicals believed that such participation would increase godliness in society.

The Episcopal conflict over voluntary societies illustrates the two parties' views of salvation, holy living, and society. For the High Churchmen, salvation was found in the Episcopal Church alone, holy living was formed by participation in its rites, and the church was a sort of "ark" in the midst of American society. Evangelicals, on the other hand, believed that men and women in other denominations could be saved, that holiness was the outworking of the transformed heart of the converted person, and that individual holiness would result in a purified social order. To them, voluntary societies were organizations of redeemed individuals seeking to live out a holy life in the world. By example, by preaching, and by exhortation holiness would spread throughout the world until the kingdom of God would be revealed in its fullness.

Millennialism and the Kingdom of God

Like other evangelicals, Evangelical Episcopalians equated the kingdom of God with a millennial reign of Jesus Christ on earth. From the early years of the nineteenth century, biblical prophecies regarding the millennium fascinated Evangelical Episcopalians. Benjamin Allen, rector of St. Paul's in Philadelphia, closely studied English works on prophecy. He prepared American editions of George Croley's work on the Apocalypse and, most important, was the American editor of Edward Irving who wrote on the books of Daniel and Revelation.[113] In the early 1820s, Allen taught his women's Bible class "a knowledge of history in connexion with the prophecies of Scripture."[114] In 1828, Allen triumphantly proclaimed, "We are within forty years of the Millennium."[115] Although he died young, Allen was extremely influential: among his close friends were McIlvaine, Tyng, and Virginia Bishop William Meade. But Allen was no eccentric or isolated student of millennialism among Evangelical Episcopalians; Episcopal ministers John P. K. Henshaw, Isaac Labagh, Edward Winthrop, Richard C. Shimeall, and George E. Hare all published books or magazines devoted to millennialism.[116]

Two views of the millennium were current in nineteenth-century America. *Premillennialism*, the view promoted by Edward Irving and John Nelson Darby, stated that Christ's second coming would be followed by the millennium, a literal 1,000-year period of peace and happiness. *Postmillennialism* argued that the present age would grow in righteousness and become the millennium, and after 1,000 years of earthly peace, Christ would return to establish a new heaven and earth.[117] Supposedly, premillennialists had a pessimistic view of the future: the world would be destroyed before Christ would return. Postmillennialists, conversely, were optimists: they worked to bring about the kingdom because they believed that the world would improve before Christ's return. The millennial views of Evangelical Episcopalians are not so neatly categorized, however. Allen, for example, seemed to have been a postmillennialist early on and then switched to premillennialism: in both instances, his millennialism contained elements of optimism and pessimism. The imagery of Revelation – of destruction and triumph – fill the pages of Evangelical works on prophecy.[118] The real point for Evangelical Episcopalians was that there would be a millennium, a golden age of Christ's triumphant rule; how it came about was secondary to the fact that it would be. Thus, unless an Evangelical Episcopalian spelled out his exact position, it was often difficult to tell whether he or she was pre- or postmillennial in theology.

That there would be a millennium (regardless of how it arrived) was key to the Evangelical worldview. In the world, the kingdom would always be, in some measure, invisible. No church, no nation could encompass it. During the millennium, however, the kingdom would be made visible; in it, the corporate body of all believers would finally be seen. These believers would live without sin, in eternal triumph with Jesus over the evil of the world and Satan. In the millennial age, the world would be completely transformed from sin into glory.

There is an analogy here between personal and communal salvation. As the revival was an instrument to save individuals, so the voluntary society was an instrument to save society: through the revival, individuals were saved; through the voluntary society, society was saved. As instruments of reform and redemption, these societies spread the good news of the kingdom. Voluntary societies were a communal expression of individual salvation: Christians banded together to make visible, in some small way, the peace and unity that awaited the world in the millennium. Evangelical Episcopalians wholeheartedly participated in this effort to bring about millennial glory in the world. St. Ann's Episcopal Church in New York City was an ideal place for McIlvaine to work to bring about the kingdom of God. New York was the headquarters for numerous benevolent enterprises; it was the headquarters of the Protestant evangelical benevolent empire.

The Church and the Kingdom

McIlvaine arrived at St. Ann's after a good deal of controversy. The church's previous rector, Henry U. Onderdonk, had opposed McIlvaine's call to St. Paul's in Rochester. Onderdonk wrote St. Paul's vestry and accused McIlvaine of being a "half-churchman, a great opponent of Bishop Hobart, and a zealous promoter of the schemes that would blend us with Presbyterians." After Onderdonk wrote his letter, and had it published in a Philadelphia newspaper, he was elected assistant bishop of Pennsylvania. His parish, St. Ann's, promptly called McIlvaine as their rector! Of 105 pew-holders, seventy-five signed the call to McIlvaine. St. Ann's knew they were getting an evangelical rector, and they were getting a rector clearly disliked by their own former minister. Onderdonk had "avowed the determination to leave no stone unturned to prevent [McIlvaine's] election at Brooklyn."[119] So, winning the call to St. Ann's was no small victory for McIlvaine. Charles McIlvaine was going into an Evangelical lion's den: he was elected rector of the church of one of his bitterest critics—a church under the supervision of Bishop John Henry Hobart. McIlvaine and his friend James Milnor were the lone Evangelical Episcopal ministers in New York City.

When Onderdonk charged McIlvaine with being a "promoter of schemes that would blend us with the Presbyterians," everyone knew what he meant. Onderdonk was referring to McIlvaine's participation in and support for voluntary societies. The Presbyterians had been so instrumental in establishing such organizations that other denominations considered them a Presbyterian plot.[120] McIlvaine freely confessed "the only societies or schemes out of the Episcopal Church with which the accused is connected, are the *American Bible Society* and the *American Tract Society*."[121]

Since its organization in 1815, the American Bible Society had caused controversy among New York Episcopalians. Hobart disliked such interdenominational organizations and urged Episcopalians to support only the work of Episcopal societies to distribute the Bible along with the *Book of Common Prayer*. Rejecting the idea that evangelism could be conducted separately from the particular form of a church, he argued against Christian cooperative ventures for evangelism: the gospel could not be presented without presenting some sort of church tradition. Hobart could not conceive of Christian truth separate from the form of the Episcopal Church.[122]

Not so for McIlvaine. He believed that Episcopalians could and should "unite and mingle with . . . brethren of other churches in the promotion of those schemes for the extension of the knowledge of 'the truth as it is in Jesus.' "[123] Accordingly, a common core of "the grand essential doctrine of the cross of Christ" united all true Christians and transcended denominational particularities. By embracing the grand essential doctrines of Christianity, men and women experienced salvation. It was possible, therefore, to promote these essential doctrines without promoting a particular denomination.

Evangelical Episcopalians separated the gospel core from Episcopal particularity. They also distinguished the visible church from the invisible church. The *visible church* expressed various forms of Christianity based on nonfundamental issues of faith and practice; therefore, it existed on earth in different forms. Evangelical Episcopalians believed that the Episcopal Church was the "truest" and most primitive of all visible churches; still, other churches were legitimate expressions of the Christian faith. The *invisible church* comprised all those who were true believers regardless of denominational affiliation. Made up of all born-again persons, the invisible church was known only to God and could not be seen in it fullness on earth. It was primarily a spiritual entity. For Evangelical Episcopalians, then, it was possible to be a member of the visible church and not a member of the invisible church. Membership in the invisible church resulted from an inward experience of grace. The visible church and the invisible church were not necessarily congruous. Wrote McIlvaine:

> However great the value and necessity of visible ordinances and sacraments to the visible form of the otherwise invisible house of God . . . we cannot keep too distinct the great truth, nor urge it too plainly, that it is not these which constitute the true Church of God, whatever their office as parts of, and as essential to, its visible form; that the great constituent act on which the whole being of the true Church depends, is just that on which all true peity in each soul depends–the coming of sinners, each for himself, unto Christ, by faith.[124]

The visible church consisted of all "professing Christians"; the invisible church "only real Christians." The visible church is "seen of men, in the mixed mass of the true and false, the genuine and the counterfeit, people of God." In contrast, the invisible church is "seen only of God, in the unmixed company of all His faithful people."[125]

Discontinuity between the visible and invisible church was one of the distinguishing marks of Evangelical Episcopalianism; salvation could, and did, occur outside the Episcopal Church. High Church Episcopalians, on the other hand, believed that the salvation of non-Episcopalians was left to the "uncovenanted mercies of God." McIlvaine believed that other Christians may be wrong about particular points of church polity or worship, but they certainly were within the grasp of God's grace:

> Should [an Episcopalian] offer his Christian brethren of other churches no better consolation than "uncovenanted mercy," he would think it equivalent to an opinion that their souls are utterly destitute of hope. But blessed be God, he is not obliged to regard them as in a condition so miserable. With all his heart, he can carry to them, as beloved brethren in Christ, the overflowing "cup of blessing"; and can say to "all that love the Lord Jesus in sincerity," of whatever name of form, "He that believeth in the Son hath everlasting life."[126]

Since all born-again Christians shared in the hope of Christ's salvation and were members of the same invisible church, Evangelical Episcopalians participated with other denominations to promote general evangelical truth. McIlvaine, and numerous Evangelical Episcopalians, gladly joined in the American Bible Society's crusade to publish the Bible without note or comment. Appealing to common sense, Evangelical Episcopalians believed that the Bible could communicate its truths to the human heart without ecclesiastical interference, and through it, many people would be spiritually transformed.

By participating in voluntary interdenominational organizations, Evangelical Episcopalians subordinated the form of the Episcopal Church to general Christian cooperation. They did not do this, however, because they disregarded the church. Instead, they had greater regard for the *invisible* church–the church of all believers– that would become visible only in the last days. The visible form of the Episcopal Church (or any other church, for that matter) was of secondary importance to the unified Body of Christ. They did not, therefore, disregard the church, as was claimed by High Churchmen; they had a different conception of the church. This concept was closely tied to their millennial views.

Christian cooperation signified the beginning of millennial glory. In an address to the American Tract Society in 1826, McIlvaine preached on Christian cooperation and praised the prospect that "Christians are rapidly learning, while they differ in opinion upon subordinate subjects, to differ in heart upon none." This "unity of hearts rather than of opinion" exhibited mature Christian character and the Holy Spirit's work. McIlvaine argued that it was wonderful when Christians in the same church displayed such "harmony and love." How much more wonderful, therefore, "when you behold the members of many different denominations and the advocates of as many varieties of secondary opinions, maintaining those opinions not in anger and strife, but with . . . charity . . . and delighting to forsake the arena of sectarian . . . controversy, to mingle their minds, and hearts, and labours in the spread of that knowledge of Christ."[127] To McIlvaine, this kind of Christian cooperation was a sign and symbol of the kingdom of God; it was a union of real peace and love. McIlvaine prophesied:

> The more extensive [such cooperation] shall become, the more will the Gospel triumph in the world, and the day when it shall pervade the whole militant church, and animate the hearts of its members, of every kindred and tongue, will be the day of the bursting forth of that millennial glory, when Barbarians, Scythian, Bond and Free, shall stretch out their hands unto God, and when at that "name which is above every name, every knee shall bow, of things in heaven, and things in earth, and things under the earth."[128]

The goal of all Evangelical endeavor was to bring forth this kingdom in the world. The voluntary societies were key to that goal: they functioned both as instruments to further the kingdom and as harbingers of its approach. Evangelical Episcopalians recognized this dual purpose. In his sermon to the American Tract Society, McIlvaine saw the Christian union promoted by the societies as a sign of the increase of Christian love in the last days. The voluntary societies did something the visible church could not do: through Christian cooperation, they embodied the invisible church. Pragmatically, the books published by the tract society would spread the Gospel and bring many more people into the kingdom, thus enlarging the reign of God.

No one nation could encompass this reign of millennial glory. McIlvaine did not believe that America would be God's new Israel.[129] The kingdom that was spreading throughout the world was a kingdom of God's peculiar people. "They are not," argued McIlvaine, "separated from all nations; but scattered among all nations. . . . Not restricted as of old to one territory, but citizens of all territories." The kingdom of God, "the commonwealth of Israel," was outside the boundaries of nationality. "With regard to country and language and time, [the new Israel] is the Catholic Church," proclaimed McIlvaine, "catholic, as it is for all people and is to be among all people; catholic, as it endures to all generations. This kingdom of God is the purchased possession of Christ. . . . It is his mystical body." This kingdom was not to be confused with any nation. "All things in the movements of nations," argued McIlvaine, "are made to work together for the final good and triumph of his church." Nations, including America, are required by God's plan to serve the church—"in other words to serve that Gospel of which she is the honored depository, to serve the Christ and God of the Gospel, in the ways and through the outward ordinances of the church of the Gospel."[130] No nation can encompass the kingdom; all nations must serve the kingdom. Any nation that refused to serve God and his church would be destroyed.

America was not God's new Israel. The new Israel, the millennial rule of God, comprised all believers throughout the world. The best that America, as a nation, could hope for was to be a part of that new Israel. The nation was responsible to recognize "the existence of God as the Ruler of nations" and to model national laws after the laws of God. With this basic obedience, a nation created a climate of stability and provided "a wholesome measure of morality" for the furtherance of the work of the church.[131] If these conditions were met, God would bless any nation (America included), and freedom and prosperity would increase.

At this juncture, millennialism, voluntary societies, and their theory of society came together for Evangelical Episcopalians. America was not the millennial kingdom. Nonetheless, it could participate in that kingdom by virtue of national obedience. The possibility existed to be part of the new Israel, or to be destroyed (as God had allowed France's political power to be diminished following the French Revolution). Voluntary societies served both the millennial and the national kingdoms. The societies spread the gospel (and brought more people into the kingdom of God), and they promoted general morality (by which the nation would be more obedient to God's laws). McIlvaine was under no illusions: voluntary societies could not bring forth Christ's reign on American soil; they could only restrain national wickedness and promote national obedience. Voluntary societies were, bringing forth the kingdom from the soil of the invisible, universal church, however; they were indeed the precursors and the instruments of the millennium. Insofar as America would allow the untrammeled growth of the church, that invisible body of believers, she would, as a nation, be blessed.

Because McIlvaine did not conceive of America's voluntary societies as the only harbingers of the millennium, he rejoiced in the multiplication of such societies throughout the Protestant world. The kingdom was coming forth from all Protestant nations, not just America. Charles McIlvaine's first exposure to the spread of the kingdom in the rest of the world came in 1830. During his third year at St. Ann's, he was taken ill and sent to Europe to rest. He spent most of his time in England, with his friend James Milnor, who had addressed most of the British benevolent societies during their May meetings.[132] McIlvaine arrived in time to address two seamen's societies and the British Sunday school society meetings. In addition, he attended the Islington conference, held at the home of Daniel Wilson.[133] He met Hannah More and attended the meetings of the British Anti-Slavery Society, where he met William Wilberforce. He spent a week in Cambridge, where he dined with Charles Simeon. For nearly eight months, he traveled with Milnor; together they met and visited all of England's evangelical leaders (including many non-Anglican evangelicals). This visit laid down a pattern of cooperation between the evangelical societies of the two countries that would remain in place throughout the nineteenth century.[134] For McIlvaine, Britain was as important in bringing forth the millennium as was America.[135] The goal for all evangelical believers—everywhere in the world—was the spread and promotion of the kingdom of God.

Conclusion

By 1832, Charles McIlvaine was well known as a leader of both the Evangelical party in the Episcopal Church and transdenominational evangelicalism. Like other America evangelicals, he stressed the importance of a transformed heart: revivalism was an instrument through which the heart was transformed. McIlvaine also believed that the millennium—the period of perfect unity, harmony, peace and love; the time of Christ's reign on earth—was dawning. To hasten the millennium, he participated in voluntary societies. He believed these societies, which were composed of Christians from many evangelical denominations, would bring in the kingdom of God. At that time, the church—now invisible and divided—would become visible and united.

Episcopal High Churchmen like Bishop Hobart rejected all these concepts. The visible church, they insisted, was the only instrument of the kingdom of God, and the only true expression of that visible church was the Episcopal Church. They rejected both revivalism and evangelical millennialism. They refused to cooperate with other Protestants in voluntary societies. All such things were "innovations" that ruined the primitive gospel truth of the Episcopal Church.

Evangelical religion had not won the day in the Episcopal Church, but it was fast becoming a formidable force. Before 1820, Evangelical Episcopalianism was little more than a loose network of like-minded persons. By 1830, the clergy had succeeded in turning this network into a church party complete with its own defined theology, periodicals, influential parishes, well-known leaders, and a theological seminary. Eighteenth-century evangelicalism may have faded because of lack of effective leadership; the nineteenth-century clergy were motivated to ensure that the same would not happen. McIlvaine's mission, to bring the Episcopal Church back to its evangelical heritage, was being accomplished. It was, however, being achieved by institutionalizing the spirit of true Christianity—a difficult maneuver under the best of circumstances. It was made more difficult in the Episcopal Church because of the conflicts between evangelical spirituality and the forms of Episcopalianism. The more power Evangelicals gained, the more compromises they would be forced to make. This, however, was not obvious as these young clergymen organized themselves into a party determined to shape the identity of the church.

In 1832, a strategic opportunity opened up for Charles McIlvaine. Ohio Episcopalians elected him as their bishop. As a parish priest, he might convert many people. As a bishop, he could help shape an evangelical direction for the entire church. For a man on a mission, the authority and power of being bishop overcame any feelings of inadequacy or insecurity he may have had. God had called him, and as an obedient slave, he had no choice. The cultivated, Princeton-educated McIlvaine left his cosmopolitan New York parish for the wild west.

Notes

1. For the character of Princeton at the time, see Mark A. Noll, *Princeton and the Republic, 1768–1822: The Search for a Christian Enlightenment in the Era of Samuel Stanhope Smith* (Princeton, 1989).

2. Rev. Ashbel Green, "Letter XVIII" in the Appendix to William B. Sprague, *Lectures on Revivals of Religion* (Albany, New York, Philadelphia, and Boston, 1832), 133–134. Some of this is a reworked version of idem, *A Report to the Trustees of the College of New Jersey; Relative to a Revival of Religion Among the Students of Said College, in the Winter and Spring of the Year 1815* (Philadelphia, 1815). For Alexander's account, see James Alexander, *The Life of Archibald Alexander, D.D.* (New York, 1854), 392–394. For a student's view of the revival, including McIlvaine's participation, see A. A. Hodge, *The Life of Charles Hodge, D.D., LL.D. Professor in the Theological Seminary, Princeton, N.J.* (New York, 1880), 30–38. For the Princeton revival, its aftermath, and its effect on American culture, see Thomas J. Wertenbaker, *Princeton, 1746–1896* (Princeton, 1946), 165–166, and Noll, *Princeton and the Republic*, 272–291, especially 279–280.

3. Charles P. McIlvaine, *Bishop McIlvaine's Address to the Convention of the Diocese of Ohio, on the Revival of Religion* (Cincinnati, 1858), 7.

4. McIlvaine's mother became a communicant after his conversion. For a brief memoir of his time at Princeton, see Carus, *Memorials of McIlvaine*, 9–12.

5. Most notably, the Rev. John Johns, who later became Episcopal bishop of Virginia, and Dr. Charles Hodge, Presbyterian minister, one of the most influential theologians in America in the nineteenth century.

6. On Wharton, see Sprague, *Annals of the American Pulpit*, V: 335–342, and Christopher M. Agnew, "The Reverend Charles Wharton, Bishop William White and the Proposed Book of Common Prayer, 1785," *Anglican and Episcopal History* 58 (1989): 510–525.

7. For more on White, see Woolverton, "Philadelphia's William White," and Sydney A. Temple, Jr., *The Common Sense Theology of Bishop White* (New York, 1946). For more on White's list, see Mullin, *Episcopal Vision/American Reality*, 11–18, and Prichard, "Theological Consensus."

8. McIlvaine was not the only awakened Episcopalian to consider the Presbyterian ministry. The Rev. Dr. James May, later to become professor of church history at two Episcopal seminaries, reported a similar experience. After having converted at Presbyterian Jefferson College, May almost entered the Presbyterian ministry before finally deciding to become an Episcopal clergyman. See Alexander Shiras, *Life and Letters of Rev. James May, D.D.* (Philadelphia, n.d.), 12–21.

9. Carus, *Memorials of McIlvaine*, 16.

10. Preceding quotes from "The Minister of Christ Exhorted to Growth in Grace," in *The Truth and the Life: Twenty-Two Sermons*, by Charles P. McIlvaine. (New York, 1854), 489–490.

11. Ibid., 501.

12. All quotes this paragraph from Charles P. McIlvaine, *Origin and Design of the Christian Ministry: A Sermon* (Gambier, Ohio, 1839), 10–12.

13. Ibid., 11.

14. Carus, *Memorials of McIlvaine*, 199–200.

15. Ibid.

16. Ibid., 14.

17. In his *Popular Mood of Pre-Civil War America*, Lewis Saum explores the melancholic aspects of evangelical religion among common people. Although no common person, McIlvaine's private writings reflect the same sort of fears and religious doubts Saum describes.

18. Evangelicalism arose as a response to "dead orthodoxy" in seventeenth- and eighteenth-century Europe. In the years following the Reformation, Protestants were surprised that their rejection of Catholicism did not result in holy living. A division developed between "orthodoxy" and "piety." Puritans, Pietists, and Evangelicals attempted to instill orthodox Protestant doctrine with an experience of holy living. The classic statement of the problem of "dead orthodoxy" is probably Philip Jacob Spener's *Pia Desideria* appearing in 1675, trans. and ed. Theodore G. Tappert (n.p., 1964). For the development of the experiential religious movements of Pietism, Puritanism, and evangelicalism, see Ted A. Campbell, *The Religion of the Heart: A Study of European Religious Life in the Seventeenth and Eighteenth Centuries* (Charleston, S.C., 1991). In addition to the Protestant reaction to lifeless orthodoxy, Campbell also looks at the Catholic and Jewish experiential movements that occurred in Europe at the same time.

19. For the pervasiveness of evangelical religion in antebellum America, see Martin Marty, *Righteous Empire: The Protestant Experience in America* (New York, 1970), 67–99, which states that evangelicalism was "a kind of national church or national religion."

20. His abilities as an evangelical pastor were widely known by High Church Episcopalians as well. As early as 1822, fellow ministers were complaining to Bishop Kemp of McIlvaine's popularity. The Rev. William Rafferty refers to him as an ignorant youth–in spite of his abilities in the pulpit. William Rafferty to Bishop Kemp, June 12, 1822, in EA, MD Dio. Arch.

21. Ethan Allen, "Annals of the Protestant Episcopal Church in the District of Columbia," unpublished manuscript, p. 106, in ibid.

22. William H. Wilmer to Rev. William M. Stone, April 8, 1812, in ibid.

23. All quotes this paragraph from "Prospectus," *Washington Theological Repertory* 1 (1819): 1, 3ff.

24. Charles P. McIlvaine, *Contrasted Hopes* (New York, n.d.), 3, 6.

25. "The Doctrine of Man's Depravity," *Washington Theological Repertory* 1 (1819): 7.

26. Ibid., 6. This is a surprisingly strong statement of human sinfulness given the climate of American theological debate in 1819. Belief in inherent sin passed down through the generations from Adam was becoming an unpopular notion in American theology. Americans softened the extent of human depravity, and such Calvinistic sentiments as we "cannot even think of any thing good of ourselves" were declining in popular influence. Even the Calvinist theologians were modifying their notions of sin and its effects. Just eight years after the *Washington Theological Repertory* published those words, Congregational theologian Nathaniel W. Taylor pronounced that sin occurs only in the action of sinning– that it is not an inherent disposition passed down through the human race. See his *Concio ad Cerum* which is reproduced in many places, including H. Shelton Smith, Robert Handy, and Lefferts Leotscher, *American Christianity: An Historical Interpretation with Representative Documents, Vol. 2, 1820–1960* (New York, 1963), 28–36. For Taylor's liberalization of Calvinism, see Sidney Mead, *Nathaniel William Taylor, 1786–1858: A Connecticut Liberal* (Hamden, Conn., 1967). For the decline of Calvinism in antebellum America generally, see Joseph Haroutunian, *Piety Versus Moralism: The Passing of the New England Theology* (New York, 1932); Bruce Kuklick, *Churchmen and Philosophers: From Jonathan Edwards to John Dewey* (New Haven, 1985); and Allen Guelzo, *Edwards on the Will: A Century of American Theological Debate* (Middleton, Conn., 1989). See also H. Shelton Smith, *Changing Conceptions of Original Sin: A Study in American Theology Since 1750* (New York, 1955).

27. For a survey of Episcopal attitudes toward Calvinism see Prichard, "Theological Consensus," 70–102. For the importance of Reformed doctrine in English evangelicalism, see Elliot-Binns, *Early Evangelicals*, and Hylsen-Smyth, *Evangelicals in the Church of England*. For American Evangelical Episcopalians and Reformation theology, see also Chorley, *Men and Movements*, and Zabriskie, "Rise and Major Characteristics of the Anglican Evangelical Movement," 7–10.

28. All preceding quotes from "Editorial," *Washington Theological Repertory* 3 (1821): 2–3. Much of this argument is drawn from the Anglican Bishop Horseley.

29. Kilgour to Kemp, July 25, 1822, in EA, MD Dio. Arch.

30. James Kemp, *Pastoral Letter* (1822). For the controversy surrounding the seminary, see Hawks, *Contributions to Ecclesiastical History*, 437ff.

31. Stephen Tyng tried to solve the matter between himself and the bishop through private correspondence which still survives in the Maryland Diocesan Archives. These letters are reprinted in Tyng, *Life and Work of Stephen Tyng*, 67–70. Tyng was dissatisfied with the bishop's response and decided to issue a public letter defending his position.

32. It is clear from this argument that Hawley, McIlvaine, and Tyng did not know very much about Anglican theology at this early point of their careers. They mix up theologians and centuries here. The main point, however, is still that many early Anglican divines were "Calvinists" in the way Hawley, McIlvaine, and Tyng considered themselves "Calvinist." William Hawley, Charles P. McIlvaine, and Stephen H. Tyng, *Letter to the Right Rev. James Kemp, D.D. in Defence of the Clergy of the District of Columbia Against Certain Charges Preferred Against Them in His Late Pastoral Letter* (Washington, 1822), 19–21.

33. Ibid., 21–22.

34. Prichard "Theological Consensus," 87–102, argues that Evangelical Episcopalians believed in ecclesiastical election–that God chose the church and then chose certain individuals in the church for salvation–a doctrine they drew from Richard Laurence, *An Attempt to Illustrate Those Articles of the Church of England Which the Calvinists Improperly Consider as Calvinistical* (Oxford, 1805), via William White. McIlvaine himself supported the ecclesiastical election position that came from his reading of George Stanley Faber, an English evangelical theologian.

35. Hawley et al, *Letter to Kemp*, 23–24.

36. This position is outlined by Prichard, "Theological Consensus," 87–102. See also Robert W. Prichard, "Nineteenth Century Episcopal Attitudes on Predestination and Election," *Historical Magazine of the Protestant Episcopal Church* 51 (1982): 23–51.

37. Charles P. McIlvaine, *Oxford Divinity Compared with That of the Romish and Anglican Churches with a Special View to the Illustration of the Doctrine of Justification* (Philadelphia, 1841), 320–321.

38. Quoted from Simeon's preface to *Horae Homileticae* in Hugh Evan Hopkins, *Charles Simeon of Cambridge* (Grand Rapids, Mich., 1977), 174–175.

39. Carus, *Memorials of McIlvaine*, 189. McIlvaine's regard for Simeon is attested to in numerous places in ibid. and in McIlvaine's introduction to the American edition of William Carus, ed., *Memoirs of the Life of the Rev. Charles Simeon, M.A.* (New York, 1847).

40. I have always had doubts with this term, but I use it here because of its widespread use in scholarly literature on Anglican Evangelicalism. I have always thought *modified Calvinism* would be more accurate because even most Anglican Evangelicals were in some ways "Arminianized," but not full-blown Arminians. To describe this tendency, *moderate Calvinism*, nevertheless, was first articulated by J. D. Walsh, "The Yorkshire Evangelicals in the Eighteenth Century, with Special Reference to Methodism" (Ph.D. diss., Cambridge University, 1956), and has since remained a standard feature of the scholarly interpretation of Anglican Evangelicalism. The difficulty of this point may demonstrate that the Calvinist

Arminian theological grid is more confusing than helpful when looking at Anglican and Episcopal Evangelicalism.

41. "The Doctrine of Man's Depravity," *Washington Theological Repertory* 1 (1819): 41.

42. "Exposition of the Editor's Views," *Washington Theological Repertory* 1 (1819): 4.

43. Charles P. McIlvaine, *The Importance of Consideration* (New York, n.d.), 3–4.

44. This is true for all evangelicals–Episcopal and otherwise. David Bebbington, in his *Evangelicalism in Modern Britain*, lists "conversionism" as one of four central and unchanging marks of evangelical belief. Of it, he says: "Conversions were the goal of personal effort, the collective aim of churches, the theme of Evangelical literature" and that conversion "was the one gateway to vital Christianity" 4, 7.

45. "Backsliders," those who once experienced grace but are not living according to the power of God, are often classed with nominal Christians. Charles McIlvaine addressed an entire tract to the problem of nominal Christianity called *Spiritual Declension* (New York, n.d.).

46. Evangelical literature is full of stories of pious women and blacks, who by their experience of conversion, are actually wiser in spiritual things then well-educated white men who depend on their wits and intelligence for salvation. See for example, McIlvaine's *Contrasted Hopes* in which a man of position "of property, intelligence, vigor in business and ability in matters of this life" rejects Christ's salvation. In contrast, "a negro-man and his little son" testify to the grace of God in their lives. The climax of the story is McIlvaine's joy at praying with the black man "before the throne of our common Lord" and his hope to talk again with that "poor, but rich negro man."

47. For Episcopalians, unlike some other evangelicals, the act of becoming born again need not be a particular moment in time. Although Evangelical Episcopalians often reported dramatic conversion experiences, it was acceptable to experience a slow, and less dramatic, conversion as well. The major issue was not a momentary experience, but rather a life-changing religious commitment. The form of the experience was less important than the experience itself. For example, the much revered Gregory Bedell, Sr., whose biography was written by Stephen Tyng, experienced no adult conversion experience; instead, he could testify to a lifelong disposition to believe in and trust God for his salvation. Even the saintly Bedell records a time when, in his early ministry, he came to know the evangelical doctrine of grace more clearly. See Stephen H. Tyng, *Memoir of the Rev. Gregory T. Bedell, D.D.*, 2nd ed. (Philadelphia, 1836), 1–44.

48. Ibid., 11.

49. Sometimes they even spoke of liturgy leading people into an inward and personal relationship with God.

50. In the very earliest years of the Episcopal Church's existence, the House of Bishops–Evangelicals, High Churchmen, and latitudinarians–passed strict legislation against "vain amusements." See Charles N. Brickley, "The Episcopal Church in Protestant America, 1800–1860" (Ph.D. diss., Clark University, 1950), 199–212.

51. Jonathan Edwards wrote the definitive treatise for evangelicals on religion and the affections. See his *Religious Affections*, ed. John E. Smith (New Haven and London, 1959). The best study on Evangelical interest in the affections is Norman Fiering's *Moral Philosophy at Seventeenth-Century Harvard: A Discipline in Transition* (Chapel Hill, N.C., 1981).

52. All preceding quotes from "Exposition of the Editor's Views," *Washington Theological Repertory* 1 (1819): 3.

53. All quotes this paragraph from "The Influence of Religion on the Affections," *Washington Theological Repertory* 1 (1819): 22, 23, 25, 69.

54. Ibid., 163.

55. For his thought on revivals, see Jonathan Edwards, *The Great Awakening*, ed. C. C. Goen (New Haven and London, 1972).

56. Smith, *Revivalism and Social Reform*.

57. Schmidt, *Holy Fairs*; Bernard A. Weisberger, *They Gathered at the River: The Story of the Great Revivalists and Their Impact upon Religion in America* (Boston, 1958).

58. In Finney's New York campaigns in the Rochester area, a number of Episcopalians embraced his style of revivalism. Finney's second wife, Elizabeth Ford Atkinson Finney, was an Episcopalian converted during one of these early revivals. See Keith J. Hardman, *Charles Grandison Finney, 1792–1875, Revivalist and Reformer* (Syracuse, N.Y., 1987), and Leonard I. Sweet, *The Minister's Wife* (Philadelphia, 1983), 186–189.

59. A very helpful study on Finney's new measures is Ralph Gerald Gay, "A Study of the American Liturgical Revival, 1825–1860" (Ph.D. diss., Emory University, 1977). Gay recognizes the historical roots of Finney's means and concludes that it is the "new pattern" that was his real innovation.

60. Saying that revivalism produced emotionalism should in no way undercut the fact that this system of revivalism was also very rational. Finney calculated the effects of these revival techniques and applied them "scientifically" to produce salvation.

61. Not just in America; Finney had a significant ministry in England as well. See Carwardine, *Transatlantic Revivalism*.

62. The term *anxious bench*, taken from the bench where potential converts sat while contemplating their sins, became synonymous with the whole pattern of Finney-style revivalism.

63. Claude Welch, *Protestant Thought in the Nineteenth Century*, Vol. 1 (New Haven, 1972), and Walter H. Consor, Jr., *Church and Confession: Conservative Theologians in Germany, England, and America, 1815–1866* (Macon, Ga., 1984).

64. See George M. Marsden, *The Evangelical Mind and the New School Presbyterian Experience* (New Haven, 1970); Hatch, *Democratization of Christianity*; and Carwardine, *Transatlantic Revivalism*. Some New School Presbyterians, such as Lyman Beecher and Ashel Nettleton, however, had reservations about Finney. See Stuart Henry, *Unvanquished Puritan* (Grand Rapids, Mich., 1973), and Hardman, *Finney*, 104–132.

65. This tendency is exemplified in Consor, *Church and Confession*.

66. There were other evangelical "moderates" as well. The revival theology of the moderate group was best expressed by William B. Sprague, *Lectures on Revivals of Religion* (Albany, New York, Philadelphia, and Boston, 1832). This group of clergy—mostly Presbyterian, Baptist, and Congregational—have not attracted as much historiographic attention as the extreme camps have. Evangelical Episcopal revivalism fits best with these moderate revivalists' views.

67. See Thomas G. Allen, *Memoir of the Rev. Benjamin Allen, Late Rector of St. Paul's Church, Philadelphia, Pennsylvania* (Philadelphia, 1832), 525–547, which describes the mode of conducting such classes. For McIlvaine and St. Ann's, see F. G. Fish, *St. Ann's Church, Brooklyn, New York from the Year 1784–1845 with a Memorial of the Sunday Schools* (Brooklyn, 1845), 58–62. One of McIlvaine's Bible class notebooks still survives in the archives at Kenyon College; this notebook covers Exodus. According to the class format, McIlvaine asked the class simple, leading questions about the text and theology of Exodus and then urged his hearers to think of the spiritual lessons gained from such exercises as they related to salvation and Christian living. Although social class probably contributed to Episcopal dislike of fanaticism and excess emotionalism, there was an important theological check on their acceptance of Finney's style of revivalism—the Evangelical insistence on the complete depravity of humanity. Unlike Finney, who rejected this Calvinist doctrine and opted instead for a more Arminian view of human nature, McIlvaine and other Evangelical

Episcopalians continued to insist that human beings could in no way contribute to their own salvation. Thus, the use of means was, for them, always tempered by their doctrinal commitment at this point.

68. "On Meetings for Prayer," *Washington Theological Repertory* 1 (1820): 301.

69. "On Prayer Meetings," *Washington Theological Repertory* 1 (1820): 233.

70. For a description of one such meeting in 1819, see Tyng, *Life and Work of Stephen Tyng*, 44.

71. Alexander Viets Griswold, *Remarks on Social Prayer-Meetings* (Boston, 1858), 75. This small book originally appeared as a series of articles in several publications in the 1820s. Another representative work is James May, "Letter to a Friend on Prayer Meetings," in Shiras, *Life and Letters*, 166–170.

72. Most of the Evangelical Episcopal clergy skirt the issue of women in lay leadership, but it appears that some of them were somewhat open to the idea. William Jay defended the American Bible Society's practice of female leaders against Hobart's attack. Griswold and McIlvaine never explicitly say that women were forbidden from lay exhortation or leading prayer meetings. For evidence of Episcopal women's involvement in prayer meetings in the earliest years of nineteenth-century New York, see [J. H. Taylor,] *Sketches of the Religious Experiences and Labors of a Layman with an Appendix* (Hartford, Conn., 1867). There can be little doubt that Evangelical Episcopal bishops and clergy knew of the women's practice. Their silence is most likely evidence of tacit and implicit approval of women's leadership in a lay context.

73. This incident was recorded by the woman's brother in the form of a letter included in Tyng, *Memoir of Bedell*, 79–82.

74. As admitted in "Of Prayer Meetings," by W. W. [most likely William Wilmer], *Washington Theological Repertory* 2 (1820): 20.

75. Carus, *Memorials of McIlvaine*, 17.

76. Lee, *In Memoriam*, 10.

77. Preceding quotes this paragraph from Tyng, *Life and Work of Stephen Tyng*, 61.

78. From T. L. Cuyler, *Recollections of a Long Life* (1902), 200, as quoted in "Stephen Higginson Tyng," *Dictionary of American Biography* 19 (1936), 101.

79. All quotes this paragraph from Stephen Tyng, from his lectures on preaching. Only notes of these lectures survive. Tyng, *Life and Work of Stephen Tyng*, 409.

80. Ibid., 381–382.

81. Ibid., 408.

82. Charles P. McIlvaine, *The Work of Preaching Christ* (Boston, 1871), 3.

83. Griswold, *Remarks on Prayer-Meetings*, 87.

84. For Moore's views on contemporary revivalism and the revival at St. Stephen's, see J.P.K. Henshaw, *Memoir of the Life of the Rt. Rev. Richard Channing Moore, D.D.* (Philadelphia, 1842), 70–106.

85. For the growth of the Episcopal Church in Virginia, see David L. Holmes, "Decline and Revival of the Church."

86. McIlvaine to the Christ Church vestry, October 26, 1822. Christ Church vestry records; typescript copy in the Charles P. McIlvaine papers, Diocese of Ohio Archives, Cleveland, Ohio.

87. Christ Church vestry minutes, September 18, 1827, in ibid.

88. For the political machinations surrounding this appointment, see Pugh, "McIlvaine: Faithful Evangel," 49–50, 53–54.

89. Quoted in William M. Polk, *Leonidas Polk, Bishop and General*, 2nd ed. (New York, 1915), I: 89.

90. Ibid., 92. For additional material on the revival, see Carus, *Memorials of McIlvaine*, 19–29.

91. Among the men influenced by McIlvaine's preaching and the West Point revival were Robert E. Lee and Jefferson Davis. A number of prominent military leaders of the Civil War were cadets under McIlvaine's ministry.

92. The *New England Galaxy* reported the story on December 15, 1826.

93. All preceding quotes from John S. Stone, *A Memoir of the Life of James Milnor, D.D.* (New York, 1848), 264. Pages 264–270 include letters written by Milnor to McIlvaine about the West Point revival following a visit by Milnor to West Point. In June 1826, McIlvaine brought some of his new converts to Milnor's church in New York where they also visited the offices of "the religious institutions of the city, especially the newly erected Tract Society's house." McIlvaine's side of the correspondence, unfortunately, seems to have disappeared.

94. For the High Church critique of American revivalism and the Episcopal alternative, see Mullin, *Episcopal Vision/American Reality*, especially 60–96.

95. Published letter, "Bishop McIlvaine's Revival Counsels," dated February 5, 1834, from a clipping in a family scrapbook in the Charles P. McIlvaine Collection, Thomas Greenslade Manuscripts and Archives, Olin Library, Kenyon College, Gambier, Ohio. [Hereafter referred to as McI, Kenyon College.]

96. Preceding quotes from ibid.

97. Ibid. See also Charles P. McIlvaine, "Letter XI," April 6, 1832, in Sprague, *Lectures on Revivals*, Appendix, 93–94.

98. Ibid., 92.

99. Ibid., 92–93.

100. "Bishop McIlvaine's Revival Counsels." William W. Manross, *The Episcopal Church in the United States, 1800–1840* (New York, 1938), 105, says that "these Episcopalian revivals differed from those of the more exclusively evangelical bodies in degree, rather than in kind. The object and the methods were essentially the same, but because they were sensitive to the criticism of the more conservative members of their own Church, the Episcopalian Evangelicals were more careful than others to guard against emotional extravagance." Evangelical restraint toward excess emotionalism had little or nothing to do with High Church criticism. Their restraint is a reflection of their theology and an outgrowth of their pastoral experience. To them, "emotional extravagance" was a sign that the revival was going wrong and would not result in forming Christian character; excess emotionalism would just as likely lead someone away from true salvation as toward it. Thus, they loathed overemotionalism as much as High Church Episcopalians, but for completely different reasons. They were not accommodating High Church views; instead, they were being consistent within their own worldview.

101. Sprague, *Lectures on Revivals*, articulates this same position from a moderate Presbyterian viewpoint. At the end of his work are numerous letters from other church leaders (mostly Presbyterians and Congregationalists) who sympathize with the goals of revivalism, yet are critical of the abuses of Finneyite revivalism.

102. The visiting committee of the government was not impressed by McIlvaine's proceedings at the academy. They did not report this dissatisfaction in their formal report, but pressured McIlvaine through informal channels to find a new position. One of those informal channels was his friend James Milnor. See Stone, *Memoir of Milnor*, 269–270.

103. Onderdonk wrote to St. Paul's vestry and accused McIlvaine of being a "half-churchmen, a great opponent of Bishop Hobart, and a zealous promoter of the schemes that would blend us with Presbyterians." This private letter was subsequently printed in a Philadelphia newspaper and the accusations were reprinted in McIlvaine's tract, *Rev. Mr.*

McIlvaine in Answer to the Rev. Henry U. Onderdonk, D.D. (Philadelphia, 1827). For this controversy in relation to revivalism in upstate New York, see Cross, *Burned-over District*, and Johnson, *Shopkeeper's Millennium*, 91–92.

104. St. Ann's had been Henry Onderdonk's parish during the time of his attack on McIlvaine. Meanwhile, Onderdonk had been elected bishop of Pennsylvania. It probably gave McIlvaine particular delight that he would be taking over his old enemy's parish. There was no love lost between McIlvaine and Onderdonk, or between McIlvaine and Henry's brother Benjamin T. Onderdonk. In matters of Episcopal polity, McIlvaine and the Onderdonks were at odds throughout their lives.

105. A good summary of Protestant confirmation rites is found in Cheslyn Jones, Geoffrey Wainwright, and Edward Yarnold, eds., *The Study of Liturgy* (New York, 1978), 128–132.

106. The standard High Church works on confirmation were Hobart's four sermons entitled "For Confirmation" in *The Posthumous Works of the late Rt. Rev. John Henry Hobart, D.D.*, Vol. 2., ed. William Berrian (New York, 1832); idem, *The Candidate for Confirmation Instructed* (New York, 1819); and idem, *A Catechism for Confirmation* (New York, 1819). Evangelicals generally approved of the spiritual seriousness of Hobart's approach to confirmation and quoted him widely in their own writings on confirmation. For an example of Evangelical use of Hobart, see Charles P. McIlvaine, *The Pastor's Address to a Candidate for Confirmation in St. Ann's Church, Brooklyn* (New York, 1831). A helpful article on Hobart's confirmation theology is Julien Gunn, "Bishop Hobart's Emphasis on Confirmation," *Historical Magazine of the Protestant Episcopal Church* 24 (1955): 293–310.

107. Charles P. McIlvaine, *Bishop McIlvaine on Confirmation* (n.p., [1840]), 13.

108. McIlvaine, *Pastor's Address . . . for Confirmation*, 6.

109. Stephen H. Tyng, *Guide to Confirmation* (Philadelphia, 1833), 35.

110. For example, see Charles P. McIlvaine, "Address," *Journal of the Diocese of Ohio* (Gambier, 1842): 15.

111. B. P. Aydelott, "Parochial Report, Christ Church, Cincinnati," *Journal of the Diocese of Ohio* (Gambier, 1834): 21.

112. For a complete list, see Manross, *Episcopal Church in the United States*, 55–56.

113. Edward Irving, *Babylon and Infidelity Foredoomed of God: A Discourse on the Prophecies of Daniel and the Apocalypse* (Philadelphia, 1828), and George Croley, *The Apocalypse of St. John, or Prophecies of the Rise, Progress and Fall of the Church of Rome . . . and the Final Triumph of Christianity* (Philadelphia, 1827).

114. Allen, *Memoir of Benjamin Allen* (Philadelphia, 1832), 543.

115. Ibid., 362. Irving's prophetical views were extreme. He is considered an early premillennialist. That Allen's biographer would include his interest in Irving without comment indicates that Irving was being read, and it appears being accepted, by Evangelical Episcopalians. For Irving's views and the Church of England, see Bebbington, *Evangelicalism in Modern Britain*, 76–91, and Ernest R. Sandeen, *The Roots of Fundamentalism: British and American Millennarianism, 1800–1930* (Chicago, 1970), 14–29. Sandeen argues that "only after 1840 did British millennarian thought began to attract attention in the United States." Allen's interest in British millennarianism was contemporary with Irving's own work. It does not appear that Allen was isolated in his interest. Thomas Allen, editor of Allen's memoir, published in 1832, records all Allen's millennarian comments in matter-of-fact style. It appears that he expected his audience to be familiar with British millennarianism and the study of prophecy. Evangelical Episcopalians, therefore, were thinking about the millennium a full twelve to fifteen years before Sandeen indicated, and they helped transmit British millennarian thought to other American Evangelicals. Sandeen does point

out that Episcopal ministers were keenly interested in millennarianism following 1840 (55–56).

116. Episcopal millennialist works include the following: J.P.K. Henshaw, *An Inquiry into the Meaning of the Prophecies Relating to the Second Advent of Our Lord Jesus Christ* (Baltimore, 1842); Edward Winthrop, *Lectures on the Second Advent of the Messiah*, (Cincinnati, 1843); Richard C. Shimeall, *Prophecy, Now in Course of Fulfillment* (New York, 1844); and George Emlen Hare, *Christ to Return: A Practical Exposition of the Prophecy Recorded in the 24th and 25th Chapters of the Gospel According to St. Matthew* (Philadelphia, 1840). Isaac Lebagh published the periodical *American Millenarian and Prophetic Review*. Millennialism in the Episcopal Church occasionally extended beyond the Evangelical party: Levi S. Ives, the High Church bishop of North Carolina and future convert to Roman Catholicism, wrote the preface to Hare's book.

117. Sandeen, *Roots of Fundamentalism*; Timothy Weber, *Living in the Shadow of the Second Coming: American Premillennialism, 1875–1925* (New York, 1979). Sandeen and Weber may have underestimated the extent of premillennial views in antebellum America. See E. S. Gaustad, ed., *The Rise of Adventism: Religion and Society in Mid-Nineteenth Century America* (New York, 1974).

118. James H. Moorhead makes the same point about American millennialism in general in "Between Progress and Apocalypse: A Reassessment of Millennialism in American Religious Thought, 1800–1880," *Journal of American History* 71 (1984): 524–542. See also Ruth Alden Doan, *The Miller Heresy: Millennialism and American Culture* (Philadelphia, 1987), 13–14.

119. See note 103. All preceding quotes from McIlvaine, *McIlvaine in Answer to Onderdonk*, 40.

120. Charles I. Foster, *An Errand of Mercy: The Evangelical United Front, 1770–1837* (Chapel Hill, N.C., 1960), and Marsden, *Evangelical Mind*, 19–20.

121. McIlvaine, *McIlvaine in Answer to Onderdonk*, 32. At the time this tract was written, those were the only two societies in which McIlvaine regularly participated. Within a few years, however, he was the secretary of the American Seamen Friend's Society and active in the American Colonization Society; he also lectured widely for the American Temperance Society. In addition, he was keenly interested in the work of the American Sunday School Union, various Sabbath observance societies, and missionary work to convert Jews.

122. For a more detailed explanation of Hobart's views on the Bible society, see Mullin, *Episcopal Vision/American Reality*, 50–59. Hobart carried on a protracted pamphlet war with Evangelical Episcopal layman William Jay on the nature of the Bible society and its relationship to the church. Mullin outlines the controversy, as does Brickley, "Episcopal Church in Protestant America," 173–196. Brickley finds the main point about the controversy over the Bible society to be "that the Episcopal Church would never be able to present a united front in respect to cooperation with members of other faiths of Protestantism" (195). His overall thesis is that the Evangelical party is marked by this cooperative spirit.

123. McIlvaine, *McIlvaine in Answer to Onderdonk*, 17.

124. Charles P. McIlvaine, *The Holy Catholic Church, or the Communion of Saints in the Mystical Body of Christ: A Sermon* (Philadelphia, 1844), 23.

125. Preceding quotes from ibid., 29–30.

126. McIlvaine, *McIlvaine in Answer to Onderdonk*, 16–17. For a similar expression of the same idea, see also idem, *Holy Catholic Church*, 53–54.

127. All quotes this paragraph from Charles P. McIlvaine, "Address to the American Tract Society," in *First Annual Report of the American Tract Society* (New York, 1826), 37–38.

128. Ibid., 38.

129. Historians have widely commented on the theme of America as the new Israel. The most well known of these works include Perry Miller, *Errand into the Wilderness*, (Cambridge, Mass., 1956), and Ernest Lee Tuveson, *Redeemer Nation: The Idea of America's Millennial Role* (Chicago, 1968). It is very clear from Evangelical Episcopal sources that in the antebellum period, Evangelicals did not believe America to be Israel; only the church was Israel. The division between America and Israel is very clear in McIlvaine's thought. Although he sometimes uses the image of a new Israel in America, there is never the confusion of equating America with Israel. For McIlvaine the millennial kingdom was much grander, much bigger than America. He does not confuse the two. He does, however, want America to be faithful to that kingdom, and sometimes his language can be confusing to anyone unfamiliar with his whole body of writings.

130. All quotes this paragraph from Charles P. McIlvaine, *The Necessity of Religion to the Prosperity of the Nation: A Sermon* (Gambier, Ohio, 1838), 4.

131. Ibid., 14.

132. Voluntary societies in America and England all held their annual meetings in the same week in the same city. This event was called *anniversary week*. In America, anniversary weeks were usually held in May or June, either in New York or Philadelphia (sometimes both). In England, anniversary week was usually held in May in London. That way clergy and laity could attend the meetings of a multitude of societies without traveling from city to city.

133. The Islington meeting was an annual conference of British evangelical clergy.

134. Milnor was the first officially appointed representative of the American Bible Society sent to England to contribute to and report on British voluntary societies. See Stone, *Memoir of Milnor*, 299–300, 457–459.

135. McIlvaine also had contact with French and Italian Protestants, as well as German evangelicals.

3

Episcopal Distinctiveness: Fighting the Protestant Radicals, 1832–1838

On September 10, 1831, Charles McIlvaine was elected unanimously to become the second bishop of the diocese of Ohio. Busy with parish duties and teaching a course on "Christian Evidences" at the University of the City of New York, the election genuinely surprised him. When the news arrived, McIlvaine wrote in his diary:

> I can very freely commit the matter to the Lord. I would not remain here, if it be His will that I go to Ohio; I would not go to Ohio, if it be His will that I remain here. My heart does not thirst for a bishopric. Its honour I could willingly forgo, its responsibility I am not sufficient to bear. Its duties are unspeakably holier than any spirit I could bring to them.[1] . . . When I received the official notification from Ohio, I hardly entertained a thought of accepting it.[2]

Such self-effacing spirituality masked his natural ambition: for several years, his family had privately addressed him as "the lord bishop." Seeking after a higher ecclesiastical position, however, lacked appropriate evangelical humility.

He sought advice from his friends. Stephen Tyng urged him to leave his "comparatively unimportant parish" in Brooklyn and accept a Boston position. St. Paul's was a very important parish, and Tyng believed McIlvaine could combat the Hobartian High Church influences taking hold in Massachusetts. As for Ohio, "this is out of the question, when the other place [St. Paul's] is in the way."[3] From Baltimore, J. P. K. Henshaw congratulated McIlvaine on the Ohio election. Boston was certainly important, but Henshaw, with perhaps more political acumen than Tyng, urged him to consider the "manifold advantages" of Ohio: he would be another Evangelical in the House of Bishops and he would have control over Kenyon College.[4]

Although ambitious, McIlvaine hesitated about becoming a bishop on personal and spiritual grounds. Old anxieties dogged him. In his diary, he confessed to feeling inadequate, fretted about his health, and bemoaned leaving the east coast for the west. "But my arguments," he concluded after a time of spiritual struggle, "have all been silenced. I cannot escape the belief that my Lord has called me."[5] He decided to accept Ohio's invitation to serve as bishop and president of Kenyon College.

Although McIlvaine had decided to go to Ohio, some Ohioans were having second thoughts. Shortly after the election, a small group of Episcopalians protested. Not everyone agreed they needed a new bishop. Bishop Philander Chase had not died; he had resigned from Ohio's episcopacy – the position was therefore not technically open. Perhaps the former bishop could be convinced to return. Because he had been elected for life, some Ohioans believed Chase's resignation should have been rejected by the convention. They argued that the episcopate of Ohio was not actually vacant when McIlvaine was elected. The decision whether or not he would be Ohio's second bishop was not for McIlvaine to make; the bishops of the Episcopal Church must decide whether the election was canonically legitimate.

The bishops and the standing committees of each diocese had the power to confirm the vacancy and validate McIlvaine's election. On an individual basis, they voiced their opinions on the matter through letters to the presiding bishop. Their opinions followed party lines: the few evangelical bishops, such as Griswold and Meade, concurred with Ohio's decision to elect McIlvaine; the remainder of the bishops declined to confirm the election, citing the confusion over Chase's resignation.[6] Thus, the 1831 election was invalidated. The Ohioans were required to call a new election at their 1832 diocesan convention. The results of the second election would have to be formally ratified by the 1832 General Convention – after the convention determined whether or not the see was vacant. The Evangelicals in the church were furious. Henshaw pointed out to McIlvaine that the election of all the Evangelical Episcopal appointments had, in some way, been questioned, blocked, or delayed by the House of Bishops.[7] During the intervening year, party tensions heightened. The 1832 Massachusetts convention "was the scene of an exceedingly stormy contention for the supremacy on the part of two rival parties."[8] At issue: McIlvaine's election. The High Church party wanted Chase restored to Ohio; the Evangelicals wanted McIlvaine confirmed. In Massachusetts, the Evangelicals won, and they sent a delegation to the General Convention supporting McIlvaine.

In Ohio, Bishop Chase's supporters made one last attempt to convince him to come back, but the convention was resolute. Chase resigned; he was no longer their bishop. On September 7, 1832, they once again elected Charles McIlvaine as bishop. Six weeks later, the results of this election were presented to the General Convention meeting in New York. From his parish in Brooklyn, McIlvaine awaited word from the convention. "Today," he wrote in his diary on October 19, "the General Convention is in session to decide whether I go to Ohio, or remain a contented, happy pastor in Brooklyn."[9] McIlvaine evidently thought the decision would come quickly. He was wrong. The wrangling went on for more than a week.

Bishop Chase's resignation remained a problem – the bishops still hesitated to accept it. On October 20, the committee appointed to study Chase's case presented its report. Led by High Church Bishop DeLancey, the committee recommended that the House of Bishops attempt to heal the separation between Chase and Ohio. In the committee's opinion, Chase was still bishop. Only if Chase and Ohio remained unreconciled, then, on May 1, 1833, should a new bishop be elected.[10] On the 23rd, the bishops debated the issue all day. Finally, on the 26th, they passed the DeLancey committee's recommendation. According to its provisions, Charles McIlvaine's election would not be ratified at the 1832 convention.

At seven o'clock in the evening, they sent the proposal to the House of Deputies (the "lower house," consisting of clergy and laity), and the deputies quickly vetoed the committee's report. They believed that the episcopacy of Ohio was indeed vacant and voted against depriving Ohio of yet another six months without a bishop. Since the two houses could not agree, the DeLancey motion failed.

On October 27, the bishops capitulated to the deputies and drafted a new resolution. This resolution stated that Chase had abandoned his diocese, that the episcopal see of Ohio was indeed vacant, and that the September 1832 election of Charles McIlvaine by the diocese of Ohio was valid.[11] The clergy and laity agreed.[12] With the vacancy and the election confirmed, McIlvaine finally became bishop-elect of Ohio. Four days later, bishops White, Griswold, and Meade laid hands on McIlvaine and consecrated him a bishop of the Protestant Episcopal Church. "May I be girt about with truth," he prayed, "strongly, boldly, patiently, as a pilgrim, as a labourer, ready to endure hardness as a good soldier of Jesus Christ."[13]

The Move to Ohio

The new bishop needed prayer to "endure hardness." In some ways, no one could be less suited to tackle the difficult problems of the Episcopal Church in Ohio then was Charles McIlvaine. Cultivated and cosmopolitan in his tastes, manners, education, and friendships, and given to anxiety, depression, and fatigue, the crudeness and the rigors of frontier life always taxed him. The diocese of Ohio was geographically large, yet the Episcopal Church there was pitifully small. In 1818, less than a half-dozen clergy had organized the practically nonexistent church into a diocese; thirteen years later, there were only 16 clergy serving 873 communicants in 31 functioning parishes.[14] Much of this growth can be credited to the energy and vision of Philander Chase. He preached all over Ohio, and he founded Kenyon College to provide Episcopal ministers for the west. By the time of McIlvaine's election, the church was still small, but Chase had laid a foundation for future Episcopal evangelization.[15]

In the early years of the nineteenth century, Methodists, Baptists, Congregationalists, and Presbyterians vigorously evangelized the west.[16] "As to the religious opinions of the people," wrote the Rev. Henry Caswall of Ohioans in the 1830s, "the greater part are more or less attached to the Methodist, Baptist or Presbyterian sects."[17] In his travels he noticed that the Methodists seemed to have particular appeal and attracted large numbers to their preaching and revivals. "More or less attached" appropriately described the situation: a good many Ohioans maintained no church connections whatsoever. The cities, Caswall observed, were religiously diverse. Cincinnati in particular troubled him, for there he saw a sizable number of Roman Catholics, along with visible congregations of Swedenborgians, Unitarians, and Universalists.[18]

This same religious diversity also troubled Bishop McIlvaine. After he was consecrated, he remained rector of St. Ann's for several months—reluctant to move Emily and their young children west during winter. Nevertheless, he toured his new diocese during November and December. Never having been west, what he saw amazed and distressed him. He wrote to Stephen Tyng:

> Those who call themselves Christians there, and ought to be of one mind and one heart, are most sadly divided. I do not refer to the long established and familiar partition walls which separate Christians every where into different denominations. I mean domestic divisions; household quarrels; sects convulsed in their own bowels. It is said that as many as thirty divisions of Baptists may be counted in the west. Those called Campbellites (heretics of a peculiarly plausible and anti-christ character) have led away a large portion of the western Baptists. . . . Heresies of rapid growth and short career, of new form and names, without definite shape, and often incapable of being defined by any metes and bounds, start up on every side, in a region where mind is as fertile as matter, and where the forming and controlling power of cultivation is about as dominant in the moral and the physical energies of the country. . . . It is the ignorance of active, adventurous minds, that think for themselves and will think about religion . . . and being under the influence of unsanctified hears, must be expected to branch off into the wildest and most ruinous errors.[19]

This extensive visit convinced McIlvaine that Ohio was out of control with sectarian revivalism, religious innovation, undirected enthusiasm, and non-Christian aberration.

Bishop McIlvaine was not exaggerating the religious situation in frontier Ohio.[20] Wrote one historian: "If a frontier can be defined as a zone of cultural competition, a region lacking widely accepted political institutions or social norms, a place in which values are in flux and the locus of sovereignty uncertain, then the Ohio Country in the late eighteenth and early nineteenth century qualifies on all counts."[21] Religion was one of those counts. Wrote another nineteenth-century Ohio historian:

> The action and reaction of colliding elements in the Ohio Valley struck out much intellectual heat and light. Civilized races met with savage, Christianity met Judaism, Protestant challenged Catholic, Calvinist encountered anti-Calvinist, Unitarian opposed Trinitarian, old denominations split by contention projected new sects into beings, and each new sect criticized all the others. Antagonizing churches in general, and even assaulting the bulwarks of religion itself, the agnostics, the skeptics, and the avowed atheists joined the thick combat. Extremes grappled.[22]

Bishop McIlvaine observed Ohio's freewheeling religious competition firsthand. Although the Methodists and Baptists had gained a number of adherents, diversity and division, rather than consensus and cooperation, marked Ohio's early religious culture. A multitude of popular denominations, unencumbered by ecclesiastical restrictions, made early inroads: the first Methodist circuit riders visited Ohio around 1796, and the first Methodist congregation was founded in 1801.[23] These popular, evangelical denominations with their stress on personal conversion and immediate access to God attracted many Ohioans seeking freedom and liberty.[24]

Although parts of Ohio had been settled by Anglican families from Virginia, Episcopalians still had a good deal of trouble on the frontier. In the early years of the Ohio country, they had very few clergy and churches. There simply were not enough Episcopal priests to minister successfully to Anglican immigrants. Many of these families remained outside the reach of an Episcopal parish and often converted to Presbyterianism or Methodism. In addition to Virginia Anglicans, other parts of Ohio were settled by New Englanders and upstate New Yorkers—people with a historic suspicion of Episcopalianism. In his travels, Henry Caswall met a Calvinist Baptist who offered his opinion about the Episcopal college at Gambier:

> I have fought the British in the revolutionary war; I have again encountered them in the last war; and I know something of their character. I know they would not contribute so many thousands to build a college in Ohio without a sinister object. I am, therefore, convinced that Bishop Chase is an agent employed by them to introduce British domination here. The college is in fact a fortress, all you students are British soldiers in disguise, and when you think you have an opportunity, you will throw off the mask, and proclaim the king of England.[25]

In the minds of some Ohioans at least, the Episcopal Church was antidemocratic and an anti-American front for British interests. The combination of a shortage of ministers and Yankee suspicion put Episcopalians in a difficult evangelistic position in relation to their Protestant neighbors.

Evangelizing Ohio for the Episcopal Church might have been easier if there had not been division in the Ohio church itself. Although McIlvaine wrote to Tyng that "party names do not exist here" and the Episcopal Church was in "general harmony,"[26] that was most certainly not the case in Ohio.[27] By McIlvaine's election, the church in Ohio was largely Evangelical, but the High Church party held several important parishes in the east and around Cleveland.[28] The Chase-McIlvaine problem did become a party issue, but Bishop Chase's resignation indicated that other tensions existed within the church as well—tensions that demonstrated the difficult task of Episcopal evangelization in Ohio. The Episcopal Church in Ohio was doubly divided: there was the formal and traditional division between High Church and Evangelical Episcopalians, and there was division within the Evangelical party itself. Some Evangelicals fully identified with other Protestant evangelicals, but some remained critical of aspects of evangelical Protestantism in the west.

Bishop Chase resigned over a power struggle between Evangelicals at Kenyon College. The bishop, assisted financially by wealthy and noble Anglican Evangelicals, founded the college. From his perspective, the college owed its existence and allegiance to him. The faculty thought him too high-handed in managing the college, a sentiment shared by some of the clergy who considered him authoritarian. According to the founding documents, the bishop served as college president and had "a controlling influence . . . over the whole."[29] Chase believed himself the "parent-founder" of the college. He compared his Kenyon College duties to the responsibilities of a biblical patriarch:

> Like Abraham on the plain of Mamre, it hath pitched its tent under the trees of Gambier Hill; it hath its flocks and its herds, and its different families of Teachers, Scholars, Mechanics, and Laborers; all united under one head, pursuing one common interest, and receiving their maintenance and food from one common

source. . . . This patriarchal establishment must, it is obvious, have a father, and that father must be clothed with authority to seek and effect the common good. Deprive him of this, and the family must come to ruin. Guard his power against *abuses;* but, for the common interest, preserve it entire.[30]

No wonder Caswall's Baptist friend thought Chase an agent of an antidemocratic English plot!

Chase published these sentiments in an open letter, which infuriated Kenyon's faculty. The professors considered his pretensions to patriarchal authority absurd. The bishop, they claimed, exercised a "principle of absolute and unlimited power" that was "contrary to the usage of colleges in general, and to the spirit of the age."[31] Even the Episcopalians were not immune to the democratic and antiauthoritarian tenor of the times. One popular professor, William Sparrow, encouraged students to protest against the bishop. This popular "spirit of the age" offended Chase, "who rejoiced that he belonged to a Church that was primitive, and, as he thought, in no way subject to the *Zeitgeist.*"[32] He believed the professors were poisoned by this "spirit" who dared scoff at his Episcopal authority. Chase wrote about himself in the third person:

> Both the teachers and the unsuspecting scholars had been afresh invited by "the spirit of the age" to "resist and put down authority." . . . Scarcely a living object passed him without some small sign of disrespect. Even the smallest grammar school boys . . . had learned to cry out, "it was too much power to commit to the hands of one man"; and the little guns they were allowed by the teachers to load with powder, were fired with shouts of independence of Episcopal tyranny. The very clerk in the College-store had been won over to the cause, and was heard often to boast of his belonging to the "Anti-Bishop Party."[33]

The Anti-Bishop Party gained adherents beyond the walls of the college. Along with Dr. Aydelott, the powerful rector of Cincinnati's Christ Church, the Kenyon faculty convinced the diocesan convention that "although the Right Rev. Bishop . . . is ex officio President of the College; yet as President, he cannot invoke his episcopal functions, or any powers or authority other than the customary functions of the president . . . of a theological and literary seminary."[34] Those opposed to the "arbitrary power" of the bishop won: Chase could only rule as bishop in ecclesiastical affairs—not academic ones.

Bishop Chase believed he was always a bishop—in all episcopal duties at all times. He refused to separate the offices of bishop and college president. Believing that the convention of Ohio voted "in blinded rage against the authority of Bishops" and robbed him of his rightful privilege,[35] he resigned. A day later, this upstart Episcopal convention, so thoroughly influenced by the antipatriarchal, antiauthoritarian "spirit of the age" elected Charles McIlvaine as their next bishop. If they had to have a bishop, he better be an evangelical one—and one less given to authoritarian pretensions. Everyone was in for a surprise, for during his years in Ohio, the evangelical Bishop McIlvaine became a staunch defender of the distinctives of the Episcopal Church and an unembarrassed user of episcopal power and authority. In his early years as bishop, he became increasingly committed to the distinctives of the Episcopal Church as he battled Protestant ultraism. Against extreme evangelical fanaticism, he articulated the mission of the Protestant Episcopal Church in the west—to be an evangelical haven from the heresy and schism brought about by individualistic American religion.

Against the Protestant Radicals

In the months before he left for Ohio, McIlvaine realized that he was in danger of "falling into a sectarian spirit." He feared that he might elevate his attachment to the Episcopal Church above all others. "I never knew," he confessed, "so much of the temptation to this vice. . . . It is difficult to separate the Church, as the fold of Christ, from one's own personal and earthly interest in its extension."[36] The greater success of the Episcopal Church in Ohio, the greater his own career would be. Although he desired the success of the Episcopal Church, he worried that it might create a partisan spirit in his ministry. Would he grow more zealous for the Episcopal Church than for the kingdom of God?

> It is difficult to seek the enlargement of Zion, and not be influenced by motives of a selfish and party character. . . . I desire to prefer the advancement of our own Church merely because I believe it to be the best, and most Scriptural and profitable form in which to establish the Kingdom of God. I desire to seek no extension of the Episcopal Church, but by the extension of truth and righteousness. . . . I desire to realize ever that . . . as a Christian, I am not an Episcopalian, but a member of the family of the people of God of every name under heaven.[37]

This kind of evangelical open-mindedness marked the early months of his ministry as bishop. When he went west, McIlvaine took the cooperative spirit he had developed from his work with other evangelicals in revivals and voluntary societies in New York. He praised the Presbyterians and Methodists, who welcomed him warmly, and ministers of both denominations opened their pulpits and loaned him their churches for Episcopal services.[38]

In early September 1834, the bishop attended his first convention in the diocese of Ohio. In the parish church of Chilliocothe, McIlvaine delivered his first charge to the diocese—a *charge* was a special sermon preached by the bishop and devoted to some topic of particular importance or concern to him or his diocese; Bishop McIlvaine delivered only six charges to his clergy throughout his forty-year episcopate.

A first charge was a special and solemn occasion, setting the tone for the new episcopate. He delivered it in Chilliocothe's elegant, new Gothic church building. People came from town and the surrounding counties to see and hear the new bishop from the east. The dignified, Princeton-educated McIlvaine dazzled the spectators as he preached a powerful and eloquent sermon. "How shall I speak of the scene," wrote one attendee, ". . . the fervour and animation of the Bishop— the fixed and steady gaze of the assembled clergy, and other members of the Convention,—the deep solemnity spread over a large audience . . . —above all, the uncompromising faithful instruction of this servant of Christ, in the discharge of his high and responsible duties."[39] The new bishop completely captivated his clergy and audience.

Entitled "The Preaching of Christ Crucified," the sermon laid out the bishop's views of the Christian ministry. "You are well aware," he began, "that the great work for which your sacred office was established, is the preaching of the Gospel." The primary job of the clergy, he stated, was not reading the liturgy or celebrating sacraments; ministers were called to preach the atoning work of Christ. He urged his clergy to examine the evangelical character of their preaching: "Does it bear witness to Christ?" Since the center of the gospel is Christ himself, every sermon must point to some aspect of Christ's life, ministry, or kingdom. Sin, justification, sanctification, and the final glory of believers were appropriate topics for evangelical sermons. The purpose of such preaching, proclaimed the bishop, is "to the overturning of the kingdom of Satan in the hearts of men."[40] Such gospel preaching distinguished the ministry of the early apostles, and he argued in conclusion, if the Ohio clergy preach in the same way, God will increase the church.

Throughout the sermon, the bishop never once referred to the Episcopal Church, nor did he refer to the church's distinctive polity, practices, or doctrine. In this first charge to his diocese, he preached a sermon that could have been preached in any evangelical church. This did not escape the notice of those in attendance. "There he stood before us," wrote one astute theological observer, "not descanting on the antiquity of the Church, or apostolic succession, or the glory of the liturgy, or the power of the Bishop, all excellent topics in their place, but full of another theme, the preaching of Christ and of him crucified!"[41] The bishop delivered a nonsectarian exposition of the great doctrines of evangelical belief and the responsibility of the clergy to preach those doctrines.[42] The convention was delighted. They requested copies for the clergy and voted to publish 1,000 copies of the charge for "general circulation."[43] The Bishop's first convention was a success—full of "the most entire harmony and brotherly love."[44]

Three years later, however, the bishop's tone had changed. Living in the west had taught him a few things—it tempered his optimism in regard to American revivalism. In New York, for example, it had been easy to promote revivals, and although the West Point revival had run to extremes, he nevertheless defended it. In 1828 and 1829, when some Episcopal laywomen started a prayer revival at the American Bible Society house in New York, it spread throughout the Episcopal churches in the area, and McIlvaine no doubt participated in it.[45] He proudly reported revivals and increased religious interest at St. Ann's in Brooklyn. The evangelical awakenings of some military cadets and of Episcopal laypeople, however, failed to rival the religious enthusiasm of uneducated Ohio farmers and settlers. The emotionalism and fervor of the western revivals shocked those easterners who had supported revivalism at home. Even Cincinnati's well-known Presbyterian minister, Lyman Beecher, who had long conducted revivals in New York and New England, backed away from their extreme manifestations in the west.[46] Since the days of the West Point revival, McIlvaine had criticized extreme revivalism; that he would become a more vocal critic after his move to Ohio should have been no surprise.

Ohio Episcopalians regularly reported on the revivals occurring in their parishes: twelve parishes experienced revivals between 1834 and 1837.[47] Even in his early months in Ohio, McIlvaine became concerned about the "appetite for excitement and novelty in the mode of awakening and converting sinners" apparent among some Christians in the state.[48] He warned the Rev. Ethan Allen of Dayton, one of the diocese's most successful revivalist ministers, not to let his revival meetings get out of hand. "Keep close to the Liturgy," he advised, "avoid seeking excitement—be sober—grave—temperate—all gospel & then as fervent in spirit as possible."[49] Episcopalians were not immune to radical revivalism. In February 1834, Bishop McIlvaine learned of a parish experiencing revival. He wrote to them, encouraging "the great increase of attention to the salvation of the soul" that appeared among them, but he warned them against "all efforts to kindle excitement . . . noise and all endeavors to produce animal feeling."[50]

Nothing could have been more calculated to harden the opinion of the bishop against radical revivalism than the publication of Charles Finney's *Lectures on Revivals of Religion* in 1835. McIlvaine had seen the results of Finney-type revivalism in the west; Finney's own writing must have only confirmed his worst suspicions. McIlvaine had gladly contributed to Presbyterian William Sprague's *Lectures on Revivals of Religion* just three years earlier. Sprague and McIlvaine were both in favor of orderly, clergy-led revivals,[51] but now Finney took Sprague's title and pulverized Sprague's position. Unlike Sprague, who argued that revivals were the work of God, Finney believed that a revival "is not a miracle, or dependent on a miracle, in any sense. It is a purely philosophical result of the right use of the constituted means." His means reached the common people, and those same people were responsible for employing revivalistic means to convert others. It was a pounding denunciation of the Presbyterian and Congregational clergy. By implication, it was also a denunciation of Evangelical Episcopalians like Charles McIlvaine. But is was a hugely popular success. More than 12,000 copies of Finney's book were sold in the first months of publication.[52]

Keeping the parishes in line was difficult, but there were deeper troubles at Gambier. The antiauthoritarian clergy and laity who had engineered Chase's ouster grumbled about the new bishop. Leading the antibishop faction were the Kenyon faculty and students, an independent-minded group, whom one observer thought more "western" than other Ohio Episcopalians. The Kenyon students remained unimpressed by tradition, authority, and eastern pretensions. Their "tastes," ran one report, "have become vitiated by the boisterous rant, and bathos, which have long been fashionable among their popular public speakers, who would seem to have taken their tone from the prevailing manner of the Methodists."[53]

In 1834 and 1835, people complained that the bishop was "haughty and proud" and desired "to keep at a distance from the unrefined and untutored."[54] His sister-in-law, Ellen, jokingly called him "my lord bishop" and warned that his anti-Jacksonian sentiments would get him in trouble "with the Washington demagogues." Responding to a letter he had written her, she replied "you might be proscribed as a high-church aristocrat or an aristocratical high-churchman."[55] The new Evangelical bishop was taking his office a bit too seriously for some Ohio Episcopalians. Rumors circulated as to his imperiousness. When writing McIlvaine in regard to a candidate for Episcopal orders, the Rev. Samuel Seabury (a

High Churchman of the first order) reported that the young man "expressed a fear to me today that from what he had heard of you lately he should not be *high* enough for you now–I told him in reply that you were no higher now than you ever were tho' you were probably as high as any man of sense could be."[56]

If attitude and rumor were not enough to condemn him as a "High Church aristocrat," McIlvaine's second charge–delivered in 1836–to his clergy was. "By particular nature of my duties," he explained as he addressed the convention, "I am obliged to meet every wind of doctrine, to observe the trial of every experiment and the consequences of every novelty." During his travels in the past year, he had pondered "the general aspect of religion in the land." What he saw troubled him. "Ultraism," sectarianism, and revivalism flourished in Ohio. In contrast to the religious confusion that was convulsing Ohio, he said, the Episcopal Church was growing because of its settled ministry and its "strong and increasing attachment to the order and government, the worship and ministry that distinguish our Church." Ohioans needed refuge from the prevailing religious enthusiasm. Episcopal polity and church order provided peace and spiritual comfort. "The Church, as a Church, can have no stability, no force, without [them]. . . . Inward and spiritual ties are not enough for the holding together of the several parts of the outward and visible Church."[57] This appeared to be a departure for Bishop McIlvaine. Throughout the early years of his ministry he emphasized the inward, spiritual, and invisible nature of true religion. Now, in his second charge to his clergy, he preached on the particular form of the Episcopal Church. The success of the church in Ohio was not a result of evangelical enthusiasm; it came, rather, from the unity of a visible church and the orderliness of her institutions. He proposed:

> If we would promote the spirit of vital godliness in the world, we must promote it in connexion with, and by means of, that only body–the Church–which the Lord has built as the earthly house of its tabernacle in this wilderness. You may as well expect your minds to be in health while your bodies are diseased, as that the spirit of religion will flourish, while the body of religion, the visible Church, is disordered.[58]

Episcopalians provided Ohio a church with "distinctive sobriety, dignity and purity" in the face of the "appalling exhibition of the religious temper of the times."[59]

Clearly alluding to Finney-type revivalism and Campbellite sectarianism, McIlvaine characterized the Protestantism of the day as full of the "spirit of reckless innovation, contemptuous insubordination, formal fanaticism and fanatical informality." American Protestants lacked orthodox authorities. Heresies had "grown up amidst the fragments of the broken walls and neglected gate-ways of the visible Church." Without the guidance, authority, and ministrations of a settled clergy, innocent and unwary people had been victimized by "the cold hearted but heated fanatic" who preached false doctrines and divided churches. All of this confusion, argued the bishop, started when "Christians began to undervalue external institutions, putting them at the mercy of individual or local caprice and fancy." Although they intended to promote lively piety, the new measures and devices of

Protestant fanaticism would eventually harden into a new formalism. In this way, revivalism and sectarianism would become a new "popery" with "its miracle-working machinery, and its opus operandum of 'anxious seats,' and confessions." Without the authority of an orthodox church body, each leader would become the "infallible head of his party."[60] Every charismatic leader claimed the Spirit of God, and each was doing as he or she pleased. Any person who claimed such authority, who separated him- or herself from the visible authority of traditional Protestantism, undermined true religion. True Christianity, argued the bishop, never separated visible and invisible reality.

At the climax of the sermon, Bishop McIlvaine offered his solution to the religious confusion of the day:

> Permit me here to express the honest belief, in all kindness towards any that differ, that these institutions, Episcopal and Liturgical, based upon articles of faith so evangelical, so comprehensive, so catholic, and, on points controverted among true Christians, so moderate, are the only ones that bid fair to stand, unmutilated, the powers which, whether we look at things in the religious world or things out of the religious world, are more and more assaulting the order and government – the ministry and worship of the visible Church. . . . Let us be patient with these things, carefully observing the signs of the times, and waiting, in confident expectation, a day when the friends of good government, of sober piety, of dignified worship, of catholic doctrine and unity will see reason to be thankful that our distinctive institutions were maintained, unmutilated by capricious innovation; unaccommodated to temporary prejudice; preferring to be adapted to the wants of all centuries and all people, rather than change with the times and vary with the tastes of the day.[61]

Two things guarded the Episcopal Church from novelty: first, the church's return to the "old paths" of the doctrines of the Reformation, and, second, the serious attention and administration of the sacraments and the "apostolic institution" of confirmation. Finally, McIlvaine pictured the Episcopal Church as a visible institution built of "lively stones" as a "habitation of God through the Spirit." With greater grace, love, holiness, and piety, a "new beauty would spread over our external institutions." Only such a church could withstand the "tempest lulled or raging" throughout all ages.[62] The Episcopal Church offered protection against the innovation and novelty of present-day Ohio.

The Evangelical Episcopal press responded enthusiastically to the bishop's address. "We have received a copy of it," wrote the editor of the *Episcopal Recorder*, "and find it to contain much important counsel, peculiarly appropriate to the present circumstances of the Church." For a number of years, the *Recorder* reported on the growth of sectarianism and fanaticism in the west. Just a few months earlier they published a short piece by one A. C——n of Philadelphia. The writer argued that "between the errors of Romanists on the one hand, and the departures from sound doctrine on the part of some Protestants on the other," the Episcopal Church in the west was "an Ark of Refuge for all judicious and sober Christians."[63] The High Church party had long considered the church an ark of refuge; now such sentiments appeared in the Evangelical press. McIlvaine agreed; he pictured the church as a "haven" and a "tabernacle in the wilderness."[64]

The immediate reaction of the Ohio clergy was positive. In retrospect, however, some people began to question the bishop. Wrote one Ohio Episcopalian:

> I am constrained to say that I feel something of pensiveness, not to say anxiety
> and fear, for the future. Read the charge and the ordination sermon and tell me,
> what mean those so oft repeated and decisive declarations, on the subject of
> external constitution and order? There are some positions there which would not
> startle me if coming from many other men, but in this case they in spite of me
> occasion surprise and sadness. . . . That ministry, says the Bishop in the ordina-
> tion sermon, is poor and ruinous, in which the enclosures are not carefully
> guarded.[65]

The correspondent turned on the bishop. He pointed out that there had been a
revival at West Point which was not so "carefully guarded" and had not ruined
anyone's attachment to the Episcopal Church. As a matter of fact, three cadets had
become Episcopal ministers. "It was a ministry," he chided, "of prayer, of zeal and
of devotion to the spiritual interests of the soul." How did these young men
become attached to the "peculiar principles and order" of the Episcopal church?
"Because they had heard the inestimable value of order and externalism preached
from day to day?" No: preaching on externals, argued the writer, would lead
people away from true religion. "Go into almost any parish," he urged, "and you
will find that the tendency exists to become strongly attached to the rites, usages
and order of the Church, to the utter neglect of a spiritual and holy life." Finally,
the writer charged the bishop with giving "his censure upon the religious usages of
some of the most respectable denominations around us."[66]

These were serious charges. The writer of this letter mounted a classic evangelical argument: that the spirit, not the form, of religion is most important. The
spirit of true religion promoted unity among all Christians. Commitment to the
particularities of Episcopal form would divide Episcopalians from other true
believers and lead to deadening formalism. In his first charge to the clergy, and
indeed, in his own West Point revival, the bishop had preached the gospel. Now it
seemed, to at least some Ohioans, that the bishop was preaching the Episcopal
Church. Gossip around the diocese charged him with "imperiousness," "abuse of
power," and the "use of unconstitutional power."[67] Had their Evangelical bishop
changed his views?

Samuel Seabury may have gotten it right: Charles McIlvaine was as "high" as
he had ever been. McIlvaine had always preferred the forms and polity of the
Episcopal Church. To him, the Episcopal Church was the truest representation of
New Testament Christianity; the church closest to biblical purity. The 1836
sermon was not a repudiation of his evangelical principles; rather, it was an
explication of the distinctive contribution of the Episcopal Church to evangelicalism. He did not argue that externals were valuable in and of themselves. He argued
that externals were necessary to guard against the possibility of spiritual religion—
evangelical religion—to become perverted by fashion, whim, or charisma. He was
concerned that without external checks evangelical religion would be corrupted.
Thus, true religion needed some sort of authority beyond the individual.

The most biblical, primitive, and pure authority was that of the Episcopal
Church. In one sense, the Ohioans, worried by McIlvaine's "High Church"

leanings were right. Like the High Church party, McIlvaine was skeptical about the excesses of American evangelicalism. The innovations and manipulations of ultraists and fanatics obscured the gospel. Extreme individuality and extreme democratic tendencies had made each man and woman his or her own religious authority. McIlvaine agreed with the High Churchmen: the extreme evangelicalism of the day injured Christian faith. The church must act to guard true doctrine, fight innovation, and stand as a bulwark against schism and sectarianism.

This did not mean that McIlvaine had become a Hobartian High Churchman, as some in his diocese seemed to think. Hobart and McIlvaine based their proclamation of the Episcopal Church's claim to ecclesiastical authority in different theological sources. As a consequence, they diverged on defining how the church was to be guardian and refuge. Both sources came from Anglican theology. Hobart drew from seventeenth- and eighteenth-century Anglican theology—a theology that downplayed the theology of the English Reformation. Following the lead of these theologians, Hobart concluded that the Episcopal Church was an "apostolic" ark—one constructed from the material of the early Christian fathers and the first five centuries of Christian tradition.[68] From this standpoint, he rejected evangelical views on justification by faith alone, individual conversion, and the invisibility of the church. He argued instead for the external means of grace provided through the ministrations and sacraments of the visible church.

McIlvaine, in contrast, conceived of the Episcopal Church as a "protestant" ark. He buttressed this idea with sixteenth-century Anglican theology. The English Reformers, he believed, had recovered the theology of the biblical, New Testament church. They stripped away layers of human invention and revealed the English Church in apostolic purity. Although all the Reformers—Lutheran, Calvinist, and Anglican—were basically correct and biblical, the English Reformers most successfully elucidated the theology and practice of the primitive church. The English Church, and her American Episcopal progeny, was therefore, the truest, most biblical Protestant church. Because he based his view of the church on Reformation presuppositions, McIlvaine agreed with classical Protestant views on justification and salvation. What he did not like was the way those Protestant doctrines were being corrupted by the nonbiblical, non-Reformational practices of his contemporaries. Innovations, and innovators, harming the core of the gospel must be stopped. So, while Hobart assailed American evangelicalism from without, McIlvaine assailed it from within a shared theological framework. His 1836 convention charge reveals this theological commitment. In it, he repeatedly emphasized the importance of the theology of the English Reformation.

This theological heritage, however, was one that American Evangelical Episcopalians had to recover for themselves. In the late eighteenth and early nineteenth centuries, the Reformation was not a typical starting point for Episcopal theology. William White, the first presiding bishop, had an intense dislike of sixteenth-century theology.[69] As a result, American Episcopal theology was bereft of Reformed influences. Evangelicals recovered Reformation theology early in the nineteenth century with the publication of Allen's 1820 edition of Burnet's *History of the Reformation*, and with the publication of articles on the Reformation in periodicals like the *Washington Theological Repertory*. The *Repertory* had found knowledge of the Thirty-nine Articles, for example, so abysmally low, that they were compelled to print them, with biblical commentary, over the course of several issues![70]

The Evangelical rediscovery of the Reformation had three sources. First, during the eighteenth-century Evangelical Revival, Wesley and Whitefield based their preaching on rediscovery of the Reformation theology of the Thirty-nine Articles.[71] Evangelicalism within the Anglican tradition had always been linked with sixteenth- rather than seventeenth- or eighteenth-century Anglican doctrine. Second, in early America, Evangelical Episcopalians had been educated at seminaries other than Episcopal seminaries, so although they read required seventeenth- and eighteenth-century Anglican texts, their theological interests were often shaped by Presbyterian and Congregational teachers. Some Episcopalians, like Hobart, rejected the Reformation, while others, like McIlvaine, sought commonalities between Episcopalianism and the theology of their Reformed friends and colleagues. The Reformation, particularly the Reformed interpretation of the Thirty-nine Articles, provided common theological ground between Episcopalians and other American Protestants, particularly Presbyterians. Third, their Anglican evangelical cousins in England staunchly defended the Reformation foundations of Anglicanism. Evangelical Episcopalians and Anglican evangelicals were in very close contact, and their mutual concerns fostered a recovery of sixteenth-century doctrine by Americans. In addition to these three reasons particular to Episcopalians, there was a general interest in Reformation theology in antebellum America. At the same time that Episcopalians began to read Cranmer and Ridley, Presbyterians and the Reformed rediscovered Calvin.[72] In both Europe and America, church history and historical theology had really just begun to be considered academic disciplines. For Evangelical Episcopalians as well as other Americans, the recovery of the Reformation was a sign of the growing historical consciousness of their time.[73]

In his charge, McIlvaine argued that Reformation theology kept the Episcopal Church from succumbing to the spirit of innovation and novelty in American religion: "closer adherence to the evangelical principles of our old 39 Articles" protected the church from heresy; in addition, the liturgy expressed the same "evangelical principles."[74] Because his theological heritage was that of the English Reformation, which never eliminated "externals" to the same degree as did the Calvinist movements, McIlvaine was always willing to accept "form"—as long as the form was not contrary to the clear teaching of Scripture. The forms retained by the English church were biblical and thus divinely revealed. They therefore served a useful purpose in Christian life. McIlvaine referred to certain forms—particularly the form of the episcopacy—as primitive and apostolic.[75] The form of the Episcopal Church was God's appointed structure to promote the gospel and the health of the church. McIlvaine's whole conception of "externals"—the term so roundly denounced by his critic in the *Episcopal Recorder* who wrongly heard the sermon as if it was preached by Hobart—came from his commitment to the theology of the English Reformation. McIlvaine was a High Churchman all right, but not a Hobartian one. If by High Churchman one meant someone who defended the particular forms of polity and practice of the Episcopal Church, McIlvaine was a thoroughly Protestant, Anglican, evangelical, and Reformed one.

Placed in the context of British Anglicanism, this combination of traits was not at all unusual.[76] No Anglican Evangelical bishop would have ever been accused of High Churchism for preaching on the unique and biblical forms of the Church of England. English bishops were expected to uphold the distinct teaching of their church against any dissenters. Being an established church, however, they possessed the power to do this. In contrast, many Evangelical Episcopalians believed the same about their church as did Anglican Evangelicals, but the Americans were in no position to offend Presbyterians, Methodists, and Baptists. They were less willing to cut themselves off from evangelicals in other communions. They lived in a society where the church functioned on the voluntary system. Being distinct was one way of attracting converts (as Bishop McIlvaine said in his sermon), but, at the same time, cooperating with other denominations was often necessary for survival. The Episcopal Church was very small in Ohio, and it depended on the good will of its neighbors for material aid and for assistance in joint educational and evangelistic projects. Thus, the Americans tended to emphasize their commonality with other denominations.[77] Bishop McIlvaine was just preaching as any good Anglican bishop naturally would; it was preaching about the benefits of Episcopal form and distinctiveness to Ohioans that got him into trouble.

The Missionary Society and the Limits of Cooperation

McIlvaine was not only beginning to sound like a High Churchman to Ohio Episcopalians, he was cooperating with High Church colleagues in the House of Bishops in a singularly important venture: the mission of the church. In the early years of the nineteenth century, American Christians began to form national voluntary societies to promote missions and evangelism. One of the earliest societies, the American Board of Commissioners for Foreign Missions (ABCFM), was established in 1810. This board dedicated itself to the task of world evangelization, and to this purpose it sent out the first group of American missionaries in 1812.[78] Within a few years, a large number of societies had been founded with the purpose of evangelizing America; these included the American Bible Society (1816), the American Sunday School Union (1824), and the American Tract Society (1825). In 1825, a number of students at Andover seminary felt these societies inadequate to evangelize the west; they envisioned a national, domestic missionary society. Out of this group, the American Home Missionary Society (AHMS) was formed in 1826.[79]

McIlvaine and other evangelical Episcopal leaders were willing to cooperate with the national educational and evangelistic organizations. They were not willing to cooperate with the ABCFM and the AHMS, however. The national and home missionary societies, were, like the other societies, controlled largely by Presbyterians and Congregationalists.[80] But, unlike the other societies, the ABCFM and the AHMS were in the business of establishing specific churches. It was one thing for Episcopalians to print and distribute Bibles and tracts with the

Presbyterians; it was another to give Episcopal money to support Presbyterian missionaries!

Individual Evangelical Episcopalians had long been interested in missions. Besides the national excitement created by the ABCFM venture in 1812, Evangelical Episcopalians were influenced by their parent denomination in England. In 1799, Anglican Evangelicals created a voluntary foreign missionary society, the Church Missionary Society (CMS), which became a model for many American societies (including non-Episcopal ones). In 1815, as the war with England ended, the Rev. Josiah Pratt of the CMS contacted American bishops to enlist their aid in missionary work. Evangelical Bishop Griswold was eager to cooperate. In 1814, before the CMS expressed interest, the bishop urged his clergy to consider their missionary duties and chided them for being slower then other Protestants in carrying out mission work.[81] In 1818, he corresponded with the CMS with the hopes of establishing a similar society in America.[82] "To spread the Gospel," preached the Rev. Benjamin Allen, "is a paramount duty." Should not "our call be heard by the hunter on the Rocky Mountains, and the savage on the shores of the Pacific?"[83]

Other Protestants had been busily establishing their missionary societies: the Presbyterians worked with the ABCFM, but they established a home missions board in 1816, and the Methodists organized their mission efforts in 1819.[84] Evangelical Episcopalians were anxious not to fall behind. Finally in 1821, the Episcopal Church organized its Domestic and Foreign Missionary Society. Based on the voluntary model of the CMS, the new society solicited memberships costing from three to fifty dollars. Fifty dollars entitled the "patrons" to sit on the board of directors, but because so many patrons signed up, this provision had to be dropped. Early patrons included a host of Evangelicals: James Milnor, J.P.K. Henshaw, Benjamin Allen, John Jay, and Francis Scott Key.[85]

In spite of the enthusiasm of evangelical leaders, the missionary society did not live up to expectations. "I have to regret," reported the Rev. Gregory Bedell, who had been sent out by the society to elicit Episcopal support, "that my success has not been so great as I had fondly hoped for. . . . The formation of a Society for missionary purposes . . . is a circumstance yet new to the Episcopalians of our country, and will require some considerable time to produce . . . a favorable impression."[86] In the first years of its existence, the Episcopal board struggled for funds and potential missionaries. They achieved modest success in domestic fields, but failed almost completely on the foreign field. By the early 1830s, ample opportunities for Episcopal missionaries had arisen in Africa and China, and the church in the west was desperate for missionaries. But there were few candidates and little money. The voluntary system of the board of missions had failed. A special meeting of the board of directors was called in August 1835 to discuss the situation.

Charles McIlvaine was invited to give the opening sermon for the meeting. The bishop, straight from his own mission field in Ohio, preached on "The Missionary Character and Duty of the Church." The sermon is colored by his experience trying to maintain the democratic excesses of Ohio evangelicalism. The Church, he proclaimed, was the light of Christ in the world; it was "the design of the Lord of Glory in setting up his Church" to evangelize the world.[87] It was the nature, the very being, of the Church to carry out this work. Explained McIlvaine:

> We have now seen what constitutes the great office of the Church of Christ on earth, that it is no other than a great association, under a Divine constitution, of the professed people of God, for the propagation of the Gospel to every creature; and that, inasmuch as the preaching of the Gospel, by an ordained ministry, is God's chief ordinance for that propagation; so the Church is a great Missionary association, divinely constituted, for the special work of sending into all the world the ministers and Missionaries of the Word.[88]

The Church, as a missionary association, was not a *voluntary* society; "Church duty and missionary duty, Church membership, and obligation to take part in missionary work" are not distinct. He proclaimed:

> The Church is a Missionary Society, in its grand design, in the spirit and object of its Divine Founder, in the primitive commission of it ministry. . . . Consequently . . . every member of the Church, by the vows of that baptism in which he was consecrated to Christ and by his every renewal of those vows at the table of the Lord, stands committed and pledged to take part with his heart, and mind, and prayers, and substance, as he hath opportunity, in promoting the Gospel to the ends of the earth.[89]

McIlvaine urged the board of directors to take up this vision – of the whole Episcopal Church as a missionary society – to reformulate the Domestic and Foreign Missionary Board.

The directors appointed seven men to recommend "what measures should be adopted for the more efficient organization of this Society."[90] Bishops Doane and McIlvaine headed the committee; the Revs. Milnor, Henshaw, Beasley, and Kemper represented the clergy; and a Mr. Magruder was the appointed layperson. On August 21, they presented their report. "The Committee," read Bishop Doane, "unanimously recommend that the Church herself, in dependence on her divine Head, and for the promotion of His glory, undertake and carry on, in her character as the Church, and as 'The Domestic and Foreign Missionary Society of the Protestant Episcopal Church . . . ,' the work of Christian missions."[91] It was a complete triumph for McIlvaine. His platform, as presented in his sermon, had been accepted whole.[92] The General Convention of 1835 approved the recommendations: the Episcopal Church was, in its entirety, a missionary association.[93]

When it came to missions, the actual activity of establishing churches, McIlvaine rejected the cooperative, voluntary model demonstrated both by other American Protestants and by evangelicals in the Church of England. Instead, in 1835, he articulated a particular, denominational, obligatory model for mission work. He turned his back on interevangelical cooperation, and he joined with High Churchmen, like Bishop Doane, to further the interests and influence of the gospel as it was preached by the Episcopal Church. Many years later, Evangelical Episcopalians would regret this moment as the compromise that undermined their entire program. At the time, however, it seemed they finally shared real power in the direction of the church.

In Defense of the Episcopacy

McIlvaine was not the only Evangelical to defend Episcopal forms. Evangelical Episcopalians, especially the clergy, were devoted to Episcopal ecclesiology and deeply attached to its liturgy, its ministry, and the sacraments.[94] To no form, however, were they more loyal than the episcopacy itself. Virginia's Bishop Moore believed in "the divine origin and perpetual obligation of the Christian ministry under the Episcopal form."[95]

Bishop Griswold preached an ordination sermon that affirmed the scriptural warrant of the threefold office of the Christian ministry in bishops, elders, and deacons. In it, he argued that the elders, or presbyters, in some instances in the early church had seized the power of the bishop. Calling this innovation "strange" and "wicked," he proclaimed "we are sure, from all ancient history, that Episcopacy was general from a very early period down to the Reformation". Only at the Reformation was the episcopacy widely, and wrongly, discarded. Episcopal government, he concluded, was that "which God has set in his Church."[96] Of all the Reformation churches, only the Episcopal churches retained it in its primitive mode.[97]

In his 1836 sermon, McIlvaine defended the role of the clergy in establishing order and maintaining orthodoxy—ideas he elaborated throughout his career. One of his most notable sermons on the Episcopal ministry, "The Apostolical Commission," was preached at the consecration of Leonidas Polk. Polk, McIlvaine's first convert at West Point, sacrificed his military career for the Episcopal ministry and had been elected as the missionary bishop of Arkansas. McIlvaine was delighted by the request to preach the consecration sermon. The service was performed on December 9, 1838, and those hearing the sermon were deeply stirred. Three of his fellow Evangelical bishops—Meade, Smith, and Polk—urged McIlvaine to publish it.[98]

Drawing from the Great Commission in Matthew 28, McIlvaine pointed out that Jesus Christ gave the commission to the apostles, and that they were "his ambassadors to the whole world, and [invested] them with supreme authority, under himself, to plant, to rear, and to rule his universal Church." Thus, God created the church with the apostles at its head. Given all power and authority, the apostles ruled over the church and its ministry, administered the sacraments, and passed the authority of their office to chosen successors. This, he argued, was the episcopate as Christ had established it, and it was designed to remain as the structure of the church "to the end of the world." "But where," McIlvaine asked, "shall we find this office in the present church; this union of authority to preach and administer sacraments, with this individual right to ordain, and this presidency over clergy; this original, apostolic Episcopate?" This office "did descend" from the first apostles "to successors" by the "hand of the Lord." He traced this descent through the early centuries of Christian history and concluded that the apostolic office had continued from Christ's commission down to the sixteenth century (when it was thrown away by some wrong-minded Protestants) to the present day. Roman Catholics had rightly maintained the episcopacy, but they had corrupted it by placing all its power in the hands of a single bishop. Thus, the "preservation in each diocese, of an original, independent Episcopacy . . . this primitive constitution of the church" only occurred in the English Reformation and "oriental Christendom."[99] The only place, in other words, where Americans could find the true apostolic ministry of the church was in the Episcopal Church.

Ten months later, at an ordination service in Gambier, the bishop argued again for a distinct office of bishop and the threefold order of ministry:

> It is clearly the doctrine of the Church that not only ancient authority, but the *Holy Scriptures*, teach the *apostolic origin* of an episcopal ministry, in *the three orders* . . . It is evidently the doctrine of the Church that, from the Apostles' times, and by the evidence of Scripture, there was *no other ministry* than that which subsisted under the several gradations of Bishop, Presbyter and Deacon.[100]

As a consequence, the *"Episcopacy is the only form of Church-order contained in the Scriptures and manifested from ancient authors."* Sermons such as these marked McIlvaine as a defender of his own church.

"Bishop McIlvaine was no half-hearted or lukewarm son of the church," recalled Bishop Alfred Lee years after these sermons were preached, "His conscientious preference was given to his own Communion, as in his judgement most closely conformed to the Apostolic model."[101] McIlvaine believed that the Episcopal Church was the present-day equivalent to the New Testament church of the apostles.

Claiming that one's church structure was the primitive order of the Bible was hardly unique in antebellum America. Both mainstream and sectarian Protestant groups claimed to historically recreate or reproduce the biblical community of Scripture.[102] Many Protestants, such as the Presbyterians and Congregationalists, however much they believed in their own polity, nevertheless recognized each other's clerical orders as valid. Only the more sectarian Protestants claimed exclusive orders for their churches. Episcopalians, however, no matter how evangelical they were, and how much they cooperated with other Protestant groups, still refused to allow non-Episcopalians to preach in their churches and reordained ministers converted to the Episcopal Church. To other Protestants, most Episcopalians – even Evangelical ones – acted like sectarians in relation to church government. They claimed that church government was neither adiaphoristic, nor expedient. They believed they were the only truly apostolically constituted Protestant church. An Episcopal minister could pray and preach in a Presbyterian or Methodist service, but at Episcopal services, even Evangelical Episcopal services, Episcopal ministers retained their exclusive right to perform explicit church functions.[103]

Other Protestants expected such exclusivist claims from High Church Episcopalians. But the Evangelical party in the Episcopal Church had always stressed its common faith with other Protestants, and believed, as did non-Episcopal evangelicals, that the true and universal church was an invisible church. When McIlvaine preached his 1836 charge, his critic argued this very point. Preaching on the visible church, the externals, divided them from other evangelicals. It made them exclusivists, and it made them sound like the close-minded High Churchmen.

McIlvaine, however, persisted. The invisible could no more be separated from the visible than the soul could be separated from the body. The spirit of true religion was best exemplified in the forms of the Episcopal Church. Scripture and the early church attested to this fact.

His sermon "The Apostolic Commission" came back to haunt McIlvaine. Sixteen years later, in 1855, Presbyterian theologian Charles Hodge published a review of McIlvaine's collected sermons. In this gracious review of his former classmate's and close friend's work, Hodge claimed that although McIlvaine was "disposed to lay more steps on externals then we think the free spirit of the gospel warrants," he and the bishop were essentially agreed on the nature of the church. "The great evangelical doctrine," stated Hodge, is "that the true Church consists only of true believers." He and McIlvaine agreed that "the 'Idea of the Church' and the 'Organization of the Church' are two distinct subjects."[104] The true church knows no denominational bounds. The review was high praise from America's most influential Presbyterian thinker.

In May 1855, Hodge addressed the Presbyterian historical society and laid out the distinctives of Presbyterian polity. A few months later, the High Church *Church Review* published Hodge's lecture. To refute Hodge's argument, the *Church Review* reprinted McIlvaine's sermon "The Apostolic Commission." "A man," wrote the editor, "might as well question the demonstrations in Euclid, as to contest either its premises or conclusions."[105] Pitting McIlvaine against Hodge was a move of High Church genius. It showed McIlvaine as inconsistent, maintaining Episcopal exclusiveness on one hand and evangelical interdenominational inclusiveness on the other. In addition, it would create a rift between McIlvaine and his most loyal Protestant supporters – the Old School Presbyterians.

Never having read this particular sermon before, Charles Hodge was shocked. "Granting what you say," he protested, "I am no minister, and if a Christian, am in a state of rebellion against one who has a divine right to my submission to him as the bishop of New Jersey." He continued:

> It is not reasonable to expect that Presbyterians can silently submit to these claims of Episcopacy. So long as they emanated only from professed Anglicans or High-Churchmen, I for one, cared little about them. But when I found to my surprise that they had been advocated by one of your high character as an evangelical Christian, I felt bound, when specially by name called upon, to say what I have said in reference to the whole matter.[106]

He enclosed a copy of an article that was going to appear in the January 1856 issue of the *Princeton Review* in which Hodge demolished his old friend's arguments. McIlvaine, he asserted, misconstrued the nature of the Great Commission and, consequently, the nature of the episcopacy: the commission was not given to just the apostles; it was given to the whole church. "Bishop McIlvaine has attempted," he argued, "to walk on a paper bridge over a sea of fire." What disturbed Hodge most, however, was that "until recently the doctrine of apostolic succession as involving the perpetuity of the apostleship was confined to the Laudean faction in the Episcopal Church," but now "the heads of the evangelical party have gone over to the enemy."[107]

Hodge asked McIlvaine to explain himself. McIlvaine received his letter and immediately responded. He wrote off the *Church Review*'s article as an attempt to destroy their long friendship and the fruitful cooperation between Evangelical Episcopalians and Presbyterians. McIlvaine pointed out to Hodge that in his sermon he said nothing about the state of other Protestant orders; Hodge had only inferred that he considered Presbyterian orders invalid. McIlvaine replied:

> It teaches Apostolical Succession, just as I understand real Presbyterians to teach it, namely, that a certain part of the authority committed to the Apostles was intended to continue in the ministry to the end of the world. The difference between the Episcopalians and the Presbyterian being that the latter hold the descent to have been in the line of Presbyters, the former in the line of diocesan Bishops. The Apostolical succession is held in my opinion as much in one Church as the other.[108]

A High Churchman would never admit this, he stated, and would deny the validity of Presbyterian orders and the reality of Presbyterian sacraments. McIlvaine dodged Hodge's attack, but Hodge remained unconvinced. McIlvaine never really answered the central question: Should Presbyterians submit to Episcopal authorities? Hodge insightfully pointed out a painful–and central–conundrum for Evangelical Episcopalians. How could they really believe that the church was an invisible, spiritual reality made up of all born-again persons and, at the same time, bind themselves to a visible body with pretensions of "divine right" and exclusivist tendencies? How could they recognize other Protestants as true Christians when those Protestants were outside the bounds of Episcopal ministration?

What did McIlvaine think of other Protestant orders? In 1839, after writing on the biblical basis of the episcopacy, McIlvaine pondered this point:

> How the belief of these views should affect our opinion as to the validity of any non-episcopal orders; whether, whilst we must consider them irregular, because wanting apostolic precedent, we should consider them also as, in all respect, invalid, the Church speaks not; but leaves the question for private judgment, and alike nourishes in her bosom those who affirm and those who deny. This is wisdom.[109]

Now, he told Hodge, he was "at full liberty to believe in and acknowledge other churches as real churches, and their ministers as real ministers. . . . I did not consider, nor do I now, Episcopal ordination essential to the being of the ministry or sacraments, any more than to the Church, though I do consider it essential to the full order and model of the primitive church. So you think of Presbyterian ordination."[110] Unlike the High Church position that episcopacy was essential to the being (*esse*) of the church, McIlvaine maintained that the episcopacy was only essential to the church's well-being (*bene esse*).

Thus, the Evangelical party maintained the private right to recognize other Protestant orders, but publicly obeyed the directive of the church to forbid non-Episcopal ministrations. In 1836, McIlvaine reminded the clergy of this position. Quoting William White, he stated that the Anglican Reformers

> unequivocally affirmed the Apostolic origin of Episcopacy *as a fact;* and then, as a suitable consequence, they ordained that there should be no other ministry

within its bounds. The same is the limit in our church. If any should carry the subject beyond this, it is *private opinion and cannot be acted on*.[111]

McIlvaine believed that Episcopal polity was primitive and apostolic; he upheld the Church's laws, but still privately "recognized" the ministry of other churches. The Episcopal Church might be more primitive and biblical, but God still blessed other churches anyway. "It is one thing to maintain certain doctrines," McIlvaine confessed to Hodge, "and another to give them a certain relative position."[112] Depending on the circumstances, McIlvaine could preach on the invisible or the visible church, but, he asserted, the invisible church had always claimed his primary allegiance. Hodge knew that; he printed as much in his article on McIlvaine's ecclesiastical views only a year earlier. Although McIlvaine did not recognize it himself, the circumstances in Ohio in the 1830s led him to emphasize the visible and external aspects of the church. By the 1850s, the time of Hodge's articles, McIlvaine was in the midst of a new controversy and, as he had in his early ministry, preached more often on the invisible church.

Admitting he had been uncharitable, Hodge regretted attacking his old friend. He did not believe that McIlvaine's argument was logically consistent, however, nor did he grant that Presbyterians believed in a permanent apostle-ship—an idea that Hodge argued would always undergird Roman Catholic claims of papacy. Although he understood his friend's reasons and arguments, Hodge still believed "if the doctrines of your sermon can be established it is all over with Protestantism and Evangelical religion."[113]

McIlvaine resisted this conclusion, as did the other leaders of the Evangelical party. Wrote one Evangelical Episcopal missionary:

We believe, that Christ and his apostles set up his Church under a distinct and specific external organization, and intended that that particular form should be preserved and maintained in all ages and countries. . . . As for our brethren of other denominations, who have repented and believed on the Lord Jesus Christ, we can have no doubt as to their final salvation. We may think that it would be better for them, and more acceptable to God, if they were within the pale of our communion, but of their safety we can cherish no doubt.[114]

The primitive forms—structure, liturgy, and theology—of the Episcopal Church did propagate Protestant and Evangelical religion. "We do believe," wrote McIlvaine about the institutions of the Episcopal Church, "that they are primitive, derived from the Apostles, of the same origin as the Bible, binding upon our consciences, and a full warrant for our standing a separate denomination, till all others become Episcopal."[115] With such statements, it was no wonder other evangelicals suspected Episcopalians of ecclesiastical imperialism. To them, evangelical unity on the "grand essentials of doctrine" always seemed at odds with Episcopal exclusiveness.

In spite of near-constant criticism on this point from other evangelicals, Evangelical Episcopalians refused to recognize this as a problem. The invisible church was, to them, one thing; the visible church, another. They saw no contradiction between being "one in Christ" and extolling the glories of Episcopal polity and liturgy. McIlvaine therefore persisted. He had witnessed the "success" of non-Episcopal ministers in Ohio. Freed from the burdens of ecclesiastical machinery, they preached and taught wherever and however they wanted, spread heresy, and divided churches. McIlvaine believed that the episcopacy, with its divinely appointed authority, was best suited to confront such problems on the mission field. Ecclesiastical order was a necessary part of mission work. To that end, he joined forces with the High Church Episcopalians to evangelize both the west and the world.

Conclusion

In the early years of the nineteenth century, American evangelicals from a number of theological traditions cooperated in a multitude of revivals and interdenominational organizations to promote the gospel. But as the decades progressed, particularly in the 1830s, American Protestants, even committed evangelicals, rediscovered and reasserted the claims of their particular denominations. The Baptists, for example, refused to participate in the American Bible Society when the society was unwilling to substitute the word *immersion* for baptism. In the west, Antimission Baptists refused to cooperate with any interevangelical organizations at all. Some Presbyterians and Congregationalists questioned the wisdom of participating in revivals. Although the large voluntary organizations held together, they were joined by a host of small organizations, also run by evangelicals, which stressed Baptist, Presbyterian, Methodist, or Episcopal distinctives. Evangelical Episcopalians continued to work with the large national organizations—with the exception of missionary organizations—and, at the same time, they defended the institutions of the Episcopal Church.

In the same decade, tensions between Evangelical and High Church Episcopalians lessened. Part of this was no doubt due to the growth of fanaticism and ultraism in America. The differences between the High Church and Evangelical parties were no less; but when forced to choose whether to cooperate with Protestant extremists or High Church Episcopalians, Evangelicals, like Charles McIlvaine, choose their co-religionists. Episcopal order was the need of the day. As a consequence, McIlvaine preached and wrote a great deal about Episcopal distinctiveness. He defended the "externals" of liturgy and church order, he extolled the primitiveness of the apostolic ministry, and he rejected voluntary cooperative societies for missions—preferring instead to extend the borders of his own Episcopal Church.

McIlvaine's turn toward the church should not be regarded as a modification of his evangelical commitment. Rather, the crisis in Ohio over Chase's resignation and McIlvaine's subsequent troubles point to another conclusion: the Evangelical party itself was divided. No formal division existed, but two tendencies within the party were evident. First, there existed a *democratic* branch of the party, well represented by the anonymous letter writer to the *Episcopal Recorder* and the Kenyon faculty and students. These evangelicals wanted to associate fully with the surrounding evangelical ethos; they were uncomfortable with the power of bishops and institutional structures. Second, the *authoritarian* evangelicals, like

Bishop McIlvaine, shared evangelical theological beliefs and spirituality, yet they criticized the lack of order and restraint exhibited by many American evangelicals. They were comfortable with the power structure of the church, and they rarely failed to use it to their advantage. These tendencies within the Evangelical party, democratic and authoritarian evangelicalism, were often at odds in Ohio. In the 1830s, High Church–Evangelical party tensions lessened only on an official level, mostly because authoritarian evangelicals made common cause with the High Church party against all forms of democratic evangelicalism.[116]

McIlvaine's concern for church authority matched that of other American Protestants at the time. Yet for him, the trend toward denominationalism was exacerbated by his experience in the west. Against the backdrop of religious competition in Ohio, he asserted his authority as a bishop, an apostle of the most primitive of all churches. He worked to contain the spill of democratic evangelicalism that was seeping into his churches. Clearly, not all the laity were listening to the message of "orderly evangelicalism" preached by their bishop. He wrote to his mother:

> I go from the most refined society of the State perhaps next to the most uncultivated–now charging the clergy, horse and foot, next scolding some parish in the woods for abolition lectures in the Church, or protracted meetings, or even perfectionism. . . . It is well that I have the gift of tongue, for I have to preach for the times.[117]

That McIlvaine felt obligated to contain the spread of radical evangelicalism– abolition, revivalism, and perfectionism–within the Episcopal Church showed how much even his own church had been influenced by the surrounding religious culture. The times in 1830s Ohio were turbulent. In the face of that turbulence, the bishop preached on Christian order as proclaimed by the Episcopal Church. For Bishop McIlvaine, "denominational authority clashed with the egalitarian values" of the American west.[118]

The times, however, were changing, and shortly Bishop McIlvaine would stop worrying about extreme evangelicalism and start to worry about a new challenge to his orderly gospel. Within his own communion, the communion he had so vigorously promoted and defended in the 1830s, arose a movement that threatened to wipe out the primitive, evangelical, and apostolic genius of the English Reformation–the Oxford Movement had begun. For Evangelical Episcopalians, John Henry Newman would prove a much greater threat than Charles Finney ever had.

Notes

1. Carus, *Memorials of McIlvaine*, 65.
2. Ibid., 66.
3. Tyng to McIlvaine, September 21, 1831, in McI, Kenyon College, 310921a.
4. Henshaw to McIlvaine, September 21, 1831, in ibid., 310921b.
5. Carus, *Memorials of McIlvaine*, 66.

6. The letters from each bishop pertaining to Chase's resignation and McIlvaine's election are in McI, Kenyon College.

7. Henshaw to McIlvaine, note 4.

8. Stone, *Memoir of Griswold*, 168.

9. Carus, *Memorials of McIlvaine*, 67.

10. This report is in *Journal of the Proceedings of the Bishops, Clergy, and Laity of the Protestant Episcopal Church* (New York, 1832): 23–24.

11. The second resolution is found in ibid, 33–34.

12. The vote was not unanimous, however. Clergy: 27 aye, 19 nay. Laity: 18 aye, 10 nay. Although not an absolute correlation, there is a general geographic concurrence between the High Church and Evangelical tendencies of these dioceses and the way their delegates voted. Delegates–both clergy and laity–from Evangelical dioceses in Maine, Massachusetts, Rhode Island, Virginia, Kentucky, and Ohio voted overwhelmingly aye (there were only two dissenting lay votes from all six delegations). Delegates from High Church strongholds, such as North Carolina and Maryland, voted unanimously nay. Pennsylvania, split in its church tendencies, also split its votes. However, High Church Connecticut also split its votes: the clergy voted nay, while the laity voted aye. Surprisingly, New York was also split: one clergyman voted aye; two nay. The real surprise in the New York vote was that all four of the lay delegates, including the vocal evangelical, William Jay, voted in favor of McIlvaine. See ibid., 35.

13. Carus, *Memorials of McIlvaine*, 70.

14. Some of these parishes were little more than a family or two meeting in a home. Besides the functioning parishes, there were some dozen or so parishes with drawn boundaries, but no people whatsoever. The statistics are taken from "Statistics of the Diocese–1830," *Journal of the Diocese of Ohio* (Gambier, 1831): 38–39.

15. There were also some very faithful Episcopal lay persons who maintained the Episcopal Church before the arrival of a bishop or the formation of a diocese. For example, cousins of Bishop Griswold of Massachusetts conducted Episcopal services in Worthington, Ohio, during the War of 1812. The Worthington parish had been organized in 1804 by Bishop Griswold's brother, Ezra Griswold. A good article on the early years of Ohio is Evelyn A. Cummins, "The Beginnings of the Church in Ohio and Kenyon College," *Historical Magazine of the Protestant Episcopal Church* 6 (1937): 276–298. For Philander Chase's work in early Ohio, see Philander Chase, *Reminiscences: An Autobiography*, 2 vols. (Boston, 1848); Laura Chase Smith, *The Life of Philander Chase, First Bishop of Ohio and Illinois: Founder of Kenyon and Jubilee Colleges* (New York, 1903); George Franklin Smythe, *A History of the Diocese of Ohio Until the Year 1918* (Cleveland, 1931); idem, *Kenyon College: Its First Century* (New Haven, 1924); and James A. Muller, "Philander Chase and the Frontier," *Historical Magazine of the Protestant Episcopal Church* 14 (1945): 168–184.

16. For the success of these groups in the West, see William Warren Sweet, *Religion on the American Frontier*, 4 vols. (Chicago, 1931–1946), and T. Scott Miyakawa, *Protestants and Pioneers: Individualism and Conformity on the American Frontier* (Chicago, 1964).

17. Henry Caswall, *America and the American Church*, 1st ed. (London, 1839), 32–33. Caswall was an Anglican minister who served in Ohio and Kentucky for ten years. *America and the American Church* was a tract to enlist other English clergy to become missionaries to America's western frontier.

18. Ibid., 56.

19. McIlvaine to Tyng, January 19, 1833. Published in the *Episcopal Recorder* (January 36, 1833): 170. McIlvaine wrote a series of letters to Tyng conveying his impressions about his new diocese. Tyng, for missionary purposes, thought these letters so important he secured McIlvaine's permission to publish them in Philadelphia's *Episcopal Recorder*. They

were also published, with a few week's lag time, in Ohio's *Gambier Observer*. The letters were edited, rearranged, and published in pamphlet form (unfortunately omitting some of McIlvaine's most interesting insights on the west) as Charles P. McIlvaine, *The Respectful Address of C. P. McIlvaine, ... to All Who Would Promote the Progress of Learning and Religion in the Western States* (New York, 1833).

20. There is little in the way of first-rate historical studies on religion in nineteenth-century Ohio. Peter Williams published a bibliographic essay on the subject, indicating the lack of recent historical scholarship—"Religion in the Old Northwest: A Bibliographical Essay," *Old Northwest* 5 (1979): 57–73. In addition to the works of Sweet and Miyakawa, there is a very suggestive chapter on the role of religion in shaping community in Ohio in Andrew R. L. Cayton and Peter S. Onuf, *The Midwest and the Nation: Rethinking the History of an American Region* (Bloomington, 1990). There are scattered references to religion in some Ohio histories; these usually follow the Turnerian line of interpretation. See, for example, John D. Barnhart, *Valley of Democracy: The Frontier Versus the Plantation in the Ohio Valley, 1775–1818* (Bloomington, 1953). Timothy L. Smith's recent "The Ohio Valley: Testing Ground for America's Experiment in Religious Pluralism," *Church History* 60 (1991): 461–479, seeks to point out religious diversity, but seems to have the underlying thesis that Methodism was really the determinative Christian tradition in Ohio. This leads him to identify McIlvaine and Evangelical Episcopalians as influenced by the Methodist tradition. Although many lay Episcopalians were friendly toward Methodism, McIlvaine kept his distance. Not until well into the 1850s did McIlvaine sound anything like a Methodist. He and his clerical colleagues were self-consciously developing an evangelical tradition in the Episcopal Church without reference to Methodism. There are also a number of denominational studies on religion in the Ohio Valley.

21. Andrew R. L. Cayton, *The Frontier Republic: Ideology and Politics in the Ohio Country, 1780–1825* (Kent, Ohio, 1986), x. Cayton draws this definition of frontier from a number of sociological and historical studies, including works by Richard Hofstadter, Lee Benson, Frederick Jackson Turner, and Don H. Doyle. Although Cayton's work is strictly secular (there is for example, only one reference to Methodism), his categories and thesis proved helpful in this study. He argues that the political history of Ohio is one of conflict and compromise. Two groups, the democratic-leaning Jefferson Republicans, whose ideology emphasized "personal independence or liberty," and the Federalists, who "preached the necessity of social interdependence," fought each other to control the territory. He argues that the Jeffersonians won Ohio's statehood and early political control, but they were eventually forced to modify Ohio's government, borrowing from the Federalist vision of national power. He concludes "the citizens of Ohio reached a basic consensus about government and society only when they abandoned the extremes of individual and local independence, and national control and institutional authority" (153). Thus, by 1825 Ohioans concluded (politically at least) that "neither absolute power nor absolute liberty could effectively govern Ohio" (153). Cayton's thesis replaces Turner's frontier thesis—that popular democracy was the guiding ideological force in the West—with a thesis of compromise between two conflicting ideological impulses. I believe Cayton's thesis helps explain the religious tensions between Episcopalians and sectarian groups, along with some of the tensions within the Episcopal Church, in the diocese of Ohio.

22. W. H. Venable, *Beginnings of Literary Culture in the Ohio Valley* (Cincinnati, 1891), 225. I disagree with Venable that this sort of competition created antiintellectualism, but I think his observations on the religious competition in the area are sound.

23. One early Methodist circuit rider, Joseph Dodderidge, had some success in Ohio. After the Methodists split from the Episcopal Church, Dodderidge remained an Episcopalian. For accounts of the growth of Methodism in Ohio, see William Warren Sweet's *The*

Rise of Methodism in the West (New York and Cincinnati, 1920); idem, *Circuit Riders Days Along the Ohio* (New York and Cincinnati, 1923); and idem, *Religion on the American Frontier, 1783–1840*, Vol. 4 (Chicago, 1946). See also Samuel W. Williams, *Pictures of Early Methodism in Ohio* (Cincinnati and New York, 1909), and John M. Versteeg, ed., *Methodism: Ohio Area, 1812–1962* (n.p., 1962).

24. This is the traditional interpretation of popular evangelicalism on the frontier. Following the lead provided by Frederick Jackson Turner, William Warren Sweet and others formulated the thesis that Methodist and Baptist beliefs "matched" the popular, individualistic, and democratic ethos of the West. Therefore, they "succeeded" where other groups "failed." I believe that historians who have followed this line of interpretation have failed to take account of the authoritative and hierarchical aspects of even the most consistently "popular" of these denominations. Miyakawa, *Protestants and Pioneers*, points out that the popular denominations supplied a sense of order on the frontier. Donald Mathews, "The Second Great Awakening as an Organizing Process, 1780–1830: An Hypothesis," *American Quarterly* 21 (1969): 23–43, who does not focus on the frontier in particular, has also identified a strain of authority and order in evangelicalism. It is at this point that Cayton's thesis of the conflict between liberty and authority might help present a more nuanced picture of frontier religion.

25. Caswall, *American Church*, 1st ed., 46.

26. McIlvaine to Tyng, note 19.

27. These statements were for publicity purposes. McIlvaine was trying to raise funds to support Kenyon College. He certainly knew that the diocese was wracked with dissension. There are numerous letters in the McIlvaine collection, Kenyon College, from the years 1831 and 1832 filling the new bishop in on all the local controversies.

28. There were some High Church congregations in the state, notably in the north and northeast. These strongholds of "Connecticut Churchmen" were pointed out to McIlvaine by Dr. Aydelotte of Cincinnati in letters dated February 20, 1832, and September 17, 1832, McI, Kenyon College, 320220 and 320917.

29. Smith, *Life of Chase*, 233; also Chase, *Reminiscences*, II: 91.

30. Chase to B. B. Smith, July 14, 1832, published in Chase, *Reminiscences*, II: 122.

31. These charges are addressed to the bishop in a leaflet dated July 25, 1831, signed "The Professors of Kenyon College." See also William Sparrow, *A Reply to the Charges and Accusations of the Rt. Rev. Philander Chase, D.D.* (Gambier, Ohio, 1832), and Smythe, *History of the Diocese of Ohio*, 153–159. To meet deconstructionist criticism, I grant that it is questionable as to how much of this democratic rhetoric the Kenyon professors believed and how much was simply an attempt to gain power at the college. They were a very independent-minded group, however, and throughout the century there would be tension between the Kenyon faculty and the diocese. In addition, it is telling that in their attempt to gain control, they used such unmistakable democratic-sounding language. They clearly allied themselves with popular democratic sentiment—whether or not they believed it. I think they really did believe that Chase's episcopal pretensions would harm the cause of the Episcopal Church in the west. By identifying themselves with democratic belief against episcopal authority, their battle against Chase gained a great deal of popular appeal. For William Sparrow's point of view on this battle, see Walker, *Life and Correspondence of Sparrow*, 62–72.

32. Smythe, *History of the Diocese of Ohio*, 170.

33. Recorded in Chase, *Reminiscences*, II: 103, and in Edward Waylen, *Ecclesiastical Reminiscences of the United States* (London, 1846), 124.

34. "Statement," *Journal of the Diocese of Ohio* (Gambier, 1831): 27.

35. Smythe, *History of the Diocese of Ohio*, 165. Bishop Chase always had supporters. Almost all the parishes in eastern Ohio, an area heavily settled by New Englanders, supported him and tried, in the 1832 convention, to get him to come back. This was the area of "Connecticut churchmanship" to which Aydelotte referred. Aydelotte was convinced that this was a diocesan battle between the southern, and more evangelical, part of Ohio and the High Church northeast. Chase himself was really more of an evangelical. Nevertheless, his appeal to authority pleased the High Church Ohioans more than the evangelicals. They became Chase's staunchest defenders.

36. Carus, *Memorials of McIlvaine*, 77.

37. Ibid.

38. Charles P. McIlvaine, "Bishop's Address," *Journal of the Diocese of Ohio* (Gambier, 1833): 6–12, especially 7, 10–11.

39. "Your Friend" to the Editor, *Episcopal Recorder* (September 27, 1834): 102.

40. All quotes this paragraph from Charles P. McIlvaine, *The Preaching of Christ Crucified* (Gambier, Ohio: Acland Press, 1834), 3, 5. In this sermon, McIlvaine was clearly following the lead established by the great Anglican Evangelical, Charles Simeon, who also emphasized in his preaching the atonement and Christ's crucifixion for salvation above other doctrines.

41. "Your Friend," 102.

42. McIlvaine thought this sermon so important, its message so basic to all Christian understanding, that he recast the entire sermon and preached it in a longer and more contemporary form in 1863–twenty-nine years later–in his sixth and final charge to his diocese. Both the original sermon and the 1863 revised sermon, *The Work of Preaching Christ*, went through numerous editions in both the United States and England. William Carus, an Anglican Evangelical minister in Cambridge and compiler of McIlvaine's memoirs, attested to the enduring popularity of this sermon among English evangelicals. See Carus, *Memorials of McIlvaine*, 88.

43. *Journal of the Diocese of Ohio* (Gambier, 1834): 6.

44. "Your Friend," 102.

45. Although I found no record of his reaction, it is inconceivable that McIlvaine was not a participant. Since he was extremely active in the American Bible Society and the women who started the revival were Episcopalians, he must have known about it, and it would have been entirely in character for him to support it. There is little information on this revival. The only reference I have found is from [Taylor,] *Sketches of the Religious Experiences*, 93–109, which portrays this revival as quite significant. It could be that it was not recorded in any of the clergy biographies because it was initiated by the laity.

46. For a good survey of revivalism in the west, see Miyakawa, *Protestants and Pioneers*, 159–173. Although this is an older interpretation of frontier revivalism, Miyakawa surveys a number of firsthand accounts that provide helpful insights into the confusion created by western revivalism.

47. Churches reporting significant revivals between 1834 and 1837 include Christ Church, Cincinnati; the parish at Dayton; St. James, Boardman; Trinity Church, Newark; St. James, Hanover; St. James, Piqua; Harcourt Parish, Gambier (whose seventeen Sunday schools comprised 800 children); Trinity Church, Cleveland; Trinity Church, Troy; and St. James, Zanesville. A number of churches reported a significant increase in communicants– an important statistic since in most Ohio churches a person was required to give testimony of having been born again before being admitted to communion. Further, the churches at Piqua and Troy seem to have been especially affected by revivals. The parish reports come from the *Journal of the Diocese of Ohio* (1834–1837). For the period 1825–1835, one social

scientist identified 351 evangelical revivals in Ohio. See John L. Hammond, *The Politics of Benevolence: Revival Religion and American Voting Behavior* (Norwood, NJ, 1979), 50ff.

48. McIlvaine, *Preaching of Christ Crucified*, 21

49. McIlvaine to Ethan Allen, October 21, 1834, Allen correspondence, in McI, Kenyon College, 341021.

50. McIlvaine to ——, February 5, 1834, published in Carus, *Memorials of McIlvaine*, 81–82.

51. McIlvaine was considering writing a book about revivalism at the same time Sprague had begun his. When McIlvaine heard of Sprague's work, he willingly gave up the idea. Believing that Sprague would be of the same opinion on the subject as himself, he wrote: "I rejoice that the undertaking has fallen into hands so much more qualified, in every sense, to do it justice." McIlvaine to William Sprague in Sprague, *Lectures on Revivals*, appendix, 87.

52. This discussion closely follows Hardman, *Finney*, 276–286. The quote is from page 277 and is probably one of the most often quoted parts of Finney's lectures on revival.

53. All quotes this paragraph from Glen King to McIlvaine, January 9, 1833, in McI, Kenyon College, 330109.

54. McIlvaine reports hearing these rumors in a journal entry dated June 1, 1834, in Carus, *Memorials of McIlvaine*, 86.

55. Ellen and Reid McIlvaine had lived for some time in Kentucky. The tone of her letter is lighthearted, but she had real insight into the different temperaments between east and west and the political temper of the times. Ellen McIlvaine to McIlvaine, December 4, 1833, in McI, Kenyon College, 331204b. I have not been able to locate McIlvaine's letter to her.

56. Rev. Samuel Seabury to McIlvaine, September 11, 1835, from the family scrapbook, p. 11. Typescript copy in McI, Kenyon College.

57. All quotes this paragraph from Charles P. McIlvaine, *The Present Condition and Chief Want of the Church: A Charge to the Clergy of the Protestant Episcopal Church of Ohio* (Gambier, 1836), 3–4. The office of bishop itself probably did influence the change in McIlvaine's tone and thought, making him more authoritarian and inflexible in his ideas of church order. After all, he was responsible for the well-being of the Episcopal Church in Ohio and accountable to the House of Bishops for problems of order and orthodoxy.

58. Ibid., 4–5.

59. Ibid.

60. All quotes this paragraph from ibid., 6, 16–18. The disciples of Alexander Campbell were quite successful in Ohio in the 1830s. For an interesting nineteenth-century account of Alexander Campbell in Ohio, see A. S. Hayden, *Early History of the Disciples in the Western Reserve of Ohio* (Cincinnati, 1875). For a modern interpretation of the radical doctrines preached by Campbell and his disciples, see Richard T. Hughes and Leonard Allen, *Illusions of Innocence: Protestant Primitivism in America, 1630–1875* (Chicago and London, 1988).

61. Ibid., 19.

62. All quotes this paragraph from ibid., 9–11, 20, 24–25.

63. This letter was reprinted in the *Episcopal Recorder* (May 23, 1835): 32, from the High Church paper, *The Churchman*.

64. He used both terms several times in *Present Condition*.

65. Unsigned letter to the editor, *Episcopal Recorder* (October 1, 1836): 106.

66. All quotes this paragraph from ibid.

67. Smythe, *History of the Diocese of Ohio*, 189.

68. See Mullin, *Episcopal Vision/American Reality*. The most extensive anthology of seventeenth-century High Church theology is Paul Elmer More and Frank Leslie Cross, eds., *Anglicanism: The Thought and Practice of the Church of England Illustrated from the Religious Literature of the Seventeenth Century* (1935). Even though High Churchman downplayed the Protestant theology of the sixteenth century, they still conceived of themselves as Protestants rather than Roman Catholics.

69. For the theological sources of the early American Episcopal Church, see Prichard, "Theological Consensus," and Mullin, *Episcopal Vision/American Reality*, 9–25.

70. See "The Thirty-nine Articles Collated with Texts of Scripture," *Washington Theological Repertory* 1 (1820): 309ff. The editors explained to readers: "That this summary of our faith, containing the most important doctrines in religion may be regarded not only as the voice of the Church, but the echo of the word of God, and may produce the proper effect on the life and character of professing Christians is devoutly to be wished" (309).

71. For Whitefield and the articles, see Henry, *George Whitefield*, 98ff. On Wesley's use of the articles, see Baker, *John Wesley*, 92, 235–239, 249–251. Whitefield argued that he strictly and literally interpreted the articles, while Wesley demonstrated more flexibility. The difference between the two men in their approach became clear when Wesley revised them in 1784 and omitted six points. Different stances toward the Thirty-nine Articles, as illustrated by Whitefield and Wesley, account for some of the differences between Methodism and Anglican Evangelicalism. Anglican Evangelicals, I believe, are identified as Calvinists because they did not reject the article on predestination and election. Although they did not reject it, they certainly felt free to interpret it in a variety of ways.

72. In addition to reading Cranmer and Ridley, Evangelical Episcopalians read Luther, Calvin, and other Lutheran and Reformed works as they became available. They also read Puritan writers, Whitefield, some Wesley, and other eighteenth-century evangelicals, such as Henry Venn, William Romaine, and William Wilberforce.

73. Although the bulk of his book is concerned with the post–Civil War period, Henry Warner Bowden's *Church History in an Age of Science: Historiographical Patterns in the United States, 1876–1918* (Chapel Hill, N.C., 1971) nevertheless looks at this developing historical consciousness in the works of Philip Schaff in the antebellum period as well.

74. McIlvaine, *Present Condition*, 10.

75. By apostolic, McIlvaine usually means "biblical," or of the first twelve apostles. Only on rare occasion does this term indicate any apostolic tradition borrowed from the early centuries of the Christian church.

76. Archbishop J. B. Sumner, who was a good friend of McIlvaine's, is another example.

77. At the same time in England, Anglican Evangelicals and evangelical dissenters moved further apart as the Anglican Evangelicals became even more vocal supporters of the establishment. Donald M. Lewis, *Lighten Their Darkness: The Evangelical Mission to Working Class London, 1828–1869* (Westport, Conn., 1986), 17–22.

78. The story of the ABCFM and its influence can be found in John A. Andrew, *Rebuilding the Christian Commonwealth: New England Congregationalists and Foreign Missions, 1800–1830* (Lexington, Ky., 1976); Clifton J. Phillips, *Protestant America and the Pagan World: The First Half-Century of the American Board of Commissioners for Foreign Missions, 1810–1860* (Cambridge, Mass., 1968); and William E. Strong, *The Story of the American Board* (New York, 1910).

79. For the history of the AHMS, see Colin Brummitt Goodykoontz, *Home Missions on the American Frontier, with Particular Reference to the American Home Missionary Society* (Caldwell, Idaho, 1939).

80. Even the Presbyterians were at times skeptical of the AHMS as a Congregationalist scheme to "subvert Presbyterianism," Ibid., 178–179.

81. Although the sermon was preached on September 28, 1814, it was not published until 1816. Griswold, *A Charge . . . September 28, 1814* (n.p., 1816), 11, reprinted in Stone, *Memoir of Milnor*, 602–620. See also Manross, *History of the Church*, 253.

82. Stone, *Memoir of Milnor*, unabridged edition, 236–237, and Griswold, *Address*, (n.p., 1818), 4.

83. This is a good example of an early Evangelical Episcopal mission sermon–Allen, *Memoir of Benjamin Allen*, 192. The text of the sermon, "The Duty of Spreading the Gospel," appears in full on pages 188–202.

84. Old School Presbyterians stopped support for the ABCFM in 1837 and formed their own society. See Arthur Judson Brown, *One Hundred Years: A History of the Foreign Missionary Work of the Presbyterian Church, U.S.A.*, 2nd ed. (New York, 1936), 27–42.

85. There are two older histories of the Domestic and Foreign Missionary Society: S. D. Denison, *A History of the Foreign Missionary Work of the Protestant Episcopal Church*, 2 vols. (New York, 1871), and Julia C. Emery, *A Century of Endeavor, 1821–1921: A Record of the First One Hundred Years of the Domestic and Foreign Missionary Society of the Protestant Episcopal Church in the U.S.A.* (New York, 1921).

86. Bedell's report to the board of directors, 1823, quoted in Denison, *History of Missionary Work*, I: 37.

87. All quotes this paragraph from McIlvaine, "Missionary Character and Duty of the Church." Reprinted many times in the nineteenth century, this copy appeared in Charles P. McIlvaine, *Select Family and Parish Sermons. A Series of Evangelical Discourses* (Columbus, Ohio, 1838), II: 311.

88. Ibid., 314.

89. Ibid., 322–323.

90. Denison, *History of Missionary Work*, I: 250.

91. Ibid., 252–253.

92. Every one of the recommendations made by the committee was either directly mentioned or alluded to in McIlvaine's sermon.

93. Two years later, in 1837, the Presbyterians made a similar move when they established the denominational Board of Missions under the control of their General Assembly. See Brown, *One Hundred Years*, 38–42.

94. The examples of this devotion to Episcopal form is evident in an immense number of tracts and books written by the Evangelical clergy. A particularly good example is William Meade, *Reasons for Loving the Episcopal Church*. Chorley, *Men and Movements*, 67–70, points this out as well.

95. Henshaw, *Memoir of Moore*, 290.

96. All quotes this paragraph from Griswold, "On the Apostolic Office." This sermon went through several reprints in the nineteenth century. The quote is from the sermon in the anthology edited by McIlvaine, *Select Family and Parish Sermons*, II: 278–279.

97. The *Episcopal Recorder* did a series of articles in which they recognized that the Moravians had also maintained a primitive episcopacy.

98. James Otey, the High Church bishop of Tennessee, also requested its publication.

99. All quotes this paragraph from Charles P. McIlvaine, *The Apostolical Commission. The Sermon Preached at the Consecration of the Rt. Rev. Leonidas Polk, D.D., Missionary Bishop for Arkansas in Christ Church, Cincinnati, December 9, 1838* (Gambier, Ohio, 1838), 4, 14–15, 25–27.

100. All quotes this paragraph from McIlvaine, *Origin and Design of the Christian Ministry*, 4–5.

101. Lee, *In Memoriam*, 21.

102. Hughes and Allen, *Illusions of Innocence*; and Richard T. Hughes, ed., *American Quest for the Primitive Church* (Urbana and Chicago, 1988). Or, as in the case of the Mormons, to rewrite scripture to be more in line with supposed ancient practices.

103. Some Evangelicals, like Stephen Tyng, were looser on this point than was Bishop McIlvaine. But, even among the Evangelicals, this practice was widely enough spread as to illicit unfavorable comment from non-Episcopal evangelicals. Tyng's unconventional practices got him into trouble in the 1870s, See Tyng, *Life and Work of Stephen Tyng*, 468ff.

104. Preceding quotes from Charles Hodge, "Bishop McIlvaine on the Church," *Princeton Review* (1855): 350–351, 354.

105. *Church Review and Register* 8 (October 1855).

106. Preceding quotes from Hodge to McIlvaine, December 18, 1855. Published in Hodge, *Life of Charles Hodge*, 414.

107. Preceding quotes from "The Church Review on the Permanency of the Apostolic Office," *Princeton Review* 28 (January 1856): 11, 19.

108. Preceding quotes from McIlvaine to Hodge, December 22, 1855, in Hodge, *Life of Charles Hodge*, 415.

109. McIlvaine, *Origin and Design*, 4

110. McIlvaine to Hodge, in Hodge, *Life of Charles Hodge*, 416.

111. Charles P. McIlvaine, "Address," *Journal of the Diocese of Ohio* (Gambier, 1836): 10–11.

112. McIlvaine to Hodge, note 110.

113. Hodge to McIlvaine, December 29, 1855, in ibid., 417.

114. John A. Clark, *Letters on the Church* (Philadelphia, 1839), 13. Clark's tract provides interesting insights into the problems encountered by Episcopal missionaries in antebellum America.

115. Charles P. McIlvaine, "Address at the Laying of the Corner Stone at Bexley Hall," *Gambier Observer* (October 26, 1839): 182–183. To be fair to the bishop, it should be noted that in the section preceding this quote, he spoke of the need for the seminary, the liturgy, and the lives of clergymen to be filled with holiness and true piety.

116. *Democratic* does not imply the rejection of all authority; it is used to connote a certain disposition toward centralized and established authorities. Even the most rabid democratic evangelical believed in authority – that authority usually rose from individual choice or conscience. Conversely, *authoritarian* does not imply that these evangelicals were opposed to democracy. They favored a democracy with the checks of established, and often centralized, authority. In political terms, *Jacksonian* and *Whig* could easily be substituted. Democratic evangelicalism is superbly described in Hatch, *Democratization of American Christianity*. Although there appear to exist only scattered sources, some Episcopal clergy and laypeople were attracted to this form of evangelicalism. Charles Finney's second wife, for example, was an Episcopalian. The laity often exhibited a considerable amount of rebellion against even Evangelical bishops. The best work describing authoritarian evangelicalism is Daniel Walker Howe, *The Political Culture of the American Whigs* (Chicago, 1979).

117. McIlvaine to Maria McIlvaine, October 8, 1839, in Carus, *Memorials of McIlvaine*, 121.

118. Butler, *Awash in a Sea of Faith*, 268.

4

"To Your Tents, O Israel!": The Advance of "Puseyism" and the War Within the Church, 1839–1852

By the end of the 1830s, High Churchmen and authoritative Evangelicals had made a tenuous peace. High Church bishops originally opposed to McIlvaine's election must have been pleased by his stand against radical revivalism, his defense of the episcopacy, and his participation in the church's missions organization. By the 1830s, the orderly Evangelicals had secured their position within the Episcopal Church's institutions and hierarchy.

During the same decade, McIlvaine successfully defended Episcopal institutions against the incursion of democratic evangelicalism. In 1839, he finally extended his episcopal authority over the ever-troublesome Kenyon College faculty, exerting far more power than his predecessor, Philander Chase, ever dared attempt.[1] He removed the faculty from the Board of Trustees, appointed a new college president, and gained the power to act on behalf of the trustees without their consent. He completely controlled the institution. William Sparrow, Kenyon's most outspoken opponent of episcopal control and the power broker behind McIlvaine's election in the first place, was infuriated. "Dr. Sparrow is here," wrote student Henry Calhoun, "but too mad (and not without reason) to have anything to do with the college. . . . Rest assured I have seen enough of Episcopal power to set me forever against Bishops and Monarchies in the Church.[2] The Kenyon malcontents tried to charge him with abuse of authority but failed. Sparrow soon left to teach at Virginia Theological Seminary, and Calhoun left the Episcopal Church and became a Presbyterian minister. The argument between Sparrow and McIlvaine was not theological; it was over the issue of episcopal control and church authority.[3] It illustrates that, as Evangelicalism moved into a position of respect in the Episcopal Church, small fissures developed in the Evangelical party between those who held more institutional views and those who were more individualistic. Those who stayed at Kenyon submitted to McIlvaine's authority; those who could not submit left.

The fissures were almost invisible to outsiders, however, and the Evangelical party appeared united in their program of spreading true Christianity in the

Episcopal Church. Well represented by the successes of Bishop McIlvaine, the party had consolidated its position on two fronts. First, it offered a strong, and acceptable, alternative to the High Church conception of Episcopal identity. As did the High Churchmen, Evangelicals considered the Episcopal Church an ark of refuge from extreme American evangelicalism, but the latter constructed this ark from the materials of the Protestant Reformation and the eighteenth-century Evangelical Revival. Working within the church to further the interests of all Episcopalians, they established an alliance with the High Churchmen. Second, it remained distinctly evangelical and continued to cooperate with non-Episcopal evangelicals to further the broader interests of the gospel. Although Evangelicals rejected any radical or sectarian beliefs, they retained friendly associations with many other evangelicals. As long as the interests of the gospel, as they defined it, did not conflict with the interests of the Episcopal Church (and they worked to make sure the two did not conflict), Evangelical Episcopalians remained secure with their dual identity.

Evangelical Episcopalians rejoiced in the "bond of peace" in their church.[4] While other denominations were convulsed by sectarianism and division, the Episcopal Church, on a formal level at least, was unified. Unity signified that God had blessed the Episcopal Zion. During the coming millennium, all divisions would cease, and to Evangelical Episcopalians unity foreshadowed the approaching reign of God. In the 1830s, proclaiming Episcopal unity, as opposed to evangelical sectarianism, became an important evangelistic strategy. Calvin Colton, for example, converted from Presbyterianism to Episcopalianism because of the unity of the Episcopal Church. As an apologetic for this conversion, he published his *Thoughts on the Religious State of the Country*. The High Church paper, the *Churchman*, explained how Colton

> found himself almost in a strange world, where discord had been exchanged for peace, confusion for order, and where the waves of infidelity and fanaticism were breaking over fields that he had left so promising. In investigating the causes of this change, and searching for its remedy, his mind has seized upon *episcopacy* . . . as furnishing the identical principle of order, the want and violation of which had produced the evils which have defaced so large a portion of the American Zion.[5]

The *Episcopal Recorder*, the staunch Evangelical paper, reprinted the *Churchman*'s review of Colton's book and praised it as expressing "much of our own thoughts and opinions on the subject."[6] Episcopal unity proved, to Evangelical Episcopalians at least, that their church was a "truer" church—made obvious by divine blessing—than the churches of other evangelicals.

Formal Episcopal unity with informal theological diversity might have continued indefinitely if not for a new theological movement, the Oxford Movement, that began in the Church of England in the late 1820s. This movement threatened both aspects of Evangelical Episcopal identity. First, it threatened their position in the church by articulating a non-Protestant theology, which challenged the basis of Evangelical theology—without the theology of the Protestant Reformation, the Evangelical Episcopal ark would sink. Second, the Oxford Movement confirmed the long-lingering fears of non-Episcopal evangelicals that evangelical religion could never be maintained by the Church of England or its offspring, the Protestant Episcopal Church. Fears of prelacy and Romanism threatened to force Evangelical Episcopalians out of their own church and to break up their alliance with other Protestant evangelicals. Unless Oxfordism was stopped, Bishop McIlvaine and his colleagues might lose everything they had gained.

On March 15, 1839, the *Gambier Observer* ran an article entitled "The Oxford Tracts" signed "Cranmer." William Whittingham, professor of church history at the General Theological Seminary, immediately recognized it as the work of his friend Charles McIlvaine.[7] Three weeks later, the *Episcopal Recorder* ran the article and hinted that McIlvaine was its author. Wrote the editor: "Few have enjoyed forming a juster or more intelligent estimate of the heresies of the *Tracts for the Times*, than our correspondent 'Cranmer.' "[8] The *Tracts* were about to be published in their first full American edition. McIlvaine opposed this. He wrote to the *Gambier Observer*'s editor:

> You have wisely abstained from saying much thus far concerning the "Tracts for the Times," better known by the name of "Oxford Tracts." Till there was danger that the poison contained in them would be propagated in this country, you were not called to make known to your readers the fact that, in another continent, such poison existed. But that danger is now apparent. The poison is to try its force on the constitution of the Episcopal Church in this land. You may be sure that the sore trial which the Church of England is now undergoing, and which threatens the introduction of Popery within the very strongest bastions of that bulwark of the Reformation, and which has raised the cry so widely among the champions of that *Protestant* Church "*To your tents, O Israel*," you may assuredly expect that . . . trial will be vouchsafed to us.[9]

Even some High Churchmen, McIlvaine pointed out, recognized that the *Tracts* "were in danger of effacing those lines which broadly discriminate us from Rome and Geneva, and an adherence to which has formed . . . the distinctive character and glory" of the Protestant Episcopal Church.[10]

Why then, argued McIlvaine, publish the *Tracts*? The distinctiveness of Episcopalianism, as opposed to both Roman Catholicism and extreme Protestantism, held together the High Church–Evangelical coalition of the 1830s. Although High Churchmen and Evangelicals disagreed on the particular points of that distinctiveness, they both maintained that the church was Protestant and that it retained the truest forms of biblical and primitive religion. Both parties maintained that the church was an ark of refuge from democratic evangelicalism. The *Tracts* articulated a new theology—a theology outside the established bounds of American Episcopal theological debate—and appeared, from McIlvaine's perspective, more Roman Catholic than Anglican. They threatened the identity, mission, and unity of the American Episcopal Church. "Let them not be republished," McIlvaine warned, "any more than you would offer poisoned meat in the shambles. They will disgrace the church that publishes them and corrupt the minds that receive what they contain."[11] As much as Evangelicals valued unity, if the High Churchmen insisted on publishing the *Tracts*, the High Church–Evangelical truce was finished. The bond of peace was broken. The war for the soul of the Episcopal Church was on.

Background

War over the Oxford *Tracts for the Times* was nothing new. The Church of England had been brawling over them for some time. At Oxford University in the late 1820s, a group of young men—led by John Henry Newman, Richard Hurrell Froude, John Keble, and Edward Bouverie Pusey—began to espouse a theology that emphasized the apostolic constitution of the Church of England. Against the backdrop of growing political liberalism and ecclesiastical latitudinarianism, they argued for the authority of the Church of England, divinely maintained through a succession of bishops. Anglicanism, they argued, was neither Roman Catholic nor Protestant; it was, rather, the continuation of the catholic church in England from the early centuries of Christian history. The young men at Oxford wanted to reform the spirituality and practice of the English church along true catholic—but not Roman—and apostolic lines.[12] To this end, they issued a series of ninety tracts, the *Tracts for the Times*, beginning in September 1833.[13] They laid out their reform program by discussing the episcopacy and the liturgy, always appealing to the first five centuries of Christian practice as their authority. In addition to the *Tracts*, the *Tractarians*, as Newman and company came to be called, published sermons, occasional works, and a library of early Christian writings.

Much of the early program of the Oxford divines resembled that of America's John Henry Hobart.[14] As American Evangelicals had been suspicious of Hobart's appeal to tradition and what they perceived to be his overemphasis on form, so English Evangelicals were suspicious of the new *Tracts*. Tractarianism resembled too closely the moralism and formalism of seventeenth- and eighteenth-century Anglican theology—always a bête noire to Evangelicals. Nevertheless, Evangelicals shared the Tractarian concern for piety and new theological liberalism, and they were equally upset by the political liberalism that threatened to disestablish the Church of England.[15] In America of the 1820s and 1830s, Evangelicals and High Churchmen fought together against radical, democratic evangelicalism. In England of the early 1830s, Evangelicals and Tractarians opposed both dissenting Evangelicalism and latitudinarianism. On both sides of the Atlantic, somewhat tenuous alliances—based on a shared dislike of religious and social extremism—formed between authoritative Evangelicals and their High Church colleagues.[16]

During the early years of the *Tracts*, Evangelical reaction was mixed. In 1833, the radical London newspaper, the *Record*, opposed them as "spiritual weapons to the armoury of the 'Man of Sin' " and stated that they would surely lead to Rome;[17] after this initial blast, however, the *Record* was silent about the *Tracts* for a few years. In 1833–1836, the more moderate *Christian Observer* contained both critical and favorable evangelical responses to the *Tracts*. In spite of some initial hostility, the middle years of the decade passed with only a few angry incidents. Evangelicals and Tractarians were uncomfortable allies in the defense of the established church and in their opposition to democratic tendencies in British political culture. Neither group wanted to see a Parliament influenced by Roman Catholics and dissenting voters making decisions for the Church of England. The parties were not unified in the way they wanted to protect the church from democratic encroachment, however;

Anglican Evangelicals wanted the establishment to remain intact; some Tractarians wished to retain the primacy of the Church of England but wanted to sever it politically from an increasingly liberal Parliament.

In 1836, the wait-and-see attitude of Anglican Evangelicals toward the Tractarians began to change. In that year, Pusey published his tracts on baptism, which laid out a clear doctrine of baptismal regeneration and placed responsibility for sin committed after baptism on the penitential believer.[18] This surprised even some English High Churchmen. Instead of scattered criticism of this "Puseyism" (a term used derisively by Evangelicals to describe the Oxford Movement) in newspapers and journals, the Anglican Evangelicals mounted a sustained attack through tracts, treatises, and sermons. Leaders like Edward Bickersteth, John Bird Sumner, and Daniel Wilson opposed what they believed to be the "innovations" of Oxford theology. By the time of the 1837 Islington clergy conference, the yearly Evangelical association meeting, Anglican Evangelicals opposed Tractarianism without exception.[19]

The following year, two new books shocked Anglican Evangelicals: Froude's *Remains* and Newman's *Lectures on the Doctrine of Justification*.[20] After Froude died in 1836, Newman edited and published his *Remains*. The first volume, issued in 1838, deeply offended and outraged Evangelicals: Froude revealed his complete contempt for the Protestant Reformation and displayed a peculiar affection for medieval ascetic practices. Evangelicals had suspected that the Tractarians hated the Reformation heritage of the Church of England; Froud's *Remains* proved that suspicion true. To them, Froude had as good as admitted that Tractarianism was a Roman Catholic plot.[21]

Newman's *Lectures on Justification* alarmed them even more. Since the eighteenth century, Anglican Evangelicals had emphasized their commitment to justification by faith alone as the leading theological tenet of the Protestant Reformation. They believed that the Reformers had recovered the primitive doctrine of justification from Scripture. It was, to them, the formal principle upon which all Protestant Christianity was built: Christians were justified, made righteous, when God imparted Christ's righteousness to sinful and repentant believers through an act of personal faith. Nothing intrinsic to the human condition contributed to justification; it was God's action alone. George Stanley Faber, a leading Evangelical theologian, made this position clear in his *Primitive Doctrine of Justification*, published a year before Newman's work.[22] Evangelicals believed Newman's work promoted a doctrine of infused – not imparted – righteousness by which the believer participated in justification. According to this theory, at baptism God infused righteousness to a Christian, which enabled one to cooperate with grace for salvation. To Evangelicals, Newman had betrayed the most basic theological principle of Protestant theology.[23] Controversies raged over Newman's work, and, by 1839, Anglican Evangelicals were united in their opposition to Pusey, Newman, and the Tractarian theology. The tenuous coalition of the early 1830s was completely destroyed.

Charles Pettit McIlvaine followed all these developments. He had most likely been made aware of the *Tracts* through the *Record* and the *Christian Observer*, two papers he read regularly. In 1834 and 1835, he visited England, staying with his friend John Hill, the evangelical vice-principal of St. Edmunds Hall in Oxford, where he no doubt witnessed some of the Oxford controversy first hand.[24] In January 1835, he attended the Islington conference. The theme of that year's meeting was "the present condition and prospect of the Church of Christ." Although in just two years Tractarianism would be Islington's all-consuming topic, in 1835 there was only passing concern over Oxford's lack of piety, especially as compared to Cambridge's evangelical fervor. McIlvaine reported Anglican worry over the spread of "popery" in England and concern over the disestablishment of the church.[25]

During the early years of the Oxford Movement, Anglican Evangelicals were more concerned with the possible disestablishment of the Church of England than by the theological implications of the Oxford Movement, and McIlvaine's early perceptions of Tractarianism were colored by this opinion. In his correspondence to Anglican friends in the early 1830s, there is little mention of Newman or the *Tracts for the Times*; instead, there is a good deal of discussion on the merits of a voluntary system of denominationalism. Against the establishment, McIlvaine defended American religious freedom and become known to the British as a champion of "voluntaryism." When the London *Christian Observer* rather snidely published a convention address of McIlvaine's decrying the lack of funds to pay clergy, they concluded by pointing out that if "any reader should prefer the casual and scanty dripping of voluntaryism to a well-regulated national provision for the clergy, we can only say that we wonder at their judgement."[26] These views were a serious point of difference between Anglican Evangelicals and Evangelical Episcopalians. It was an awkward situation for McIlvaine: he agreed with some of the Tractarians (and the dissenters, for that matter) who believed that church-state connection should be severed, and he disagreed with Anglican Evangelicals over their intractable commitment to establishment. Although he certainly worried about the Roman Catholic tendencies of the *Tracts*, as long as the controversy remained an English controversy, he seemed willing to stay out of it.

Had it not been for Pusey's tracts on baptism, along with Neman's and Froude's controversial publications, McIlvaine might have tried to completely ignore the Oxford controversy. In 1838, however, Charles Girdleston, vicar of Sedgley and outspoken opponent of Tractarianism, sent McIlvaine all of the volumes of the *Tracts* published to date. McIlvaine was startled by what he read: "We shall feel their influence in this country. We have much tinder for such sparks—I exceedingly deprecate the results." McIlvaine feared the *Tracts* would hinder the progress of the Episcopal Church in America. "I am horror struck," wrote McIlvaine, "at the advances towards Rome in the publications of Oxford." He worried that the *Tracts* would lead to extremism on "matters of polity and discipline" and that they would divide the Episcopal Church.[27]

In addition, McIlvaine was outraged by Newman's *Lectures on Justification*. "The veins of justification," he wrote to Girdlestone, "by Mr. Newman, I cannot hold."[28] This outrage was shared by the editors of the *Episcopal Recorder*. Beginning in January 1839, Stephen Tyng (then editor of the *Recorder*) reprinted a two-part article from the London *Record*, which criticized both Froude's *Remains* and Newman's *Lectures on Justification*.[29] The *Record* article attacked "Puseyism" for having revived the "stinking puddles" of human tradition; it was a tool of Satan and Rome to destroy the evangelical success of Wilberforce, Simeon, and Venn.

The *Record*'s attack reflected increased hostility of the Anglican Evangelicals amidst the growing tensions of 1838. Until this point, American periodicals had been relatively quiet about Oxford theology. Historians have pointed to the American publication of the *Tracts* as the reason for the sudden Evangelical Episcopal interest in them beginning in 1839.[30] Certainly the call in March 1839 by the *Churchman* for an American edition of the *Tracts* initiated a vigorous anti-Oxford response from the Evangelicals, but the Evangelicals began their attack before an American edition was seriously proposed. The increased hostility of Evangelicals toward the *Tracts* only makes sense when placed in trans-Atlantic context. In the Anglican Evangelical press, 1838 had been a particularly tense year: publication of Newman's *Lectures* and Froude's *Remains* verified the anti-Protestant sentiments of the Oxford Movement. What had been suspected was proved true: the Oxford Movement, at its heart, was an attack on all forms of evangelicalism—even evangelicalism within the Church of England. From across the Atlantic, Evangelical Episcopalians felt threatened: What would keep their own High Church colleagues from adopting Oxford theology and destroying the gains of evangelicalism in the American Episcopal Church? Those well informed of the British religious scene, like McIlvaine and Stephen Tyng, started an anti-Oxford campaign to protect the position of Evangelicals in the church; Oxfordism must be stopped—before it got as far in America as it had in England. Following the lead of the vigorous anti-Oxford critique from the British press and their Anglican Evangelical colleagues, in January 1839, the *Episcopal Recorder* ran the *Record*'s attack on Puseyism months before the announced publication of the American edition of the *Tracts for the Times*. After the controversial publication and the ensuing debates in the Church of England in 1838, American Evangelicals abandoned their neutrality. When the Oxford Movement attacked Protestant theology, McIlvaine and his colleagues could not be silent. The peace of the Episcopal Church, as McIlvaine feared it would be, was destroyed by the John Henry Newman and the Oxford *Tracts*.

The Tracts and the American Spirit of the Times

The polemical literature of 1839 clearly identified the Oxford Movement's chief threat to the Episcopal Church: the *Tracts*, declared McIlvaine, "teach Popery, where they should teach the Gospel."[31] Anti-Roman Catholicism was at the core of the Evangelical Episcopalian fear of the Oxford Movement. This should not be surprising. They had built their whole theory of the Episcopal Church on the theology of the Protestant Reformation and the practices of the eighteenth-century Evangelical Revival. To them, the Episcopal Church was catholic because it perpetuated the universal practice of the episcopacy, promoted devotional worship through its liturgy, and embraced biblical truth regarding the nature of salvation. The Episcopal Church was catholic, but not in any way *Roman* Catholic. The Reformers, they argued, had completely broken with the corrupt innovations of Rome and restored biblical purity to the English Church. Any practice or theology that sought to restore Roman Catholicism betrayed the Episcopal Church's primitive catholicism.

The truce between High Church and Evangelical Episcopalian occurred, in part, because the two parties essentially agreed on the primitive and apostolic vision of the Episcopal Church. They differed only on their theological sources for such a vision. When the Oxford Movement started, and while it sounded like Hobartian High Churchmanship, Evangelicals looked askance at it, but they were willing to tolerate it—even as they tolerated the High Church bishops in their own communion. With the publication of Newman's *Lectures* and Froude's *Remains*, however, everything changed. Newman and Froude declared war on primitive catholicism as the Evangelicals understood it (through the lens of the English Reformation), and seemed to proclaim their loyalty to Roman Catholicism. Many High Churchmen were still unwilling (or unable) to recognize this shift, but the Evangelicals believed that the Oxford Movement betrayed the primitive and Protestant catholicism of the Episcopal Church.

Anti–Roman Catholic sentiment had a long history within the Church of England and the early American colonies.[32] Although it abated somewhat in the early days of the Republic, anti-Roman sentiment grew in the 1820s and 1830s. Immigration from Roman Catholic countries caused tension in American cities, and increased Roman Catholic criticism of Protestant political and social monopolies created a climate of hostility. In addition, Roman Catholics quickly saw the potential of missions and evangelization in the new western territories and moved to expand their church in the Mississippi Valley. In October 1829, the Roman Catholic Church held its first Provincial Council in Baltimore. The council "revealed to non-Catholic Americans in no uncertain terms that the Roman church was a substantial, growing, and well-organized reality."[33] Protestant Americans were worried. Denominations, missions, and voluntary organizations; religious periodicals, clergymen, and laymen and -women—all issued forth a veritable flood of anti–Roman Catholic literature, the most famous being Maria Monk's *Awful Disclosures of the Hotel Dieu Nunnery of Montreal*. Monk's tract graphically described her supposed experience with sexual immorality and infanticide in a Roman Catholic convent, thus confirming in the minds of many Protestants the evils of Romanism.[34] Anti-Catholicism in mid-century America culminated with terrible 1844 Philadelphia riots and the formation of anti-Roman political parties. By the late 1830s and early 1840s, at the same time the Oxford *Tracts* were being published in America, anti–Roman Catholic sentiment had reached one of its nineteenth-century peaks.

Charles McIlvaine shared this American anti-Roman prejudice. He was worried about the number of Irish immigrants to Ohio and the "constant tide of Popery."[35] In 1839, he visited Paris and wrote in his diary: "I never had such an impression of a state of general rebellion against God. . . . This is no city for a Christian to remain in, unless duty calls him to do so."[36] The Roman Catholic Church, he believed, had destroyed true religion in France.

Romanism in a Roman Catholic country shocked McIlvaine's provincial eyes, but even worse were residual medieval Roman Catholic practices in the Church of

England. He found the liturgy of Winchester Cathedral "barbarous" where the "service of the church is *performed*—not *read*, literally *performed*—by three clergymen . . . and about 15 singing men and boys in white surplices. The whole, whether of anthem or prayer was *sung*."[37] As much as McIlvaine loved England, he thought that much of the Church of England had never been reformed enough.

> The whole business had such a completely popish appearance and sound, that I could easily have fancied myself in the midst of the mummeries of a cathedral in Paris. I felt indignant at such mockeries of devotion and remnants of popery in a Protestant Ch. and ceased to feel any wonder that the soldiers of Cromwell, excited as they were by still worse conformities with Rome, should have laid a mutilating hand on so many beautiful specimens of sculpture. . . . The cause of religion would suffer no loss, whatever would be the case as to that of antiquarians taste, were every cathedral in England levelled with the ground.[38]

Winchester College was hardly better because it had kept "all the antiquated usages of barbarous ages . . . with ridiculous absurdity."[39] To McIlvaine, Roman Catholicism and all its residual practices went against the spirit of the nineteenth century and the spread of the kingdom of God.

McIlvaine's dislike of medievalism points out one of the discontinuities between Anglican Evangelicalism and Evangelical Episcopalianism. Anglican Evangelicals lived with the cultural remnants of their church's medieval heritage; within historically proscribed limits, singing choirs, chanted liturgies, and processionals did not necessarily offend them. Evangelical Episcopalians, appalled by all traces of the "dark ages," believed that Roman Catholicism (and by implication, the Oxford Movement) was a throwback to a less enlightened, less democratic age. To Evangelical Episcopalians, medievalism was mysterious and unappealing and completely at odds with modern reason and taste.

The anti–Roman Catholicism of the Evangelical Episcopalians was closely tied to their view of the millennium. Since the days of the Reformation and the subsequent Puritan rebellion in England, Protestants identified the pope as the Antichrist. The Reformation had destroyed the Babylon of the Roman Catholic Church as predicted in the biblical Revelation. In the nineteenth century, the prophetic implications of Romanism took a new turn in relation to evangelical millennialism. Since most nineteenth-century evangelicals—Evangelical Episcopalians included—believed that the millennium was about to begin, the advance of Roman Catholicism in England and America took on ominous overtones. The Bible predicted that in the last days the church would spread throughout the whole earth, but it also predicted a concurrent surge of infidelity under the reign of the Antichrist. The invasion of Romanism into the Protestant world was nothing less than this final incursion of the Antichrist.

To Evangelical Episcopalians, the Oxford Movement heralded the approach of the last days. It was Satan's last desperate attempt to destroy true religion in the Episcopal Church before the kingdom of God arrived in its fullness. Millennial prophecy had fascinated Evangelical Episcopalians since the early 1820s, and in the late 1830s and early 1840s, America was rocked by millennial fervor. William Miller's millennial movement gained a number of adherents in the 1830s, but his message reached a national audience beginning in 1839 under the leadership and organizational genius of Joshua Himes.[40] Although Evangelical Episcopalians rejected Miller's date setting, they nevertheless, were confident that the kingdom was imminent. Publication of the Oxford *Tracts* coincided exactly with the increased millennial expectations of 1839 onward.

Evangelical Episcopalians quickly identified the connection. The *Episcopal Recorder* reprinted an article from the London *Churchman* by "Phoenix," which identified "a Papal conspiracy to root out Protestantism from Christendom" as a present fulfillment of biblical prophecy.[41] To McIlvaine, the *Tracts* were part of the "signs of the times" pointing to the Roman attempt to subvert Protestant America.[42] Bishop Manton Eastburn of Massachusetts spared no apocalyptic imagery in describing the *Tracts*: "The Tractarian Movement was of Rome, the work of Satan; if allowed to continue, it will destroy the Evangelical faith and tradition which had descended from the Reformation; and while suasion has its place, condemnation and even force must be brought to bear to silence these advocates of the Dark Ages and followers of the Scarlet Woman."[43]

William Jay, social reformer and spokesman for the rights of black Americans, violently opposed the *Tracts*. The *Tracts* would surely undo the good of Protestant benevolent organizations—long opposed by the Roman Catholics and Roman-leaning Episcopalians—and lead to a new, repressive Dark Age. Jay wrote to McIlvaine about the *Tracts*:

> Where all this is to end I know not but have not doubt it all tends to laxity of morals. My observation through life has convinced me that a dependance on rite and ceremonies has very little connection with holiness of life and that religious superstition is very consistent with ungodly practice. . . . Formality as far as I have witnessed it in our Church is preeminently anti-philanthropic and closely associated with worldly conformity. I do not profess to read the spirit of the times, but to me they [the *Tracts*] seem to portend much evil to both Church and State.[44]

It was clear to Jay that the *Tracts* were a Roman Catholic plot to destroy Protestant America: "The Man of Sin is recovering from his would received at the Reformation, is everywhere displaying his restless authority and promise . . . to exercise a blighting influence in our own country."[45] He bemoaned the "extension of Mormonism, puseyism and popery" as evils of the age and asked, "When the Son of Man cometh shall he find faith on earth?"

> The reign of righteousness it would seem is to *follow* not precede his coming. So far as I understand the Prophecies, they predict the personal reign of Christ upon earth. Of the times and seasons I pretend not to judge, but it is highly probable that the coming of the Lord drawth nigh.[46]

Until the Oxford Movement, Evangelical Episcopalians were generally convinced that the millennium was proceeding without interuption; after the Oxford Movement, their millennial optimism began to wane. The growing Romanism within their own church certainly set back the coming of the kingdom. Although Episcopal millennialism continued to be an admixture of post- and premillennial views, Tractarianism helped to push Evangelical Episcopalians toward a less optimistic view of the coming of the kingdom during the middle decades of the nineteenth century.[47]

The *Tracts* were dangerous: they were a Roman Catholic plot to subvert the advance of evangelicalism in the Episcopal Church; they threatened holy living and Protestant social reform; and they surely signified the beginning of the reign of the Antichrist. Oxfordism threatened both the Episcopal Church and the kingdom of God. The last days must be upon both England and America. Evangelical Episcopalians rallied to beat back the enemy so the kingdom of Christ could arrive in its fullness. They opened three fronts in their holy war on the *Tracts*: in theology, in church politics, and by forming societies to promote the Evangelical vision for the Protestant Episcopal Church.

Theological Response of the Evangelicals

McIlvaine and other Evangelical leaders believed that right doctrine and right living were inseparable. "The worship of the sanctuary," preached McIlvaine to his fellow bishops, "will be maintained in spirit and in truth, only so long as the Gospel shall be preached in purity and faithfulness. . . . Hence comes . . . the injuction, 'take heed unto the doctrine.' "[48] Doctrine was the front line of defense against all errors—especially errors in Christian worship and practice. Upon it were built "the permanent interests of true religion in the whole church."[49] In 1839, nothing threatened true religion more than Newman's attack on the Protestant doctrine of justification by faith alone. Evangelicals, so thoroughly convinced of the rightness of Reformation theology, rallied to defend themselves, their church, and the progress of "true religion."

Because of his acquaintance with the Oxford developments, Charles McIlvaine was the first American to elaborate a sustained defense of the doctrine of justification. As he reported to Girdlestone, he had read Newman on justification during the months following its publication. The Oxford divines, he insisted, "cannot be cleared of the charge of downright Popery on the subject of *the Justification of the sinner before God*." He pointed out the main theological problem of Rome and the Romanism of the Tractarians: Roman Catholicism was "a substitution, substantially, of the merits of man, for the merits of Christ; works for faith."[50] This criticism of the Oxford Movement remained at the center of Evangelical theological debate for the remainder of the century.

Although McIlvaine first protested Newman's theology of justification in his short article "The Oxford Tracts," the topic received his full attention in his third charge to Ohio's Episcopal clergy, *Justification by Faith*. At the 1839 convention, he delivered this address on justification by faith alone "as long as three common sermons" which had to be interrupted by a time of hymn singing to give him a rest.[51] The published version ran over 150 pages. In it, the bishop proposed that the doctrine of justification by faith "is of the most vital importance of the system of Gospel truth" and is the central doctrine of both Scripture and Anglican theology.[52] Without it, the whole system of Christian living, piety, and spirituality of true religion in the Episcopal Church would crumble.

Mounting this argument, McIlvaine contrasted two views of justification: first, the Protestant view that justification – the "righteousness of God" – is imputed forensically to the believer by God through no human merit at all; second, the Roman Catholic view that a person is justified through inherent righteousness infused to him through the merit of Christ given in the church.[53] According to Protestants, justification and sanctification are two separate acts of God: in justification God declares the sinner righteous, and through sanctification God creates righteousness within the believer. Justification is complete in God's declaration; sanctification becomes complete through the cooperation of the justified believer – it always follows the forensic declaration of God. Roman Catholics, argued McIlvaine, had essentially conflated justification and sanctification and thus made salvation contingent on works of merit. Such teaching, because it made Christians believe they had to participate in salvation through the church, had led to all the Roman abuses of the medieval church. This, he argued, contradicted the plain teaching of Scripture. "This it was which," he proclaimed, "in the great revolt of the 16th century, against the usurpations of Popery, combined the whole Protestant host in one array of indignant opposition." Roman Catholicism was a "maze" constructed by the "Man of Sin" on a corrupted doctrine of justification.[54]

In his charge, McIlvaine only alluded to the Oxford Movement. Anyone who holds Roman views, he argued, did not rightly belong to the Protestant Episcopal Church. He did not examine the "doctrine of certain gentlemen of the University of Oxford" to see if they indeed believed such.[55] In his charge, he rearticulated the classical Protestant forensic view of justification in terms set by sixteenth-century theology. He reminded his clergy of the absolute importance of maintaining this Protestant doctrine. In this he was successful. *Justification by Faith* was heralded. Wrote the editor of the Presbyterian *Princeton Review*:

> Although we knew that Bishop McIlvaine was a truly evangelical man, we did not
> expect to find him coming out so decidedly and boldly in defence of this great
> cardinal doctrine of the reformation. . . . He has come out with the genuine
> courage of a reformer, and has thrown himself into the front of the battle, which
> is now commencing between evangelical truth and Popish error. We have seldom
> ever read a publication from any quarter with so much unmixed pleasure.[56]

In *Justification by Faith*, McIlvaine defended traditional Protestant views on justification; the attack on Oxfordism was secondary to this main purpose. He promised his readers that his fuller examination of Oxford theology on the doctrine of justification was forthcoming.

Published simultaneously in New York and London a year later, that work, *Oxford Divinity Compared with That of the Romish and Anglican Churches*, would stand for several decades as a bulwark of Protestant doctrine for Episcopalians. In it, McIlvaine proposed that the "vital principle" of Oxford divinity "is precisely the same as that to which are to be traced all the various and gross departures from truth and godliness in the Church of Rome." That vital principle: an erroneous view of justification. Oxford divinity, therefore, "is little else than Popery restrained."[57]

To prove his thesis, McIlvaine borrowed heavily from Faber's *Primitive Doctrine of Justification*. Faber had proved, to McIlvaine's satisfaction, that the doctrines of Irish lay theologian Alexander Knox were substantially the same as those of Rome on justification. Newman, argued McIlvaine, had fallen into the same theological morass as Knox had; since Knox was guilty of Romanism, so, therefore, was Newman. Knox, Newman, and Rome had all removed "the cross of Christ from its central position in the system of Christian verity" and replaced it with a doctrine of works.[58]

Although this guilt-by-association argument may at first seem simplistic, McIlvaine's work was actually quite complex. In the 500-plus pages of *Oxford Divinity Compared*, he displayed a deep knowledge of Protestant theology—continental and English—from the sixteenth century onward. He argued as he had in his charge: only two views of justification were possible. The first view, the Roman one, was that justification occurred through a personal change in the moral nature; this view, McIlvaine argued, confused justification with sanctification. The second view, the Protestant one, was that justification occurred through a change in a person's state in relation to God; this view separated justification and sanctification into two distinct acts of God. "The whole of Oxford Divinity," McIlvaine wrote, "is founded upon the denial of that distinction."[59] The key to Oxfordism, also the key to Romanism, is that righteousness is internal and inwrought. Such righteousness leads to justification only as the Christian progresses in holy living.

Historians have argued that Newman came to his views through reading the theology of Eastern Orthodox Christianity. Even Peter Toon's sympathetic account of evangelical reaction to the Oxford Movement criticizes Faber and McIlvaine on this point. The evangelicals, therefore, did not really understand Newman—who was not arguing the Roman position of *inherent* righteousness, but the Eastern position of *adherent* righteousness. Such analysis implies that if only evangelicals had understood the Eastern sources, the Oxford Movement would not have been pictured as "Romanism," and possibly much of the polemics and division would have been avoided.

It is difficult to imagine an evangelical like McIlvaine to have read Newman with anything other than Roman Catholic theology in mind, however. First, McIlvaine was not well acquainted with Eastern Orthodox theology (with the exception of ecclesiology). To a nineteenth-century American bishop, Rome and Constantinople were equally far from Wittenberg. Second, the publication of Froude's *Remains*—filled with anti-Protestant venom and pro–Roman Catholic sentiment—must have influenced the bishop's analysis of Newman. Finally, given that the theological compass of the Evangelicals was the Protestant Reformation, it was obvious that to them Newman's attack on the Protestant doctrine of justification would point to the old debates against Rome.

McIlvaine was right in identifying the major Evangelical difficulty with Newman's work. Whatever his theological source, Newman rejected the Protestant conception of justification. "Justification and sanctification," wrote Newman, "were in fact substantially one and the same thing; . . . that in the order of our ideas, viewed relatively to each other, justification followed upon sanctification." McIlvaine recognized this was not the theology of the Protestant Reformation. Newman made himself very clear: to him, Luther's doctrine was "an utter perversion of the truth."[60]

Newman's statement directly attacked Protestant evangelicalism—an attack no Evangelical apologist could ignore. The whole system of evangelical doctrine was founded on the doctrine of justification by faith alone. According to McIlvaine, the difference between the theology of the Church of England and Oxford-ism was "a difference upon grand primary questions, involving all that was so nobly contended for by the martyrs of the Reformations, and all that is precious to the sinner in the Gospel of Christ."[61] To reject the Protestant doctrine of justifica-tion did two things: one, it undercut the theological base of the Church of England and the Episcopal Church; two, it destroyed Christian hope and assur-ance. For McIlvaine, this was more than a theological argument over the principles of the Reformation. It went straight to the heart of evangelical practice: without justification by faith alone it was impossible to preach salvation through the free gift of God's grace. It betrayed the atonement and left the sinner in a hopeless state with no assurance that his or her sins are forgiven. McIlvaine pleaded:

> Alas! reader, what shall we do to be saved, so as to have any consolation in Christ, if all our refuge is in such a system? It is a change of great fundamental doctrines; a new creation of our whole belief of the way of salvation. . . . The cross of Christ lifted up on high for every soul to be ever looking at, as the single object of his justifying faith, and foundation of his only hope, must be borne away from its central position in the grand panorama of gospel truth, and laid down almost out of sight, and Baptism be set up in its stead. . . . Thus must we change our hopes, and desert our consolations, and bring a cloud of dark uncertainty over our eternal prospects, and refuse to rejoice in Christ.[62]

Tractarianism "is an abandonment of all that we have been taught by our Church to believe to be true, the narrow, the only way that leadeth unto life."[63] To McIlvaine, the Oxford Movement betrayed Christ's good news to men and women in need of a saviour.

Although justification was the major issue in *Oxford Divinity Compared*, other aspects of Tractarian theology offended McIlvaine as well: the elevation of tradi-tion over Scripture, the doctrine of baptismal regeneration, and the proposed doctrine of "reserve." Because he connected these issues to the doctrine of justification, McIlvaine criticized them on the same grounds: each rejected the theology of the Reformation. The doctrine of "reserve" especially galled him. In Tract 87, Isaac Williams proposed that some religious knowledge be kept "re-served" until a Christian had sufficiently progressed in religious life to be able to hear and properly act on that reserved knowledge. Williams singled out the doctrine of atonement of sin as one such doctrine. He accused evangelicals of having so elevated the doctrine that they had disconnected the life of obedience from the life of grace. Teaching on the atonement should therefore be "reserved" until a person had progressed to a life of good works and would, at that time, be unlikely to separate grace from works.[64]

McIlvaine believed that the very center of Christian theology was "the preach-ing of Christ crucified." To him, all other doctrines were based on the atonement. Christ's saving work on the cross was to be preached openly and without reserve; to do less would be to disobey God and contradict the clear teaching of Scripture. "St. Paul," he argued, "waited not till men were well initiated into Christian mysteries, before he unveiled the grand subject of atonement and justification through the blood of Christ." According to Evangelical theology, the atonement, when embraced and believed by contrite sinners, was the only sure ground for "unreserved obedience."[65]

This point divided the two parties. Tractarians argued that good works made a good person and that progressive sanctification would lead to acceptance with God.[66] Works, therefore, must be done by the faithful Christian who wanted to cooperate with God's grace in salvation. The Evangelicals, on the other hand, believed that only a good person—and no person was good unless made righteous through God's justifying grace—could do good works. All good works, works of Christian mercy and love through which the believer cooperates with God's sanctifying grace, were impossible to separate from God's imputed righteousness. Good works must follow justifying grace.[67]

The argument over the relationship between the atonement and good works had a profound impact on the practical theology of the two parties. The Tractarians opposed antinomianism and therefore stressed the role of works of mercy in shaping Christian character; they relegated the theology of the cross to a lesser position to combat "cheap" grace. The Tractarians misunderstood Evangelical theology at this point. Evangelicals were not antinomians; they believed that good works flowed from a truly regenerate heart. Any real Christian must do good works because those works were part of the sanctified life—works could not be separated from grace. Evangelical philanthropy was based on this principle: works were the free and loving response of a person saved by God's grace. Obedience to God's will was impossible by those still under the curse of sin. To reverse the order, therefore, by placing works before salvation, would place a yoke of slavery on unsaved men and women. This, believed the Evangelicals, was the curse of Romanism. True Christian benevolence was not coerced; it issued forth from a heart freed of the constraints of sin. This relationship between salvation and works was the foundation of all Evangelical benevolence. Personal redemption was the only sure ground of true charity. Without it, the whole Evangelical philanthropic superstructure would collapse. "Unreserved obedience," wrote McIlvaine, was "the necessary expression of a new heart" and the sure result of the "full preaching of justification by faith."[68] To "reserve" the doctrine of the atonement was, to the Evangelicals, like withholding food from a starving person.

When the Oxford Movement rejected the Protestant doctrine of justification by faith, it was much more than an academic or theological quarrel. It amounted to a complete rejection of all the most cherished principles of evangelism. If the Tractarians gained a powerful position in the Episcopal Church, the Evangelicals and their message would be destroyed. The Evangelicals could see the Oxford Movement as nothing other than a full attack on their hard-won standing and respect in the church.

The Evangelical response to McIlvaine's *Oxford Divinity Compared* was overwhelming. "I have purchased your book," wrote William Jay, "and read it with an entire concurrence in its sentiments."[69] James Milnor wrote, "I have read with great delight, your interesting and elaborate examination of the principles of the Oxford divinity, and earnestly hope it may have a wide-extended circulation."[70] From far-off

Calcutta, missionary bishop Daniel Wilson praised McIlvaine's work. Joseph McIlvaine, McIlvaine's son, wrote to his father after a visit with Milnor: "Dr. Milnor requested me to tell you that he had received a letter from the Bishop of Calcutta who said that your book on Oxford Divinity was the best book that had appeared since the Reformation."[71] The editor of London's *Christian Lady's Magazine* praised the work: "The Bishop has anatomized this system as no other man has yet done. . . . It [is] one of the most delightful, as well as most valuable, books we ever opened. God has not forsaken his Church."[72] The British *Christian Observer* recommended the work to its readers in a twenty-four page review that said it is "seasonable and valuable" and handles the question of justification "with great piety, ability and solid argument."[73] Anglican and Episcopalian Evangelicals embraced McIlvaine's *Oxford Divinity Compared* as a definitive refutation of Newman and the Oxford Movement.[74] By 1841, McIlvaine had laid the foundation for the Evangelical party's theological critique of the Oxford Movement for the remainder of the century.[75]

Political Battles of the Church

The theological polemics of the early 1840s prepared the way for the political battles within the church during the rest of the decade. In the months following publication of *Oxford Divinity Compared*, John Henry Newman's Tract 90 appeared. In it, Newman attempted to reconcile the theology of the Thirty-nine Articles with Roman Catholicism, arguing that the English reformers were only opposed to the corruptions of medieval Roman Catholic practice, not Roman Catholic theology per se. "The Protestant Confession," wrote Newman about the articles, "was drawn up with the purpose of including Catholics; and Catholics now will not be excluded."[76] Tract 90 resulted in a huge controversy in England, and as a result of the furor, Newman resigned his Oxford position and retired to a country parish. Newman's remarks proved that Oxfordism was an assault on the Protestant identity of Anglicanism.

In America, Roman Catholics praised the Oxford Movement. In July 1841, the Roman Catholic bishop of Philadelphia, Francis P. Kenrick, invited Episcopal bishops to "come back" to Rome.[77] Newman's tract and Kenrick's letter steeled Evangelical resolve to rid the church of Oxford's Romanist "poison." "The Oxford heresy," McIlvaine told his clergy, "is becoming more and more developed and bold." He lamented its overt tendencies toward Rome; "I have never believed that any thing less would be the result; but I confess the bud has opened much faster than I expected."[78]

Nowhere had the "bud" opened faster than at the General Theological Seminary in New York under the control of Bishop Benjamin T. Onderdonk. "He was a high-churchman of the highest type," stated then-student Clarence Walworth. "He was a fearless and tenacious polemic, and strongly inclined in favor of the Oxford movement."[79] The seminary reflected Onderdonk's openness to the Oxford Movement. Recalled Walworth:

> Some called it Catholic; some called it Romish and superstitious; some called it a spirit of reform, and return to true doctrine and genuine piety; and others

regarded it as a relapse into religious darkness and barbarism. Whatever it might be, however, the seminary was recognized by all as the focus of a new religious life in the Episcopalian body.[80]

The seminary was America's "little Oxford." Arthur Carey, a student at the time, formed and led a discussion group promoting the new theology. "His doctrine," wrote a fellow student, "was all on the High-Church side, and gave no countenance to what is known as Evangelical Protestantism."[81] Carey and his classmates turned the seminary into a hotbed of anti-Protestantism.

When he applied for ordination in New York in 1843, Carey himself became a political target. During most of his seminary years, he worked for Dr. Hugh Smith of St. Peter's Church as a Sunday school teacher. Smith, an evangelical, was aware of Carey's fondness for Oxford theology, but he agreed to sign Carey's ordination testimonials. A few weeks before the ordination, however, Smith having been recently "informed of expressions used by Mr. Carey, which, in my judgement, rendered it very questionable whether the testimonial could justly be accorded to him," refused to sign the papers without a thorough examination of Carey's theology.[82]

Eight clergymen and Bishop Onderdonk conducted the examination. Six of the eight, and the bishop, were satisfied with Carey's responses. The other two— Smith and St. Mark's rector, Henry Anthon—were startled by some of Carey's thoughts on Roman Catholicism. The objectionable points: Carey admitted that if he was refused ordination in the Episcopal Church, he would consider Roman orders; he did not see any differences between the Episcopal and Roman churches on matters of faith; he believed in the real presence of Christ in the eucharist; he did not object to purgatory; he admitted to having denounced the Protestant Reformation; he refused to accept any "close and rigid construction" of the Thirty-nine Articles.[83] His friend Walworth proudly proclaimed that, for these answers, Carey was indebted to Newman's Tract 90. In spite of these beliefs, Onderdonk accepted Carey for the priesthood. He would be ordained the following Sunday.

At the outset of the service, the bishop asked if anyone protested the ordination. Smith and Anthon rose and read prepared statements accusing Carey of holding doctrines "in too close conformity with those of the Church of Rome."[84] The bishop rejected the protest; Smith and Anthon walked out, and Carey was ordained. The reaction was sensational. A virtual flood of pamphlets and newspaper articles appeared, either defending Onderdonk's action or demanding an explanation.[85] Almost all the Evangelicals protested Carey's ordination; almost all the High Church party defended it.[86] In the middle of the war of polemics, Arthur Carey died. He had long ceased being the issue anyway. The real issue, the Evangelicals maintained, was "between *the Church and Romanism*."[87]

As long as the Tractarians had only opposed "ultra-Protestantism," McIlvaine did not complain. He himself opposed ultra-Protestantism. However, when the Oxford theology started to "un-protestantize" Anglicanism, then the movement must be publicly—and virulently—resisted. When Carey confessed that he might seek Roman orders if not ordained by the Episcopal Church, he revealed the extent of the "unProtestant" tendencies of the Oxford theology in America. "Mr

Carey's avowal," wrote McIlvaine, "in substance it is—*I could be a preacher of Romanism without changing my present doctrine.*"[88]

From the point of view of the Evangelicals, the Carey case symbolized a larger, national problem as well. About eight years earlier, New Jersey's Bishop Doane had suggested that the Protestant Episcopal Church change its name to the "Reformed Catholic Church." Although his suggestion predated American Tractarianism, it was, nevertheless, picked up by Oxford partisans and became an issue of Protestant versus Catholic identity for the Episcopal Church. Evangelicals championed the Protestant nature of the church, and when a few High Churchmen styled themselves as "Reformed Catholics," controversy followed. The suggestion for a name change became a symbol of Tractarian efforts to "un-Protestantize" the Episcopal Church.[89] Because the Carey case occurred in the midst of the controversy over the Episcopal Church's commitment to Protestantism, the Evangelical response to Carey's ordination was fraught with their worries over what they perceived to be the larger attempt to undermine their historic Protestantism.

In his address to the diocese in September 1843, McIlvaine defended the actions of Smith and Anthon. He argued that when a bishop ordained a candidate, that bishop represented the whole church; thus Onderdonk was responsible to the whole church for upholding the errors of Arthur Carey. Ordination was not simply local concern; the welfare of the national church depended on whether or not a candidate could hold to Roman theology and be ordained an Episcopal priest. If the Carey ordination stood unchallenged, the whole character of the Protestant Episcopal Church was at risk. The Ohio clergy agreed: they passed a resolution condemning the ordination and called for an investigation into the General Theological Seminary.[90]

No diocese had taken stronger action against the advance of the Oxford Movement in the church. Before the convention, the Rev. Richard Killin, rector of St. James Church, Piqua, published an article in the *Episcopal Recorder* urging his fellow Ohioans to stop the Oxford heresy: "This is no question then of high or low Churchmanship, of Calvinism or Aminianism, of this or that shade of doctrine, in which a latitude may be allowed." No, he argued, this was a matter of "life and death."[91] He continued:

> When we see men among ourselves who would lead us to a system of many mediators instead of one—a system of mortification and bondage which our fathers were not able to bear, and for this deserting the glorious liberty of the Sons of God—a system which changes the whole foundation of a sinner's acceptance with God—a system to which is emphatically another gospel . . . God forbid that that we should glory save in the Cross of Christ.[92]

Killin urged that the Episcopal Church must remain free from Romanism. "A system of externals," he lamented, "a lengthened ritual service will crush us." Episcopal liturgy and church order, he maintained, were not a system of "externals," rather it was "true Catholicism" as demonstrated in the scriptures; Romanism was legalism—a system grown out of poisonous tradition invented by men.[93] The gospel of the Bible and the Episcopal Church was freedom; the gospel preached by the Tractarians was Romanist bondage.

McIlvaine mounted much the same argument in his 1843 charge to the clergy of Ohio. He identified the five objectionable theological points of Tractarianism: (a) dependence on tradition as an authority above Scripture; (b) holding to a theory of infused rather than imputed righteousness; (c) confusing justification with sanctification; (d) lessening the importance of the atonement; and (e) elevating the sacraments over the plain preaching of the word. These arguments paralleled his previous work in *Oxford Divinity Compared*.

> The whole system is one of Church, instead of Christ; priest, instead of Gospel; concealment of truth, instead of 'manifestation of truth'; ignorant superstition, instead of enlightened faith; bondage, where we are promised liberty – all tending directly to load us with whatever is odious in the worst meaning of priestcraft, in place of the free, affectionate, enlarging, elevation and cheerful liberty of a child of God.[94]

Tractarianism pushed McIlvaine to modify his evangelicalism once again – he admitted as much himself in an 1844 sermon: "Under some circumstances, we feel called to preach . . . upon the *visible institutions* of the Church. Under other, upon the *invisible structure* of the Church."[95] In the 1830s, McIlvaine had preached on order and authority of the visible church against democratic evangelicalism. By the 1840s, McIlvaine emphasized "freedom" and "liberty" of spiritual and inward religion as opposed to the rigid formalism and legalism that he perceived in Tractarianism. McIlvaine might agree with the Oxford partisans that the Episcopal Church was apostolic in form and primitive in its liturgy and that it should be commended to other Christians; however, he could not abide these forms elevated to such a point as if salvation depended on them. Salvation came only from Christ. McIlvaine believed that form was always secondary to salvation. The Tractarians had erred in making form primary – and exclusive. They had confused Christ with the church. The Tractarians replaced God's free gift of salvation with *formalism* – a system of salvation by adherence to laws and works.

As a result of the Carey case, Evangelicals defined the issues threatening the Episcopal Church. They pictured that threat in stark terms: liberty versus bondage; freedom versus form; Christ versus the Pharisees; the true catholicism of the Episcopal Church versus Roman Catholicism. They defended liberty, freedom, true religion, and Protestantism; they attacked anything that resembled Roman Catholicism – anything perceived to impede the free preaching of Christ's salvation. On the national level, they instigated an investigation of the General Theological Seminary.[96] Evangelicals brought charges against three pro-Oxford bishops. After painful and protracted church trials, the two Onderdonks were dismissed from their offices in New York and Pennsylvania on charges of immorality and intemperance.[97] New Jersey's Bishop Doane was eventually acquitted of charges of mismanagement of funds.

These national cases attracted much interest. Historians have written a great deal about the trials of the 1840s – usually from the point of view sympathetic with the Oxford Movement and hostile to the Evangelicals. McIlvaine and his colleagues have generally been pictured as narrow-minded crusaders. Because of the complexity of the national cases, bitter polemics and invective, and long-standing personality conflicts, the rationale behind the Evangelical complaint against the Oxford Movement has often been lost.[98] As important as the national controversies might have been, however, it is difficult to get at the issues behind the party labels.

The historical treatment of these controversies has obscured important elements of the Evangelical worldview. Since their inception within the Episcopal Church, Evangelicals used the forms of the Episcopal Church to promote true religion. They argued that the liturgy and doctrine of the church contained, or in some cases was compatible with, the spirit of evangelical piety. By the 1820s, this evangelical interpretation of Episcopal forms was accepted, or at least tolerated, by most of the Episcopal churches. Evangelical Episcopalians promoted revivals through use of the *Book of Common Prayer*, penitential seasons, and the symbolism of the sacraments; they extolled the Protestant theology of the Thirty-nine Articles; they praised the spiritual unity of their church through the ministry of bishops, priests, and deacons. Episcopal forms had buttressed their call to true piety and evangelical faith.

As a result of the Oxford Movement, forms once again became a source of controversy. The Tractarians were "un-Protestantizing" the forms of the Episcopal Church. In Tract 90, for example, Newman argued that the form of the church's confession, the Thirty-nine Articles, was compatible with the spirit of Roman Catholicism. Offended Evangelicals rejected this view; any attempt to replace the biblical, evangelical, Protestant spirit of Episcopal forms with Roman Catholicism met with intense opposition. The Oxford Movement, according to the Evangelicals, subverted Protestant meaning of Episcopal forms and attempted to fill those forms with new—and foreign—meaning.

An Ohio controversy illustrates this aspect of Evangelical Episcopal religion during this period. In 1846, Bishop McIlvaine refused to consecrate the new parish church of St. Paul's, Columbus, because the church had an altar instead of a communion table. The controversy points out the real fear of Evangelicals over the "de-Protestantizing" of their church and the threat they perceived to Episcopal forms.

French Roman Catholics settled the Ohio Valley in the late seventeenth century and began missions in the area shortly thereafter. When the region changed to English control, Roman Catholic settlers from Maryland arrived in Ohio; French and English Roman Catholics had always been part of Ohio's religious mix. Then, in the 1830s and 1840s, large number of Irish and German Catholics arrived as settlers and laborers for the new canal system. Non-Catholic native Ohioans, frightened by all these foreign Roman Catholics, reacted with anti–Roman Catholic polemics and persecution.

Cincinnati Presbyterian Lyman Beecher's *A Plea for the West* articulated Protestant fears. In this work, based on a millennial text in Isaiah 66, Beecher praised the "rapid and universal extension of civil and religious liberty" as "introductory to the triumphs of universal Christianity." He contrasted the "light of our republican prosperity" with the "dark prison house" and "primeval darkness" of Europe. Recent European immigrants, most of whom were Roman Catholics, imprisoned "through the medium of their religion and priesthood" posed a great danger to

American liberty. "The Catholic system," he warned, "is adverse to liberty." Beecher called Catholicism "the inflexible enemy of liberty of conscience and free inquiry," which were essential for a free republic.[99] Although American Catholics denied these charges, Beecher accused them of concealing their true intentions: Catholics really desired to convert Protestants and subvert the institutions of the republic. Two years later, Alexander Campbell mounted a similar argument in his debate with the Roman Catholic bishop of Cincinnati.[100] To many antebellum Ohioans, Protestantism was the religion of freedom, democracy, and light; Catholicism that of slavery, totalitarianism, and darkness.

Such sentiments also lie behind Bishop McIlvaine's fight against the spread of Tractarianism in Ohio. In 1842, the bishop ordained the Rev. Henry Richards as rector of St. Paul's, Columbus. As a graduate of Kenyon College and a protégé of the bishop, Richards had read both *Justification by Faith* and *Oxford Divinity Compared*. In the early years of this ministry, however, the young man read the *Tracts* for himself, rejected McIlvaine's arguments, and became convinced that Newman was right. "The change soon showed itself," wrote a sympathetic biographer, "not only in his sermons but was made manifest to the very eyes of the congregation in the altar and other fixtures of the church."[101] When a new building was constructed, Richards discarded the old communion table and installed an altar. McIlvaine refused to consecrate the church until the altar was removed and replaced with a table.

A few Ohio Episcopalians were angered–a handful wanted to charge the bishop with heresy and schism.[102] Obliged to explain his actions in his address to the 1846 convention, McIlvaine stated that in England, the Oxford Movement had reached a crisis point.[103] In the previous year, John Henry Newman had joined the Church of Rome. "Nothing seemed less probable," McIlvaine lamented, "than that Romish corruption of Christianity should make head in the Protestant Churches of England and this country." Before the spread of the Oxford heresy, McIlvaine continued, some things were "looked upon as a matter of indifference," and as a result "such alarming changes have compelled us to regard [some things] as of serious importance in connection with the growth of heresy and corruption."[104]

One such matter was the shape of the structure on which the communion was celebrated. Before the advance of Puseyism, it did not matter if this structure was a table or an altar (a closed box with solid sides); it was strictly a matter of architectural preference and taste.[105] It had not been an issue of doctrine. McIlvaine admitted in the past he had consecrated Ohio churches with altars, but that was before the Oxford Movement. Since then, the Tractarians had demonstrated a preference for altars, reflecting their notion of the real presence of Christ in the Lord's Supper. They believed the minister to be a " 'sacrificing Priest' at the altar–a mediator between God and sinful humanity." These notions repelled the Evangelicals who believed that communion was a memorial of Christ's sacrifice and emphasized the Protestant notion of the priesthood of all believers. "This," stated McIlvaine referring to Tractarian eucharistic theology, "is Popery at its essence."[106] The altar had therefore become doctrinally significant: a closed structure in the front of the church, on which Christ was "re-sacrificed," now represented the theology of Rome. To McIlvaine, the Tractarians had taken a form, an altar, which had previously been a matter of taste, and invested it the symbolism and theology of Roman Catholicism. Whenever altars had signified priestly power and sacrifice, the bishop argued, true religion in the church declined. Therefore, McIlvaine demanded a table. To support his argument, he marshalled evidence from the Bible, early Christianity, and the English Reformation. Ohio Episcopalians agreed with him. They backed his actions against Richards with a nearly unanimous vote.[107]

Underneath McIlvaine's formal doctrinal argument is also an informal, cultural argument against Roman Catholicism—one that resembled Lyman Beecher's. Throughout his address, McIlvaine likened Roman Catholicism to slavery. "It forges the chains of superstition," he charged, "and priest craft, and riveting them around the reason and the consciences of men, fastens them down under bondage to whatever terrors a despotic priesthood may emply." Altars fostered the growth of "astonishing superstition," whereas tables represented "edifying and inspiring associations, arising out of the recollection of the primitive and pure ages of the gospel."[108] The altar, McIlvaine proposed, is

> an oblong chest or ark, of stone or wood, closed in on all sides, as if some sacred mysteries were concealed therein. . . . It [is] a mere martyr's tomb; its top, the birth-place of the idolatry of the Mass; its interior a depository of worshipped bones; a most fit symbol of that whole system of spiritual bondage and death . . . under which the Church of Rome has always, since she became what she is, buried the gospel, and imprisoned the minds of men, wherever she has held dominion.[109]

Priest, altar, and the sacrifice of the Christ in the real presence were all corrupt innovations of the darkest days of Romanism.

When McIlvaine's invective is placed next to Beecher's and other anti-Roman Catholic writings of the time, it becomes clear that part of the Evangelical charge against the Oxford Movement was that Tractarianism was foreign and unrepublican. The contrast is clear: Oxfordism represented the barbarism of medieval Roman Catholicism; evangelical religion represented the freedom and purity of biblical religion. McIlvaine had always disliked medievalism; to him, it represented mystery (used negatively as "concealment") and barbarity. Medievalism was a remnant of corrupt European kingdoms: wherever medievalism was present, as in France, true religion and holy living could not flourish.

McIlvaine used the same language of slavery, bondage, and concealment as did Beecher. He believed that Oxfordism stood against all Protestant and republican values. Evangelical religion was a more fit companion to American liberty. To Evangelical Episcopalians, the Oxford Movement posed both a theological and a cultural threat: theologically, it threatened to undo the basis of Evangelical belief and practice; culturally, it threatened to replace American freedom with European despotism and liberty of conscience with an enforced system of belief. While any Anglican Evangelical could have mounted the theological arguments, McIlvaine's secondary, cultural argument was an American one. Facing the double threats of anti-Protestantism and anti-Americanism, the Evangelicals vigorously proceeded to root out Romanism. Tractarianism, if victorious, would replace the Protestant forms of the Episcopal Church with Roman Catholic meaning. This betrayed McIlvaine's heritage as both an Episcopalian and an American.

As if this dual threat was not enough to energize the Evangelical crusade against Tractarianism, a third factor entered the picture: Tractarianism threatened the evangelical family. This aspect of the Evangelical-Tractarian argument is best illustrated in the 1844 ecclesiastical trial of Bishop Onderdonk, who had been charged with intemperance, immorality, and impurity. This sensational trial has most often been interpreted as an act of party vengeance following Onderdonk's ordination of Arthur Carey. Onderdonk's action, stated one historian, "was neither forgotten nor forgiven by the Low Churchmen. Henceforth he was marked as a man dangerous to the peace of the church."[110] When the Evangelical party failed to secure a churchwide condemnation of Tractarianism at the 1844 General Convention, they began to persecute various individuals. Onderdonk was a logical candidate. Within a year, he was tried, found guilty, and suspended from office. Wrote one Episcopal historian:

> It is impossible not to see in this verdict the influence of the bitter party feeling which prevailed at the time, especially as the voting throughout the trial was pretty much along party lines, all of the Evangelicals voting to condemn Bishop Onderdonk and most, though not all, of the High Churchmen voting to acquit him.[111]

On one level, this assessment seems true enough, but letters written by Anna Pierrepont, a wealthy New York Evangelical Episcopalian, to her friend Bishop McIlvaine, as well as some of the documents surrounding the case, reveal that it was not a simple party issue of doctrinal differences and ecclesiastical vengeance between clerics: Bishop Onderdonk was accused of drunkenness and impurity. The specific charges included "thrusting his hands into ladies' bosoms" and reaching up women's skirts to "their central parts." As Pierrepont grieved in one letter, "If indeed all clergymen & Bishops looked upon these acts as unimportant in themselves no lady would sit an instant in clerical society."[112]

During the trial, which lasted until early January 1845, Bishop McIlvaine was in New York and often stayed at Pierrepont's Brooklyn home. Her letters to him report the follow-up events after he returned to Ohio: "You have escaped from the worrying reports and inuendos & disagreable things that are constantly flying about us here. My heart often sickens as I listen and look on. . . . It is truly abominable, I could not help thinking of a line of 'Haylets triumph of temper,' 'The powers of mischief met in dark divan.' " Such "powers of mischief," Pierrepont believed, resulted from Onderdonk's High Church theology. She understood one of the basic tenets of Tractarianism to be "that the Church is the Mediator between God & the individual – that is the clergy – that the salvation of a man's soul is not effected solely by change of light wrought by Christ's Spirit, but through the Church."[113] Hence, tremendous power rested in the hands of male clerics. Bishop Onderdonk's offenses revealed the corruption of placing the power of salvation in the church rather than in Jesus alone. Tractarianism threatened respectable Episcopal ladies by placing immoral mediators between them and Jesus. Oxford theology was nothing less than an attack on women's equal spiritual standing before God.

Tractarianism also attacked female purity.[114] Pierrepont believed, as did other Evangelicals, that any kind of Catholicism would result in immorality. For her, however, it took a very particular form. She was distressed that Onderdonk's supporters did not believe the "lady witnesses." She wrote to comfort one of them, Mrs. Butler, from the attacks she suffered in the press. The High Church press adopted the tactic of discrediting the testimonies of the women who accused the bishop and implied (some of them stating outright) that the women themselves were of impure and dishonest character and had actually enjoyed and encouraged the bishop's advances.[115] "If indeed," Pierrepont railed, "one witness could not establish a fact in an Ecclesiastical court though that witness were a communicant in good standing and under solemn oath then it were unsafe to be a moment alone with one of the clergy or a Bishop."[116] The "lady witnesses" were in a terrible bind: they were required to preserve their purity, yet at the same time be submissive to the male authorities over them. The bishop had not only attacked their purity but had undermined female trust in the system of male authority in the church—a fact that Anna Pierrepont was quick to point out.

The dual threats to Episcopal ladies and clerical authority over women proved a strong incentive for some Evangelical men to bring Onderdonk to trial. The Rev. James Richmond, called "crazy Richmond," by the High Church supporters of the bishop, wrote to his brother:

> I am satisfied, too, that [Bishop Onderdonk's indecency] is now a matter of notoriety in the female portion of the Diocese here, there, and everywhere . . . No lady is safe from the grossest, most palpable, and almost open insult . . . I write this only for the sake of the Church, and because there are female candidates for confirmation who will not be confirmed by him. . . . This alas! is too true.[117]

Even his supporters admitted "to have acquitted him would have hurt the church" because of the sexual issues involved.[118] No denomination—comprised of majority of women—could afford to alienate its female communicants around such a sensitive issue. Anna Pierrepont expressed it well: "Oh what corruption has not this affair shown! What unsoundness both in faith & practice in doctrine & morals, I am bowed to the dust by the developments made since this trial begun!!" Through this affair, she believed God had judged New York Episcopalianism and found it wanting, because it was infected with Oxford theology which dared to "wink at iniquity." Perhaps the bishop's suspension might turn his "heart toward the right,"[119] by which she meant be converted to the Evangelical gospel.

If Tractarianism posed such a terrible threat to the piety and purity of Episcopal ladies, it was no less threatening to their children. The Evangelical home was the center of piety—the place where children learned the gospel from their parents and prayed around family altars. Like other nineteenth-century Protestants, family piety was important for Evangelical Episcopalians as they recited family liturgies, read from the *Book of Common Prayer* and the Bible together, and instructed their children in the faith.[120] Anna Pierrepont belonged to several groups of women that met regularly in homes for prayer, devotional reading, and spiritual encouragement. Her letters are full of reports to Bishop McIlvaine regarding her childrens' (especially her daughters') spiritual progress.

In November 1845, a new worry appeared in her correspondence. Speaking of her concerns for her son, Henry, she fretted: "Who ever loved and venerated a tender Mother enough? What child can ever repay the cares and love & sorrow of a

Mother?" She continued: "I do not know what plans are in embrio! My dear friend, but I am sure something is going on—Henry has hired a pew in Immanuel Church!! Mr. Vinton visits there frequently."[121] Henry Pierrepont was the oldest son and heir of the family; Mr. Vinton was the Rev. Francis Vinton, a graduate of the General Theological Seminary, a supporter of Tractarianism, and the rector of Immanuel Church in Brooklyn. Anna Pierrepont's son, in other words, had gone over to the enemy. There is talk "of building a church for Mr. V," and it had long been expected that the Pierrepont family would donate land and money toward the next Episcopal Church in Brooklyn. She wrote:

> I cannot consistently with my feeling give to that church . . . It was expected and intended by my dear Husband that land would be given for a church on his estate, and as it was not done in his lifetime, all the heirs agreed to give when the proper time came, & I told Henry I would give what was owed me by the estate thinking as we all did that we were to have a voice in the building & in the preacher.[122]

However, if that preacher was Francis Vinton, Anna Pierrepont refused to cooperate; "The more I hear and see of Mr. Vinton, the more I sorrow that he should have influence over any I love."

The Rev. Mr. Vinton *was* influencing her loved ones. "Theresa goes to Henry's pew . . . attends Saints days and told me Mr. V's lecture was very excellent, when Mr. Sands told me he thought it stuff—baptism he held up as salvation etc. & instead of sending on to the Bible, he directed to the prayerbook!!!"[123] Two of her children had become fascinated with High Church theology: "I hear Bishop Hobart often brought up now a days by Mr. Vinton's congregation." When Vinton was offered the bishopric of Indiana, Pierrepont confessed, "I wish he had been anywhere but here."[124] She fumed over Vinton's ritualistic procession held for the laying of the foundation stone for Grace Church in Brooklyn, but Theresa was entranced by the beauty of the service. Anna wrote to McIlvaine:

> You know how I feel and think and lament the novelties which carry away so many I love . . . I think his insinuating manner draws away many silly women (and men) captive, he is never idle—I will not if I can help it say any more, but it is a sore subject & calls for patience and prayer.[125]

She felt she was fighting against "the Legions" for Theresa's evangelical faith.

Tractarianism, focused on Mr. Vinton's influence over her children, had undermined Anna Pierrepont's own position as a Christian mother. She reserved special venom when Vinton dared encroach on her territory. It appalled her that he offered to rebaptize in the church all those who had been baptized at home—thus moving a central ritual out of the control of the family and home into the clerical and institutional setting. When Vinton preached on the "pains and perils of childbirth," she was furious that a man would treat such a subject from the pulpit. In another sermon, Vinton shocked her by emotionally re-creating the suffering and sorrow of "the blessed Mother"—she stated that this was not a subject a man should depict "in such an unfeeling manner with a parade of feeling."[126] When Bishop Doane, another High Churchman, prepared to confirm Anna's granddaughter without proper instruction, Pierrepont expressed similar anger over such men misrepresenting the gospel. She wrote the girl, urging her not to submit to the rite without having been born again, and she confided to McIlvaine: "I have prevented the child from coming forward uninstructed & entirely ignorant of what she was going to undertake."[127] Tractarianism threatened the evangelical home by moving the learning, rituals, and symbols of family piety into the church building. Anna Pierrepont saw this as a loss of control of the spiritual growth and development of her own family and an attack on her world. Anna Pierrepont identified Tractarianism as a threat to the women's sphere.

There is an interesting contrast here with other Protestant evangelical women. Throughout the nineteenth century, evangelical women used "motherhood" as a justification to enter, often conservatively, the political sphere—especially well illustrated in the case of "home protection" and temperance. Evangelical Episcopal women generally appropriated such arguments as well, and thus participated in the "politics of domesticity."[128] But Anna Pierrepont's comments suggest that Evangelical Episcopal women believed that resistance to High Church theology was also a kind of "home protection" against the insidious advance of "Romanism." By preserving the evangelical character of their church, they remained the moral guardians of their homes, protected themselves from impurity, and saved their children from idolatry and eternal damnation. Thus, Anna Pierrepont constructed a "church politics of domesticity" against the assaults of Tractarianism. Sounding much like her friend Bishop McIlvaine, she directed her energies to preserve the teaching of "Christ crucified, to dying sinners, as the resurrection & the life & the great doctrine of justification by a simple excercise of faith in the Righteousness of Christ without any aid from good works."[129] Tractarianism threatened to move family piety out of the home—out from the control of saintly, pure, and pious mothers—into an institutionalized church that was controlled by male clerics of the likes of Bishop Onderdonk. If Tractarianism won the day, no mother or her children would be safe.

Within this context, the political battles of the church reached a fever pitch. Sensing anti-Protestant, anti-American, and anti-family tendencies in Tractarianism, highly motivated Evangelicals won many of these battles. In Ohio, the Rev. Richards relented and knocked the sides off his altar, turning it into a table. Henry and Benjamin Onderdonk lost their ecclesiastical positions. Students at the General Theological Seminary were admonished and expelled; the seminary was disgraced. Bishop Doane retained his episcopal office, but he looked inept. Although the Evangelicals lost in their attempt to have the 1844 General Convention condemn the Oxford Movement, through the series of national trials, and their victories in local disputes, within a few years of Carey's controversial ordination, they believed that they had gotten Oxfordism under control. Their successes indicate just how strong their party had become and how willing they were to use any means to retain their power and position in the church.

Uneasy Evangelical Relations

If the Oxford Movement threatened Evangelicalism within the church, it also threatened the relationship between Evangelical Episcopalians and non-Episcopal evangelicals. There was always a certain amount of suspicion between the two groups. Most non-Episcopal evangelicals came out of English dissenting traditions with long histories of hostility toward Anglicanism. They remained suspicious of Episcopal commitment to the separation of church and state. They protested that Episcopal liturgy had not been reformed enough. They questioned whether Episcopalians recognized their orders and ministrations as valid. Presbyterians, Baptists, Methodists, and Congregationalists all had long-standing quarrels with the Church of England that affected their relationships with American Episcopalians.

In the early years of the Republic, Evangelical Episcopalians overcame a good deal of this prejudice. They won the respect of other evangelicals for their warm support of various voluntary organizations.[130] They were recognized for their defense of Protestant theology and were commended for their revivals. Evangelicals feared that this friendly relationship with other evangelicals would be ruined if Oxford theology gained a large following in the Episcopal Church.

McIlvaine worried at Ohio's 1841 convention:

> I much lament to say that our Church has suffered great dishonor in the sight of a large part of the Christian people of these United States . . . by the efforts which have been made in some quarters of our Communion, to defend the lamentable wanderings of what is . . . called Oxford Divinity, as being not inconsistent with the doctrines of our standards."[131]

Other Protestants, he said, were already prejudiced against the Episcopal Church. They believed that the church had never really eradicated Romanism. Tractarianism reinforced this prejudice. Admitted McIlvaine: "Probably the reputation of our Church has suffered more by prejudices and aversions against our peculiarities, in consequence of what has been written and done by individual Episcopalians in the United States, in favor of Oxford Divinity, during the last three years" than by all the good that had been done by evangelical ministers in the decades before.[132] He was probably right.

Other evangelicals had taken notice of Episcopal problems. Episcopalians, who had long boasted of their unity as a protection against American sectarianism, were at war with one another. Presbyterians, Methodists, and Baptists must have felt somewhat vindicated: their denominations were undergoing painful splits and schisms at this time.[133] The Episcopal Church looked like it might be heading in a similar direction.

As if to underline the division in the Episcopal Church, a Presbyterian in Burlington, New Jersey, published a pamphlet in 1843 with the ironic, and somewhat snide, title *"One Faith," or Bishop Doane vs. Bishop McIlvaine on Oxford Theology*.[134] In it, the Presbyterian editor placed quotes from McIlvaine and Doane on Tractarianism side by side to show the radically different opinions of the two bishops on the subject. The editor admitted a two fold purpose: first, "to exhibit Oxfordism and Romanism in contrast with evangelical doctrine" and, second, "to beseech those prelates and others, who boast of 'one church,' 'one faith,' 'one Apostolic succession,' &c., not to chant their plea of 'UNITY' with notes of discord. Silence would be far more becoming, during the continuance of 'divisions' among them."[135] Although "Presbyterian" thought Bishop McIlvaine had succeeded in the first point, he targeted both Doane and McIlvaine with the second.

The editor was impressed by McIlvaine's refutation of Oxford theology and agreed with the bishop's analysis: Oxfordism was essentially Romanism. As a result, the editor argued, the Episcopal Church was preaching two conflicting gospels. "Presbyterian," however, was not content to end his observations there. He concluded this pamphlet with an examination of his own: the "fallibility of forms" in the Church of England! These forms, argued the editor, had never preserved true religion. Even after the great Evangelical Revival ("no period in the history of the established Church . . . has probably witnessed more evangelical piety"), corruption of forms was likely. Look what had happened: amidst the success of evangelical Anglicanism, "the Oxford heresy burst forth."[136] Liturgies, he concluded, did not necessarily promote orthodoxy.

> We see nothing in them that is calculated to preserve religion. . . . Nor do we see any thing in mere forms that is specially adapted to cherish spiritual influences. If the BIBLE fails to keep religion alive in the heart, man's inventions and Liturgies will accomplish nothing, except to made formalists more formal.[137]

The final blow: "It is impossible to boast of 'ONE FAITH,' in a Church, where, notwithstanding one Liturgy, there are at this very moment TWO GOSPELS."[138]

To McIlvaine, and other Evangelicals who read the pamphlet, these were the worst possible accusations. They had long maintained that theirs was an *evangelical* liturgy designed to best promote true religion. It had occasionally been corrupted by formalists, but, in itself, the liturgy was biblical, pure, and spiritual. This Presbyterian polemicist argued *no*: the liturgy itself was corrupt, and only spiritual religion could salvage what little good there was in it. The attack on the liturgy added insult to the injury inflicted by pointing out Episcopal disunity. Evangelical Episcopalians believed that charity and unity signified the blessings of Zion; *"One Faith"* revealed the deep divisions in the church over fundamental doctrines.

Even more alarming was the attack by the New School Presbyterian leader, Albert Barnes. Barnes had debated Episcopal claims for a number of years.[139] In 1834 and 1835, he took on Henry U. Onderdonk on the claims of the episcopacy. Barnes concluded that the episcopacy was not scriptural and objected to Episcopal exclusivism. Episcopalians, he asserted, should admit that their church was simply one church among many.[140] In 1843, immediately after the Carey ordination, Barnes published another work attacking the Tractarian view of the episcopacy. Then, in January 1844, Barnes took a new approach. In a series of articles in the *New Englander*, instead of attacking the Oxford Movement, he turned on Evangelical Episcopalians. The articles were published as a pamphlet entitled *The Position of the Evangelical Party in the Episcopal Church*. Barnes proclaimed that Episcopal claims to unity were a sham and Evangelical attempts to revitalize Episcopal forms were hopeless. The Tractarian crisis proved, once and for all, that Evangelical religion was antithetical to the nature of the Episcopal Church.

Barnes went right to the heart of the Evangelical Episcopal synthesis: "the attempt to unite the religion of forms with the gospel." The Oxford crisis proved this synthesis was impossible. He proclaimed, "THAT IT HAS NEVER BEEN POSSIBLE

PERMANENTLY TO CONNECT THE RELIGION OF FORMS WITH EVANGELICAL RELI-
GION." Evangelicalism, he argued, had been "engrafted" onto the Episcopal
system; it had not developed naturally out of Anglicanism. Tractarianism, on the
other hand, was a "fair development of the system." Barnes believed that Evangelicalism was borrowed from "the spirit of the age" and through contacts with
Christians of other denominations. Although he admired Episcopal revivalism,
Evangelical zeal for "spiritual religion," and Christian benevolence, Barnes proposed that it was ultimately impossible for such things to be maintained with
evangelical purity in the Episcopal Church. If Evangelicalism remained within the
church, he argued, it would become hopelessly polluted by prelacy and papacy. If
Evangelicals tried to maintain their position, the two parties within the church
would remain constantly at war. The only real hope for Evangelical Episcopal
survival was schism. "The spirit of truth," he believed, "will not be bound. It does
not breathe and act freely when fettered with forms."[141]

To support his thesis, Barnes argued four major points: (a) Evangelical Episcopalians were "compelled to use a liturgy which counteracts the effect of their
teaching"; (b) "there are no arrangements or provision in the liturgy for promoting
their peculiar and distinctive efforts"; (c) their "efforts are all at variance with the
doctrinal views of the church"; and (d) they refused to recognize the rights and
ministrations of other Protestant clergy and implied, therefore, that the Episcopal
Church was the only true church. The "Episcopal sect," argued Barnes, was no
evangelical church; it is the religion of forms. To proclaim it evangelical "was both
unkind to Episcopacy, and it was morally certain that it would be a failure."[142]
Anglicanism always tended toward Romanism; Evangelicalism was little more
than a short Protestant detour.

In a final blow, Barnes resorted to the Episcopacy-is-un-American argument.

> We regard the prevailing spirit of Episcopacy, in all aspects, high and low, as at
> variance with the spirit of this age and of this land. This is an age of freedom, and
> men *will* be free. The religion of forms is the stereotyped wisdom or folly of the
> past. . . . The spirit of this age demands that there shall be freedom in religion;
> that it shall not be fettered or suppressed; that it shall go forth to the conquest of
> the world. . . . [Episcopacy] might be appropriate in lands where religion is
> united in the state
>
> > – "like beauty to old age
> > For interest's sake, the living to the dead,"
>
> but it does not suit our times, or country. It makes a jar on American feelings. It
> will not be tolerated.[143]

No amount of evangelical adaptation could ever change the essential nature of
episcopacy: it was, and always would be, a religion of "forms," a "cold, dead, dull,
formal thing."[144] Nothing was more out of step with the energy and freedom of
American evangelicalism. Formalism was the wineskin of the old world; evangelicalism was the wine of the new. The Episcopal Church could never hold the
spirit of true religion.

Barnes's argument demonstrates the deep suspicion of "forms" by some
Americans in the young republic. Established forms undermined democratic

individualism. Only a "free" religion, a religion of choice—unfettered by the nonbiblical innovations and formalistic restrictions of the old world—was suitable for the new republic. Other Americans, however, such as Evangelical Episcopalians, maintained a sort of "whiggish" approach to traditional forms. Forms were not necessarily good or bad; they took character from the content given them. Some forms served as a necessary check against sinful behavior or unorthodox belief. Admitting that form was necessary did not deny the importance of freedom. This whiggish commitment to forms recognized that freedom could only exist within limits.

Barnes's argument angered Evangelical Episcopalians. Along with Barnes, they believed that formalism deadened true Christianity, but they separated *forms* from *formalism*. Forms could be good or bad; what mattered was the spirit that enlivened the form. The Episcopal liturgy, in particular, they believed was essentially helpful, or good. It embodied the theology of the New Testament. These forms had been misused by formalists, but by themselves Episcopal forms did not deaden spiritual religion. On the contrary, Episcopal forms were admirable guides to a converted heart.

When Barnes's attack appeared anonymously in serial form, the Evangelical press noted but did not review the work. When it was published as a pamphlet, a writer in the *Episcopal Recorder* confessed that "the only circumstance of the least consequence about this book is the name of the author."[145] Only Barnes's reputation as an evangelical leader prompted an answer. In three unsigned articles, the *Recorder* defended the position of Evangelicals in the Episcopal Church, refuting Barnes point by point; as a result, the articles are somewhat disjointed. Nevertheless, some common themes run throughout.

The first article tackles Barnes's claim that Evangelicalism was not within the nature of the Episcopal Church. If it were, the *Recorder* argued, how is it that so many evangelical movements have appeared with such regularity within Anglicanism? "The more rational conclusion would be," stated the *Recorder*, "that there was something in the nature of that Church, which he calls a mere religion of forms, adapted to produce a result which has been so uniformly seen to flow from it." Evangelical Episcopalianism "is not to be considered wholly a Presbyterian gift"; rather it was a long-standing tradition within the Church of England.[146]

The second article deals with a number of Barnes's points that had one common issue: "compulsion." Freedom, the *Recorder* evidently agreed, was more in keeping with the spirit of the age. Arguing that Episcopalianism was a free choice, the *Recorder* said that no one was compelled to believe it. Moreover, anyone who chose to be an Episcopalian freely consented to use the liturgy, and clergymen voluntarily bound themselves to this form of worship. "The public worship" of the church, admitted the *Recorder* "is fixed,"[147] but is a voluntarily chosen form of worship a denial of freedom? In his battles against revivalism, Bishop McIlvaine maintained that revivalism, of the sort practiced by Barnes, had produced a number of new forms, which were so corrupted that they had become a new formalism. Revivalists imposed these forms without regard to free choice. Revivalistic religion was guilty of that which they accused Episcopalians.

On matters other than the form of the liturgy, the *Recorder* pointed out that Episcopal clergy "have a liberty conceded and secured to them, and universally practised by them . . . of which the Presbyterian minister is perfectly destitute."[148] This retort must have irritated Barnes. Episcopal ministers were theologically freer than Presbyterians. Within the bounds of Protestant theology, Episcopal clergymen were not required to subscribe to a particular interpretation of the Thirty-nine Articles, and there existed a good deal of latitude on Arminianism and Calvinism. Presbyterians, on the other hand, were bound to certain Calvinist creeds; there was no freedom to modify or reject such creeds without fear of recrimination. The *Recorder* was too polite to mention its directly, but Barnes himself had been charged with heresy in 1831. American Presbyterianism was wracked by questions of freedom and limits in theological belief. The *Recorder* turned Barnes on his head. Yes, free religion for a free land. But whose denomination was actually freer? Episcopal bishops were not despots; perhaps Presbyterian elders actually were.

The third article defended the form of the liturgy in relation to American evangelicalism. The *Reformer* argued that the liturgy was full of evangelical concern for missions—it particularly suited revivals. "As for the adaptation of this Liturgy to revivals of religion," stated the *Recorder*, "we have seen it used day after day, for weeks and months, in just such works of grace, and every day the interest in it became deeper, and the love of it the more intense. The peculiar application of it to such awakened feeling is very remarkable."[149] The liturgy was full of references to the sinful state of the unconverted sinners and admirably displayed the atoning grace of Christ. Argued the writer:

> The single prayer of the Litany, 'O Lamb of God, who takest away the sins of the world, have mercy upon us, grant us thy peace,' seems in itself to outweigh in worth, all the formal, theoretical, discursive prayers, we have ever heard from Presbyterians.[150]

True spiritual awakenings "have been uniformly and always the legitimate fruits of this very Liturgy." The more evangelical the congregation, stated the writer in classic Evangelical Episcopal fashion, "the more dear to them, and appropriate to their necessities and tastes does the Liturgy become."[151]

One issue that particularly galled Barnes (as well as other non-Episcopal evangelicals) was the issue of Episcopal exclusivity in regard to ministry. If a Presbyterian minister wanted to become an Episcopal priest, he must submit to reordination. If a Roman Catholic priest, however, wanted to become an Episcoal priest, he would be received into the ministry without reordination. At the center of the issue was whether or not one had been episcopally ordained. It seemed outrageous to Barnes that a Protestant church would recognize the ministry of Roman Catholics as superior to that of Presbyterians. From his perspective, this proved his point: the Episcopal Church was fundamentally hostile to true religion.

The editor of the *Episcopal Recorder* strained for an answer. "When the Prayerbook was formed," he responded, "there were no others [referring to denominations] in existence." How could the Prayer Book make provision for a multitude of Christian "sects" which had not yet come into being? This response was woefully inadequate since the American Prayer Book had been revised in 1789, long after other Protestant churches had been formed. The *Episcopal Recorder* attempted to dodge Barnes's complaint. As to the fact that Episcopal pulpits were closed to non-Episcopal ministers, the *Recorder* pointed out that Presbyterians excluded Quakers from their pulpits. "There must be," wrote the *Recorder*, "some line and limit of admission into the pulpit."[152]

In conclusion, the writer dealt with the issue of schism. Was not Mr. Barnes, he asked, satisfied with having divided one church already?

> But Mr. Barnes urgently and affectionately invites us to secede from a Church, in which we are so trammelled and confined. . . . We desire not to "go forth of the ark"—and least of all, while the floods are raging around us as they are now. There is nothing abroad which yet equals in attraction, the joys and comforts of our still comparatively peaceful and united home.[153]

"Comparatively" was the key: in comparison to the other major Protestant churches, Episcopalians were still "one." Once again, Evangelical Episcopalians insisted that unity was a primary mark of the work of the Holy Spirit and true Christianity. In spite of the Tractarian crisis, they refused to leave the church. They maintained that the Tractarians had abandoned the heritage of Anglicanism, and Evangelical Episcopalians would not surrender their church to such interlopers. Even if unity was only "comparative," schism was not a genuine possibility.

Barnes was neither convinced nor impressed by these arguments. In a second series of articles, he blasted right back: "When will Episcopalians so far modify *their* views as to believe there is any true church besides their own?" In this tract, Barnes emphasized the issue of the Episcopal Church's relationship with other Protestant churches. He rearticulated and clarified many of the points from his first pamphlet and concluded that evangelicals within the Episcopal Church were "engaged in a hopeless warfare" in which true Christianity would be "overshadowed and crushed by Puseyism or Romanism."[154]

G. W. Ridgely, an editor of the *Recorder*, published a response to this second attack of Barnes. In a better argued and much wittier piece than the original reply, Ridgely admitted to Barnes's central point: "it never has been possible permanently to connect the Religion of Forms with Evangelical Religion." Having given Barnes the point, he submitted a second proposition: "it is equally true of a religion WITHOUT forms."[155] To prove his point, Ridgely traced the history of Presbyterianism and New England Puritanism from Scotland and Geneva to New School Presbyterianism and the Unitarianism of nineteenth-century Harvard College. Reformed religion, he concluded, was just as likely to be hostile to evangelicalism as was Episcopalianism!

In his discussion, Ridgely identified four—not two—parties in the Episcopal Church: Ultralow Churchmen and Moderate Churchmen (both "Evangelical") and High Churchmen and Hyper-Churchmen (both called "High Church"). These groups were distinguished by their varying views toward Episcopal government and ministry. The Ultralow Churchmen, he explained, "consider all forms of Church government good." The High Churchmen and the Hyper-Churchmen believe that episcopacy is necessary to the "being" of the church and "infer" from this doctrine that all non-Episcopal ministries are invalid. The Hyper-Churchmen push the idea to the extreme, however, and insist on strict compliance with Episcopal canons in every instance—whereas High Churchmen are "content to hold these inferences as matters of 'private opinion.' " The Moderate Churchmen, the category in which Ridgely placed the majority of the Evangelicals, "consider Episcopacy essential not to the *being*, but only to the *well*-being of a Church. . . . They consider it not indispensable to the existence, but only to the perfection of a Church." According to his analysis, the two middle parties—the moderates and the High Churchmen—differed in interpretation regarding non-Episcopal ministers, but they agreed to allow a certain amount of personal latitude in interaction with non-Episcopalians. It was these two groups that had forged the successful alliance of the 1830s. "On the subject of non-Episcopal Churches and ministers," Ridgely concluded, Evangelicals, "as a Party, hold no opinion; as individuals, there is a diversity of sentiment among them." How one interpreted the church's exclusion of non-Episcopal orders was strictly a matter of private inference. This diversity of opinion, insisted Ridgely, was "recognized and allowed" by the church. All Episcopalians united on the great "fact" of the episcopacy; inferences from that fact were left up to the free judgment of the individual. The formal doctrine of the Episcopal Church, quite simply, did not *necessarily* invalidate the orders of other Protestants. That was only the opinion of some Episcopalians. Because of this freedom, the Protestant Episcopal Church, Ridgely maintained, was an "Ecclesiastical Republic"—a church well suited to American democracy.[156]

Support for Evangelical Episcopalians in their battle against Barnes came from an unexpected quarter: the Old School Presbyterians of the *Princeton Review*. Charles Hodge and his colleagues had long disliked Albert Barnes and warmly supported Bishop McIlvaine's defense of the Reformation against Tractarianism. Hodge criticized Barnes's attack as uncharitable and unproductive. "The assumption," wrote Hodge, "on which the whole book is founded, we believe to be erroneous. . . . That assumption is that Puseyism is the true doctrine of the Episcopal Church, and consequently that the evangelical party are in conflict with their own doctrinal standards." Hodge defended the Anglican liturgy and the Thirty-nine Articles as perfectly evangelical—allowing for a few points that seemed to "favour the Tractarian system." He did express his reservations about Episcopal attitudes toward other denominations, however. On the whole, Hodge applauded the success of the Evangelicals in the Episcopal Church and rebuked Barnes. "We do not wish," he proclaimed, "to be numbered among the abettors of Tractarianism as the true doctrine of the Episcopal church."[157]

In spite of Hodge's charitable defense, Barnes's tract was met with "unusual attention" and excitement by gleeful Tractarians and non-Episcopal evangelicals.[158] Although Evangelical Episcopalians had worked productively with other evangelicals for more than two decades in leading Christian benevolent work and promoted the same religion of the heart as they, the Oxford Movement confirmed the suspicions of non-Episcopal evangelicals of the continued Romanist tendencies of Anglicanism. Old hostilities between "dissenters" and Anglicans lingered. The specter of "popery" brought back unhappy memories of prelacy and persecution. "A Church without a Bishop," ran one popular political song of the day, "and a State without a king."[159] To some, like Barnes, "Evangelical" and "Episcopal" appeared irreconcilable. The alliance between the Evangelical party and transdenominational evangelicalism was shaken by the advance of Puseyism within their church.

Conclusion

In spite of the loud denial of Barnes's accusations, Evangelicals were clearly shaken. They recognized that their position was weakened. Tractarianism might one day be powerful enough to push them completely out of the church. The questions were painful: If schism was rejected, what to do instead? How could they protect the cause of true religion in the Episcopal Church? How could they, in addition to heresy trials, beat back the Oxford threat?

Instead of schism, they resorted to the solution of "a church within a church". In the years following the Oxford crisis, they created their own Evangelical Episcopal organizations: a publishing house—the Protestant Episcopal Society for the Promotion of Evangelical Knowledge (PESPEK); a separate and voluntary mission society—the American Church Missionary Society; and a fund to provide for the education of Evangelical clergy—the Evangelical Education Society.

The earliest of the three societies, the PESPEK, also known as the Evangelical Knowledge Society, or E.K.S., was founded in 1847. The Protestant Episcopal Sunday School Union had been founded in 1826 as a nonpartisan society. By the early 1840s, however, the society was under the control of Bishop Onderdonk. In 1846, Virginia's Bishop Meade published a pamphlet showing how High Church doctrine and Tractarianism had infiltrated the publications of the Sunday School Union.[160] At the 1847 General Convention, a number of Evangelical bishops, Meade and McIlvaine included, met to discuss the situation. They decided to withdraw their support from the Sunday School Union and form a new society, the PESPEK. Although publications for Sunday school were the immediate concern, they conceived of a much larger society, along the lines of the American Tract Society, which would publish books and tracts to propagate "the principles and doctrines of the Gospel embodied in the Articles, Liturgy, and Homilies of the Protestant Episcopal Church."[161]

In the society's first address, the founders announced that they were "distinctly Evangelical" in doctrine and "distinctly Protestant Episcopal" in church order. Nothing more succinctly described the Evangelical Episcopal synthesis. In a pamphlet, *Statement of the Distinctive Principles*, they laid out their understanding of the position of the Evangelical party in the Episcopal Church. Evangelical doctrine included belief in all the major doctrines of the Protestant Reformation and the experiential knowledge of salvation through conversion and subsequent holy living. Protestant Episcopal polity, as they defined it, was simple, primitive, and biblical and not at variance with Evangelical doctrine. This, they believed, was an inclusive vision of Christianity. They believed that the church was the invisible body of *all* true believers in Christ made visible "under the form" of rightly administered sacraments.[162] They did not imply that other Protestants were excluded from the true, invisible church.[163] They maintained that Jesus alone mediated on behalf of sinful human beings before God the Father. They rejected sacerdotalism and proclaimed that the sacraments were signs, seals, and pledges of convenantal grace. In no way could the sacraments "save" a person. They stated their fidelity to the Bible and praised the liturgy as being unencumbered "with human invention."[164]

The Oxford Movement forced Evangelical Episcopalians to state definitively their theological and ecclesiastical position. The outlines of these "distinctive principles" had been drawn for many years, but now the Evangelicals were forced to refine and defend them within the Episcopal Church and to evangelical detractors. Their position was clear and well defined: Evangelical in doctrine and experience; Episcopal in polity and order. By the late 1840s, after the trials and the immediate crisis receded, Evangelicals began to feel as if they might succeed.

In 1852, an event occurred that seemed to vindicate the Evangelical position. Tractarianism, they had argued, would always lead to Rome. Those attracted to the Oxford Movement denied this. Then North Carolina's Levi Ives, the most zealous Tractarian bishop, while on a visit to Rome submitted himself to the pope. Ives's conversion humiliated his High Church defenders. His "perversion" was unanimously condemned by the House of Bishops,[165] and Oxfordism suffered a severe setback. The moderating alliance between old-fashioned High Churchmen and the Evangelical party held, and the Evangelicals were jubilant.

They were not convinced they had achieved complete victory, however. The PESPEK produced a large number of works on Evangelical theology and spirituality, but they also published a steady stream of apologetic pamphlets defending the very existence of something called Evangelical Episcopalianism.[166] Although McIlvaine and his colleagues made loud objections to the contrary, they were clearly shaken. The Oxford Movement and Albert Barnes both raised a terrible and uncomfortable question: Could Evangelical Episcopalianism survive within the church? George Dashiell had raised the same question more than twenty-five years earlier; concluding that it was impossible, he left the church and set up his own. Since that time, the leaders of the party had done everything they could think of to secure their position in the church while remaining committed to American transdenominational evangelicalism. Yet, here was the same accusation again: Evangelicalism and Episcopalianism were fundamentally incompatible. Dashiell had long since disappeared, but Tractarianism and Albert Barnes would never completely go away. Although McIlvaine and others wanted to believe that they had successfully defended the Evangelical Episcopal synthesis, the question of schism would continue to haunt Evangelical Episcopalians.

Notes

1. For McIlvaine's complete triumph over the Gambier institutions, see Smythe, *History of the Diocese of Ohio*, 186–194, and idem, *Kenyon College*, 118–130.

2. Calhoun in a letter to a friend, quoted in Smythe, *Kenyon College*, 173.

3. The depth of Sparrow's anger can be read between the lines in Sparrow's biography, Walker, *Life and Correspondence of Sparrow*. After Sparrow left Ohio, the volume never again refers to McIlvaine—not even to note his death in 1874. The breach between the two men seemed never to have been overcome in spite of their shared theological commitments and common vision for the Episcopal Church. For Sparrow's theology, see J. Barrett Miller, "The Theology of William Sparrow," *Historical Magazine of the Protestant Episcopal Church* 43 (1977): 443–454.

4. For McIlvaine's discussion of the "bond of peace" versus "the unity of the Spirit," see his *Holy Catholic Church*, 51.

5. Quoted from the *Churchman*, reprinted in the *Episcopal Recorder* (May 28, 1836): 34. See Calvin Colton, *Thoughts on the Religious State of the Country with Reasons for Preferring Episcopacy* (New York, 1836).

6. *Churchman*, note 5.

7. William R. Whittingham to McIlvaine, April 3, 1839, in EA, MD Dio Arch. This letter was apparently never sent to McIlvaine. Whittingham and McIlvaine maintained a cordial correspondence throughout the 1830s; their friendly tone is indicative of the good relationship between McIlvaine and some High Churchmen. Whittingham later became bishop of Maryland.

8. "Cranmer," "The Oxford Tracts," *Gambier Observer* (March 15, 1839), reprinted in the *Episcopal Recorder* (April 6, 1839): 6. Internal evidence points to McIlvaine as the author as well.

9. Ibid.

10. Ibid.

11. Ibid.

12. There is an immense amount of literature on the Oxford Movement in England. The standard works include the following: Owen Chadwick, *The Mind of the Oxford Movement* (London, 1960); idem, *From Bossuet to Newman: The Idea of Doctrinal Development* (Cambridge, 1957); idem, *Newman* (Oxford, 1983); idem, *The Spirit of the Oxford Movement: Tractarian Essays* (Cambridge, 1990); Yngve Brilioth, *Three Lectures on Evangelicalism and the Oxford Movement* (Oxford, 1934); idem, *The Anglican Revival: Studies in the Oxford Movement* (London, 1925); R. W. Church, *The Oxford Movement, Twelve Years: 1833–1845* (n.p., 1891); Geoffrey Faber, *The Oxford Apostles* (London, 1936); and Geoffrey Rowell, *The Vision Glorious* (Oxford, 1983).

13. The *Tracts for the Times* appeared in numerous editions throughout the century.

14. For the similarities and dissimilarities between American High Churchmanship and Tractarianism, see Mullin, *Episcopal Vision/American Reality*, 149–159.

15. In this period, Anglican Evangelicals moved further away from dissenting Evangelicals than previously. See Lewis, *Lighten Their Darkness*, 9–27.

16. The American political situation was already more politically liberal than that of England. The Americans were all democrats who did not believe that church and state should be formally connected. Within those bounds, they were conservatives who opposed the extremes of democratic liberalism. The English Evangelicals were conservatives who resisted democratic reform and the disestablishment of the church. Peter Toon has admirably traced the relationship between English Evangelicals and Tractarians in his *Evangelical Theology, 1833–1856: A Response to Tractarianism* (Atlanta, 1979). For the cordiality of the early years, see also Brilioth, *Three Lectures on Evangelicalism*, 28; Horton Davies, *Worship and Theology in England. Vol. 3. From Watts and Wesley to Maurice, 1690–1850* (Princeton, 1961), 244–522; Dieter Voll, *Catholic Evangelicalism: The Acceptance of Evangelical Traditions by the Oxford Movement During the Second Half of the Nineteenth Century* (London, 1963), 29–39; and David Newsome, "Justification and Sanctification: Newman and the Evange-

licals," *Journal of Theological Studies* 15 (1964): 33–37. The most notable instance of Evangelical-Tractarian cooperation was their common opposition to the appointment of liberal theologian R. D. Hampden to the Regis professorship of theology in Oxford in 1836. For the Hampden controversy, see Owen Chadwick, *The Victorian Church: An Ecclesiastical History of England* (New York, 1966), I: 112–121.

17. *Record* (December 5, 1833) quoted in Toon, *Evangelical Theology*, 18.

18. E. B. Pusey, *Scriptural Views of Holy Baptism* (London, 1836).

19. Toon, *Evangelical Theology*, 31.

20. Richard H. Froude, *Remains of the Late Richard Hurrell Froude* (London, 1838–1839), and John Henry Newman, *Lectures on the Doctrine of Justification* (London, [1838], 1885).

21. For a good summary of the impact of Froude's *Remains*, see Chadwick, *Victorian Church*, 172–181.

22. See George Stanley Faber, *The Primitive Doctrine of Justification Investigated Relatively to the Several Definitions of the Church of Rome and the Church of England* (London, 1837).

23. For a detailed explanation of the controversy over justification see Toon, *Evangelical Theology*, 141–170. The controversy over infused and imparted righteousness had a long history within the Church of England. See C. FitzSimmons Allison, *The Rite of Moralism* (Wilton, Conn., 1966).

24. Although Oxford has been seen as the center of Tractarianism, there were a significant number of committed Evangelicals at the university as well. See J. S. Reynolds, *The Evangelicals at Oxford, 1735–1871: A Record of an Unchronicled Movement* (reprint, Appleford, Abingdon, and Oxford, 1975).

25. Extracts from McIlvaine's visit to England were published without his permission or knowledge in the *Episcopal Recorder*. The Islington meeting is reported in *Episcopal Recorder* (April 4, 1835): 2, and in ibid, (April 11, 1835): 6.

26. See "Bishop McIlvaine and the Voluntary Principle," *Christian Observer* 33–34 (1840): 546–549, 607–609. Quoted from p. 549.

27. All quotes this paragraph from McIlvaine to Charles Girdlestone, February 20, 1839, in McI, Kenyon College.

28. Ibid. Samuel Seabury, editor of the *Churchman*, had reservations about Tractarian views on this issue as well, but was willing to publish those views.

29. See the *Episcopal Recorder* (January 19 and 26, 1839).

30. The best statement of this viewpoint is Kenneth M. Peck, "The Oxford Controversy in America: 1839," *Historical Magazine of the Protestant Episcopal Church* 33 (1964): 49–63.

31. "Cranmer," "Oxford Tracts," note 8.

32. I use the terms *anti–Roman Catholic* and *anti–Romanism* because they are more precise than *anticatholic*. Most evangelicals—of all different denominations in the nineteenth century—were not opposed to "catholicism." Evangelicals interpreted catholic as "universal" and generally referred to the universal practices and doctrines of the New Testament. They also used the word to denote their shared belief in heartfelt religion and conversionism with all other evangelicals. Evangelicals believed that Rome had particularized and claimed catholicism for itself—this was their one major objection to Roman Catholicism. Evangelicals were not anticatholic; they embraced catholicism as they defined it. They did oppose Rome's exclusive claim to catholicism and were vigorously anti-Roman. The definitive study of anti–Roman Catholicism is Ray A. Billington, *The Protestant Crusade, 1800–1860: A Study of the Origins of American Nativism* (New York, 1952). Billington, however, nowhere points out evangelical claims and definitions of catholicism.

33. Ahlstrom, *Religious History of the American People*, 540.

34. For the reception of Maria Monk's work, see Billington, *Protestant Crusade*, 99–108.

35. Charles P. McIlvaine, *The Respectful Address of McIlvaine . . . to All Who Would Promote the Progress of Learning and Religion in the Western States* (New York, 1833).

36. Diary entry, June 16, 1830, in Carus, *Memorials of McIlvaine*, 51.

37. McIlvaine, partial journal of his visit to England in 1835, written for his wife. Date of the particular entry missing; next entry dated July 20, in McI, Kenyon College.

38. Ibid.

39. Ibid. McIlvaine clearly did not believe, as some as his non-Episcopal evangelical critics did, that the episcopacy itself was an "antiquated usage" of the Middle Ages.

40. Himes later became an Episcopal priest. For the Millerites, see Ruth Alden Doan, *The Miller Heresy: Millenialism and American Culture* (Philadelphia, 1987).

41. "Phoenix," "Millennnarianism," *Episcopal Recorder* (May 11, 1839): 28.

42. "Cranmer," "Oxford Tracts," note 8.

43. No source given; quoted in Chorley, *Men and Movements*, 203.

44. William Jay to McIlvaine, January 25, 1842, in McI., Kenyon College, 420125.

45. William Jay to McIlvaine, April 15, 1843, in ibid., 430415.

46. Ibid. The most complete biography of Jay is Robert A. Trendel, "William Jay: Churchman, Public Servant and Reformer" (Ph.D. diss., Southern Illinois University, 1972), but Trendel skirts the issues of Jay's millenialism, his anti–Roman Catholic sentiments, and his vigorous opposition of the Oxford Movement.

47. Millennial optimism became widespread again following the great revivals of the late 1850s.

48. Charles P. McIlvaine, *The Sermon Before the Bishops, Clergy and Laity of the Protestant Episcopal Church in the U.S.A. in General Convention, at the Consecration of the Rev. Alfred Lee. D.D. . . . October 12, 1841* (New York, 1842). The sermon was later reprinted as *How a Minister of Christ May Both Save Himself and Them that Hear Him. A Sermon Delivered at the Consecration of the Rt. Rev. Alfred Lee* (Philadelphia, 1850).

49. Charles P. McIlvaine, *Justification by Faith: A Charge Delivered Before the Clergy of the Protestant Episcopal Church in the Diocese of Ohio . . . September 13, 1839* (Columbus, Ohio, 1840), 9.

50. Preceding quotes from "Cranmer," "Oxford Tracts," note 8.

51. McIlvaine to Maria McIlvaine, October 8, 1839, in Carus, *Memorials of McIlvaine*, 122.

52. McIlvaine, *Justification by Faith*, 10.

53. Although the Protestant and Catholic positions on justification had been argued for a couple of centuries, McIlvaine seems to have borrowed his dualistic explanation of justification from Faber's *Primitive Doctrine of Justification*. Faber's work was not an attack on Newman; it was published in 1837 as a defense of justification against the teachings of Alexander Knox.

54. Preceding quotes from McIlvaine, *Justification by Faith*, 23, 32.

55. Ibid. "Advertisement," no page number.

56. "Justification by Faith," *Princeton Review* 12 (October 1840): 566–567.

57. Preceding quotes from McIlvaine, *Oxford Divinity Compared* i, x.

58. Ibid., 51.

59. Ibid., 63.

60. Preceding quotes from John Henry Newman, *Lectures on the Doctrine of Justification*, 6th ed., (London, 1892), 63, 60.

61. McIlvaine, *Oxford Divinity Compared*, 511.

62. Ibid., 526–527.

63. Ibid., 527.

64. Isaac Williams, *On Reserve in Communicating Religious Knowledge*, Tract 87, 2nd ed. (London, 1840).

65. All quotes this paragraph from McIlvaine, *Oxford Divinity Compared*, 547.

66. Williams, *On Reserve*, 58–63.

67. Their theology of works and grace follows the parameters established by Martin Luther during the Protestant Reformation. See Luther's *Freedom of a Christian* for the classic Protestant statement of this position. Of particular importance for Evangelical Episcopalians was Thomas Cranmer's explication of the problem in "An Homily or Sermon of Good Works Annexed unto Faith," *Miscellaneous Writings and Letters of Thomas Cranmer* (Cambridge, 1846), 141–149.

68. McIlvaine, *Oxford Divinity Compared*, 547.

69. Quoted in McIlvaine to Maria McIlvaine, May 7, 1841, in Carus, *Memorials of McIlvaine*, 124.

70. Milnor to McIlvaine, January 15, 1841, in Stone, *Memoir of Milnor*, 548.

71. Joseph McIlvaine to Charles McIlvaine, February 21, 1842, quoted in Carus, *Memorials of McIlvaine*, 126.

72. "Oxford Divinity," *Christian Lady's Magazine* 15 (1841): 462.

73. "Bishop McIlvaine on Oxford Tract Divinity," *Christian Divinity* 39 (1841): 177.

74. McIlvaine is the only American theologian discussed in Toon's *Evangelical Theology*.

75. *Oxford Divinity Compared* was republished twenty years later in a revised edition entitled *Righteousness by Faith* and went through several American and British editions in 1860s. Used here is Charles P. McIlvaine, *Righteousness by Faith, or the Nature and Means of Our Justification Before God*, 2nd ed. (Philadelphia, 1864).

76. John Henry Newman, *Remarks on Certain Passages in the Thirty-Nine Articles*, Tract 90 (London, 1841), 83

77. Kenrick's letter appeared in the *New York Observer* on July 24, 1841.

78. Charles P. McIlvaine, "Address," *Journal of the Diocese of Ohio* (Cincinnati, 1842), 24.

79. All quotes this paragraph from Walworth, *Oxford Movement in America*, 5. Walworth made this comment after he himself had converted to Roman Catholicism.

80. Ibid., 8.

81. Ibid., 10.

82. Hugh Smith and Henry Anthon, *The True Issue for the True Churchman* (New York, 1843), 6. High Church writers disputed Smith and Anthon's interpretation of Carey's response.

83. Ibid., 8–9. Also Walworth, *Oxford Movement in America*, 42–50.

84. William B. Sprague, *Annals of the American Pulpit*, Vol. 5, *The Episcopal Church* (New York, 1857), 800.

85. The two most important pamphlets were Smith and Anthon, *True Issue for the True Churchman*, and [Samuel Seabury, editor of the *Churchman*,] *A Full and True Statement of the Examination and Ordination of Mr. Arthur Carey* (New York, 1843). These tracts illustrate the anti- and pro-Carey positions, respectively.

86. There were shades of opinion on both sides, and occasionally a surprise or two. Stephen Tyng, one of the most radical of the evangelicals, published a pamphlet supporting Onderdonk's action, *A Letter Sustaining the Recent Ordination of Mr. Arthur Carey* (New York, 1843). In it, Tyng argued that if Carey's ordination were deemed invalid by some bishops, other bishops would have the right to refuse to ordain anyone whose theology they happened to dislike. This would lead to a "patchwork church." Tyng was no friend of Tractarianism, he was trying to protest the Evangelicals' position in the church by support-

ing Onderdonk's right in this matter. John Henry Hopkins, the High Church bishop of Vermont, published *The Novelties Which Disturb Our Peace* (Philadelphia, 1844), protesting Carey's ordination.

87. Smith and Anthon, *True Issue for the True Churchman*, 43.

88. [McIlvaine] "Scrutator," "Notes on the Case Presented by Drs. Smith and Anthon," *Episcopal Recorder* (July 29, 1843): 74.

89. This controversy is described by Robert W. Shoemaker, *The Origin and Meaning of the Name "Protestant Episcopal"* (New York, 1959), 187–200. Shoemaker's account covers the whole history of the debate between Protestant and Catholic conceptions of Anglicanism, is heavily biased in favor of his ecclesiastical agenda promoting a twentieth-century name change, and is not always fair to Evangelicals.

90. *Journal of the Diocese of Ohio* (Gambier, 1843): 33–34.

91. R.S.K., "An Address to the Protestant Episcopal Church of the Diocese of Ohio," *Episcopal Recorder* (August 20, 18424): 89.

92. Ibid.

93. Ibid., 90.

94. Charles P. McIlvaine, *The Chief Danger of the Church in These Times: A Charge Delivered to the Clergy of the Diocese of Ohio* (New York, 1843), 20.

95. McIlvaine, *Holy Catholic Church*, 38–39.

96. See Powell Mills Dawley, *The Story of the General Theological Seminary. A Sesquicentennial History, 1817–1967* (New York, 1969), 145–179; Walworth, *Oxford Movement in America*, 133–145; and E. Clowes Chorley, "The Oxford Movement in the General Theological Seminary," *Historical Magazine of the Protestant Episcopal Church* 5 (1936): 177–201. McIlvaine was involved in this investigation and probably wrote a number of the questions to the faculty. In the McIlvaine papers at Kenyon College there exists a list of the questions in McIlvaine's own hand.

97. The case against Benjamin T. Onderdonk elicited stronger public debate than that against his brother, and there is a great deal of material surrounding his trial. See in particular *The Proceedings of the Court Convened for the Trial of the Rt. Rev. Benjamin T. Onderdonk* (New York, 1845); Benjamin T. Onderdonk, *A Statement of Facts and Circumstances Connected with the Recent Trial of the Bishop of New York* (New York, 1845); John Jay, *Facts Connected with the Presentment of Bishop Onderdonk: A Reply to Parts of the Bishop's Statement* (New York, 1845); Charles King, *Review of the Trial of the Rt. Rev. B. T. Onderdonk* (New York, 1845); *No Church Without a Bishop, or, A Peep into the Sanctuary! Being a Succinct Examination of the Right Rev. B. T. Onderdonk, Bishop of New York . . . by a High Churchman* (Boston, 1845). A good secondary source is E. Clowes Chorley, "Benjamin Treadwell Onderdonk, Fourth Bishop of New York," *Historical Magazine of the Protestant Episcopal Church* 9 (1940): 1–51.

98. For example, McIlvaine's participation in the General Theological Seminary case and the Onderdonk trial have been pictured by historians as a result of his anger over an unfavorable book review given his *Oxford Divinity Compared* in the *Churchman*. According to this interpretation, McIlvaine wanted to get revenge on Bishop Onderdonk of New York. This idea seems to have begun with Richard G. Salomon's "The Episcopate on the Carey Case: new Sources from the Chase Collection at Kenyon College," *Historical Magazine of the Protestant Episcopal Church* 18 (1949): 240–281. It is repeated in Dawley, *Story of the General Theology Seminary*, 149.

Hard feelings existed between McIlvaine and both of the Onderdonk brothers, but it was not simply the case of wounded ego on McIlvaine's part. Henry Onderdonk had attacked McIlvaine in 1827 over his "half" churchmanship, and both Onderdonks conspired to keep the young minister out of the diocese of New York. In 1821, Benjamin

Onderdonk criticized McIlvaine's liturgical practices in a curt series of letters. In the McIlvaine collection at Kenyon College: B. T. Onderdonk to McIlvaine, October 10, 1832, and October 12, 1832; McIlvaine to Onderdonk, October 15, 1832; Onderdonk to McIlvaine, no date, file 321322; McIlvaine's "Explanation of This Correspondence," no date file 321332a. McIlvaine was clearly bothered by the bishop's admonitions – especially since, at the very same time, Onderdonk was busy rallying the opposition to McIlvaine's election to Ohio's episcopate. No wonder McIlvaine did not like the Onderdonk brothers. for fifteen years they questioned his ministry, attempted to block his appointments to churches, refused to validate his election to the episcopacy, and criticized his churchmanship.

99. all quotes this paragraph from Lyman Beecher, *A Plea for the West*, 2nd ed. (Cincinnati, 1835), 9. 54, 56–57, 61, 85–86.

100. *A Debate on the Roman Catholic Religion: Held in the Sycamore-Street Meeting House, Cincinnati . . . Between Alexander Campbell and the Rt. Rev. John B. Purcell* (Cincinnati, 1873). This must have been quite a spectacle to the Evangelical Episcopalians since they considered both Campbell and Purcell heretical.

101. Walworth, *Oxford Movement in America*, 168. Richards later left the Episcopal Church and was received into the Roman Catholic Church on January 25, 1852.

102. See Smythe, *History of the Diocese of Ohio*, 247–249.

103. In the *Journal of the Diocese of Ohio* (Mt. Vernon, Ohio, 1846): 29–54. Later reprinted separately as Charles P. McIlvaine, *Reasons for Refusing to Consecrate a Church Having an Altar Instead of a Communion Table* (Mt. Vernon, Ohio, 1846).

104. Preceding quotes from McIlvaine, *Reasons for Refusing*, 3.

105. The argument about "taste" provides some clues about the Evangelical truce with the older High Church party. Evangelicals may have regarded some High church practices under the rubric of "taste." Therefore, while Evangelicals might have objected to various devotional practices, they regarded them as having insignificant doctrinal content. The arguments over taste should not obscure the fact that the early English reformers objected to altars on the basis of doctrine. See, for example, Thomas Cranmer, "The Council's Letter to Bp. Ridley to Take Down Altars and Place Communion Tables in Their Stead" and "Reasons Why the Lord's Board Should Rather be After the Form of a Table Than of an Altar," in *Miscellaneous Writings and Letters of Thomas Cranmer*, Parker Society ed. (Cambridge, 1846). McIlvaine was fully aware of this tradition and used it in his own polemic against altars.

106. Preceding quotes from McIlvaine, *Reasons for Refusing*, 5.

107. Forty clergy voted to support the bishop and only two against, one being Richards himself. *Journal of the Diocese of Ohio* (1847): 9.

108. All quotes this paragraph from McIlvaine, *Reasons for Reusing*, 5, 11–14.

109. Ibid., 14.

110. Chorley, "Benjamin Onderdonk," 17.

111. Manross, *History of the Episcopal church*, 280–281.

112. Anna Pierrepont to McIlvaine, January 24, 1845, in McI, Kenyon College, 450124.

113. All quotes this paragraph from Ibid.

114. For purity and female spirituality during this period, Barbara Welter's "The Cult of True Womanhood: 1820–1860," *American Quarterly* 18:2 (1966): 151–174, remains the standard.

115. See, for example, *No Church Without a Bishop*.

116. Pierrepont to McIlvaine, note 112.

117. James Richmond, *The Conspiracy Against the Late Bishop of New York Unravelled* (N.p.), 5.

118. *No Church Without a Bishop*, 32

119. Preceding quotes from Pierrepont to McIlvaine, note 112.

120. The best study on family piety and the home in nineteenth-century America is Colleen McDannell, *The Christian Home in Victorian America, 1840–1900* (Bloomington, Ind., 1986). For Episcopal home piety in particular, see pages 80–81.

121. Pierrepont to McIlvaine, November 1, 1845, in McI, Kenyon college, 4511101.

122. Ibid.

123. Ibid.

124. Preceding quotes from Pierrepont to McIlvaine, April 1, 1847, in McI, Kenyon College, 470401.

125. Pierrepont to McIlvaine, July 1, 1847, in ibid., 470701.

126. Pierrepont to McIlvaine, n.d., in ibid., 471332.

127. Pierrepont to McIlvaine, August 10, 1849, in ibid., 490810.

128. Barbara Leslie Epstein, *The Politics of Domesticity: Women, Evangelicalism and Temperance in Nineteenth-Century America* (Middletown, Conn., 1981).

129. Pierrepont to McIlvaine, April 6, 1847, in McI, Kenyon College, 470406.

130. An example of the good relationships between Evangelical Episcopalians and other evangelicals is found in *Forty Years' Familiar Letters of James W. Alexander, D.D.* (New York, 1860). Alexander, a Presbyterian church leader, suggested to a friend that an Evangelical Episcopalian ought to preach on behalf of a voluntary society board of directors because they were well liked by everyone. "Some active, zealous, affectionate Episcopalian . . . would encounter least prejudice, yet great talent or eloquence would not be thrown away. . . . I should feel an emotion of more than common joy, if I could hear that Dr. Tyng, Mr. Suddards, and a few such men, had made an arrangement to five sermons" (282).

131. *Journal of the Diocese of Ohio* (1841): 23.

132. Ibid., 23–24.

133. For a comparative work on these schisms, see C. C. Goen, *Broken Churches, Broken Nation: Denominational Schisms and the Coming of the American Civil War* (Macon, Ga., 1985), and H. Shelton Smith, *In His Image, But . . . Racism in Southern Religion, 1790–1910* (Durham, N.C., 1972). For the Presbyterians, see Marsden, *Evangelical Mind and Presbyterian Experience*; for the Methodists, see Emory S. Bucke, Ed., *The History of American Methodism*, Vol. 2 (New York, 1964).

134. *"One Faith": or Bishop Doane vs. Bishop McIlvaine on Oxford Theology; Exhibited in Extracts from Their Writings . . . by a Presbyterian* (Burlington, 1843). To emphasize his point, "Presbyterian" printed two Bible verses on the cover: "One Lord, one Faith, one Baptism" (Eph. 4: 5) and "I hear that there be division among you; and I partly believe it" (I Cor. 11: 18).

135. *"One Faith,"* 3.

136. Ibid., 66.

137. Ibid.

138. Ibid., 67.

139. For a summary of Barnes's quarrels with Episcopalians, see Edward Bradford Davis, "Albert Barnes, 1798–1870: An Exponent of New School Presbyterianism" (Th.D. diss., Princeton Theological Seminary, 1961), 252–273.

140. Albert Barnes, *The Scriptural Argument for Episcopacy Examined* (New York, 1835).

141. All quotes this paragraph from Albert Barnes, *The Position of the Evangelical Party in the Episcopal Church*, 3rd ed. (Philadelphia, 1844), 21, 9, 30.

142. All quotes this paragraph from ibid., 331, 50, 59, 63, 68.

143. Barnes, *Position of the Party*, 69.

144. Ibid., 28.

145. The *Reply* appeared in serial form in the *Episcopal Recorder* in March and April 1844 and was published later as *Remarks on Mr. Barnes' Inquiry into the Position of the Evangelical Party in the Episcopal Church* (Philadelphia, 1844), 1. From evidence elsewhere, it was most likely written by Stephen Tyng.

146. Preceding quotes from ibid., 12, 11.

147. Ibid., 18.

148. *Remarks on Mr. Barnes' Inquiry*, 18.

149. Ibid., 35.

150. Ibid., 36.

151. Ibid.

152. Preceding quotes from ibid., 37–38, 40.

153. Ibid., 40.

154. Preceding quotes from Albert Barnes, *Reply to a Review of the Tract on the Position of the Evangelical Party in the Episcopal Church* (1844; reprint Philadelphia, 1875), iv, 31.

155. [G. W. Ridgely,] *An Examination of Mr. Barnes' Reply to the Episcopal Recorder by One of the Editors* (Philadelphia, 1844), 27.

156. All quotes this paragraph from ibid., 118, 117, 120, 123, 129–144.

157. All quotes this paragraph from Charles Hodge, Review of "The Position of the Evangelical Party in the Episcopal Church," *Princeton Review* (April 1844): 319, 323, 324.

158. Ibid., 319.

159. Ridgely reports on the popularity of this song with "solemn Presbyterian Elders" in a litany of anti-Episcopal persecution in *Examination of Barnes' Reply*, 6–7.

160. For William Meade and the early development of these societies, see John Johns, *A Memoir of the Life of the Rt. Rev. William Meade, D.D.* (Baltimore, 1867), 204–252.

161. [Charles Wesley Andrews,] *An Apology. The Protestant Episcopal Society for the Promotion of Evangelical Knowledge: Its Origin, Constitution, Tendencies and Work* (New York, 1854), 6.

162. *Statement of the Distinctive Principles of the Protestant Episcopal Society for the Promotion of Evangelical Knowledge* (New York, 1850), 26.

163. But it continued to be *inferred* that other Protestants had less than fully biblical ministrations in their visible communications.

164. *Statement of Distinctive Principles*, 41.

165. *Perversion* was the nineteenth-century term used to describe a conversion to Roman Catholicism. For more on Ives, see Michael T. Malone, "Levi Silliman Ives: Priest, Bishop, Tractarian and Roman Catholic Convert" (Ph. D. diss., Duke University, 1970).

166. There were four notable defenses: [Andrews,] *Apology*; John Seeley Stone, *Christian Toleration: A Sermon Before the New York Auxiliary to the PESPEK* (New York, 1849); [J. A. Shanklin,] *Some Objections to the Episcopal Church Considered and Answered* (New York, 1858); and *Evangelical Religion in Its Historical Connection with the Church of England and the Protestant Episcopal Church: A Letter to a Friend* (New York, 1857).

5

Standing Up for Jesus: The Evangelical Episcopal Quest for Purity, 1853–1865

On Tuesday, April 13, 1858, the Rev. Dudley Atkins Tyng, son of Stephen Tyng, got up from his books and left his study for a brief walk. He entered his barn to watch some of his servants operating a mill. Unnoticed by him or his servants, the sleeve of his gown caught in a cogwheel of the machine. Before anyone could stop the mechanism, Tyng's right side was crushed between the gears. "The cogs," recalled his father, "had ground the flesh from the bone, from the elbow to the shoulder."[1] For a week, doctors tried to save the young minister—having amputated his arm—to no avail. Six days later, on Monday, April 19, Dudley Tyng died.

Dudley Tyng was nearly as famous as his father as an evangelical leader in the Episcopal Church. He had been rector of parishes in New York, western Virginia, Ohio, and Pennsylvania. In Ohio, he led Cincinnati's prestigious Christ Church, the parish church of Bishop McIlvaine. There McIlvaine befriended the son of one of his closest friends, and the younger Tyng preached a clear evangelical and anti–Oxford Movement theology. He gained fame for his "pulpit presence and eloquence."[2] In 1854, he was honored with a call to a former parish of his father's, the well-known evangelical parish, Philadelphia's Church of the Epiphany.

In Philadelphia, in 1857 and early 1858, Dudley Tyng was at the center of a massive revival that was sweeping the east coast. He was one of the founders of the YMCA and shared in the leadership of the revival prayer meetings and preaching services at the association.[3] In spring 1858, when the revival was at its height, the gruesome accident killed Tyng. Among his last words was a message for the revival participants. "Tell them," he implored his father, "let us all stand up for Jesus."[4]

Tyng's sensational funeral attracted so many people that it had to be held in the Concert Hall on Chestnut Street rather than a church. Bishop McIlvaine conducted the liturgy and preached the sermon, and a number of non-Episcopal clergymen testified as to Tyng's influence in the revival. Tyng's last words, "Stand up for Jesus," were repeated throughout the service. A reporter for the *Boston Courier* wrote:

> A noble standard-bearer of the cross has fallen upon the battle-field, but his last words of divine cheer will still multiply in power in every Christian heart. No more touching incident has ever met an eye, in the range of Christian biography, than is presented in the dying moments of this young soldier of the cross.[5]

136

Tyng's friend and fellow revival worker, Presbyterian George Duffield, captured the emotions of his friend's death in a poem, "Stand Up for Jesus." The first stanza ran:

> Stand up, stand up, for Jesus,
>   Ye soldiers of the cross!
> Lift high his royal banner!
>   It must not suffer loss:
> From victory unto victory
>   His army shall he lead;
> Till every foe is vanquished,
>   And Christ is Lord indeed.

Shortly thereafter, it was set to music and became one of the most popular and well known of all nineteenth-century revival hymns.[6]

These words, written to commemorate the death of an Episcopal priest, reflect the growth of northern evangelical triumphalism in the years preceding the Civil War. Although written by a New School Presbyterian minister, Dudley Tyng no doubt shared similar sentiments. The hymn points toward a change in the priorities of the Evangelical party. In the 1820s and 1830s, before the Oxford Movement, McIlvaine and his colleagues were preoccupied by questions of unity, peace, and church order; in the 1840s and 1850s, after the Oxford Movement, they become absorbed by questions of institutional and ideological purity. Because of the Oxford Movement, they lost confidence in the Episcopal Church. The need to "vanquish every foe," therefore, grew out of a real desire to purify their compromised church. In the 1850s, Evangelical Episcopalians became preoccupied with perfectionistic dreams, and they could no longer tolerate compromise of any kind. For them, compromise became identified with sinfulness, error, and evil. No evangelical could tolerate such things. As God purified the heart, so must he purify the church. Eventually, Evangelical Episcopalians extended their quest for purity to national political life. Jesus, they believed, must finally and completely be Lord of all.

Loss of Confidence: The Episcopal Church

In the 1820s and 1830s, Evangelical Episcopalians and High Church Episcopalians worked out a common identity for the Episcopal Church based on their shared ideas of church order. Against a backdrop of extreme evangelical revivalism, moderates of both parties agreed that the polity of the Episcopal Church was a divinely appointed "check" against religious extremism. The Episcopal Church, they argued, was an ark of refuge in American religious culture. Its unity and peace offered protection from the religious chaos of the day.

In the 1840s, this coalition fell apart during the controversies over the Oxford Movement. Evangelicals believed that Oxfordism deviated from true Anglicanism and was little more than a Roman Catholic plot to undermine the Protestant mission of the Episcopal Church. Although some High Churchmen agreed with this interpretation, many were reluctant to condemn the movement outright. Some were rather mild in their criticism, and some even supported it wholeheartedly. Thus, in the 1844 General Convention, Evangelicals were unable to secure a majority of votes in order to censure Tractarianism. Although they were initially successful in stemming the movement, without the help of the "old-fashioned" High Church party, they never could completely eradicate it. They felt betrayed and deserted by the High Church party's political manipulation of the national church.

Dudley Tyng articulated this sense of betrayal in a pamphlet he published anonymously while rector of Christ Church, Cincinnati. In *Vital Truth and Deadly Error*, Tyng argued that two erroneous theological systems actually existed in the Episcopal Church. By identifying two errors, Tyng elaborated on *Oxford Divinity Compared* in which McIlvaine had only identified one: Tractarianism. The first error—Tyng called it *legal Christianity*—was a system in which justification occurred at baptism and Christians were required to obey moral law in order to gain complete acceptance with God. Tyng identified legal Christianity with the views of "old-fashioned High Churchmen." McIlvaine had not attacked these views in *Oxford Divinity Compared*; he had disagreed with High Church ideas, but he did not question their right to exist within the Episcopal Church. The second erroneous view—he called it *ceremonialized Christianity*—was a system in which a person was saved not by morality but by the sacraments of the church. This Tyng identified with the newer Oxford Movement. The first system, he believed, if carried to its logical extreme, would result in Unitarianism; there would be no real need for Christ's atonement in a system of morality. The second, he argued, would result in popery. "Thus, it is," he concluded, "that there must ever be . . . two false systems claiming each to be the way of life."[7] Tyng's modification of McIlvaine was significant: whereas McIlvaine tolerated older High Churchmanship, Tyng argued against it. According to his analysis, the Evangelical party now faced two enemies in Episcopal ranks: both High Churchmen and Tractarians.

Both systems, Tyng believed, were that "which the Apostle Paul has condemned as 'another Gospel.' "[8] The only true gospel in the Episcopal Church was being taught by the Evangelicals: a gospel of total trust on Jesus for salvation—not works and not sacraments. Yet all three "gospels" were held by different members of the Episcopal Church. This worried Tyng. Could one church contain three gospels? It could not. "If those who hold them are true to their own principles," Tyng concluded, controversy was inevitable:

> It is impossible that these different systems should consent to live together in fraternal and equal communion. They are as opposite as light and darkness. The only way in which they could be held without collision, would be for the advocates of each to become wholly indifferent to truth and error. . . . It is in vain for well-meaning men to entreat for peace. Even peace is less important than truth. And 'the wisdom which is from above must be *first pure*, then peaceable.'[9]

He blasted the fiction of a unified Episcopal Church, calling it a body full of "serious diversities of doctrine." It had been a mistake to make peace with the High Church party; the "peace spirit" had allowed error to grow unopposed. "The only way," Tyng urged, "to prevent the continued increase of this mischief, is to 'put the battle in array' between truth and error."[10]

The early 1850s were not particularly good years for the Evangelicals. Although they believed that Bishop Ives's conversion to Rome had proved their point (that Oxford theology would always end in Roman Catholicism), they were convinced, to their complete consternation, that Ives would not be the last Episcopal clergyman to convert to the Roman church. From 1817 to 1858, more than thirty Episcopal ministers left the church for Rome. Of those conversions, seventeen occurred in the years 1850–1853. That many of these converts came from Evangelical backgrounds was extremely unsettling.[11] In 1853, the year of Tyng's pamphlet, it probably appeared to Evangelical Episcopalians that Ives's conversion might be part of an unstoppable hemorrhage. It was almost as if, in their own insecurity, they failed to see how much power they held in the church. Failing to recognize the position of the moderate Evangelicals, they began to push their cause to the limits.

Evangelical insecurity was evident in McIlvaine's 1853 address to Ohio's diocesan convention. After announcing that Ives had "embraced the apostasy of Rome," he lamented that a number of Episcopal clergy had done the same. Ives, McIlvaine said, "is only, *at present,* the last of those who, having been thus confident, have been seduced by the very dangers they derided, and have fallen over the very precipice which they would not believe to be near."[12] McIlvaine decried the duplicity of such ministers:

> Have they not gone on keeping up the profession, eating the bread, occupying the pulpit of the Protestant ministry, long after they had secretly, but entirely, renounced in heart and mind the Protestant Gospel? And have they not continued thus disguised, and thus knowingly deceiving, till it was *convenient* to appear in their true colors; so that the marvel appeared, of men who *yesterday* were Protestant ministers, in all appearance and profession . . . coming forth *tomorrow* full grown Romanists: every Romish doctrine espoused . . . every Protestant doctrine rejected as false . . . ?[13]

McIlvaine clearly believed that such conversions were part of a Roman Catholic plot to subvert the ministry of the Episcopal Church. It unnerved him that Roman Catholic doctrine could grow within the heart of the trained ministry. Those most able to defend and articulate the faith, those educated at the Episcopal Church's colleges and seminaries, had publicly betrayed the very doctrine they had sworn to defend. The Ives conversion was therefore a little like a double-edged sword: it confirmed the Evangelical's criticism of the Oxford Movement, but it also proved, to them at least, that the Romanizing heresy was probably more widespread than even they suspected. How could they trust any of the church's institutions if even a bishop converted to Rome?

In this pessimistic mood the Evangelicals went to the 1853 General Convention held in New York in October. The theme that year was missions—in honor of the 150-year anniversary of the Society for the Propagation of the Gospel. McIlvaine preached the opening sermon, "The Harvest and the Labourers." In it, he bemoaned the lack of clergymen and missionaries in the church: "Was there ever a time," he asked, "since our present means of theological education were established, when the number of candidates for orders, in proportion to our churches, was less encouraging?" The Church, he accused, was lukewarm. "We have the primitive order," he reminded; "what we greatly need is the primitive spirit." He called for a new Pentecost: "Ah! What strength the Church of these days would have if, only in the spirit of prayer, it were like the Church of the Apostles' days."[14]

A sense of worry and need for renewal marked this opening sermon. A similar concerned tone permeated a proposal presented to the convention, which became known for the name of its author as the Muhlenberg Memorial. William A. Muhlenberg was the rector of New York's Church of the Holy Communion. For a time, he had been attracted to the Oxford Movement, but eventually rejected it. "I flew back," he recalled, "not to rest on the pier of High Churchism, from which this bridge of Puseyism springs, but on the solid rock of Evangelical truth, as republished by the Reformers."[15] He styled himself an "Evangelical Catholic" and won friends for himself among the Evangelicals for his anti-Tractarian pronouncements, his benevolent activities, and his interest in Protestant intercooperation.[16] Among the signers of his memorial were Evangelical leaders Gregory T. Bedell, later McIlvaine's assistant in Ohio; Alexander Vinton, Boston's most prominent Evangelical clergyman; and Charles Wesley Andrews, a Virginia rector and apologist for the Evangelical Knowledge Society.

The memorial itself was a proposal for church reform in which Muhlenberg argued for liturgical reform and a more flexible, evangelically oriented ministry. Muhlenberg shared the Evangelical's overall sense that the church's institutions were inadequate in the present crisis:

> The divided and distracted state of our American Protestant Christianity, the new and subtle forms of unbelief adapting themselves with fatal success to the spirit of the age, the consolidated forces of Romanism bearing with renewed skill and activity against the Protestant faith, and a more or less consequence of these, the utter ignorance of the Gospel among so large a portion of the lower classes of our population . . . [cause many clergymen to wonder if the Episcopal Church] is competent to the work of preaching and dispensing the Gospel . . . in this land and this age?[17]

His solution: greater flexibility of ministry and liturgy, along with an extension of episcopal powers.

It is no puzzle why the Evangelicals liked this proposal. The memorial had two ends: greater effectiveness in the work of evangelization and Christian unity; these were also the goals of the Evangelicals. For years, they had argued their right to adapt the liturgy to evangelistic needs and were frequently criticized by High Churchmen for their supposedly lax attitude toward the liturgy. McIlvaine, albeit sounding somewhat cautious, praised the memorial's attempt to "remove and relax" certain liturgical restrictions.[18] Evangelicals had also wanted more clergy: the proposal to ordain men to a sort of secondary, missionary ministry appealed to them as a practical way of allowing more preachers to spread the gospel.[19] In addition, Muhlenberg's call for unity of all Protestant churches under the form of the episcopacy resonated with their desire for union between all evangelical churches and their concern for church order. To them, Muhlenberg's proposal appeared to be an expansion of their own program and goals. From their perspective, these proposals would secure the Evangelical position within the church and limit the influence of both the High Churchmen and the Tractarians. The 1853 General Convention signified that better times might be ahead for the Evangelicals. Even Dudley Tyng was satisfied by "the very peculiar and very delightful harmony, and mutual courtesy and concession, which certainly did prevail" there.[20]

The Muhlenberg Memorial failed to inaugurate large-scale institutional change, although the General Convention did vote in a number of minor changes, including the appointment of an Episcopal commission on church unity and making McIlvaine, ever committed to ecumenism, its chair. In spite of its failure to change the institution, the memorial pointed out the deep dissatisfaction of the Evangelicals with the state of the Episcopal Church. Throughout the six years of discussion following the memorial, the Evangelicals consistently supported the need for change. High Church clergy (in general) resisted the proposal to modify the liturgy. One Maryland High Churchman proposed a "countermemorial" and argued for less flexibility and stricter adherence to Anglican doctrine and discipline.[21] While High Churchmen advanced the theory that only a more decided expression of Anglican distinctiveness could further the gospel, the Evangelicals worked to open the church to liturgical reform for the purposes of evangelism. Other Protestant evangelicals were not fond of the memorial, either. One Old School Presbyterian, while confessing a desire for Christian unity, still believed that "greater union would operate in favour of the Episcopacy"–a situation not altogether to his liking. A Baptist respondent decried the continuing elitism of the Episcopal Church and praised any possible reform that would "strike for the masses."[22] The memorial, in short, lacked support from both High Churchmen and non-Episcopal evangelicals.

In 1853, therefore, the memorial offered only small hope to the Evangelicals. They basically approved of the document, but there was no guarantee that its provisions would be accepted by the church. Immediately following the "harmonious and delightful" convention, the Evangelical Knowledge Society held its second triennial convention. Stephen Tyng preached the opening sermon– proving the "harmonious and delightful" rhetoric little more than pious sham. After defending the Protestant doctrine of the individual right to interpret the Bible and contrasting it to that of Roman Catholicism, Tyng quoted the prophet Elijah to his hearers:

> "How long halt ye between two opinions? If the Lord be God, follow him; but if Baal, then follow him." This is a question in which there is, there can be, no middle ground. We can yield, in matters unimportant and expedient merely, to peace and union, or the weakness of conscience in our brethren. But when it comes to the great question between the Lord and Baal, –between the flesh and the Spirit, –between Christian and the authority of men, –we can neither yield nor halt.[23]

The Evangelicals were in no mood for compromise on issues of churchmanship. "Far rather would I hide my face with Elijah on Carmel," concluded Tyng, "than ride with Ahab in his chariot in temporary victory over all the interests of righteousness and truth and God."[24]

There was one particular compromise galling a number of Evangelicals: the church's Domestic and Foreign Missionary Society. Although Bishop McIlvaine had won the day in 1835 with his proposal of the church as missionary society, a number of Evangelicals had always questioned this strategy. The Rev. Heman Dyer referred to the church's missions policy as a "strange blunder" and recalled the moment he first heard of the new missions society: "I was then a young man, at Gambier, Ohio. When the news reached us of what had been done, Dr. Sparrow and myself happened to be together, and we exclaimed, 'What a mistake! What a mistake!'"[25] The biggest mistake, according to Dyer, was the tacit agreement between Evangelicals and High Churchmen to divide the fields of missionary endeavor between themselves. Evidently done to secure the future of a church-based missions society, McIlvaine and Doane had unofficially agreed to assign all foreign work to the Evangelicals and all domestic missions to the High Churchmen. In 1835, this division appeared fairly even, and the parties were at peace. Over the next twenty years, the country grew rapidly by western expansion, and the High Church party had become more aggressive and "Romanized" in its views. All the new domestic missionary positions created in the west were going to bishops and priests of High Church sentiments. As a result, the High Church party was expanding into the territories, while the Evangelicals were exiled to foreign fields and in danger of becoming an isolated minority party in the national church. Of the new western dioceses created before the Civil War, only Iowa and Kansas went to the Evangelicals. The rest of the west—including the new diocese of California—was under the control of High Church bishops. Evangelical leaders clearly saw the problem and called for their party's emancipation from "all complicity with an organization which for the last thirty years has proved its greatest hindrance."[26]

In the winter of 1851, a group of troubled Evangelicals met to discuss the situation. Evangelical churches and laypeople gave a considerable amount of money to domestic missions, but when their money was directed toward such projects as the Rev. James Breck's semi-monastic, Roman-like missions in Wisconsin and Minnesota, Evangelicals began to withdraw their financial support.[27] The Evangelicals meeting that winter believed that Episcopal missions had always been an *Evangelical* project—one then being coopted by the High Churchmen to force them out of their own church. They proposed that a separate, Evangelical domestic missionary society be formed. Until such time, this group organized the Missionary Society for the West, through which they raised funds for the church's domestic missions but retained control over how their money was spent.[28]

Several clergymen who attended this meeting anonymously published a pamphlet stating their dissatisfaction with the Episcopal Church's missions: they argued that the church's unity was in name only and that missions had suffered because the two parties could never really coexist. Tractarianism, they believed, only served to bring out the already existing divisions in a church divided over the core issue of justification by faith alone. Evangelicals were separated from both High Churchmen and Tractarians. This issue was "of a more serious nature than any thing which divides the Church from Methodism, or Presbyterianism." The Domestic Missionary Society of the church was guilty of spreading a non-

Evangelical gospel: "High Churchmen have been almost exclusively employed as Domestic Missionaries. . . . Very many of them have been of the extreme Tractarian and Romanizing stamp."[29] This situation had become intolerable.

The remedy, according to the Evangelical clergymen, was a return to the voluntary principle of missions. They wished to withdraw from the church's society and form their own society based on the English Church Missionary Society. *"We say, without hesitation, that the only remedy which the case admits of, is in a return to the voluntary principle."*[30] They defended this action by appealing to the right of individual conscience for members of each party:

> Let each interest work by itself, under the laws of elective affinity. Let the right so to work be universally and freely conceded, for it is a right which the General Convention cannot justly take from the members of the Church. All Christian work cannot be done "by authority"; and it is by constantly enlarging the boundaries of authority, that authority comes to be a grievance, and a party majority becomes the real author of schism.[31]

A separate missionary society, according to High Church critics, could only result in schism. The Evangelicals responded that if a schism occurred, it actually would be the fault of the General Convention—an authority under the control of the non-Evangelicals. The Evangelicals argued that their missionary society was only a separation from a corrupt institution. Membership in an ideologically pure voluntary society was the only way to soothe the conscience of those holding evangelical convictions. Withdrawal from the missions board was the only protection *against* schism in the Episcopal Church:

> Division will not become a necessary evil, until such time as a majority in the General Convention may impose regulations or canons which would wound the consciences of the minority and bind them to that which they believe to be sinful. If such a time should ever come, the fact of the majority being found at the time to have the missionary work of the whole Church under their control, would not hinder a final separation of the parties, but the contrary. . . . Let each party be free to do good, in accordance with their own conscientious views of truth and duty, without hindrance from the other.[32]

The Evangelicals wanted to stay within the church, but they had staked out their territory. The threat was real: an Evangelical Episcopal schism was a genuine possibility.

"Of what value," asked Dudley Tyng of his Cincinnati congregation, "is the Protestant Episcopal Church, if she is not the candlestick from which shines the pure Gospel of Christ?"

> What do we care about a Bishop in California or Oregon, if he does not carry with him that saving truth which bishops were commissioned by Christ to preach? . . . The Gospel before the Church, is the great principle of Evangelical Episcopalians.[33]

As far as the Evangelicals were concerned, false doctrine was being spread by their own church. Tyng pronounced: "God forbid that they should succeed!" The clerical deputies from Ohio, reported Tyng, had told the General Convention, "we can not support you as missionaries; we can not allow you to select missionaries for us; and we can not join with you in the work of missions."[34] Only an

Evangelical missionary society would be able to salvage the preaching of a pure gospel in the Episcopal Church and avert a possible schism in the church as well.

Tyng ended his sermon on an ominous note. Referring to the 1835 compromise, he stated, "we were then completely deceived":

> And for eighteen years our Domestic Missions have been . . . spreading abroad, by contributions mainly derived from Evangelical Churches, High Church and Tractarian error, to the great dishonor and detriment of our Church, and the great injury of souls. If we are again betrayed by a foolish and false desire for union, the work of Romanizing the Church may go on again for eighteen years to come. How much more of Christian confidence and opportunity of usefulness we shall by that time have forfeited, and how many more of our "Bishops and other clergy" will have apostatized to Anti-Christ, God only can tell. If we are a divided Church, let us have the honesty to acknowledge it. Let us be true to our Master, and to the faith once delivered to the saints![35]

Even McIlvaine, one of the originators of the 1835 compromise, complained about the Domestic Missionary Society of the Church.[36] In the years before 1854, the society cut funds for missions in Ohio and directed its money to dioceses further west that had High Church missionaries. Ohio was left to fend for itself with its own Diocesan Missionary Society, a fund chronically short of money. McIlvaine praised the new Evangelical missionary fund established in 1851 for supporting Ohio missions. It had been McIlvaine's and Bishop Doane's vision that a primitive ministry, under the authority of a unified church, was best equipped to carry out the missionary work of Christ. Evangelicals believed that missionary strategy had not only failed, but had backfired on them and now compromised their position within the church. In his address to his clergy in 1854, McIlvaine implied the High Churchmen had manipulated the church's money to exclude Evangelical missions, such as those in Ohio, in favor of their own missions further west. A year earlier, it had been McIlvaine's own Ohio clergy who protested so vigorously against the Domestic Missionary Committee at the General Convention.

Now Dudley Tyng, rector of the bishop's own parish church and son of one of his closest friends, preached on the virtues of institutional purity over church unity. In the 1830s, unity with the High Church party initially secured the Evangelical's position in the church. By the 1850s, Evangelicals interpreted this part of the bargain as the right to maintain their distinctive principles. After the Oxford Movement, however, the Evangelicals felt that Tractarianism was being foisted upon them; their freedom had been betrayed and deceived by a "foolish and false" union with the High Churchmen. Charles Rockland Tyng, another of Stephen Tyng's sons, wrote:

> In this unity had been the comprehensiveness of the Church in all its history; for this, the liberty to hold their own principles and act in accordance with them, the Evangelical party alone contended. They sought by manifestation of the truth, not by legislative or judicial action, to establish the prevalence of their principles. . . . When they found, however, that the machinery of the Church was used to propagate the views which distinguished the opposing party, and they

seemed to be forced into bondage by it, the time came when they were compelled to take a stand in their own defense.[37]

The Evangelical party, insisted its leaders, had not changed. The church had changed on them. It had abandoned the old ground of unity on Christian freedom in favor of High Church "repression."

Part of the stand for evangelical freedom resulted in the formation of the American Church Missionary Society—finally organized in 1859. The Evangelicals desired to be free to preach a pure gospel. Explained Stephen Tyng:

> No longer can we permit ourselves to labor and pay for the extension and support of a system which we conscientiously believe to be fundamentally erroneous, under the plea of an external but heartless union. For this great work of spreading the Saviour's gospel, in its purity and power, by a faithful Evangelical ministry, over a large, open and unoccupied field, we are here united.[38]

Unity was still important to the evangelicals; it was still a mark of the charity and love that would reign in the millennial kingdom. But union, built on erroneous principles, had been a lie and a disaster.

Unity, they believed, could only be built on a foundation of agreement on principles. Parties holding fundamentally different doctrines could never be unified; thus, the union with the High Church had been misguided from the beginning. According to Ohio clergyman and Kenyon College professor, J. T. Brooke, it was no more than "apparent union." He asked: "If we can not hold together in a voluntary association, how can we hold together as a church? Must we not divide?" It was more important to separate and purify themselves from error than to share the Episcopal Church with non-Evangelical Episcopalians under a pretense of union. "To tolerate such error in a fellow-churchman is one thing," continued Brooke; "voluntarily to co-operate with him in promoting it is quite another matter."[39]

In spite of the rhetoric of schism, which was quite prominent in the 1850s, Evangelical Episcopalians were still unwilling to leave the church. They hoped that, by separating from some church institutions, they could purify the whole. They hoped that, by freely preaching "that sinners may be converted in heart, born again of the Spirit, and made new creature in Christ Jesus," the Episcopal Church would return to her "Evangelical and Apostolic" glory.[40] Unity was still desired, but not at the expense of an impure and compromised union. *Real* Christian union would grow out of purity, righteousness, and truth. Even the radical Brooke admitted that "imperfect church unity, allowing within its limits sincere differences . . . will result in a more rapid extension of the truth."[41] The Evangelicals maintained their right to form separate and free institutions, but they wanted to stay within the church—still believing that a unified church was a powerful evangelical witness to nineteenth-century Americans. By 1855, however, the situation was grim. From the Evangelicals' point of view, their freedom was threatened, they had been dupes of the High Churchmen, and the unity of the Episcopal Church existed as little more than a pious-sounding hope. The Episcopal ecclesiastical house was divided in every way except deed.

Loss of Confidence: The Nation

Concurrent with the Evangelical's loss of faith in the Episcopal Church was a loss of faith in the national union. The rhetoric over the possible schism in the Episcopal Church paralleled the increasing national rhetoric over a possible political division. In 1860, McIlvaine wrote to an old friend after he had visited West Point. The campus was still beautiful, reported McIlvaine, but "like the government of the country, and for the same causes, there is a running down, a decline, an unpinning of the machine."[42] By that time, it seemed that the Union would not survive without war. "But war seems, alas, too certain!" wrote McIlvaine to an English friend; "what desolations must attend it!"[43] The time for national unity at any cost had passed; a stand must finally be taken for truth and principle.

The 1850s were a time of disappointment for Evangelical Episcopalians in their church. Institutional unity was on the brink of failure, and, in response, the Evangelicals argued that only greater purity could save the church. Lost confidence in their church disillusioned Evangelicals over the desirability of compromise. A similar dynamic was at work in the nation's political institutions at the same time. In the 1850s, many Americans felt the democratic process had failed them and the democratic experiment appeared endangered. In such a setting, many northerners blamed national troubles on southern slavery and argued that the nation be made ideologically—and morally—pure. After all, how could the Constitution and America's cherished freedom be taken seriously if nearly 4 million Americans lived in bondage? Such arguments appealed to evangelical Americans whose piety had always scorned any kind of worldly compromise with sin. Northern Evangelical Episcopalians were not immune to the strength of the new antislavery arguments.[44] For them, as "Tractarian power" threatened their Christian liberty, so the growth of southern "slave power" threatened the basis of American democracy.

A series of political and social events pushed the nation toward a crisis point from the mid-1840s onward: the annexation of Texas, the Fugitive Slave Act, the publication of *Uncle Tom's Cabin*, the Kansas-Nebraska Act, the "civil war" in Kansas, the attack on Senator Charles Sumner, and the Dred Scot case—all fueled growing discontent.[45] With every concession to southern "slave power," it seemed to many northerners that America was further away from being the free republic it was meant to be. They felt dictated to by a southern minority. American politics had become an effort at preserving the union of north and south at any cost, and some northerners wondered if that cost included not only the liberty of slaves but also their own political liberty.[46] As Frederick Douglass aptly observed: "The cry of Free Men was raised, not for the extension of liberty to the black man, but for the protection of the liberty of the white."[47]

In the midst of the political turmoil, a new ideology developed in the north regarding slavery—an ideology that became the driving force behind the new Republican party. In the 1840s and 1850s, Republican ideology brought together existing antislavery thought with "the idea that slavery posed a threat to northern free labor and democratic values."[48] Not only was slavery a moral wrong, but also it undercut all the values of a progressive, democratic, and capitalistic society. As such, the south became an "alien and threatening" society whose particular institution was "an intolerable obstacle to regional and national development."[49] At the same time, many southerners rearticulated their commitment to slavery, and the two sections grew further apart.[50] Religious antislavery, free labor, and "slave power" ideologies together forged the new Republican party. While the admixture of evangelical religion and politics was different in the south, in the north, the resulting Republican political platform greatly appealed to evangelicals: for religious reasons, northern evangelicals allied themselves with the politics of Republicanism.[51]

The attitude of the Episcopal Church to slavery and the growing national crisis was as complex as the parties involved. High Church Episcopalians were extremely reluctant to condemn slavery. Their theology of church and state led them to avoid most political issues, and their disdain of evangelical reforming crusades led them to distance themselves from much antislavery agitation. In addition, they believed that the question of slavery would probably divide the church, and since the Episcopal Church was one of America's few undivided institutions, most Episcopalians felt an obligation to maintain church unity.[52] Although some High Church Episcopalians might have opposed slavery on a personal level, they nevertheless kept such issues far from their ecclesiastical life. Before the 1840s, many Evangelical Episcopalians held views similar to their High Church colleagues. They too were reluctant to enter into political issues and, in spite of their problems with the Tractarians, jealously guarded their church's unity as a witness to biblical fidelity.

The tensions of the 1840s and 1850s, however, pulled at the fabric of the Evangelical party. Although reluctant to enter politics, Evangelicals were closer to the American political mainstream than were High Church Episcopalians, and, eventually, they were forced (some more reluctantly than others) into the political fray. As north and south diverged politically, the social and political thought of the Evangelical party began to reflect the views of their respective regions. A good example of this dynamic is the development of McIlvaine contrasted to that of his friend, Virginia Bishop William Meade.[53]

In the early nineteenth century, many Evangelical Episcopalians held the view that slavery was wrong and should be abolished gradually. Leaders like McIlvaine and Meade shared similar sentiments: neither approved of slavery; both wanted to see the practice ended. They therefore worked together in the American Colonization Society (ACS). When McIlvaine served as one of its editors in the 1820s, the *Washington Theological Repertory* regularly reported on the efforts and successes of the society. Based on a British plan to resettle slaves in Sierra Leone, the ACS had been founded in 1817 with the purpose of repatriating American slaves to Africa as a means of ending slavery. Many of the early organizers of the society were Episcopalians—including Meade, who freed most of his family's slaves and publicly advocated emancipation.[54] "Slavery," wrote a close associate, "as a civil institution, was never to his taste. He had, however, no conscientious scruples as to its lawfulness, because he believed it to have been distinctly recognized, and formally legislated about, by divine authority in the Sacred Scriptures."[55] This view was typical among evangelicals. Slavery, although repugnant as a practice in a democratic society, was nevertheless permitted by biblical teaching. The ACS's plan for gradual emancipation was based on this principle of "evangelical repugnance."

As the century progressed, however, Evangelical Episcopalians, along with many other evangelicals, withdrew their support from colonization plans. The abolition movement in the north discouraged evangelical support by pointing out the moral—and racist—failures of colonization. In the south, colonization, once considered a "liberal" social experiment, became unpopular and even Meade stopped working for the society. Although his public work for colonization ceased, Meade continued to believe that repatriation to Africa was the best hope for ex-slaves. His own manumission experiment, he confessed, had failed because there were no opportunities for freed blacks in America. "If the persons freed," wrote his assistant bishop, "were to remain in this country . . . [Meade] decidedly advised against it."[56] By the 1840s and 1850s, having abandoned all but his personal hopes for emancipation, Meade preached a gospel of southern evangelical duty toward slaves and the obedience of servants to masters. His views were still considered rather liberal in the increasingly reactionary south, however: he praised the Africans for their sensitivity to the gospel, and he condemned slaveholders who denied the humanity of their slaves. Meade even included a prayer in his *Manual of Devotion*, which asked of God on behalf of slaves: "Convince me of sin if I be wrong in retaining them another moment in bondage."[57]

Meade's conservative, but still compassionate, gospel of "happy, contented and faithful servants" contrasted sharply to the beliefs of other southern Evangelical Episcopalians. Bishop Polk of Louisiana, McIlvaine's beloved West Point convert, for example, owned over 300 slaves. Northern Evangelical Episcopalians were not at all convinced that Polk even treated his slaves with Christian compassion. William Jay commented rather snidely to abolitionist Gerrit Smith that "Polk had more unpaid laborers than any other bishop in the world."[58] Southern Evangelical Episcopalians largely accepted the "necessity" of slavery. Some, like Meade, believed in the hierarchy of master and slave they found in the Bible, but they nevertheless tried to mitigate the worst excesses of the practice by urging masters to convert, baptize, and confirm their slaves. Others, like Polk and an anonymous writer in the Petersburg *Democrat*, accused Meade of speaking about slavery "in a way calculated unduly to elevate the slaves, socially and politically, and of course to render them dissatisfied and lead to insurrection."[59] The south as a whole, however, had moved in a substantially conservative direction, so that even the views of Meade appeared liberal and threatening to some. Evangelical Episcopalians were not immune to the spread of southern conservative thinking on slavery. As socially prominent as they were in the south, they were among the leaders of the reactionary trend.[60]

Although there is only scattered evidence as to his exact thinking on the subject, McIlvaine ultimately rejected colonization. Two factors—the influence of Anglican Evangelicalism and the personal persuasion of antislavery friends—probably influenced his change of mind. First, in 1830, he attended the great anniversary meeting of the British Antislavery Society and met William Wilberforce. He and his friend James Milnor were much impressed by the practically canonized evangelical saint. "The anniversary meeting of the Antislavery Society," wrote Milnor's biographer, "was a scene of most intense excitement." McIlvaine and Milnor had "to force their way through the dense crowd" to hear Wilberforce, "the distinguished champion of African liberty" speak.[61] When McIlvaine visited Hannah More in June, she pressed him on the issue of slavery, an issue that interested her greatly.[62] In 1833, the long, hard work of the British evangelicals finally culminated in the British Slavery Abolition Act. McIlvaine's Anglican Evangelical friends were appalled by American slavery, and they no doubt encouraged McIlvaine to reject colonization and become more vigorously opposed to slavery.[63]

A second factor was probably McIlvaine's developing correspondence with William Jay.[64] McIlvaine certainly knew of Jay, the most well-known Evangelical Episcopal antislavery activist, but the two men did not become friends until the 1840s, after Jay wrote to McIlvaine praising *Oxford Divinity Compared*. As early as 1835, Jay condemned the American Colonization Society's refusal to repudiate slavery. Its true tendency, he argued, was in "vindicating and prolonging slavery, and in augmenting the oppressions of the free blacks."[65] Slavery was sin, and sin must be abolished. "Yet of this system," accused Jay, "the Episcopal Church is a mighty buttress, and certain of her bishops its reckless and unblushing champions."[66]

Bishops Ives, Hopkins, Freeman, and Onderdonk, all High Churchmen, were objects of Jay's particular scorn.[67] At this point, Jay made a connection that probably proved quite compelling in drawing northern Evangelical Episcopalians toward the antislavery position. In *Oxford Divinity Compared*, McIlvaine had linked theories of justification to sanctification and proved, to Jay's satisfaction, that only a pure Protestant doctrine of justification by faith alone could sustain holy and righteous Christian living. "A dependence on rite and ceremonies," wrote Jay to McIlvaine, "has very little connection with holiness of life."[68] Roman Catholicism itself bound the free individual and inculcated sinful rather than holy behavior. Evangelicals rejected the Oxford Movement on the grounds that it was a system of slavery. It only followed, Jay believed, that Romanist-leaning bishops, with their weak understanding of sin, salvation, and holy living, would refuse to speak out against the wickedness of human bondage. To him, slavery was yet another example of Tractarian immorality. During Bishop Onderdonk's trial, Jay accused Onderdonk of "Puseyism, proslavery and immorality"—crimes inseparably linked by Onderdonk's Tractarian theology.[69] Using the rhetoric of sin and slavery, some Evangelicals eventually made a connection—whether one actually existed or not—between the spiritual bondage of "Romanism" and the actual bondage of black men and women.

This argument did not play well in the largely evangelical south, and it poignantly proved that northern and southern Evangelicals had diverged in their social and political views. While the southerners retained their historic "hands-off" policy toward political matters, northern Evangelicals slowly and reluctantly entered into the political arena, believing that their Christian commitment demanded such action. Within the Episcopal Church, the southerners had defended Protestant evangelicalism as aggressively as their northern colleagues. They stood together in favor of conversion and holiness and together against Tractarianism. Yet slavery, with all its regional and political implications, drove the Evangelicals apart. More moderate leaders like McIlvaine, sensitive to the implications of Jay's argument, rarely linked Tractarianism to slaveholding. When ecclesiastically convenient, however, some northerners did not fail to condemn both slaveholders and Tractarians on this sort of moral ground. In reality, Jay's argument was probably wrong anyway: more southern Evangelicals held slaves than the northern bishops who supported their right to do so. The "moral failure" of slavery arose out of certain political and social views rather than out of nonevangelical piety. Jay was right, however, in pointing out a linkage between the two: that link was the fear, almost a paranoia, that both movements created within the worldview of northern Evangelicals. By the 1850s, the northerners were convinced that both the church and their country were being dictated to by powerful, aristocratic, and nondemocratic minorities—Tractarians and slaveholders—whose agendas could destroy Christian and political liberty.

Probably more important than Jay in McIlvaine's antislavery evolution was his close friendship with Salmon P. Chase. Chase, the Ohio antislavery leader, Free Soil party organizer, presidential candidate, and senator and Republican governor of Ohio, was an Evangelical Episcopalian. The nephew of Bishop Philander Chase, he grew up in his uncle's strict and pious evangelical home. As a teenager, young Chase entered Dartmouth College, where during an 1826 revival, he experienced conversion. He wrote to a friend: "It has pleased God in his infinite mercy to bring me to the foot of the cross and to find acceptance through the blood of His dear Son."[70] Chase was active in his own Episcopal parish in Cincinnati, in Sunday schools, the Bible cause, and temperance reform.[71]

Political historian Eric Foner has maintained that Chase was the single most important individual in transforming 1830s antislavery moral activism into the 1850s primary national political issue: "He helped develop the idea that southern slaveholders organized politically as a Slave Power, were conspiring to dominate the national government, reverse the policy of the founding fathers, and make slavery the ruling interest of the republic."[72] Chase—with his persuasive political power and savvy combined with his religious beliefs—served as a linchpin holding together the worlds of Republicanism and evangelicalism. In the 1840s and 1850s, he both created and embodied the politicization of evangelical antislavery ideology. During that same period, Charles McIlvaine and Chase corresponded discussing slavery, church affairs, and, eventually, Republican politics. Chase's Evangelical Episcopalianism and his relationship with McIlvaine provided a natural door for the entrance of Republican ideology into the leadership center of the Evangelical party in the Episcopal Church.

Writing on June 29, 1843, McIlvaine admitted to being as revolted as Chase over the refusal of the diocese of Pennsylvania to admit black ministers and lay delegates to seats at their convention.[73] Just one month earlier, the Pennsylvania convention, led by High Church bishop and McIlvaine's old nemesis, Henry U. Onderdonk, had passed the following resolution:

> No church in this diocese in like peculiar circumstances with the African Church of St. Thomas, shall be entitled to send a clergyman or deputies to the Convention, or to interfere with the general government of the church.[74]

McIlvaine reported to Chase that this had so angered him that at the recent Board of Missions meeting he "took occasion to declare what has always been on my mind" on the issue of slavery. Evidently, McIlvaine came down hard against the issue, and he tried to force the board to condemn a recent article in their publication, the *Spirit of Missions*, which suggested the Episcopal Church start a kind of slave trade to support mission schools.[75] The *Spirit of Missions* article suggested that the church buy a plantation, have slaves work it, and pay them so they could eventually buy their own freedom. Any profit from the plantation would go to missionary projects. This plan resembled older schemes of colonization. That McIlvaine objected to it demonstrated his complete rejection of colonization to end slavery. By the early 1840s, he was attempting to deal with the problem of slavery in new ways.

McIlvaine was only partially successful in taking the missions board to task, however. Although the article was "universally condemned" by the board in private, the public pronouncement was mild.[76] The editor was blamed for the article, and the board disclaimed responsibility for its inclusion in the magazine; they did not condemn the plan itself. William Jay pointed out that to do so would offend the southern bishops—particularly Polk and Elliot—and he publicized the embarrassing position of the Episcopal Church's Board of Missions in the pages of the *Emancipator*.[77]

While McIlvaine condemned the *Spirit of Missions* article, the Evangelical diocese of Rhode Island took a more radical step and protested Pennsylvania's action by admitting four African-American laymen to their diocesan convention. Rhode Island had recently elected J.P.K. Henshaw as its bishop; Henshaw had long supported the ordination of black ministers and had preached at an ordination service in an African Episcopal church in Baltimore. When he arrived in Rhode Island, Henshaw called his friend, the Rev. Eli Stokes, to be the second black Episcopal clergyman in Rhode Island.[78]

June 1843, therefore, was somewhat of a turning point in the worldview of some Evangelical Episcopalians. The Carey case, with all its symbolic and political importance for the fight against Tractarianism, began during that month. At the same time, a few, but significant, Evangelical Episcopal leaders begin to protest against slavery.[79] Before 1843, William Jay thought he was alone in the Episcopal battle against slavery, but afterward, he knew he had at least some support. Another Episcopalian, the Rev. E.M.P. Wells, became a vice-president of the Anti-Slavery Society.[80] Between the actions of Pennsylvania, the noxious article, and the growth of the Oxford Movement, a small number of influential Evangelical Episcopalians became increasingly offended at the treatment and situation of American slaves.

During this period, McIlvaine's personal opposition to slavery grew in intensity. He believed that human bondage was reprehensible, though he still did not favor immediate abolition. He wanted the church and the nation to deal with the evil in some way that would ensure ecclesiastical and national unity. Unlike his old friend, Bishop Meade, McIlvaine no longer believed that slavery could be supported scripturally. The institution itself—not simply the practice—was a moral evil. As an evangelical, he could not compromise with any kind of sin. The slow divergence between the northern and southern Evangelicals became complete.

When the Republican party began, McIlvaine joined it, and his views on national unity and slavery were like those of many other mainstream Republicans. Wrote Foner: "The Republicans saw their anti-slavery program as one part of a world-wide movement from absolutism to democracy, aristocracy to equality, backwardness to modernity, and their conviction that the struggle in the United States had international implications did much to strengthen their resolve."[81] McIlvaine shared all these sentiments. To them, however, he brought some additional ideas. Slavery was not simply an international political struggle; it was part of a universal, spiritual struggle between God and Satan for the souls of all humanity. Slavery threatened the extension of God's kingdom and the progress of holiness in America. God had judged the nation and found it wanting. "We are a sinful nation," McIlvaine wrote: "we deserve to be cast down."[82] Evangelicals of all denominations added an eschatological expectation to Republican ideology: the tribulation was at hand, and Jesus' return was immanent. "We have failed," confessed McIlvaine regarding the inevitability of war, "and now it is just about time, looking at the guidances, to expect our Lord to come again to reign."[83]

In 1860, McIlvaine supported Abraham Lincoln for president. McIlvaine was never quite as liberal as Chase (and certainly not as radical as Jay), but never quite as conservative as Lincoln. Although he had not been an abolitionist, during the war McIlvaine—along with Chase—worked to convince the president to make slavery *the* issue of the conflict and urged him to emancipate the slaves on religious and moral grounds.[84]

McIlvaine's slow, but eventual, rejection of colonization and his acceptance of antislavery ideology are probably best understood within the context of his position as an Evangelical leader within the Episcopal Church. His own Evangelical party was rather evenly divided geographically between north and south, so that radical antislavery activity would split both the church and the party. If Evangelical Episcopalians split along sectional pro- and antislavery positions, the Episcopal Church would be left to the politically conservative and theologically "Romanist" High Churchmen. Most of the northern Evangelicals were in a terrible bind of conscience: whether or not to condemn slavery and lose the southern Evangelicals and, thus, open the way for increased influence and power of the Tractarianism. McIlvaine was forced to make a disturbing choice between the evils of slavery and the evils of Romanism. For some time, he seemed to conclude that the southern slaveholders—as reprehensible as they were (at least most of them were Evangelicals)—were preferable to the Tractarians. Personally strongly opposed to slavery, he tried to stay neutral in public political debates. Like most Episcopalians, he simply did not believe that it was the place of a bishop to participate in political affairs.

Even as late as 1858, when requested by Chase to sign a resolution produced by an antislavery convention in Cincinnati, McIlvaine declined. Chase knew his friend's personal feelings about the issue and was probably a little surprised by McIlvaine's refusal. "There is little difference of opinion," McIlvaine explained to Chase, "between myself and many that will sign the paper," but he refused to sign because he did not "think that good such as is sought is likely to be the result from such a convention."[85] By 1858, he had nearly given up hope that the slavery question could be solved without conflict and division, an opinion that was shared by many Americans. "We are not one people," proclaimed the *New York Tribune*; "We are two peoples. We are a people for Freedom and a people for Slavery. Between the two, conflict is inevitable."[86]

McIlvaine had already seen plenty of conflict and division in another organization, the American Tract Society (ATS). For a number of years, the society had refused to publish abolitionist literature. They defended this action by restating the organization's commitment to publish only those doctrines and issues about which all evangelical Protestants could agree. They also argued that it was the role of antislavery organizations to publish antislavery tracts. In 1853 radical antislavery evangelicals, such as William Jay, mounted an attack on the society. Jay considered silence on the issue equivalent to support.[87] But moderate antislavery evangelicals and proslavery southerners both considered the society's recommitment to its original position a victory. However, in 1858, when the publication committee decided to publish a tract called the *Duties of Masters*, southerners felt deceived and angered because the tract did not biblically *justify* slaveholding. It only argued— much like Meade's "liberal" position—that slaves should be treated with Christian compassion. While they agreed with its premise, they complained that the tract did not go far enough in support of slavery. Southern evangelicals protested loudly, and the publishing committee, feeling the pressure, decided not to print it.[88]

At the 1858 convention, McIlvaine, a vice-president of the society, delivered a stirring address in which he defended the original intent of the American Tract Society's constitution and urged the delegates to support the committee's inaction on the *Duties of Masters*. He did not do this because he supported the southern position; he genuinely believed that the society needed to stay unified. By refusing to take sides on the issue, the society was only upholding its own mandate. Argued McIlvaine:

> I do not understand that, in approving the action of the Publishing Committee, we shall be taking any ground or indicating any opinion, one way or another, on the subject of slavery. I may be the most extreme antislavery man in the land, and yet approve the action of the Committee, under the limitations of the Constitution of the Society. . . . We may write and print as we please, as members of anti-slavery societies; but as members of this catholic and national Society, we cannot, in my judgement, at present at least, go beyond the action of the Committee.[89]

McIlvaine's resolution—to support the inaction of the publication committee regarding the *Duties of Masters*—passed. The tract, with its implied condemnation of slavery, would not be published. No friend of slavery, McIlvaine nevertheless wanted to maintain the unity of the society.[90] He was extremely consistent: he still valued unity more highly than purity. For him, Christian unity—whether it be in the Episcopal Church or in the American Tract Society—was still a sign of the coming millennial glory.

Other northerners disagreed; for them purity was more important than institutional unity. Not satisfied, a number left and joined the American Tract

Society of Boston, a society that combined gospel, abolitionist, and antislavery publications. In spite of the conflict, the ATS survived and even grew in the north; however, the crisis served to remind Protestant evangelicals how near they stood to the possibility of national division. Although McIlvaine was instrumental in securing its evangelical unity, the whole episode must have made him aware of how tenuous national unity actually was. If the ATS, whose members joined voluntarily and shared a common purpose and evangelical faith, could barely hold together over the issues of sectionalism and slavery, how could the nation? This episode contributed to his growing sense of hopelessness.

After the ATS debacle, and probably (in part) because he thought the political situation increasingly bleak, McIlvaine finally became more public about his views on slavery. The seminary at Kenyon College, Bexley Hall, had its first black candidate for ordination, Mr. William Alston, as a member of the class of 1859. A controversy broke out over Alston and administration of the Lord's Supper. In the antebellum Episcopal Church, separate communion was widely practiced; blacks had to wait to take the eucharist until all white communicants in the church had been served.[91] The Bexley chaplain, not having had a black student previously, followed this convention and made Alston wait to take communion apart from his white classmates. This caused an uproar in Gambier. Recalled McIlvaine's daughter:

> On arriving [at the college], the place was much agitated because the colored man, though he was studying at the Divinity School at Gambier, was not allowed by the Chaplain to received the Holy Communion with the rest of the Divinity students when, according to custom, they presented themselves after the clergy [to be communicated], but, instead, was requested to remain until the whole white population of the place had partaken, when he, the solitary colored man, was allowed to present himself.[92]

McIlvaine was furious. The next day, he refused to preach in Gambier's chapel. Having purposely left his prayer book behind, he walked into the church and sat down next to Alston, who was sitting by himself at the back of the building. The bishop asked Alston if he would share his prayer book with him. Side by side, the two men prayed the liturgy preceding the Episcopal communion. When the time came for the Lord's Supper, McIlvaine waited until the clergy had partaken; he then stepped forward "and bidding Alston follow him, advanced and knelt at the chancel, placing the colored man by his side." Alston and the bishop took communion together, before the white students. His daughter reported: "Needless to say . . . this ended the matter."[93] Thus McIlvaine's actions at the American Tract Society need to be balanced by his action on behalf of Alston. In his own diocese, where he as bishop was the guarantor of unity, had final authority, and no one else's interests to protect, McIlvaine made it clear that before God all people—white and black—really were equal. Reluctant to make such a statement in the political realm, McIlvaine never ceased to work for the rights of black Americans within the context of his church.

By 1858, Stephen Tyng had also finally reconsidered his position on slavery. Until at least 1851, he still supported colonization—sounding much more conservative than his friend McIlvaine. In 1853, he referred to *Uncle Tom's Cabin* as "the Stowe farce" and bitterly complained that "the slavery question" had ruined all the anniversary meetings of English benevolent societies.[94] McIlvaine and his wife, Emily, attended these same meetings. Although McIlvaine's letters and correspondence indicate none of Tyng's distaste, Emily McIlvaine wrote that at the Bible society meeting "some miserable Independent minister rose and with 'Uncle Tom' in his hand, instead of the Bible, made some injudicious remarks which made me feel a good deal uncomfortable." The meeting was, nevertheless, "thrilling."[95]

Throughout the 1850s, Tyng maintained that national unity was more important than the individual injustice done to black slaves.[96] In 1858, he led the party in the ATS that opposed McIlvaine. This was somewhat ironic. McIlvaine's personal antislavery views were better pedigreed; Tyng was a recent convert to antislavery. Yet McIlvaine, ever committed to order and the establishment, sided with the strict interpreters of the ATS constitution. Tyng, always ready to bend rules, urged a reformist interpretation of the constitution. Tyng's side lost, but eventually he preached a conciliatory sermon pleading for evangelical unity—perhaps not wanting to further jeopardize his friendship with McIlvaine.

For a year, Tyng's relationship with the ATS deteriorated. In 1859, when the southerners won a victory in the society by blocking a strongly worded resolution against the slave trade, a distressed Tyng resigned and joined the abolitionist American Tract Society of Boston. In May 1860, he addressed that society praising its "calm, tranquil, and effective success . . . : We meet here this morning under a banner twofold, but never separated, the banner of purity and peacefulness. First, pure, then peaceful; first truth, then peace; first a foundation that God hath laid in Zion, then evidence that God is building up peace on that foundation." Tyng transferred the rhetoric that he had used a decade earlier to describe the crisis in the Episcopal Church over the Oxford Movement to a national political crisis. The schismatic tract society was ideologically pure and therefore peaceful. Without purity, peace was a farce. The nation (and that other, compromised and "tepid" American Tract Society, of which McIlvaine would soon become president), Tyng argued, should follow the example of the American Tract Society of Boston.[97]

Tyng's antislavery "conversion" most likely occurred as a result of the death of his son Dudley. The younger Tyng had been a vigorous temperance crusader, and he applied the same sort of reforming convictions to the practice of slavery.[98] In 1856, in an almost unheard of move, Dudley Tyng used his Episcopal pulpit to preach against slavery. Tyng preached on a litany of southern evils—a classic statement of Republican political rhetoric: "It is a mooted question how far the Christian pulpit may, and ought to be enlisted in the consideration of current events . . . [but] the Christian ministry may be criminal if it does not speak out boldly in behalf of right." Tyng denounced the violence in Kansas resulting from the nefarious Kansas-Nebraska Act. He condemned slavery being forced on the people of Kansas as an antidemocratic fraud. He accused southerners of being an "invading army, whose agents established slavery against the wishes of the people." He deplored the assault on Senator Sumner in Congress. To Tyng, these events signified the overthrow of American freedom. "How long," he wondered, if ministers keep silent, "before the freedom of the pulpit shall be also at the mercy of a popular majority or of a reckless and excitable bully?" All these incidents had one source: "the aggressive spirit of slavery."[99]

Tyng, not an abolitionist, believed that slavery should be isolated to the south. But "to strive to extend and perpetuate it" was evil. "Left to itself," Tyng argued, "it impoverishes, in the long run, both land and owner, and would gradually work out its own extermination." He condemned slave-breeding, argued that there was no natural right to hold a person in slavery, and stated that slavery lowered the moral, intellectual, and laboring character of the whole society: "The question is not whether there shall be maintained the rights of a few thousands slave-holders, but whether shall be maintained the rights of millions of freeman." The whole nation was guilty for giving into the pressure of slave power. "Whatever may be said," Tyng concluded, "in the way of temporary extenuation, slavery and human right, slavery and the Christian law of love are in irreconcilable opposition."[100] To extend such evil into the west would bring God's curse upon the whole nation.

Even though Tyng's condemnation of slavery was based more on the threatened freedom of whites than on the need to free black slaves, this was a radical sermon for Episcopalians; his congregation heard it as a purely politically speech. Their reaction proved that not all Evangelical Episcopalians were as convinced of Republican ideology as was Tyng. When the young minister returned from his summer vacation, the church was locked and closed to him. Within a few weeks, the vestry forced him to resign.[101] Some, however, agreed with him. A remnant of his former congregation split from Epiphany and founded the Church of the Covenant, an evangelical Episcopal congregation opposed to slavery and openly pro-Republican in sentiment. They called Tyng as their rector. There, freed from the constraints of his former parish, Tyng preached a damning sermon condemning slavery and the weak wills of white Americans who valued expediency over principle. This was the great tragedy of American history: "Principle and expediency were in collision." He decried the slave trade, the Fugitive Slave Act, and the "curse of bondage." He deplored that black men had been crushed "into constitutional non-entity."[102] He believed that God held America in account for these evils, as he had held Israel in account, and Tyng called for personal and national repentance. Expediency must never again triumph over principle. Compromise was the worst of all evils.

When Tyng died, he became a martyr for the antislavery cause. Wrote George Cheever: "His faithfulness in rebuking the great iniquity of slavery, and defending the claims of the colored race . . . was an example of integrity, power, and true patriotism in the pulpit." Tyng's final words, "stand up for Jesus," Cheever stated, meant "beyond all question, 'Plead, in Jesus name, the cause of the oppressed, and defend the freedom of them that are in bonds.'"[103] Stephen Tyng, grieved by the tragedy and convinced by his son's example, became vigorously antislavery. Tyng thanked God for his son's ability "to plead for the oppressed, and to rebuke the oppressor, and to accept and improve the privilege of suffering for the name of Christ."[104] After this point, the elder Tyng moved in an increasingly radical—and eventually abolitionist—direction. The men's group at Church of the Puritans praised Dudley Tyng as "a Christian hero" and pledged themselves to "stand up for Jesus" by imitating him and resisting slavery.[105]

By 1858, there were a variety of views and responses within the northern Evangelical party to slavery and the national crisis. William Jay and Salmon Chase's antislavery views were public and political. Charles McIlvaine confessed to Chase that his views were very much like Chase's, but, on most occasions, McIlvaine resisted public antislavery pronouncements. He clung to hopes for unity: national, evangelical, and Episcopal. Dudley Tyng's views were radical for an Episcopal clergyman, and, by 1856, he could no longer refrain from using his pulpit for public protest. Only after his son's troubles and terrible death did Stephen Tyng finally abandon colonization and speak out against slavery. As the lines between politics and religion blurred, all these northern leaders supported Republicanism and condemned slavery.[106]

Robert Bruce Mullin has maintained that lack of both direction and certainty guided the Episcopal avoidance of the issue of slavery.[107] As a group, this was true; however, indirection (of opinion, at least) was not the problem of a number of significant northern Evangelical leaders who held moderate-to-strong antislavery convictions. Two issues hampered their ability to mount a concerted group attack on slavery: (a) the context of the Oxford Movement and (b) the divided responses of the northern Evangelicals. Evangelicals seemed genuinely reluctant to break up their party unity over the slavery issue, but, had the Tractarian threat in the Oxford Movement not been present in the church, northern Evangelicals might not have been so inhibited. As it was, however, they judged the Roman Catholic tendencies of the Episcopal Church to be a greater problem than slaveholding. The loss of southern Evangelicals, especially the Virginians and the theological seminary in Alexandria, would be a huge setback to the Evangelical battle against Tractarianism. As the southerners moved in a more reactionary direction, party splintering became inevitable, however, and northern Evangelical caution on the issue eventually disappeared.

However united they were in their personal opinion about slavery, northern Episcopal Evangelicals were divided as to what their response should be to the problem. Two attitudes guided their actions in regard to reform. The first attitude was illustrated by Jay and McIlvaine, both of whom resisted schism (even in spite of Jay's radicalness), argued for institutional reform, and praised unity. They believed the way to change an institution was to work within it. The only organization Jay ever abandoned over the issue of slavery was the American Bible Society. In regard to the Episcopal Church, he wrote:

> I know of no church which, judged *by its authorized standards*, is more scriptural and more conducive to holiness in this life and sanctification in the next. . . . No sanction of slavery can be found in any of her standards, and hence I can very consistently hold the doctrine of the church and join in its prayers and rites and at the same time regard American slavery as the sum of all villainies. There are in the church slaveholding bishops, clergymen, and communicants, plenty of them. . . . There never has been, and I suppose there never will be, a widely extended church without unworthy pastors and members. A *pure* church composed of fallible and sinful men is a figment of the imagination.[108]

McIlvaine, repulsed as he was by southern slavery, fought to keep the both the Evangelical party and the American Tract Society together. In spite of their "no compromise" politics, both he and Jay retained the idea that complete ecclesiastical purity was not possible; unity remained a higher value to them than purity; witness to the truth from the inside was a more effective strategy than schism. In addition, McIlvaine felt a burden as a bishop and as a national leader of the Evangelical party to try to hold the church together. His close relationships with southern Evangelicals, and his almost instinctive institutional loyalty, kept his politics at a distance (at least for a time) from his religion.

The second attitude was more evident in the Tyngs. Already leaning in the direction of schism over Tractarianism, the Tyngs were quicker than McIlvaine and Jay to condemn the Episcopal Church's neutrality on slavery. Stephen Tyng, after his rapid antislavery conversion, left the ATS for the radical Boston tract society. Once he was convinced, he also became quite radical. As a New York rector, and not a bishop, Stephen Tyng had less invested in national church unity than did McIlvaine. Dudley Tyng, a young man of strong convictions and relatively minor ecclesiastical position, had no qualms about starting an antislavery Episcopal parish from the remnants of his own congregation. The Tyngs thus seemingly suffered a greater loss of confidence in the church, the evangelical societies, and the nation than did McIlvaine or Jay; they elevated ideological and institutional purity over unity and believed that it was necessary to separate themselves from all sin. Their views parallel the general trend in northern culture toward "no compromise" on ideological issues.

But none of these leaders was happy with the state of the church or the country; all had come to the conclusion that slavery was a terrible evil; all had come to wonder if the national government could solve America's problems. They all turned to the new Republican party for political hope that American freedom could be preserved.[109] "In the prospects of our country," wrote Jay to McIlvaine, "I see much to excite apprehension, and little to inspire hope." Years before Dudley Tyng, Jay had denounced a politician's "right of expediency" and political platforms that "fluctuate with every election."[110] By 1857, Evangelical Episcopalians bemoaned financial irresponsibility, party politics, the loss of freedom, and public dispiritedness.[111] The country, as McIlvaine so eloquently reported to Sylvanus Thayer, was "running down."[112]

A Sign of Hope: The Great Revival, 1858

McIlvaine had felt the country—and the church—"running down" for quite some time. In 1851, he addressed the convention of his diocese and bemoaned that a "general declension of religion has taken hold of the Christian Church, at least in our country." This address, *Spiritual Regeneration*, illustrates a genuine change in the bishop's priorities. Not since McIlvaine's first address to his convention almost twenty years earlier, did he preach an entire sermon on heartfelt religion. In his three charges between 1834 and 1851, McIlvaine had preached almost exclusively on the form of the Episcopal Church—either extolling or correcting its doctrine and order. In 1851, however, Bishop McIlvaine switched the emphasis in his preaching. He remarked on this change: "I do not undervalue the importance of those external marks and institutions of the Church which make it visible in this world. . . . They are not religion, but only its form." The time had come, he confessed, to cease preaching about external form and to once again preach on "the great common work of 'Ambassadors for Christ,' and hence with the salvation of sinners."[113] Even McIlvaine, although not calling for a schism in the church, felt a sense of the inadequacies of the external institutions of the Episcopal Church, and he, once again, turned his attention to the invisible unity of all born-again believers in Christ.

The sermon also illustrates another change in McIlvaine's thought. Throughout the 1840s, he emphasized the doctrine of justification by faith alone in his preaching and writing. In *Spiritual Regeneration*, he turned his attention to the doctrine of sanctification. The issue of holy living had certainly been present in his earlier work, and it played a significant part of his critique of the Oxford Movement. But in this sermon, he placed a stronger emphasis on the doctrine of sanctification:

> Unquestionably, the two great doctrines of the Gospel . . . are those which treat of our justification before God, and our sanctification by His Spirit. To be delivered from condemnation, so that sin is not imputed unto us, and to be delivered from the unholiness of our fallen nature, so that sin hath no dominion over us; thus to be restored to the image of God, that we may be meet for His kingdom . . . certainly, is salvation.[114]

Throughout the sermon, he emphasized the "newness" of life in Christ, the "radical transformation" of believers, and the need for the presence of the Holy Spirit in Christian life. He preached of being reborn in Christ: "There is a continual tendency in the human mind, under all names of orthodoxy, to degenerate into a low, feeble, compromising impression of the magnitude and radical extent of this spiritual change." Without these things, the church would wither. "There is needed," he urged, "a greater honoring—in our hearts, in our faith, in our ministry—of the office of the Holy Ghost as the sanctifier of sinners." He encouraged his ministers to seek "a personal, abiding, vivid experience of the work of the Spirit of God."[115] This, he believed, was the hope of all evangelical Christians. Although the Oxford Movement may have caused him to lose hope about the state of the Episcopal Church, and slavery made him a pessimist about the nation, he was more optimistic than ever about the power of personal transformation in Christ and the Holy Spirit.

In the sermon, McIlvaine backed away from the exclusive claims of the Episcopal Church and turned back to the common concerns of American evangelicals. He hoped for a revival of true Christianity; it alone was the cure for mere externalism.[116] Throughout the 1850s, he reemphasized the preparation for confirmation as a time of self-examination, repentance, and birth of "lively faith," and he urged his clergy not to present candidates who had not been born again. He argued that a "religion of externalism" would crush "religion of the heart." As a result, he fought against formal liturgical innovations such as processions and paid choirs. These things, he believed, inhibit true "spiritual worship" given in simplicity by the Holy Spirit to the whole people of God.[117]

McIlvaine's concern was contemporaneous with that of other American Protestants. As he was longing for, and preaching about, a need for a new revival, so were other evangelicals. During the 1850s, Baptists, Methodists, Lutherans, and Presbyterians all experienced a resurgence of revivalism.[118] In Ohio, McIlvaine once again preached on the need for revival and added a new emphasis on the power of the Holy Spirit and the radical, pervasive nature of sanctification.[119]

McIlvaine's renewed interest in revivalism had some effect. During Pentecost 1856, Kenyon College and the town of Gambier experienced a remarkable revival that resulted in fifty-eight confirmations. Of that number, thirty-six were students, making the number of undergraduate communicants seventy-six. Fifteen percent of all the confirmations in Ohio for the year occurred in this one small town. Three-fourths of the student body had "been truly converted to God, and changed in heart by the Holy Ghost."[120] This revival was particularly important because of the large number of men who converted; Evangelicals believed this signified a great work of God.[121] Preaching to Kenyon's students about the revival one year later, the Rev. Noah Schenk reminded them:

> You remember it was in the early summer, or rather just as spring was maturing into summer, just at the ripening of the first fruits, that the Holy Spirit came among us. . . . [The confirmation,] was a moving spectacle. . . . Near three-score souls uniting in one voice, and making covenant dedication of themselves to God. . . . How it pictured the power of the Spirit, the abounding mercy of God.[122]

This revival, Schenk asserted, was completely the work of the Holy Spirit. As the rector of Gambier parish, he had employed no means other than preaching the word.

The Kenyon revival of 1856 proved to be the first fruits of a larger revival in the diocese. Over the next four years, the diocese experienced a jump in confirmations, communicants, and missions giving.[123] The revival at the college continued through 1857 and 1858 by means of a student prayer meeting in the chapel basement. A number of these students subsequently became ministers or missionaries.[124] The revival spread throughout the diocese. In 1858, McIlvaine could rejoice with his ministers in "that blessed work of grace, which God has so mercifully and so widely and wonderfully vouchsafed to the churches of our land." Many parishes, stated the bishop, "have been greatly blessed. I pray that all may receive the power of the Holy Ghost, in such converting and sanctifying power . . . [that they] may live as they have never lived before."[125]

McIlvaine's enthusiasm was due only in part to the new fervor of Ohio Episcopalians. He had spent a considerable amount of time earlier in the year in the east raising funds for Kenyon. He arrived in Philadelphia just days after Dudley Tyng's accident, who was, he said, "to me as a son." McIlvaine conducted the funeral and preached one of the sermons. He was grateful "to see the universal grief; to feel the universal tribute; to witness scenes of united manifestation of affliction at the loss" of young Tyng.[126]

Tyng had been one of the leaders of the 1858 revival in Philadelphia. This revival began in New York the previous fall—the Fulton Street prayer meeting in

September 1857 was regarded as its inception. Throughout the winter and spring, revival interest spread through the major eastern cities and the midwest. The revival was marked by its interdenominational character, its prayer associations, and the leadership of laymen and -women. Tyng had preached and worked for "union" prayer meetings in the city, urging Christians of different denominations to unite for revival, and finally the idea caught on. In Philadelphia, huge prayer services were held in Jaynes Hall and other concert halls under the auspices of the YMCA. Tyng preached two particularly memorable sermons at the Jaynes Hall meeting to crowds of over 5,000.[127] Hearing Tyng's preaching, one person observed, as many were "slain of the Lord" as had been from "any sermon in modern times."[128] In some ways his funeral was yet another of the spring's massive revival meetings. Wrote one participant: "With the death of the lamented Tyng came a new epoch in the history of the revival. . . . The mantle of his active and fraternal spirit fell upon them all. One *in* Christ! One *with* Christ! One *for* Christ!"[129] The Evangelical Episcopal commitment to unity made an impact on this revival through the ministry of Dudley Tyng.

Even the Episcopal Church was affected by the revival. Large congregations at regular evening services of the Church of the Ascension, New York, caused the Rev. Dr. Benjamin C. Cutler, a staunch Evangelical, to remark:

> Twenty years ago such a meeting as the present one would have been denounced as Methodistical, but now [I feel] that [I] could almost say with Simeon of old, "Now, Lord, let thy servant depart in peace," for [I] had witnessed that glorious "Leviathan," the Episcopal Church, which for forty years [I] had lamented to see, with all its noble qualities and precious gifts, being fast in the stocks, at last launched and making full headway in the River that flows from the City of God.[130]

Throughout his visit to the East that spring, McIlvaine witnessed the great revival, preached when asked, and joined in united prayer meetings. When he returned to Ohio in June, he addressed his diocese and reported on the excitement of the revival. He used as his text a prophecy from Joel: "It shall come to pass in the last days, saith God, I will pour out my Spirit on all flesh." He compared the revival to the day of Pentecost and the apostolic era of the church calling it "a great and genuine work of the Spirit of God." "So far as I have had personal opportunities of observing it means, and spirit and fruits," he told his clergy, "I rejoice in the decided conviction, that it is 'the Lord's doing,' unaccountable by any natural causes, entirely above and beyond what any human device or power could produce; an outpouring of the Holy Spirit of God upon God's people."[131]

McIlvaine believed the revival genuine because it was free of means. The revivals of the 1830s, he recalled, had been produced by disingenuous preachers. In contrast, this revival simply appeared at the time of Christians' need: "Then it was just in that time of rebuke, and darkness, and apparent deep discouragement, that God's hand appeared and this present work of grace began."[132] He identified six marks which proved it was of God: (a) the "simplicity of the means," (b) the lack of "unwholesome excitement," (c) the "brotherly love and union among Christians of different evangelical denominations," (d) the high regard for clergy and the church among the participants, (e) the extent of the revival, and (f) the "respect" given to the event by those who usually disdained revivalism.[133]

Of all these evidences, McIlvaine was particularly moved by the ecumenical character of the revival's prayer meetings:

> Where brotherly love prevails, where it increases, the spirit of holiness certainly is. The true people of God are scattered through various ecclesiastical communities, under a variety of names and forms. However I may lament such dispersion and separation, I cannot but rejoice when they recognize and love one another as brethren of the same Christian family.[134]

To McIlvaine and other evangelicals, Christian union was a sign of the coming kingdom. The bishop's preoccupation with unity was evident in his private journal, as well. In a meditation on I Corinthians 7:17, McIlvaine extolled the virtues of union with Christ: "He that is joined to the Lord is one Spirit. He that is really joined to the Lord, not merely by the external bonds of visible ordinance, through an ministration, but by the invisible operation of God's grace . . . he is a 'partaker of Christ,' a member of Christ's abiding in him as 'one Spirit.' "[135] Heaven, it seemed, would be like the Jaynes Hall meetings: an innumerable crowd of people, undivided by human innovations, singing and praying in simplicity to Christ, filled with and unified by the Holy Spirit alone.

McIlvaine believed that the revival signified the near completion of the last days when the Spirit would be "poured out on all flesh." "This present revival," he proclaimed, was a "foretaste, in its diffusion, of what is to be, and must be, wider and wider, more and more wonderfully, till the whole promise" of Pentecost "is fulfilled."[136] The end of the world was very near. He confided to his English friend, William Carus, that he believed the millennium would begin in 1866. "Do not," he asked, "these revivals stand in interesting connection with that event?"[137]

In fall 1858, McIlvaine went to Europe, where he was invited by many evangelicals to speak about the revival; he encouraged them to establish union prayer meetings.[138] J. B. Sumner, archbishop of Canterbury, was so moved by these reports that McIlvaine observed: "I have seen no one in England who more entirely appreciates the Revival at home, understands it, confides in it, and sees the hand of God in it."[139] For this to be truly a new Pentecost, McIlvaine believed that the Holy Spirit must "be poured out" on all nations. Thus, for the next two years, he closely followed revival reports and encouraged his English friends; he praised revivals in England, Ireland, Scotland, and Wales as a "mark of an era," and he anticipated the continuation of the revival in America. The sedate London *Christian Observer* praised McIlvaine's tract on the revival for its sobriety and intelligence. Although the editors were reluctant to see the American revival as "the morning star of a second Pentecost, or as the ushering in of a millennium of holiness and joy," they were impressed by McIlvaine's endorsement, and they, too, praised the prayer meetings. With a modicum of British reserve, the *Observer* commended the revival to Anglican Evangelicals and encouraged them to "promote similar movements" in "our own country, parish, home, or heart."[140]

The revival in the last years of the decade was, for McIlvaine, a great sign of hope in the midst of serious ecclesiastical and national crises. More than anything else, it symbolized the unity of Christians. The Episcopal Church and the United States were unified only in name, whereas, McIlvaine believed, evangelicals were truly unified in prayer and hope. For him, unity remained a primary concern; it was the paradigm of the kingdom of God. But the locus of unity had shifted from his own communion to that of interdenominational evangelicalism. McIlvaine's movement toward panevangelicalism probably began in the late 1840s with his involvement with the Evangelical Alliance.[141] The shift away from strictly Episcopal concerns toward broader evangelical issues was evident in his 1851 clergy charge. But, at a time of institutional crisis, the 1858 revival sealed this new relationship: it brought Evangelical Episcopalians into closer contact with other evangelicals than at any other time in the century.

Northern Evangelicals and the War

If American evangelicals hoped to avert a coming disaster by means of the revival, they did not succeed. McIlvaine himself took a dim view of this possibility: although the revival was a sign of the coming kingdom, various political threats, such as the growth of Roman Catholic and Muslim empires, were also signs of Jesus' imminent return. So was the coming American war.[142] The revival was no escape; it was only a great foretaste of the coming glory. Before that time, however, as McIlvaine warned in his address on the revival, the kingdom of Satan would grow as well. "Antichrist follows Christ," he predicted, "Satan's kingdom is the more awake as that of our Lord is mighty and progressive." Some great evil; some disaster would surely follow the revival: "the more manifest the spiritual blessing, the more reason to watch against the contrary."[143] Still believing unity as a chief mark of the kingdom, disunity was a mark of Satan's work. A divided union was a fitting counterattack of the kingdom of darkness; it was part of "the great tribulation."[144] "Not Americans against Foreigners," bewailed McIlvaine after it had begun, "but Americans and Americans. Christians, Protestants, against one another. Men hitherto united together most closely not only in civil & social relations, but in the churches and in operations of Christian benevolence."[145] The division of those with a common heritage and purpose was the worst sort of evil.

McIlvaine mused on the relationship between slavery and the growing division of the country. Wrote the bishop in April 1860:

> War, I suppose, has come. I am not desirous of the recovery of the seceded states. It is a relief to get rid of that much slavery. But I would the separation could be in peace. If not, my heart is with the Sword of Govt. against a doctrine of disunion which makes all govt but a name and a doctrine of slavery the logical consequence of which is the African slave trade as a *blessing and a duty*.[146]

Although not wanting war, when it did come a year later, McIlvaine and other northern Evangelical Episcopalians (still somewhat reluctantly) joined the crusade against the south. McIlvaine was personally still convinced that slavery was the central moral issue dividing north and south, but he cited southern rebellion against the established government as the immediate cause of the war.[147] Rebellion against a duly established government was an even greater evil than that of slaveholding.[148] He elevated dedication to the Constitution – that is, nationalism – over slavery as the most crucial issue in the Union cause. He urged his own clergy to be charitable and not to preach sermons on war. "The more the trials and burdens of the public mind," he reminded his ministers, "the more important our office. . . . Remember that the appropriate subjects for your preaching are just those which at all times are the most important for sinners soon to die."[149]

McIlvaine's "stay out of politics" policy was short-lived, however. In a remarkable diplomatic endeavor, he was sent to England by Abraham Lincoln to influence the British to keep them from taking the side of the south in the conflict.[150] In itself the mission was important to the Union cause, but, in addition, this tactic illustrates a striking shift in Episcopal attitudes toward politics. In the 1850s (to a degree), and certainly in the early years of the war, Evangelical Episcopalians had become more public about their political views, and this move had prompted a mental crisis in the Evangelical party. This new involvement in secular politics cut them off from three things: (a) their own historical distance from American political affairs, (b) the High Church party who maintained an aloof attitude toward secular affairs, and (c) the southern evangelicals who had used political noninvolvement as part of their defense of slavery. During the war, northern Evangelical Episcopalians were completely drawn into Union nationalism and politics.

McIlvaine gave in to this trend. In autumn 1861, Lincoln himself contacted McIlvaine with the request to serve as part an unofficial diplomatic commission to England. The bishop was surprised and extremely reluctant to accept: "My great doubts have been as to the aspect of secularity it may wear."[151] Even at that time, McIlvaine wondered if it would be proper to engage in politics. The Ohio clergy heard about the offer, however, and unabashedly urged their bishop to go. From their reaction, McIlvaine concluded that service to his country was part of his duty – even if the mission was "secular." In the history of the Episcopal Church to that point, McIlvaine's mission was unique: a bishop sent at the behest of a president on a diplomatic mission. His participation illustrated how politicized the northern Evangelicals had become.[152] He proved himself an apt diplomat, political advisor, and even informant: the mission was a success, and the English stayed out of the war. Although McIlvaine was not solely responsible for this result, the archbishop of Canterbury wrote of McIlvaine's participation, "Few men living have done so much to draw England and the United States together."[153]

While in England, McIlvaine developed a new perspective on the slavery issue. He arrived, coincidentally, shortly after news of the Trent affair had reached England. English public opinion had been running against the north, and the Union capture of two Confederate commissioners from an English ship increased anti-Union feeling. When McIlvaine reached England, it appeared as if the British would declare war on the United States and become allied with the Confederacy. After observing the intensity of British feelings on the matter, the bishop urged Chase and the president to release the Confederate captives to the British. The American government followed this advice,[154] and the Trent affair was over.

McIlvaine's mission continued, however. He quickly discerned that British evangelicals were not in favor of supporting the Confederacy because of their own historic stand against slavery. McIlvaine confided to Bishop Bedell:

> They sympathize in our trials, and in our vast effort to sustain government against unprovoked sedition and conspiracy. They are moreover more strongly opposed to anything that would place the strength of England in any helping relations to a Confederation which begin professedly, as well as really, built on the claims, and for the preservation of slavery, they religiously abhor.[155]

Lord Shaftesbury convinced McIlvaine that Confederate cotton was not really needed by the British, who could supply their fabric industry with raw materials from India to avoid trade with a nation of slaveholders.[156] In short, McIlvaine realized that making an issue of the slavery question could mobilize English evangelical public opinion against the south. If slavery were *the* central issue of the Union cause, England–especially the English church–could never support the Confederacy. In a letter to Chase, he praised the abolition of slavery in the District of Columbia, adding that "such things will have great influence here."[157] Confederate slaveholding became part of his argument against English participation in the war. McIlvaine's personal antislavery convictions finally found a public and political voice. He had long hoped that slavery would be abolished, but lacked confidence that it could ever be accomplished. During the English mission, he realized that emancipation served a useful, and urgent, political purpose. The war to secure the nation might become a war against slavery. With this in mind, he urged Lincoln to free the slaves.[158]

Upon his return to America, McIlvaine continued in his pro-Union political activities. His fears about "secularity" vanished. He visited and preached at Union camps, worked for the interdenominational Christian Commission, corresponded with military leaders, secured commissions for friends and relatives, and advised political leaders.[159] He was elected president of the American Tract Society. Since the southerners had left the society, McIlvaine turned it into a proemancipation and pro-Union propaganda machine–another evidence of the politicization of the northern Evangelicals during the war years.[160]

Another evangelical leader, Stephen Tyng, identified the northern cause for "national liberty" with that of Moses and the Exodus–the southerners were the slaveholding pharaoh. Tyng urged:

> Take all the Word of the living God, all its principles, promises and commands, can there be a moment's doubt on which side they are arrayed, or by the success of which side they are to maintained and propagated? . . . Speak to the children of Israel, that they go forward. If they go forward in prayer, victory will crown their nation. If they stand still to cry, or vainly court a sinful peace with crime, because they are afraid to resist it, they may invoke the pardon of Pharaoh, they may yield to his slave-bearing authority, but they will find no peace. . . . We cannot afford to rest as a nation keeping the truth, till by the blessing of God, we have made that truth triumphant.[161]

The amount of God-and-America rhetoric, something that had been noticeably absent in Evangelical Episcopal sermons only twenty years earlier, radically increased.

In the years before the war, Evangelical Episcopalians had dreamed of unity without compromise. What they got was division. Ideology and politics eventually forced northern and southern Evangelical Episcopalians—who shared the same evangelical vision for the Episcopal Church—into two churches in rival, warring countries. Southern Episcopalians formed their own Protestant Episcopal Church in the Confederate States. Meade and McIlvaine, respectively, became articulate defenders of the Confederacy and of the Union. Although they remained close personal friends and were heartbroken by the developments in their church, they could not avoid the conflict that arose over slavery. The national crisis changed both men: one remained convinced that slavery, though not particularly desirable, could be within the divine order of things; the other became convinced that the moral evil of slavery stood between America and God. As America divided over political ideology, so did the Evangelical party in the Episcopal Church.

During the Protestant Episcopal (USA) General Convention of 1862, the House of Bishops issued a pastoral letter about the war, declaring the church's dedication to the Union. The political nature of the letter caused consternation to the older generation of High Church leaders who wanted to retain the Episcopal Church's neutrality. As a result of the competing visions of political involvement present in the northern church, two letters were actually drafted. The first, by Bishop Hopkins, avoided all political issues and instead discussed Christian charity in a time of war. The second, by McIlvaine, was a strong, pro-Republican, pro-Union statement. The bishops rejected Hopkins's milder letter in favor of the McIlvaine pastoral.[162] Part of the bishops' rejection of Hopkins probably came from political motives. In 1861, Hopkins published his *Bible View of Slavery* in which he outlined biblical sanctions for slavery, a position rejected by northern Evangelical Episcopalians. Hopkins came under fire from both Evangelicals in the church and political critics for his prosouthern, pro-Democratic position.[163]

In the Episcopal Church's official pastoral, McIlvaine decried silence as complicity with evil. The war was God's retribution for American's greed, selfishness, and sin. Rebellion against the ordained government of the United States "we hold to be a *sin*; and when it stands forth in armed rebellion, it is *a great crime* before the laws of God, as well as man."[164] McIlvaine took the final step toward the complete politicization of Evangelicalism: he identified the Union with righteousness and the Confederacy with sin. God's will was the defeat of the southerners and slavery; only this would save America from God's wrath. With this statement, McIlvaine incorporated the Evangelical party (and the Episcopal Church along with it) into the Puritan jeremiad tradition of American destiny.[165]

The war, therefore, provided Americans with an opportunity to repent from sin: to be free—finally and completely—from slavery. As the hoped-for emancipation became a reality, McIlvaine urged his clergy to support, as he himself supported, missionary work among the freed slaves. In June 1864, he wrote:

> God be praised for what, in His good providence, has been wrought the past year,
> in turning the rebellion of slave-holding States into a great instrument for the
> destruction of slavery. God has made a way in the sea, and a path in the mighty
> waters of this awful war . . . for the ultimate deliverance of the whole land . . .
> from that which has been so long its curse and dishonor.[166]

Writing at the war's end, in April 1865, McIlvaine praised peace, the death of slavery and the "wonder" God brought about "in the resurrection of the nation":

> Its deliverance from a curse and heritage that seemed so fastened on us that we could never get rid of it. The Rebellion opened the prison door and put into our hands the hammer to smite off the chains. By nothing else, so far as we can see, could we have found the way, without revolution, to smite it.[167]

To McIlvaine, the end of the war, slavery, and national sin meant the beginning of a new world—perhaps even the long-awaited millennium.

> Lord God of grace and glory, who art no respecter of persons, to whom bond and free, the black and the white are alike in the view of thy saving love and in the promises of thy salvation—May thy hand be over us, that by the due guidance and government of the several powers of this nation and the will of all the people, this legal abolition of slavery may be a full deliverance from all the evils engendered by slavery against the whites and the colored—and the beginning of a new era of prosperity, happiness, peace, godliness to all.[168]

God, McIlvaine believed, had brought forth his sovereign purpose through the Union victory.

Evangelical Episcopalians were jubilant: an unrestrained Stephen Tyng proclaimed "the victory is a gift of God." John Brown had been "the Wickliff of the coming day—the morning star of a new reformation," and Lincoln was likened to an "ancient ruler in the Theocracy" who led his people back to God. Lincoln's blood was the seal of a new American covenant: "the priceless blessings of liberty" would rule throughout the land "that God may be glorified in all and by all forever."[169] Northern Evangelical Episcopalians believed that, in the conflict with the south, they had stood up for Jesus, Christian righteousness, and the truth of God.

In 1858, in his famous "House Divided" speech, Abraham Lincoln said:

> "A house divided against itself cannot stand." I believe this government cannot endure permanently half slave and half free. I do not expect the Union to be dissolved—I do not expect the house to fall—but I do expect it will cease to be divided. It will become all one thing, or all the other.[170]

Seven years later, the nation had become all free. The quest to maintain the union had become, for northern evangelicals, a religious crusade for political purity. The nation had been scourged from the sin of slavery. Two conflicting ideas of freedom could not exist in one political entity, and the north had succeeded in securing their version of freedom, liberty, and unity for the whole Union—even at the cost of schism and war.

The war, however, put off some troubling questions for Evangelical Episcopalians: Could their church remain unified if the Tractarian impurity remained? Could two gospels remain within one church? In the years following the Civil War, some Episcopalians became convinced that the Episcopal Church was on its way to becoming all one thing—Tractarian—at the expense of the other—Evangelicalism. God's righteousness had been defended in the nation, but what about their church? John Brooke's question, "Must we not divide?," remained unanswered.

By 1865, the fate of national union had been decided: reunion at the price of war. The fate of the Episcopal Church was far less certain.

Notes

1. Tyng, *Life and Work of Stephen Tyng*, 267.

2. J. Wesley Morris, *Christ Church, Cincinnati, 1817–1967* (Cincinnati, 1967), 40.

3. Russell E. Francis, "The Religious Revival of 1858 in Philadelphia," *Pennsylvania Magazine of History and Biography* 70 (1946): 69–70.

4. *"Stand Up for Jesus," Last Hours and Funeral Services of the Rev. Dudley A. Tyng* (Philadelphia, 1858), 67.

5. From the *Boston Courier*, quoted in Tyng, *Life and Work of Stephen Tyng*, 271.

6. Some confusion exists regarding the circumstances of the hymn's origin. Another "Stand Up for Jesus" was recited as verse at Tyng's funeral. For this less well known version, see *Stand Up for Jesus! A Christian Ballad: with Notes, Illustrations and Music* (Philadelphia, 1858). Duffield composed his verses after the funeral and used them in a sermon; these verses were later printed in a Baptist newspaper and became the famous hymn. Henry Wilder Foote, *Three Centuries of American Hymnody* (Cambridge, Mass., 1940), 212–213.

7. [Dudley Tyng,] *Vital Truth and Deadly Error* (Cincinnati, 1853), 38. This summary follows the argument on pages 15–38.

8. Ibid., 55.

9. Ibid., 56.

10. Preceding quotes from ibid., 56, 57.

11. Statistic taken from George DeMille, *The Catholic Movement in the American Episcopal Church* (Philadelphia, 1950), 106–107. See also "Romish Perverts: Where Do They Come From?" *Church Review* 13 (July 1860): 254–255.

12. Charles P. McIlvaine, "Bishop's Annual Address," *Journal of the Diocese of Ohio* (Columbus, 1853): 18.

13. Ibid., 19.

14. Preceding quotes from Charles P. McIlvaine, *The Harvest and the Labourers* (New York, 1853), 12, 15, 25.

15. Anne Ayres, *The Life and Work of William Augustus Muhlenberg* (New York, 1880), 173.

16. For more on Muhlenberg, see ibid., which is a highly enjoyable nineteenth-century biography. Also, William Wilberforce Newton, *American Religious Leaders: Dr. Muhlenberg* (Boston and New York, 1890), and Alvin W. Skardon, *Church Leader in the Cities: William Augustus Muhlenberg* (Philadelphia, 1971). Muhlenberg left a massive amount of written material, yet he is in some ways still an elusive character. He has been pictured by historians as a Broad Churchman, an early social gospel minister, a liturgical innovator, an ecumenical leader, and a Ritualist. All these portrayals seem to better indicate the position of the historians and biographers and the later preferences of the Episcopal Church than they do Muhlenberg. For the memorial itself, see E. R. Hardy, "Evangelical Catholicism: W. A. Muhlenberg and the Memorial Movement," *Historical Magazine of the Protestant Episcopal Church* 13 (1944): 155–192.

17. *Journal of the General Convention of the Protestant Episcopal Church* (Philadelphia, 1853): 182.

18. Charles P. McIlvaine, "Bishop's Annual Address," *Journal of the the Diocese of Ohio* (Columbus, 1855): 35.

19. One of the provisions of the memorial called for an itinerant ministry of less educated men who might not be able to agree in full with Episcopal doctrine and standards. The memorial has often been interpreted as the first document of the modern, liberal, and ecumenical Episcopal Church. The itinerancy provision convinces me that it might better be interpreted as an attempt to accommodate the Episcopal Church to the successes of American Methodism and, perhaps, to attract back to the Episcopal Church those who had left for the Methodist Church. Muhlenberg and the memorial movement need to be more closely examined within the context of nineteenth-century American Protestantism, rather than that of what the twentieth-century Episcopal Church would become.

20. Dudley Tyng, *The State and Prospects of Our Church, as Indicated by Her Last General Convention: A Sermon in Christ Church, Cincinnati* (Cincinnati, 1854), 7. Other works as well point to a general "lull of party feeling" in 1854. See *Two Views of the Episcopacy: Old and New* (Philadelphia, 1854), 1.

21. See Hardy, "Evangelical Catholicism," 184, and [C. M. Parkman,] *A Counter Memorial* (Philadelphia, 1856).

22. These responses are found in *Memorial Papers*, ed. Alonzo Potter (Philadelphia, 1857), 417–444.

23. Stephen Tyng, *The Duty and Responsibility of Private Judgement in Religion: A Sermon* (New York, 1853), 29.

24. Ibid., 30.

25. Heman Dyer, *Records of an Active Life* (New York, 1886), 216–217.

26. *Voluntary Principle in Missions* (N.p.), 16.

27. Emery, *Century of Endeavor*, 145. See also DeMille, *Catholic Movement in the Episcopal Church*, 45–46.

28. Manross, *History of the Episcopal Church*, 262; *The Voice of Experience, or Thoughts on the Best Method of Conducting Missions in the Protestant Episcopal Church in Its Present State* (Philadelphia and New York, 1852), 27.

29. Preceding quotes from *Voice of Experience*, 14, 17.

30. Ibid., 24.

31. Ibid.

32. Ibid., 25.

33. Tyng, *State and Prospects of Our Church*, 8.

34. Preceding quotes from ibid., 9.

35. Ibid., 13.

36. Charles P. McIlvaine, "Bishop's Annual Address," *Journal of the Diocese of Ohio* (Columbus, 1854): 22–23.

37. Tyng, *Life and Work of Stephen Tyng*, 286. Tyng's memoir is a valuable source for information on the American Church Missionary Society, as is Dyer's *Records of an Active Life*.

38. Report of the executive committee of the American Church Missionary Society, October, 14, 1860, quoted in Tyng, *Life and Work of Stephen Tyng*, 288.

39. Preceding quotes from J. T. Brooke, *Union: How Far Consistent or Justifiable in View of the Present Differences Between Churchmen: An Address* (Cincinnati, 1859), 15.

40. Tyng, *Life and Work of Stephen Tyng*, 287.

41. Brooke, *Union: An Address*, 15.

42. McIlvaine to Colonel Thayer, October 15, 1860, in Carus, *Memorials of McIlvaine*, 206.

43. McIlvaine to William Carus, April 23, 1859, in ibid., 189.

44. Antislavery had been an impulse in more radical evangelical traditions and in liberal Protestantism (such as Quaker communities) for decades. It had been one of the factors that

led to splitting the Presbyterian, Methodist, and Baptist churches in the 1830s and 1840s. It was not until the 1850s, however, that such arguments became a prevalent political force – as well as a moral issue – for a majority of northerners. For this development, see Eric Foner, *Free Soil, Free Labor, Free Men: The Ideology of the Republican Party Before the Civil War* (New York, 1970). For the relationship between revivalistic evangelicalism and antislavery, see Bertram Wyatt-Brown, *Lewis Tappan and the Evangelical War Against Slavery* (Cleveland, 1969); Hammond, *The Politics of Benevolence*; and George M. Thomas's revisionist challenge of Hammond's thesis, *Revivalism and Cultural Change: Christianity, Nation Building, and the Market in the Nineteenth-Century United States* (Chicago, 1989).

45. While there are a number of studies on religious antislavery in the 1820s and 1830s, there are fewer sources on the effect of the political problems of the 1850s on American religious life – particularly evangelicalism. One study that attempts to correct this situation is Victor B. Howard, *Conscience and Slavery: The Evangelistic Calvinist Domestic Missions, 1837–1861* (Kent, Ohio, 1990). Helpful works on the political developments of the 1850s include Allen Nevins, *Ordeal of the Union: A House Dividing, 1852–1857* (New York, 1947); David Potter, *The Impending Crisis, 1848–1861* (New York, 1976); and Kenneth Stampp, *America at 1857* (New York, 1990). Touching on some of the religious rhetoric and implications of the Kansas crisis is Michael Fellman, "Rehearsal for the Civil War: Antislavery and Proslavery at the Fighting Point in Kansas, 1854–1856," in *Antislavery Reconsidered*, ed. Lewis Perry and Michael Fellman (Baton Rouge and London, 1979), 287–307. Louis Filler's *Crusade Against Slavery: Friends, Foes and Reforms, 1820–1860*, 2nd ed. (Algonac, Mich., 1986) covers antislavery in the whole antebellum period.

46. Stampp, *America at 1857*, particularly pages 108–109 and the whole of chapter 5, "The Heart of the Matter, Slavery and Sectionalism."

47. Quoted in Eric Foner, *Politics and Ideology in the Age of the Civil War* (New York and Oxford, 1980), 49.

48. Ibid.

49. Foner, *Free Soil, Free Labor*, 41.

50. For the importance of slavery at this time, see Eugene D. Genovese, *The Political Economy of Slavery* (New York, 1965).

51. For the relationship between Republicanism and evangelical religion in the north, see Hammond, *Politics of Benevolence*; Thomas, *Revivalism and Cultural Change*; and Paul Kleppner, *The Cross of Culture: A Social Analysis of Midwestern Politics, 1850–1900* (New York, 1970).

52. Mullin, *Episcopal Vision/American Reality*, 199. For the divisions in other Protestant churches over slavery, see Goen, *Broken Churches, Broken Nation*.

53. Meade and McIlvaine, as leaders of the northern and southern branches of the Evangelical party, are representative of the changes in their respective constituencies. Although the stories presented here are their personal journeys, it is evident that they reflect larger movements in the church and in society. Eventually, most northern Evangelical leaders moved to one or another antislavery position. William Jay and Stephen and Dudley Tyng are discussed later in this section as representative northern Evangelicals. Like William Meade, southern Evangelical leaders, such as John Johns, Stephen Elliot, R. H. Wilmer, and William Sparrow, all to one degree or another eventually supported Confederate views on the issue of slavery.

54. On the history of the American Colonization Society, see Early Lee Fox, *The American Colonization Society, 1817–1840* (Baltimore, 1919); J. H. Franklin and A. A. Moss, Jr., *From Slavery to Freedom: A History of Negro Americans* (New York, 1988); Marie Tyler McGraw, "The American Colonization Society in Virginia, 1816–1832: A Case Study in Southern Liberalism" (Ph.D. dis., George Washington University, 1980); C. Duncan Rice,

The Rise and Fall of Black Slavery (New York, 1975); and the standard work, P. J. Staudenraus, *The African Colonization Movement, 1816–1865* (New York, 1961). There is a considerable historiographic debate as to whether the society was, at its heart, radical or conservative in its view of society and race, which is well summarized in McGraw, "American Colonization Society in Virginia," 1–19.

55. Johns, *Memoir of Meade*, 476.

56. Ibid., 476–477.

57. Quoted in Samuel Wilberforce, *A History of the Protestant Episcopal Church in America* (New York, 1849), 325.

58. Quoted in Trendel, "William Jay," 295.

59. Johns, *Memoir of Meade,* 473.

60. For this trend, see Smith, *In His Image, But.* . . .

61. Stone, *Memoir of Milnor*, 351–352.

62. Carus, *Memorials of McIlvaine*, 53.

63. Among the works of varying historical interpretations on English Evangelicals and slavery are E. M. Howse, *Saints in Politics: The Clapham Sect and the Growth of Freedom* (London, 1953); Ian Bradley, *The Call to Seriousness: The Evangelical Impact on the Victorians* (New York, 1976); Ford K. Brown, *Fathers of the Victorians: The Age of Wilberforce* (Cambridge, 1961); and Roger Anstey, *The Atlantic Slave Trade and British Abolition, 1760–1810* (London, 1975).

64. For Jay and slavery, see Bayard Tuckerman, *William Jay and the Constitutional Movement for the Abolition of Slavery* (New York, 1894), and Trendel, "William Jay." Jay is often mentioned in Wyatt-Brown's *Lewis Tappan.* Wyatt-Brown is helpful because he sets Jay's activities in the context of interevangelical cooperation, but the book is not terribly nuanced in its views of Episcopalians.

65. "Inquiry into the Character and Tendency of the American Colonization, and American Anti-Slavery Societies" (1835), in William Jay, *Miscellaneous Writings on Slavery* (Boston, 1853), 20.

66. "Reproof of the American Church" (1846), in Jay, *Miscellaneous Writings,* 430.

67. With the exception of his attacks on Polk and Elliot, Jay usually ignored the fact that large numbers of *southern* Evangelical Episcopalians were proslavery. McIlvaine was more of a church politician and far more sensitive to the divisions within the Evangelical party itself. Jay accused more moderate antislavery types—such as McIlvaine—as being guilty of covering up for the moral defects of the southern bishops. In other words, he accused his fellow evangelicals of playing church politics. There is no doubt that McIlvaine and others did everything they could to maintain formal, institutional unity over the issue of slavery. Jay, however, failed to mention that those same southern bishops were Evangelicals, not Tractarians. He was guilty of a bit of a cover-up as well.

68. Jay to McIlvaine, January 25, 1842, in McI, Kenyon College, 420125.

69. Trendel, "William Jay," 294.

70. Chase to Thomas Sparhawk, March 16, 1826, quoted in Arthur M. Schlesinger, "Salmon Portland Chase, Undergraduate and Pedagogue," *Ohio State Archaeological and Historical Quarterly* 28 (1919): 129–130, and Frederick J. Blue, *Salmon P. Chase: A Life in Politics* (Kent, Ohio, 1987), 7. No biographer of Chase has examined his life, beliefs, and activities through the lens of his Evangelical Episcopal commitment. Blue mentions Chase's religion, but does not follow through on it in any systematic or analytical way. For Chase's abolitionist activities, see Albert Bushnell Hart, *Salmon P. Chase* (Boston, 1899).

71. Blue, *Chase: Life in Politics,* 16–17.

72. Foner, *Free Soil, Free Labor*, 73.

73. McIlvaine to Chase, June 29, 1843, in Salmon P. Chase papers, Historical Society of Pennsylvania, Philadelphia. [Hereafter cited as Chase, Hist. Soc. Pa.]

74. *Journal of the Diocese of Pennsylvania* (Philadelphia, 1843): 33.

75. McIlvaine to Chase, note 73. See also Trendel, "William Jay," 300, and "A letter of John McDonogh, on African Colonization, Addressed to the Editors of the New Orleans Commercial Bulletin – New Orleans, 1842," *Spirit of the Missions* 8 (March 1843): 68–75. William Jay discussed the same article in "Reproof of the American Church," in *Miscellaneous Writings*, 437–440. This episode probably fueled northern Evangelical discontent with the Domestic Missionary Society as well.

76. McIlvaine to Chase, note 73.

77. William Jay, "Memorial," *Emancipator* (January 18, 1844).

78. George F. Bragg, *A History of the Afro-American Group of the Episcopal Church* (Baltimore, 1922; reprint New York, 1968), 102–103. The first was the Rev. Alexander Crummell, who had become so disillusioned by American life that he took his family back to Africa.

79. Interestingly enough, this turn of mind never affected Stephen Tyng. Tyng never rejected the colonization policy until well into the 1850s. As late as May 1851, he still attended the New York Colonization Society's meeting. Tyng, a New Englander by birth, believed that slavery was a "temporary evil or individual injustice" that had to be suffered for the greater good of society. It was evil, but it should be abolished slowly and in accordance with the law. He hoped for the "complete and generous colonization of Africans in Africa . . . with the most glorious results, the principles of freedom, Christianity and civilization, upon the densely peopled continent." The union, he argued in 1850, was the only possible guard against the abuses of slavery, and it must be maintained without violence or revolution. Tyng, *Life and Work of Stephen Tyng*, 303–304. Tyng might have been more conservative on this issue because he had lived for a number of years in Maryland and, as his son testified, observed "the system during his ministry in the South." Ibid., 303. McIlvaine, on the other hand, spent only two years in the "south," that being Washington, D.C., and the rest of his career in the north. In contrast to Maryland, Ohio had a very small black population and was a hotbed of antislavery activity and a refuge for runaway slaves. It was probably much more difficult for McIlvaine to maintain a colonization position in a state where party tensions and emotions over slavery were so extreme. On slavery, sectionalism, and the political machinations in the Ohio of McIlvaine's day, see Stephen E. Maizlish, *The Triumph of Sectionalism: The Transformation of Ohio Politics, 1844–1856* (Kent, Ohio, 1983).

80. Trendel, "William Jay," 303.

81. Foner, *Free Soil, Free Labor,* 72.

82. McIlvaine to Carus, January 1, 1861, in Carus, *Memorials of McIlvaine,* 213.

83. McIlvaine to Carus, December 24, 1860, in ibid., 211. For the apocalyptic expectations of other American evangelicals, see James H. Moorhead, *American Apocalypse: Yankee Protestants and the Civil War, 1860–1869* (New Haven and London, 1978).

84. McIlvaine to Abraham Lincoln, March 27, 1862. Xeroxed copy in McI, Kenyon College, 620327.

85. McIlvaine to Salmon P. Chase, March 29, 1858, in Chase, Hist. Soc. Pa.

86. Quoted in Foner, *Politics and Ideology,* 53, from the *New York Tribune* (April 12, 1855).

87. Clifford S. Griffin, *Their Brothers' Keepers, Moral Stewardship in the United States, 1800–1865* (New Brunswick, N.J., 1960), 191–193.

88. For all the details of this conflict, see ibid., 194–197, and Stephen E. Slocum, "The American Tract Society: 1825–1975. An Evangelical Effort to Influence the Religious and Moral Life of the United States" (Ph.D. diss., New York University, 1975), 103–130. Griffin, however, misidentified McIlvaine as a Methodist. See also Griffin, "The Abolitionists and the Benevolent Societies, 1831–1861," *Journal of Negro History* 44 (July 1959): 195–216.

89. Charles P. McIlvaine, "Address to the American Tract Society," in *Thirty-Third Annual Report, American Tract Society* (New York, 1858), 10.

90. Four years later, in the middle of the war, McIlvaine was made president of the American Tract Society. At that time, the southerners had withdrawn, and all the Protestant evangelicals left within the society were northerners and opposed to slavery. Since they all agreed on the issue, McIlvaine and the publishing committee pursued a rigorously pronorthern, antislavery publication program.

91. This was true in many denominations: see "Condition of the Free People of Color," in Jay, *Miscellaneous Writings*, 387.

92. William B. Bodine, *The Kenyon Book* (Columbus, 1890), 265; see also Richard M. Spielmann, *Bexley Hall: 150 Years, A Brief History* (Rochester, N.Y., 1974), 27.

93. Preceding quotes from Bodine, *Kenyon Book*, 265.

94. Tyng, *Life and Work of Stephen Tyng*, 234–235.

95. Emily Coxe McIlvaine, "Journal, April 2, 1853–July 21, 1853," p. 13. Typescript copy from Burnham family original, in McI, Kenyon College.

96. Tyng, *Life and Work of Stephen Tyng*, 303.

97. Preceding quotes from ibid., 310–311, 670, 675–677. I am grateful to Kathryn Long for sharing with me her research on the 1858 ATS meeting and its aftermath.

98. For an example of his political crusade against liquor, see Dudley Tyng, *An Address on the Legal Prohibition of the Traffic in Intoxicating Liquors. February 1, 1853* (Columbus, 1853).

99. All quotes this paragraph from Dudley Tyng, *Our Country's Troubles: A Sermon Preached in the Church of the Epiphany, Philadelphia, June 29, 1856* (Boston, 1856), 3–5, 9, 12, 13.

100. All quotes this paragraph from ibid., 15, 19, 25. Tyng's sermon is a masterpiece of the rhetoric of free labor and slave power and is identical to the ideology outlined in Foner's *Free Soil, Free Labor*.

101. For his departure from the Church of the Epiphany, see Dudley Tyng, *Statement to the Congregation of the Church of the Epiphany, Philadelphia, of Facts Bearing on the Action of the Vestry in Requesting the Resignation of the Rector* (Philadelphia, 1856). This document supplies evidence that there was discontent at Epiphany about Tyng's evangelicalism *before* his sermon on slavery. The offensive sermon served as a catalyst for already dissatisfied parishioners to get rid of Tyng.

102. All quotes this paragraph from Dudley Tyng, *Our Country's Troubles, No. II, or National Sins and National Retribution. A Sermon Preached in the Church of the Covenant, Philadelphia, July 5, 1857* (Philadelphia, 1864), 21, 22–23.

103. Preceding quotes from *Memorabilia of George B. Cheever, D.D., Late Pastor of the Church of the Puritans, and of His Wife, Elizabeth Wetmore Cheever* (New York, 1890), 290, 210.

104. Stephen Tyng to George Cheever, May 17, 1858, in *Memorabilia of Cheever*, 212.

105. "The Late Dudley Tyng, a Tribute to His Memory from the Young Men of the Church of the Puritans," *Memorabilia of Cheever*, 215–216.

106. The variety of views among northern Evangelical Episcopalians paralleled the views of evangelicals in other denominations. For the conservative, antislavery, and aboli-

tionist views of other northern evangelicals, see Smith, *In His Image, But . . .* , 74–128. Smith is a more sure guide on southern views than on northern ones, however. He limits most of his discussion on northern antislavery to the 1830s and 1840s and does not really cover the developments of the 1850s in a systematic fashion. Because of this, he accepts the abolitionist agenda, condemns northern conservatives as racists, and does not account for the pervasiveness of antislavery and Republican politics among northern evangelicals after the first flush of abolitionist radicalism. A short and helpful account of mostly northern evangelical views of the Bible and slavery is Robert Bruce Mullin, "Biblical Critics and the Battle over Slavery," *Journal of Presbyterian History* 61 (1983): 210–226.

107. Mullin, *Episcopal Vision/American Reality*, 205.

108. Jay to "A Young Man," 1854, in Tuckerman, *William Jay*, 147–148.

109. It is difficult to determine how widely antislavery views were held by Evangelical Episcopal clergy as a whole. In Ohio, for example, already radicalized by years of antislavery agitation, it appears that Episcopal clergy were quite moved by Republican antislavery politics. Evangelical Episcopal clergy in other heavily antislavery areas tended to be more antislavery in their views than those who resided in areas with a variety of opinions on the issue. For example, in Galesburg, Illinois, which has been identified as a center of Congregationalist antislavery activity, the Rev. J. W. Cracraft, Evangelical Episcopalian and abolitionist (not just antislavery), got into a good deal of trouble with the local bishop— ostensibly over churchmanship but actually over his political views. See Bruce T. Brown, "Grace Church, Galesburg, Illinois, 1864–1866: The Supposed Neutrality of the Episcopal Church During the Years of the Civil War," *Historical Magazine of the Protestant Episcopal Church* 46 (1977): 187–208. In Philadelphia, however, Dudley Tyng was remembered because his views stood out so sharply against the rest of the Episcopal Church (Pennsylvania, in contrast to Ohio, was quite mixed in its churchmanship and its politics). Overall, I have concluded that the bishops were mostly conservatives (combining southern evangelicals and High Churchmen on the issue) and the rank-and-file northern evangelical clergy was probably slightly more liberal, but as mixed in their opinions as my sample. By the time the war began, however, McIlvaine's pro-Republican Union sentiments became endorsed by the House of Bishops and the national church.

110. Jay to McIlvaine, April 15, 1843, in McI, Kenyon College, 430415.

111. See the *Episcopal Recorder* (October 17, 1857), for financial scandal, and also Tyng, *Our Country's Troubles, No. II*, 15–24.

112. McIlvaine to Thayer, note 42.

113. All quotes this paragraph from McIlvaine, *Spiritual Regeneration*, 7, 3.

114. Ibid., 4.

115. Preceding quotes from ibid., 20, 10, 21.

116. He still rejected any use of means. Means would never produce evangelical Christianity. In an extended appendix to *Spiritual Regeneration*, McIlvaine attacked "practical Puseyism" and Roman Catholic revivalism as means-oriented by using the same logic he applied to radical evangelical revivalism in his 1836 charge to his clergy (37–45). In these pages he nowhere attacked another Protestant denomination.

117. Charles P. McIlvaine, *Pastoral Letter to the Clergy and Laity of the Protestant Episcopal Church in the Diocese of Ohio on the Subjects of Confirmation and Church Music* (Columbus, 1855).

118. Smith, *Revivalism and Social Reform*, 45–62. See also Miller, *Life of the Mind*, 88–95; William McLoughlin, *Revivals, Awakenings, and Reform* (Chicago, 1978); and idem, *Modern Revivalism: Charles Grandison Finney to Billy Graham* (New York, 1959), in particular 162–165.

119. This tendency is also obvious in McIlvaine's personal journal in the years 1859 and 1860. His entries contain a significant number of references to the Holy Spirit and prayers for "power" and "empowerment" in his ministry.

120. Charles P. McIlvaine, "Bishop's Annual Address," *Journal of the Diocese of Ohio* (Columbus, 1856): 18–19.

121. Evangelical Episcopalians were perennially worried that women converted in larger numbers than men. Thus, they emphasized the need to convert men and, when such conversions did occur, they felt that God was truly at work.

122. Noah Hunt Schenk, *Christ Our Helper: An Anniversary Discourse* (Gambier, Ohio, 1857), 12–13.

123. Smythe, *History of the Diocese of Ohio*, 257, identified an increase in missions stewardship as the greatest result of the revival.

124. Francis Wharton, "Abide with Me–Reminiscence of Gambier in 1857–1858," in Bodine, *Kenyon Book*, 260.

125. Preceding quotes from Charles P. McIlvaine, "Bishop's Annual Address," *Journal of the Diocese of Ohio* (Ironton, Ohio, 1858): 20.

126. Ibid., 26. See also, *"Stand Up for Jesus": Last Hours.*

127. For the 1858 revival, see Smith, *Revivalism and Social Reform*; Miller, *Life of the Mind*; Carwardine, *Transatlantic Revivalism*; J. Edwin Orr, *The Fervent Prayer: The World-wide Impact of the Great Awakening of 1858* (Chicago, 1974); Leonard I. Sweet, "'A Nation Born Again': The Union Prayer Meeting Revival and Cultural Revitalization," in *In the Great Tradition: In Honor of Winthrop S. Hudson*, ed. Joseph D. Ban and Paul Dekar (Valley Forge, Pa., 1982), 193–221. See also Russell Francis, "Pentecost: 1858, a Study in Religious Revivalism" (Ph.D. diss., University of Pennsylvania, 1948), and Carl L. Spicer, "The Great Awakening of 1857 and 1858" (Ph.D. diss., Ohio State University, 1935). For eyewitness accounts of the revival, see (among others) William C. Conant, *Narratives of Remarkable Conversions and Revival Incidents . . . An Account of the Rise and Progress of the Great Awakening of 1857–1858* (New York, 1858), and *Pentecost: or, the Work of God in Philadelphia*, A.D. *1858* (Philadelphia, 1859). The information on Tyng is from the latter, p. 13.

128. Quoted in Smith, *Revivalism and Social Reform*, 69.

129. *Pentecost: Work of God*, 20.

130. "Revival in the Episcopal Church," *New York Daily Tribune* (March 20, 1858): 6.

131. Quotes this paragraph from McIlvaine, *Bishop McIlvaine's Address . . . on the Revival of Religion*, 5, 6.

132. Ibid., 11.

133. Follows his argument in ibid., 12–16. It is interesting to compare these marks of a true revival to those established by Jonathan Edwards more than a century earlier. In his *Distinguishing Marks of a Work of the Spirit of God* (1741), Edwards emphasized internal transformation, love of theological truths, and charity, and in his *Religious Affections* (1746), he continued developing his thoughts on the inner nature of true religion. McIlvaine's marks are more external, objective, and mechanical than Edwards's. Simply put, McIlvaine's marks are easier to observe or "measure" than Edwards's detailed spiritual, theological, and psychological analyses. Although McIlvaine believed himself to be more in Edwards's than Finney's tradition, this list shows how extensively Finney's scientific and objective approach influenced even the moderate evangelical revival tradition by the mid-nineteenth century. For discussions of Edwards's marks of true revivals, see Edwards, *Religious Affections*, 1–52, and idem, *The Great Awakening*, ed. C. C. Goen (New Haven and London, 1972), 52–56.

134. McIlvaine, *Bishop McIlvaine's Address . . . on the Revival of Religion*, 14.

135. McIlvaine, personal journal, January 29, 1860, in McI, Kenyon College.

136. McIlvaine, *Bishop McIlvaine's Address . . . on the Revival of Religion,* 24.

137. McIlvaine to the Rev. William Carus, January 18, 1860, in Carus, *Memorials of McIlvaine,* 197.

138. Carus, *Memorials of McIlvaine,* 181–189; also Carwardine, *Transatlantic Revivalism,* 170.

139. Carus, *Memorials of McIlvaine,* 184.

140. "Review of *Bishop McIlvaine's Address to the Convention of the Diocese of Ohio on the Revival of Religion,*" *Christian Observer* 250 (October 1858): 810–812.

141. For McIlvaine and the Evangelical Alliance, see Philip D. Jordan, *The Evangelical Alliance for the United States of America, 1847–1900: Ecumenism, Identity and the Religion of the Republic,* Studies in American Religion, vol. 7 (New York, 1982), 19, 77, 88, 116. McIlvaine's chief activities on behalf of the alliance came after the Civil War.

142. McIlvaine to Carus, January 18, 1860, in Carus, *Memorials of McIlvaine,* 198.

143. Preceding quotes from McIlvaine, *Bishop McIlvaine's Address . . . on the Revival of Religion,* 18.

144. McIlvaine to Carus, January 1, 1861, in Carus, *Memorials of McIlvaine,* 213.

145. McIlvaine, personal journal, September 8, 1861, in McI, Kenyon College.

146. McIlvaine to Salmon P. Chase, April 11, 1860, in Chase, Hist. Soc. Pa.

147. McIlvaine, "Bishop's Address," *Journal of the Diocese of Ohio* (Columbus, 1861): 20–21.

148. This may be because he viewed rebellion against a government a clear violation of the biblical prohibition of Rom. 13. Although McIlvaine's antislavery stance was "radical" in relation to the Episcopal Church, in relation to other evangelicals, it was really quite moderate. Moderate antislavery evangelicals, such as McIlvaine, never developed a successful and convincing case against slavery from the scriptures. Slavery therefore, although morally and religiously repugnant, lacked a clear biblical injunction against its practice. This group of evangelicals, which would include Old School Presbyterians as well, were more highly motivated by nationalism, which they perceived to be more "biblical" than antislavery when the war finally came. For the evangelical failure to develop a clear, biblical antislavery interpretation, see Mullin, "Biblical Critics."

149. McIlvaine, "Bishop's Address," 27.

150. The most important sources for McIlvaine's involvement in the unofficial commission are Ann Heathcote Stevens, "The Unofficial Commission to England in 1861" (M.A. thesis, Occidental College, 1937); Jay H. Schmidt, "Mission to Europe, 1861–62," *Michigan Alumni Quarterly Review* 62 (1956): 311–313; Pugh, "McIlvaine, Faithful Evangel," 113–120; Carus, *Memorials of McIlvaine,* 217–236; and the McIlvaine correspondence for the period held by Kenyon College.

151. McIlvaine to George W. DuBois, November 10, 1861, in McI, Kenyon College.

152. It would be interesting to write about this mission from a Roman Catholic perspective. The other bishop on the mission was Roman Catholic Archbishop Hughes who had been sent to deal with the French. Both the Episcopal Church and the Roman Catholic Church were historically "distant" from American politics, yet both men chose to accept Lincoln's call to serve the union. Roman Catholic historians have often noted that during the Civil War, Roman Catholicism moved closer to the mainstream of American religion. Roman Catholic nuns, for example, gained a modicum of cultural acceptance through their compassionate service as nurses. Hughes's mission might be an example of that same kind of movement.

153. Quoted in Stevens, "Unofficial Commission," 77, from a clipping in the family scrapbook at Kenyon College.

154. Thurlow Weed and Adams urged the same, as well.

155. McIlvaine to Bedell, January 1862. Typescript copy in Stevens, "Unofficial Commision," 123.

156. Carus, *Memorials of McIlvaine,* 220–221.

157. McIlvaine to Chase, March 12, 1862, in Chase, Hist. Soc. Pa.

158. McIlvaine to Lincoln, note 89.

159. He was so well connected politically that his old friend Charles Hodge wrote asking him to secure a military commission for his son. In spite of Hodge's own reknown, he was unable to help his son's military career, and he asked McIlvaine to intercede with the president on young Hodge's behalf. Charles Hodge to McIlvaine, June 23, 1862. Typescript copy, Burhman family scrapbook, in McI, Kenyon College. He also secured his nephew an appointment to West Point that Lincoln granted as a personal favor in thanks for his service to the country. McIlvaine to Chase, May 28, 1863, in Chase, Hist. Soc. Pa.

160. For details of McIlvaine's work with the American Tract Society, see Slocum, "American Tract Society," 133–140.

161. Tyng, *Life and Work of Stephen Tyng,* 331–332.

162. There are indications that the High Church party did not go along with this move very willingly. Bishop Hopkins's son complained that political pressure had been placed on the bishops from Salmon P. Chase and William Seward – both Episcopalians, both opposed to slavery, and both members of Lincoln's cabinet. Manross, *History of the Episcopal Church,* 292. McIlvaine himself denied these charges and dismissed them as an "amusing fuss" in a letter written to Chase on November 21, 1962, in Chase, Hist. Soc. Pa. Nevertheless, a majority of the bishops did accept this as the official statement of the Protestant Episcopal Church (USA) on the Civil War. Elsewhere, one historian has identified most of the northern High Churchmen as "copperhead Democrats" and believed that they were not as neutral as they professed. See Brown, "Grace Church."

163. John Henry Hopkins, *Bible View of Slavery* (1861). Hopkins allowed it to be reprinted in 1863, and some people used his work to support a Democratic political campaign in Pennsylvania. This caused quite a stir, and, in response, he eventually published a fuller exposition of his views in *A Scriptural, Ecclesiastical and Historical View of Slavery* (1864). See also, Manross, *History of the Episcopal Church,* 294, and James M. Donald, "Bishop Hopkins and the Reunification of the Church," *Historical Magazine of the Protestant Episcopal Church* 47 (1978): 73–91.

164. Charles P. McIlvaine, *Pastoral Letter of the Bishops of the Protestant Episcopal Church in the U.S.A. to the Clergy and Laity of the Same, Delivered Before the General Convention . . . October 17, 1862* (New York, 1862), 9.

165. Hopkins, however, still protested the politicization of the Episcopal Church. See his "Protest Against the Political Tone of the Pastoral Letter of 1862" in John Henry Hopkins, Jr., *The Life of the Later Rt. Rev. John Henry Hopkins, First Bishop of Vermont and Seventh Presiding Bishop* (New York, 1873), 461–465.

166. Charles P. McIlvaine, "Bishop's Annual Address," *Journal of the Diocese of Ohio* (Columbus, 1864): 28.

167. McIlvaine, personal journal, August 6, 1865, in McI, Kenyon College.

168. Ibid., December 21, 1865.

169. "Victory and Reunion," in Tyng, *Life and Work of Stephen Tyng,* 364–371.

170. Abraham Lincoln, "House Divided Speech," June 17, 1858, in Henry Steele Commager, ed. *Documents of American History* (New York, 1934, 1968 ed), I: 345.

6

"The Ship in Tempest": Rationalism, Ritualism, and the Post–Civil War Evangelical Worldview, 1866–1874

In the years immediately following the Civil War, northern evangelicals, like Charles McIlvaine, expressed conflicting emotions about the future. Elation, optimism, and triumph mixed with worry, doubt, and confusion.[1] It seemed clear that American society, and the Episcopal Church along with it, was moving in new and different directions. But, in the 1860s and early 1870s, no one seemed quite sure which direction postwar America would take. "We are living," wrote McIlvaine, "in very difficult times. What is it the Lord intends? The ship in tempest, but He is on the Mount. Will he wait before he comes in power for us to get so near perishing?"[2]

In 1865, the abolition of slavery and the end of the war boosted the confidence of northern evangelicals. "The news came this morning," wrote McIlvaine to an English friend, "that yesterday the vote was taken in the House of Representatives . . . abolishing slavery."

> God has overruled the terrible calamity of civil war to that end. He shook the nation, as the earthquake shook the prison at Philippi, till every door flew open, and every man's bonds were loosed. The nation is filled with joy. Now *this* event will operate most powerfully towards peace.[3]

A "mighty Exodus" had delivered 4 million Americans "from the debasement of slavery" and opened optimistic possibilities for the advance of "the Gospel and Civilization" throughout the world.[4] The combined imagery of God's power in the Book of Acts and the Hebrew Exodus proclaimed a new age of hope for the world. An evangelical liberation had occurred; the freedom of the slaves signified the inbreaking of the millennial kingdom. God had delivered the nation from slavery; what great work would be next? McIlvaine hoped for the beginning of a new day, "the breaking up of old prejudices and barriers."[5]

At the moment of triumph, however, President Lincoln, who led the north to this great victory, was assassinated. "Oh, what horror and grief," wrote McIlvaine, "have come upon our whole land! Mourning, mourning!" The long-hoped-for Exodus occurred while the nation draped its houses and public buildings in black. "At the height of the flood of God's mercies to us," McIlvaine noted in his journal, "His great instrument in it was taken from us . . . great Mr. Lincoln." Lincoln's assassination symbolized something that McIlvaine had long believed: the work of the God's kingdom and the work of Satan would grow side by side in the world until the very last day. Evangelicals should expect opposition to the progress of the "Gospel and civilization."[6] Although they came out of the war in a triumphant mood, Evangelical Episcopalians immediately faced a series of stressful conflicts within their church which undermined any optimism they once had for postwar American society.

These conflicts centered around two issues: rationalism and Ritualism. Rationalism, or theological liberalism, which the Evangelicals also referred to as "infidelity," became an issue in the Episcopal Church during the war and would come to be promoted by a new church party, known as the Broad Church party.[7] Ritualism, or Anglo-Catholicism, manifested the Catholic tendencies of Tractarianism and promoted medieval-style ceremonial and church decoration. The rationalists and the Ritualists put both Evangelicals and old-fashioned High Churchmen on the defensive. Charles McIlvaine and A. C. Coxe, the High Church bishop of western New York, were equally appalled by these developments.

Evangelicals, however, developed a number of strategies to face these challenges, all of which differed from those of the High Churchmen like Coxe. To combat rationalistic theology, they rearticulated their views on Scripture, accepted premillennial theologies, and emphasized the need for evangelical unity. They continued their prewar drift toward mainstream American evangelicalism as they led the conservative fight against Protestant liberalism in the Episcopal Church. As a whole, the Evangelical Episcopal party was moving in a theological direction which would, by the the turn of the century, develop into American fundamentalism.

Successful as these efforts were in initially containing the spread of rationalism in the church, Evangelical strategies against Ritualist influences and innovations proved seriously inadequate. To battle it, they resorted to arguments formed in the 1840s and 1850s against the Oxford Movement–often republishing twenty-year-old works. They seemed to expect that Anglo-Catholicism would dissolve under the force of these arguments. The new style of Anglo-Catholicism, however, with its romantic views of the Middle Ages, proved a compelling vision in postwar America.[8] As it advanced, Evangelicals grew more desperate, and more divided, as to how to combat it.

Because of their responses to rationalism and the growing problems of Ritualism, there was an increasing sense among some Evangelicals that evangelicalism and the Episcopal Church were fundamentally incompatible. American evangelicalism and the Protestant Episcopal Church were choosing to go in different postwar directions. This slow, and painful, divergence tore at the Evangelical Episcopal synthesis. For some, this synthesis, as it had been formed and articulated by Charles McIlvaine, was finally destroyed.

Post–Civil War Evangelical Worldview
Rise of Episcopal Liberalism

The first crisis in the Episcopal Church actually began during the Civil War. While Americans were thus preoccupied, a group of British authors published a provocative book entitled *Essays and Reviews*. The volume of seven essays reexamined religious subjects that the authors claimed had suffered "by the repetition of conventional language, and from traditional methods of treatment."[9] Their goal: to expose the liberal theology being taught in English universities and abroad. Although the essays varied in subject, historian Owen Chadwick had identified four "leading ideas" that tied them together: (a) the need to reconcile modern thought with Christianity; (b) all truth comes from God; therefore, "new" scientific and historical truths should not be rejected; (c) Christian, or "spiritual," truth is of a different nature than factual, historical truth; and (d) Christian truth is not dependent on miracles or supernatural revelation.[10]

Essays and Reviews caused a furor in England, but the book is less important for what it actually said than for what it stood for. As one historian has noted, it was a liberal "tract for the times" that pointed toward new theological possibilities.[11] Before *Essays and Reviews*, a number of Anglican Evangelicals had showed thoughtful interest in new scientific theories; after its publication, however, Evangelical leaders and publications attacked liberalism, considering it a departure from orthodoxy.[12] Evangelicals and Tractarians joined to condemn the book, citing, in particular, the authors' damaging views on the inspiration of Scripture. Some 8,500 clergy protested to the archbishop of Canterbury and demanded the essayists be removed from clerical office. The controversy over *Essays and Reviews* continued for several years, and in April 1864, the Convocation of Canterbury issued a "synodical condemnation" of the work.[13] The *Essays and Reviews* crisis was exacerbated in 1861 and 1862 by the publication of some higher critical works on the Old Testament by the Anglican bishop of Natal, John Colenso.

Charles McIlvaine personally witnessed a good deal of the controversy over *Essays and Reviews*. In 1861, Lincoln sent him to England to try to convince the British not to support the south during the Civil War. McIlvaine remained in England for nearly eight months—at the height of the arguments over *Essays and Reviews*. He read an early edition of the work (he owned a second edition), and listened to his friends from the universities and the church discuss and debate its contents. Probably no other American Episcopalian—or American evangelical for that matter—had such intimate access to the initial debates over British liberalism as did Charles McIlvaine. Not surprisingly, his opinions on the issues closely resembled those of his Anglican Evangelical friends, particularly the bishop of Winchester, C. R. Sumner. "The Rationalistic flood," he wrote, expressing his approval of Sumner's charge on liberalism, "easily washes the minds of *thinking* men into its current, because so many have no anchorage in clearly defined, and *discriminating* views of what religion is—what the Gospel is."[14] Evangelicals needed, he believed, to respond to liberalism with "a decided grasp on the cross" and greater faith in Christ's salvation.

Rationalism was clearly on McIlvaine's mind during the war. In 1864, he reissued his *Oxford Divinity Compared* under a new title, *Righteousness by Faith*. The preface to this new edition attacked *Essays and Reviews*: McIlvaine linked the Oxford Movement to rationalism, describing the liberals as "a far more portentous evil, another Oxford Divinity, and another school of Tractarians."[15] He built this argument from an earlier work by Archbishop Whatley, the *Kingdom of Christ*, which compared Tractarianism to German rationalism. Using "slippery-slope" logic, McIlvaine claimed that the Oxford Movement had corrupted true Christianity, and rationalism took the next step by denying its very essence. In spite of Newman's dislike for theological liberalism, McIlvaine believed, he had unwittingly laid the groundwork for *Essays and Reviews*. Newman instilled doubt in the minds of Christians as to the inspiration of Scripture and replaced it with misplaced faith in the authority of the church and tradition. The rationalists, McIlvaine argued, accepted Newman's skepticism over Scripture, but rejected church and tradition as well. The Tractarian heresy had paved the way for rationalistic infidelity. He claimed:

> It was not difficult to see how minds might easily be led so far by such teaching as to place the inspiration and authority of the Scriptures upon the level of tradition and councils, and yet deny that in the confusion and contradictions of the latter there is any real inspiration or authority at all.[16]

Reduced to their most basic tendencies, McIlvaine believed that both Tractarianism and rationalism were movements against the literal authority of the Bible and led equally to skepticism.

As the Civil War drew to a close, American Episcopalians recognized that the debate over British liberalism could have a significant impact on their church. Since Church of England ministers could preach in American Episcopal pulpits, there was a direct, familial connection between the churches. Without some action by the bishops, *Essays and Reviews* could be an implicit approval for rationalistic theology in the American church.[17] At the 1865 General Convention, McIlvaine read a paper on rationalism in which he attacked both the essayists and Bishop Colenso. His fellow bishops received it with enthusiasm and commissioned McIlvaine to publish the work. They officially endorsed it as the church's position on rationalism for use by theological students.

McIlvaine criticized rationalism over its doctrine of inspiration. *Essays and Reviews*, he contended, denied both the inspiration of the scriptures and the direct, revelatory action of God in the world through the word and miracles. This, he argued, placed "the dictates of every man's own natural light" over the authority of the Bible. Rationalism, therefore, contradicted the teaching of the Episcopal Church on the nature of Scripture. McIlvaine admitted that Episcopal theology set forth "no *direct, dogmatic, definition*" of Scripture, but, instead believed that such a doctrine was found implicitly in the Thirty-nine Articles. At the time the articles were written, he argued, "inspiration [was] a matter of universal acceptance" and, therefore, not a major issue to the Reformers. The issue they faced was the authority of the Bible versus tradition. The Roman Church, he maintained, accepted the spurious traditions of the Apocrypha, early Fathers, and church councils, whereas the English church rejected these traditions in favor of the inspired canon of Scripture. The "joint and equal authority of Church tradition with the written Word of God," the fundamental error of Roman Catholicism, had been definitively rejected by Anglicanism. Everything, according to early Anglican theology, must be subjected to the final – and sole – authority of Scripture.[18]

This principle of the English Reformers, the submission of all authorities to the authority of the Bible, McIlvaine stated, "was equivalent to a declaration of infallibility as pertaining to the Scriptures, and consequently of the highest Inspiration of God."[19] Biblical inspiration was complete, perfect, and total:

> It is all God's Word *as it is written*, . . . *God's Word written*, applied to all Scripture, decides the doctrine of our Church, that God's Word is not merely *contained* in the Scriptures *somewhere*, but is the Scriptures *everywhere*; not merely that by His Inspiration *parts* of Scripture were given, leaving us to say which parts; but that all that belongs to holy Scripture was so given. This is Plenary Inspiration, in the full sense of the words, as opposed to partial. . . . Our Church avoids *theories* of inspiration, binding no man's faith beyond the *fact* of an inspiration co-extensive with the written Word.[20]

Without this fact – that "all Scripture is given by Inspiration of God" – no Christian can stand against evil in the world.[21] Without it, all the unique doctrines of Christianity are destroyed. The Episcopal Church's theological heritage, McIlvaine maintained, was that of a doctrine of verbal and plenary inspiration of Scripture. It was this position endorsed by the bishops as the official statement of the church on the nature of biblical inspiration.

McIlvaine's views on the Bible differed little from those of many other nineteenth-century American evangelicals except in his growing need to articulate and clarify the doctrine of biblical inspiration.[22] Eight years before McIlvaine's article, his friend Presbyterian Charles Hodge wrote a lengthy discussion in the *Princeton Review* on the same subject, "Inspiration," and explored many of the same themes. It would not be unfounded to speculate that McIlvaine had read Hodge's 1857 article, as McIlvaine continued to require Hodge's *Systematic Theology* as the main theological text at Kenyon and Bexley throughout the 1860s. McIlvaine's language of verbal and plenary inspiration certainly reflected Hodge's use of the terms in his essay.[23]

McIlvaine's second concern in *Rationalism* – one closely related to the inspiration of Scripture – was for supernaturalism and miracles. Since the essayists had rejected prophecy and the miraculous, McIlvaine felt it necessary to reemphasize the supernatural nature of God's communication to the world and the miracles written about in Scripture. Revelation occurred not simply through science, history, or culture, as the essayists maintained, but as God's supernatural gift through the Holy Spirit to human beings. McIlvaine believed that to deny miracles would lead to a denial of "those two great and head miracles of Christianity, the Incarnation of the Son of God and His Resurrection."[24] Early in his career, McIlvaine had likewise defended biblical miracles – at that time against Roman Catholic claims of contemporary supernatural healing. Miracles, he maintained, had ceased after the age of the apostles; Christianity no longer needed them; all Roman Catholic appeal to the miraculous was little more than unenlightened superstition.[25]

Following the 1858 revival, there was an almost imperceptible shift in McIlvaine's views. Although there is no evidence he believed in modern era miracles, it is clear that he was much more interested than earlier in the supernatural aspects of Christianity. Since he believed the last days had begun, it is possible that he believed miracles would recur as the time of Christ's earthly reappearance drew nearer. The biblical Book of Joel, and the Pentecost in Acts, formed much of his eschatological understanding. Joel 2:28–32, which McIlvaine was fond of quoting, spoke of visions, dreams, prophecy, and wonders. Miracles per se, however, were a difficult issue: admit to their existence, on one hand, and face Roman Catholic claims to the miraculous; deny them, on the other hand, and sound like the authors in *Essays and Reviews*. As a result, most Evangelical Episcopalians either linked the increase of the miraculous to the second coming of Christ or personalized the work of the Holy Spirit in the life of the believer. In a sermon, McIlvaine's assistant Gregory Bedell emphasized the mystical, internal, and spiritual effects of the ministry of the Spirit.[26] As a reflection of the Evangelicals' interest in the supernatural, the new chapel at Kenyon College was consecrated as the Church of the Holy Spirit. This fascination with the Holy Spirit, the end times, and the supernatural sharply contrasted with the views presented in *Essays and Reviews*. The shift toward the supernatural began before publication of the book, but the rationalism of *Essays and Reviews* probably helped reinforce the Evangelicals' increased interest in the miraculous elements in Christianity.

In their first battle with liberalism, the Evangelicals won by securing an ecclesiastical condemnation of it. They were supported in their antirationalistic campaign by a number of prominent High Churchmen, including Charles Chapman Grafton and John Henry Hopkins, Jr. Grafton condemned the rationalists as "Episcopalian Unitarians," and Hopkins, usually a critic of Bishop McIlvaine, praised his article as a "guard against the insidious approaches" of liberalism.[27] Although McIlvaine had clearly expressed his opinion about the connection between Tractarianism and rationalism, he was nevertheless willing to work with High Churchmen to extinguish the rationalist influence. In the paper sanctioned by the House of Bishops, McIlvaine greatly minimized the Tractarianism-leads-to-rationalism argument; to protect orthodoxy, he was willing to compromise, even on very important issues. The Evangelicals continued to believe McIlvaine was correct in his analysis, as stated in the *Episcopal Recorder*, but, as late as 1866, they could still work with their rivals. As a bishop, McIlvaine was able to cooperate successfully with High Churchmen against liberalism.

His writings, such as the introduction to *Righteousness by Faith*, however, probably prepared the way for a new Evangelical crusade against High Churchism. If Tractarianism and liberalism were inseparably linked, and if Evangelicals had been so successful in the battle against liberalism, might not the time be right to finally rid the Episcopal Church of all traces of the Oxford Movement? "So long as [Puseyism] prevails in the Church of England as one extreme," wrote the editor of the *Episcopal Recorder*, "the infidelity of the *Essays and Reviews* will prevail on the other."[28] The spirit of Dudley Tyng, arguing against enemies on two sides, was alive and well in the Evangelical party.

Millennialism and the Return of Christ

Puseyism and liberalism, working together against evangelical Protestantism, filled the minds of Evangelical Episcopalians with thoughts of the end times. Forty years earlier, both George Croley and Edward Irving, two influences on Evangelical Episcopal views of prophecy, had predicted that in the last days, in Babylon, "idolatry" [Roman Catholicism] and "infidelity" [rationalism] would join forces against Christ and all true believers in the great battle of Armageddon. Christ's final victory, at the time of his return during this battle, would be over "infidelity and idolatry."[29] The Lord would destroy both the "apostasy of the INTELLECT amongst Protestant nations . . . [and] the apostasy of SENSE" among the Catholic nations, and establish his perfect rule in the world.[30] In the post–Civil War years, the dual threat of Roman Catholicism and rationalism weighed heavily on the Evangelical psyche. McIlvaine feared "the two Antichrists–Popery and Infidelity."[31] The year 1866, the predicted year in which many evangelicals, McIlvaine included, hoped the kingdom might begin, passed without Christ's return.[32] Optimistically, Evangelical Episcopalians believed that the end of the war had secured the imminent arrival of the kingdom; pessimistically, they began to wonder if American slavery was the impediment to its arrival. Perhaps their bloody and horrible Civil War was only a prelude to the final battle of Armageddon. Prompted by Episcopal conflicts over liberalism and Tractarianism, Evangelical Episcopalians began to rethink their millennial views, and many of them eventually rejected any lingering postmillennialism in favor of the increasingly popular dispensational premillennialism that was gaining favor with other American evangelicals.[33]

Since the days of Benjamin Allen's prophecy classes in the early 1820s at St. Paul's, Philadelphia, a number of Evangelical Episcopalians published and preached on prophecy and the millennium. Before the 1850s, it was difficult to distinguish pre- and postmillennial views; as the century progressed, Evangelical Episcopal views turned decidedly toward premillennialism. Episcopal interest in the subject seems to have three nineteenth-century peaks: in the 1820s, at the time of Edward Irving's writings; in the 1840s, around the Millerite controversy; and in the 1860s and 1870s, the years of popular enthusiasm over Darbyite dispensationalism. Prominent Episcopal premillennialists included the following: Stephen Tyng, and his son, Stephen Tyng, Jr.; Richard Shimeall, rector of St. Judes' in New York; J.P.K. Henshaw, the bishop of Rhode Island; Edward Winthrop, an Ohio clergyman; Issac Labagh, a clergyman from New York and Iowa; Richard Newton, the well-respected rector of St. Pauls, Philadelphia, who wrote a considerable amount of nineteenth-century Sunday school material and championed the idea of "Children's Church"; William Newton, chaplain of Kenyon College; and clergymen B. B. Leacock and W. R. Nicholson. With the exception of Henshaw, all lived at least until 1865.

As a group, they influenced the Evangelical party rather widely. William Newton published a series of lectures on the prophetic timetable in Daniel and served at Kenyon College during and immediately after the war, at a time of record enrollment. When the millennialism of two of the professors (Newton and L. W. Bronson were targeted) was attacked as "unsound doctrine," other faculty defended their views. " 'Prof. B. is a Millennarian!' " wrote one of Newton's colleagues; "So are multitudes of the most holy men in the Church!"[34] Richard Newton's position at St. Paul's was one of the Evangelical party's premier pulpits.

Newton used the Advent season as a time to preach on prophetic themes.[35] Other Evangelical Episcopalians did the same: in 1863, McIlvaine's diocesan newspaper, the *Western Episcopalian*, championed the doctrine of the second coming. "*The Western Episcopalian*," praised the *Prophetic Times* editor, "presents an honorable exception to the common course of our denominational peridicals in this particular."[36] Both Newtons served as editors of the *Prophetic Times*, a premillennialist journal published from 1863 to 1874; its sole intent was to determine the signs of the times to predict when Christ would return. Evangelical Episcopalians were convinced that time was short: in 1869, Richard Newton proclaimed, "We are living . . . in the last days of the present dispensation. We are on the eve of great and stupendous changes."[37]

Richard Shimeall's book, *Christ's Second Coming: The Great Question of the Day*, which went through several editions in the 1860s, contained an appeal to New York's Bishop Potter (among others) to reject postmillennialism. To support his case, Shimeall pointed to McIlvaine and Tyng as premillennialists noted for "their learning, position, piety and zeal."[38] Although Shimeall had resigned his Episcopal orders around 1849 and had become a Presbyterian, he maintained close relations with Episcopalians, and numerous Episcopalians subscribed to and recommended his works.[39]

Edward Winthrop served three prominent Ohio parishes, including St. Paul's, Cincinnati, and St. Luke's, Marietta. Recalled one Marietta parishioner:

> He was known as a Second Adventist, his preaching and writing being mostly on that subject; and often when he would take up his favorite theme, he was so completely wrapt up in it and such was his control over the attention of his hearers, that neither he nor they took note of the flight of time and two hours or more would some times slip by without their knowing it.[40]

Winthrop dedicated his most well known work, *Lectures on the Second Advent*, to his friend Bishop McIlvaine.

In his 1871 New Year's address to the diocese of Ohio, McIlvaine made his premillennial views quite clear. Recalling the events of recent history, McIlvaine identified them as "predicted developments of His gracious purposes, introductory to the Second Coming of our Lord."[41] The greatest sign of Christ's return was the military occupation of Rome; to McIlvaine this was a fulfillment of the prophecy of the fall of Babylon in the Book of Revelation. The second coming, he predicted, must be very near. Jesus was coming soon, like a "thief in the night," and would draw the church to meet him in the clouds.

The specifics of Jesus' return was a matter of controversy among premillennialists. Some believed that a "secret" rapture would occur before the great tribulation, a predicted period of seven years of intense earthly suffering. After that tribulation, Christ would return in victory with the raptured church by his side. Thus, true believers, all who were prepared for this coming, would be rescued from the tragedy of the tribulation. McIlvaine rejected this theory: "I look for tribulation to increase in all the affairs of this world and the visible Church, until *that coming* which will be 'the restitution of all things.' "[42] There would be a rapture of the Church, and it would come without warning; however, it would occur simultaneously with Christ's return to rule over the earth after the great tribulation. McIlvaine's posttribulation rapture position differed from that of Stephen Tyng, Jr., whose pretribulation rapture theory indicated that the church would be protected from all tribulation and distress "subsequent to the time of their departure."[43]

Both positions, however, rejected postmillennialism and indicated a real departure from the more optimistic view that evangelicals could bring about the kingdom by spreading the gospel throughout the world. Wrote William Newton:

> Let us not deceive ourselves with the hope of a gradual and peaceful spreading of the triumphs of the gospel; until the world shall be converted to Christ. *It will not be*. There is not one text, in all the Bible, which affirms this, as taking place, before His second coming. There are very many which teach the contrary. *This is not the epoch of the world's conversion. The Gentiles are not the instruments.*[44]

Because of his views, William Newton worked tirelessly to promote the conversion of Jews and urged his fellow Evangelical Episcopalians to do the same.[45]

In the postwar years, Evangelical Episcopalians grew very pessimistic in regard to earthly achievement and expected "some great convulsion of the times."[46] McIlvaine believed this as well. The world was getting worse; the only hope was Christ's return. He was quite optimistic, however, about Christ's second coming, but despaired of any real improvement in the world before that time. He wrote in his private journal:

> The day is dark, very dark. . . . The two great enemies of the Gospel—Rationalism, scarcely distinquishable from a bold and extreme infidelity, and Popery, with its child Tractarianism, now putting on the form of a Romish Ritualism—these are assuming such alarming strength . . . that it seems as if the truth were to be cast down, and the Gospel to be driven into the wilderness. In our Church of this country there is little to encourage, much to alarm. . . . I get no comfort in looking to the future, except as that future is found in the promises of God.[47]

Of all those promises, the one that looked brightest to postwar Evangelical Episcopalians was " 'that blessed hope'—the glorious appearing of our great God and Saviour" and his coming kingdom.[48] "I want to be in the mind," wrote McIlvaine on his seventy-second birthday, "to be saying habitually, *'Come, Lord Jesus,'* whether to take me away by the taking down of the earthly house of this tabernacle, or to find me here at Thine *appearing.*"[49]

1867: Need for Christian Unity

In the years immediately following the Civil War, the restored political union symbolized possibilities for Christian union.[50] But optimism was coupled with a sense of fear: Christians faced dark days and needed to be unified against the threats of Romanism and rationalism. For Evangelical Episcopalians, this desire to unify all Christians expressed itself in three ecumenical experiments: with the Presbyterians, with other Anglicans, and with all evangelical Christians.

Evangelical Episcopalians made a spontaneous and informal ecumenical gesture toward the Presbyterians in 1867 at the National Presbyterian Convention.

This Presbyterian gathering was an event in church unity itself: on November 6–8, representatives of Old and New School Presbyterians met with United, Reformed, Reformed Protestant Dutch, and Cumberland Presbyterians to discuss their common problems and to explore the possibilities for Presbyterian union. As it happened, the Evangelical Episcopal societies (the Knowledge Society, the Missionary Society, and the Education Society) were all meeting in Philadelphia at the same time. The Rev. Richard Newton suggested that the Episcopalians pray for the Presbyterian meeting, and his suggestion was greeted with enthusiasm by the organizers of the Episcopal meetings. Prayers were included in the Episcopal liturgy for God's blessing on the Presbyterian convention.

The Presbyterians were moved by the action and dispatched Rev. Dr. Henry B. Smith, professor of church history at Union Theological Seminary, carrying official salutations to the Episcopal meetings. Bishop McIlvaine, touched by Smith's address, responded by "expressing his high appreciation of Presbyterian standards, and the sympathy he felt in their movements of reunion." Senator Drake, an Episcopal delegate to the society meetings, then made an "earnest and stirring address," pointed to the Bible, and proclaimed, "Here is the centre and bond of our union."[51] The Episcopalians decided to send a delegation of their own back to the Presbyterians.

The next morning, McIlvaine, along with Bishop Alfred Lee of Delaware, Stephen Tyng, and two laymen, "addressed the [Presbyterian] Conference in warmly affectionate language, offered extemporaneous and eloquent prayers in their behalf, and pronounced upon them the Apostolic benediction."[52] McIlvaine made the principal speech of the delegation. Wrote McIlvaine to an English friend:

> I took great pains to acknowledge them *as a Church*. There was a great deal of joy and praise in the assembly. It was intended on both sides for manifestation of essential unity in Church; while neither side saw the way of *Church-union*. It was well pleasing to the Lord I doubt not. I have no possible doubt of the propriety, but I expected to be greatly wondered at in some quarters—and have been—though the Evangelical brethren of our Church were delighted. In these days we must come together, all that love the truth, as much as possible.[53]

Princeton's Charles Hodge responded on behalf of the Presbyterians with a sentimental recollection (a reporter recorded that "there was scarcely a dry eye in the house") of his college days with McIlvaine.

> And now, sir, after these fifty odd years, here we stand, gray-headed, side by side, for the moment representatives of these two great bodies of organized Christians. Has not your Church and our Church been rocked in the same cradle? . . . What difference, sir, is there between your Thirty-nine Articles, and our Confession of Faith, other than the difference between one part and another of the same great Cathedral anthem rising to the skies? Does it not seem to indicate, sir, to say to the whole world, that we are one in faith, one in baptism, one in life, and one in our allegiance to your Lord and to our Lord?[54]

McIlvaine agreed; he quoted Bishop Hall's *Divine Right of the Episcopacy* to prove his point. "There is no difference," Hall had asserted, "in any essential matter between the Church of England and her sisters of the Reformation." The only difference was in form of "outward administration" which McIlvaine believed "*not essential to the being of a Church*."⁵⁵ The convention was wild with applause; together they sang "Blessed Be the Tie That Binds"; they recited the Apostles' Creed; and McIlvaine pronounced the benediction. "With prayers and thankful tears," wrote Henry B. Smith, "the audience dispersed, thanking God for the communion of saints." To his mother he confessed, "the coming in of the Episcopal delegation so large, and able, was a memorable event and moved all hearts." One Presbyterian, reading the reports of the convention declared: "It seems more like Pentecost renewed, than anything I have ever read. A chasm has passed."⁵⁶ "Such a scene," wrote an observer, "has no parallel . . . in the entire history of American Christianity."⁵⁷

When McIlvaine participated in the Presbyterian convention, he had just returned from another ecumenical scene without parallel: the first Lambeth Conference of worldwide Anglicanism.⁵⁸ The first calls for a pan-Anglican conference, for a worldwide Anglican synod, came from American Hobartians, most notably John Henry Hopkins of Vermont,⁵⁹ but attempts to hold an international Anglican conference in the 1850s failed. Following the American Civil War, however, a number of factors contributed to make the idea a reality. First, the British colonial churches were somewhat confused about their relationship to the Church of England and wanted to resolve the issue. Second, the growth of Anglican liberalism—for example, publication of *Essays and Reviews* and the higher critical writings of Bishop Colenso of Natal, led many Anglicans to conclude that a synod was needed to contain rationalist heresies. Finally, in February 1867, Archbishop of Canterbury Charles Thomas Longley issued invitations to a conference at Lambeth to approximately 140 Anglican bishops around the world.

McIlvaine received one of those invitations. As much as he expressed confidence on the essential unity between Presbyterians and Evangelical Episcopalians, he expressed grave doubt about the possibility of unity within Anglicanism. "I do not suppose," he wrote to William Carus, "the Conference, of such a variety of minds, could get in three days to any very important conclusions, and it is questionable whether the manifestation of an outward union, covering so much diversity and discordance, would be of much spiritual interest or benefit."⁶⁰ He was probably hesitant, in part, because the most ardent supporters of Lambeth were High Churchmen. In England, the Evangelical party was also extremely hesitant about the idea. Besides, McIlvaine was already in "union" with large numbers of Anglican evangelicals. What was the sense of a conference?

Comparing McIlvaine's responses to unity—evangelical and Anglican—provides an interesting insight into the worldview of Evangelical Episcopalians. Long before the High Church requested a conference on Anglican unity, Evangelicals had been practicing inter-Christian union in the voluntary societies. They separated *unity* and *union*. They were not opposed to unity; they were opposed to "outward" unions that had little basis in reality. Unity of heart, of experience in Christ, of God's word in the Bible—such was of greater value to them than institutional unions. Any true union must be based on inner reality of evangelical unity and on Protestant truth. Shortly before the conference began, McIlvaine wrote again to Carus: "Oh, for decision and boldness, and a right sense of the value of the truth, before all efforts at union and outside aspect of agreement!"⁶¹

Because he was so anxious to base union on truth, the opening resolution of the conference was of supreme importance to McIlvaine. He viewed it as theologically inadequate; it was neither Protestant enough nor evangelical enough. There were too many references to church councils and tradition and not enough to Scripture. In addition, he disliked the statement on reunion: "the best hope of reunion," he believed, "will be found in our drawing closer to Christ."[62] In place of the proposed statement, McIlvaine defined Christian union as

> a closer personal communion of all Christian people, by faith, with our common Lord and Life; in the diligent searching of the Scriptures, with humble reliance on the Holy Ghost, by whose inspiration they were written for our learning; in giving ourselves continually to prayers, each for himself, and all for the flock of Christ; and in the culmination of brotherly fellowship and love, according to the mind of Christ."[63]

This was the only possible basis for true unity or institutional union.

On the first day of the conference, Bishops McIlvaine and Sumner led an evangelical revolt against the proposed resolution. Much to their surprise, they won. The first resolution was changed nearly entirely—and all the words most offensive to the Evangelicals were omitted. Scripture was given the primary place of authority in the document. The definition of union was expanded and clarified to include Evangelical concerns. One historian has noted that in the proceedings of the opening day, through the powerful persuasion of McIlvaine, "the Evangelicals [were] in the ascendant, despite the presence of so many High Churchmen."[64] Because of this, and because of the strong condemnation of Bishop Colenso's higher critical views, McIlvaine left the Lambeth Conference quite satisfied. "I could heartily unite," he wrote to Carus, "in the last resolution of thanks to God for such a meeting, as all did. How little did I expect at one time to be able to do so."[65] Although the Evangelical press was still critical of the conference, McIlvaine came away from the meeting encouraged by the possibility of Anglican unity on Protestant and evangelical terms.[66]

Not surprisingly, McIlvaine's favorite organization promoting Christian unity was the Evangelical Alliance.[67] Of all the late nineteenth-century plans for union, the alliance resisted institutional union, or denominational consolidation, in favor of unity on the basis of theology and evangelical experience. "Unity," proclaimed Gregory Bedell, "does not depend on organic union. . . . Protestantism, indeed, is not a church. Evangelical Christianity is not a form of organization. . . . They are systems of positive truth, characterizing many churches."[68] By separating institutional union from the simple, inward unity of Christ, evangelicals could maintain denominational distinctiveness while proclaiming their oneness in Jesus. This idea appealed to many evangelicals. It had particular appeal for Evangelical Episcopalians, who valued their prayer book and polity, yet wanted to express their commonalties with other evangelical Protestants. As an organization, the alliance symbolized their long-standing commitment to being both Evangelical and Episcopal. When Presbyterian Henry B. Smith called for a revitalization of the American Evangelical Alliance at a World Alliance meeting in the summer of 1867, Evangelical Episcopal leaders, such as Bishops McIlvaine,

Bedell, and Johns and the Revs. Heman Dyer and Noah H. Schenck, eagerly joined the cause.[69]

McIlvaine's interest in evangelical unity had a darker rationale, as well. Although evangelical unitive efforts were optimistically based on the coming of Christ's kingdom, there was an element of fear in their ecumenism. Wrote McIlvaine:

> The state of the world, so remarkable at this time, and the gathering of the two great armies of the powers of darkness, in their joint war against the Church of Christ and His precious Gospel, are a loud call upon His people, essentially *one* to be *united* in *their* warfare for their glorious Head, and the great salvation. The contest will be such as the Church has not known before in its double aspect, against Popery and Infidelity.[70]

Some aspects of evangelical ecumenism were based on hope, but a large part of their desire for Christian unity was based on the need for concerted action against Roman Catholicism and rationalism. The reactionary and antidemocratic tone of European Catholicism in the 1860s was profoundly disturbing to American evangelicals, and new Protestant theological trends threatened to undermine the whole evangelical system of conversion and benevolence. Working together took on dramatic significance: earlier in the nineteenth century, evangelicals had fought against the infidelity of deism and the French Revolution, and they had long battled the growth of Roman Catholicism. In the years following the war, American evangelicals faced both foes at the same time. Infidelity and idolatry had finally come together; the evangelical battle against them was of universal significance. The outcome of Armageddon was in the balance.

Immediately following the Civil War, these new trends had a significant impact on Evangelical Episcopalians. The heightened fear of the age intensified, and sometimes altered, aspects of their worldview. By the late 1860s, they rearticulated and reemphasized their commitment to Scripture and the supernatural. They slowly abandoned their postmillennialism in favor of premillennialism and, eventually, dispensationalism. They looked increasingly away from their own church for Christian unity, and, instead, looked upon panevangelical unity as the greatest hope for the gospel. All of these trends started before the war, often in reaction to the Oxford Movement, but the combined threat of Romanism and rationalism hardened them and created a more militant, and more fearful, tone in the Evangelical Episcopal party than had existed anytime previously.

Tempest: The Swell of Anglo-Catholicism

The second crisis facing the Evangelical party was "popery," or the growth of Roman Catholicism. In the years following the Civil War, evangelical Protestants trembled at the strengthening of papal authority under Pope Pius IX (1846–1878). In 1870, the Vatican Council issued a declaration of papal infallibility and invited all Christians to come back to the Roman Catholic Church. Nearly all evangelicals believed that Rome was rising from the blow it had received from the Protestant Reformation; this Roman revival was an ominious portend of the end times.

Evangelical Episcopalians, who dreaded Roman authoritarianism and imperialism, were troubled by an endemic concern: the most immediate threat of Romanist expansion came from within the Episcopal Church itself in the form of Ritualism.

The older High Church party, the Hobartians, and the early Tractarians generally looked to the early centuries of Christian tradition for the formation of theology and liturgical practice. Believing that the Church of England and the Episcopal Church best preserved the apostolic purity of the early church, they were generally not liturgical innovators; instead, they insisted on strict adherence to the Anglican prayer book tradition. When a few innovators, such as Levi Ives, in the 1850s introduced auricular confession and monastic practices, even some of the Hobartians were shocked by what were described as "Romanizing" practices. The older High Churchmen and some Tractarians believed that the Episcopal Church was *catholic* insofar as it recognized its continuity with the early church – not because Episcopal liturgy resembled that of Roman Catholicism.

The new movement, which Evangelicals identified as a continuation of Tractarianism, leaned more heavily on medieval and romantic influences than did the older one. McIlvaine defined it as a movement of "form" as opposed to theology. The Ritualists sought to introduce a host of new forms into American Episcopalianism: use of incense, eucharistic vestments, crucifixes, processions, elevation of the communion bread and wine, genuflection, prayers to saints and for the dead, and vested choirs and choral services. Ritualism, also referred to as Anglo-Catholicism, was a movement to restore Roman Catholic practices from the medieval church into the Episcopal Church. Ritualists argued that these were common practices at the time of the Reformation, and that it had never been the intention of the English Reformers to rid the church of medieval ceremonialism.

In the years before the war, Ritualistic practices were not widely present in the Episcopal Church. In some High Church dioceses, altars replaced tables, candles were plentiful, and flowers were placed around the altar. But in other dioceses, Ohio for example, even slight ritualistic changes prompted huge controversy. There, McIlvaine had successfully used his episcopal authority to limit processionals, surpliced choirs, and other musical innovations.[71] By 1865, medieval ceremonialism was so well contained that some Evangelicals thought the Episcopal Church's brief flirtation with Roman Catholicism was a thing of the past. McIlvaine, however, expressed his doubts:

> I have constantly declared, amidst all the confidence that Puseyism was dead, that it was strong, and aggressive, and dangerous as ever. . . . The line of advance which Romanism makes among you in England is the same as here – *general display of ceremonial*, externalism, music, postures, crosses, vestments, processions, sacramentalism, working out our own righteousness by all such things, but all centering in *priest, sacrifice, and altar*.[72]

McIlvaine was aware of the growing medieval tendencies of English worship in the 1850s and 1860s. The Anglo-Catholic ceremonialism of such parishes as St. George-in-the-East caused such popular commotion that the bishop of London closed the parish from September to November 1859 to prevent rioting. By 1859, wrote one historian, "Anglo-Catholics were now a party of fighters. . . . Ritual troubles in English church and state began in earnest."[73] When the new Ritualistic movement began in America, McIlvaine was not surprised.

The renewal of Ritualism after the Civil War began with the publication of John Henry Hopkins's *The Law of Ritualism*. Hopkins argued that some "increase" of ceremony should be allowed in the Episcopal Church because of the biblical, especially Old Testament, precedents of such things as incense, vestments, and ornament. It was perfectly legitimate for the "Gentile church" to borrow these Hebrew forms. The Reformation, Hopkins maintained, was not an argument over these forms; it had occurred because of Roman Catholic innovations in doctrine. The Anglican reformers wanted to keep the good elements of their Catholic heritage. Modern Ritualism, therefore, was a restoration of biblical and Reformational purity in the Episcopal Church. As long as Ritualism did not include Roman Catholic corruptions—such as worship of saints, priestly celibacy, auricular confession, monasticism, and purgatory—it should not be rejected. "So long as the great doctrines of the Reformation," wrote Hopkins, "are faithfully preached by the clergy, I can see no danger that a solemn, rich, and attractive ritual will ever lead any one to Popery." Biblical ritual, he argued, "can neither be hostile to the doctrines of a pure faith, nor unfavorably to the exercise of a spiritual devotion."[74]

At a different time in history, Hopkins's biblical argument for the limited use of Ritualism might have appealed to Evangelicals. It was a tightly argued piece that paid close attention to Scripture and made careful distinctions between biblical ritual and Roman Catholic "innovations." In 1866, however, with the millennial worry about the growth of rationalism and Romanism, Evangelicals could not differentiate between "biblical" and Roman rituals: all ritual appeared equally unprotestant. The Evangelical party had been substantially influenced by the Puritan tradition on this point. It is hard to imagine that Bishop McIlvaine, who privately confessed to his sympathies with Oliver Cromwell's views on ecclesiastical ornaments, could have been convinced by Hopkins's argument. In addition, Evangelicals insisted that the Protestant doctrine of the Episcopal Church could not survive if ritualistic forms were introduced. Hopkins, therefore, was misguided when he asserted that as long as the doctrines of the Protestant Reformation were taught, a more elaborate ritual did not really matter. McIlvaine had come to believe that this was a fundamental inconsistency: form and truth were inseparable, and since Ritualistic forms were of one piece with Roman Catholicism, they all must be rejected. Although he once believed that form was a matter of taste, McIlvaine now wrote, "The form is the whole of it; indifference to that, is indifference to the truth."[75]

Form and Meaning of Ritualism: Problem of the Prayer Book and Baptismal Regeneration, 1866–1868

"The present plan" of the Ritualists, wrote McIlvaine in 1864,

> is to promote a taste for a ceremonial sensuous religion, for Church ornament, pomp, symbolism, mystery and ritual, multiplied into the details of Church

furniture, ministerial vestments, Clerical postures, and the like; under such fascination, quietly to introduce and make fast the whole Sacerdotal system of Priesthood, Sacrifice, Altar, and the *opus operatum* of Baptismal efficacy. . . . All this, of course, is of the very essence of Popery.[76]

For Evangelical Episcopalians, "baptismal efficacy" was at the center of the controversy. Once baptismal regeneration was admitted, the evangelical Protestantism of the Episcopal Church would be replaced by a system that "teaches the Church as the depository of saving grace," sacramentalism, and the mediation of priests. Against this, "every nerve in the heart of true Protestantism is braced."[77]

Baptismal regeneration, or "efficacy" as McIlvaine preferred to call it, had been a growing problem for Evangelical Episcopalians. Since the early days of the Oxford Movement controversy, Evangelicals had attacked the sacerdotal tendencies of the movement–especially the Tractarian views of baptism. In *Oxford Divinity Compared*, McIlvaine argued that Tractarianism would lead away from the Protestant doctrine of justification by faith alone to a doctrine of baptismal justification. In the Protestant view, argued McIlvaine, baptism conveyed grace contingent on the faith of the recipient; the Roman Catholic view, in contrast, argued that the sacraments were effective in and of themselves. To the Evangelicals, faith–that of the person or the person's parents–necessarily preceded baptism. The sacrament, they argued, was an outward sign of an inward change wrought by faith through the work of the Holy Spirit.[78] Infants, since they had no personal faith, were to be baptized on the basis of the covenant. Christian parents brought children on the basis of their own faith and claimed the promises of Christ on their children's behalf. The rite did not "save," nor did it take away sins. Only faith and trust in God, when appropriated by the baptized person, would save. Baptism was only a change in relative state–that is, the baptized individual was placed in covenant with God–not a change in moral or spiritual nature.[79] Moral, spiritual, and inward transformation would only occur when the person experienced faith through being born again. Thus, they believed that the Episcopal Church's doctrine of baptism was "a *badge* of Christian profession; a *symbol* of regeneration; a rite of *initiation*; a *covenanting* and *sealing* act; and an *evidence* to the identity of the church . . . from generation to generation."[80] On one hand, baptism was a rite of initiation into the visible church; on the other hand, it was simply a sign, or symbol, of the possibility of incorporation into the invisible body of Christ.

To support their baptismal theology, with its clearly Reformed bias in its covenantal emphases, Evangelicals leaned heavily on articles twenty-five and twenty-seven which supported receptionism and called baptism a *sign* of regeneration.[81] They nevertheless recognized that there was ambiguity in the language of the prayer book baptismal rite. Especially troubling to them was the pronouncement of the minister after baptism "that this child is regenerate." The Rev. John Seeley Stone confidently expressed:

Our Church can not mean by this language that the Holy Spirit in baptism regenerates the infant in the sense of working in him that great moral change from the old death in sin to the new life of holiness, in which faith and repentance are essential parts. If she meant this, she would stand up a house divided against itself, and sure to fall. She can, therefore, mean no more than that the Holy Spirit effects for the infant in baptism that of which in baptism is capable.[82]

In order to reconcile the language of the American prayer book and the theology of the Thirty-nine Articles, Evangelicals did two things. First, Evangelical seminaries taught that the prayer book was always interpreted by the articles; therefore, the Protestant emphases of the articles, with their formal theological statements, always took precedence over the poetic language of the prayer book rituals. "Every Evangelical clergyman remembers," wrote one Evangelical, "how his Theological Professor labored at expositions of the baptismal service for Infants" and how they were taught to reject the "literal and grammatical sense" of the prayer book office.[83]

The second Evangelical response to the problem of baptismal regeneration in the prayer book was to adopt a "hypothetical theory" of baptism. According to this theory, as the baptismal questions—such as "Dost thou believe all the articles of the Christian faith, as contained in the Apostles' Creed?"—were answered "hypothetically" on behalf of the infant, so the minister pronounced that the child was "hypothetically" regenerate on the basis of accepting salvation as an adult. When that infant grew to adulthood and experienced spiritual regeneration, then baptismal regeneration would be made effective. What was once hypothetical—that "this child is regenerate"—would, after spiritual rebirth, be made actual.[84]

In the decade before the Civil War, Evangelical Episcopalians were under pressure from two sources over the meaning of infant baptism and the prayer book declaration of baptismal regeneration: Church of England troubles over infant baptism and American baptismal arguments. The issue had been brought to its first crisis point in the Church of England when Bishop Phillpotts of Exeter declared the views of one of his Evangelical clergyman, George C. Gorham, unsound: Gorham rejected the idea that infants were regenerated at baptism. The case dragged on through several courts, and Anglican Evangelicals threatened to leave the Church of England if the courts decided against Gorham. Finally, in May 1850, the judicial committee of the Privy Council (a secular court), declared that Gorham's views did not conflict with Anglican doctrine. An Evangelical schism in the Church of England was averted.[85]

The Gorham case had some significant results for Evangelical Episcopalians in America: it proved that their views on baptism were in line with those of Anglican theology. In the process, it helped clarify and crystallize their baptismal theologies—Evangelicals held to some four or five different versions of their basic covenant theology.[86] Anglican Evangelicals published a significant number of the works on baptism during the case, all of which were widely read by American Evangelicals. The most important of those works was William Goode's *The Doctrine of the Church of England as to the Effects of Baptism*. Goode argued that Anglicanism rejected both baptism as *mere* sign and the position which supposed "that the sign is *invariably*, i.e. *opere operato*, accompanied by the thing signified."[87] Between these two views, Goode argued, the Church of England allowed for diversity of Protestant opinion. As a result of Goode's work, Evangelicals argued for liberty of viewpoints on the subject and recognized significant diversity within their own party. McIlvaine leaned heavily on Goode, calling it "the most elaborate, learned, and effective work on the subject . . . in modern times."[88]

A second crisis occurred as Evangelical Episcopalians were being pressured by other American Christians over the nature of baptism. In nineteenth-century America, many Baptists and some sectarian groups believed that baptism was absolutely connected to regeneration: without baptism, salvation was not possible. They argued that only adults could understand, experience, and appropriate the faith necessary to be saved and give a public profession through baptism. Roman Catholics and some High Church Episcopalians also connected baptism with salvation; however, they argued they all baptized persons – infants included – were regenerate. Against both these positions, Evangelical Episcopalians argued that baptism was not necessarily (although even Goode admitted that it sometimes might be) connected to spiritual regeneration. New birth, regeneration, was a matter of the inner work of the Holy Spirit.

The American debates over baptism, due largely to the phenomenal growth of the Baptists in the early nineteenth century, set in a frame of American revivalism, had a deadening effect on the practice of infant baptism in the historic Protestant denominations. By the 1850s, Presbyterians noticed a startling decline in the number of infant baptisms, and Charles Hodge pointed out that only a quarter of the children eligible for baptism were being presented by their parents.[89] Similar declines were evident in other Reformed denominations, as well. "All this evidence," wrote one historian, "seemed to bear out strongly the Baptist contention that the chief pedobaptist churches in America were rapidly coming to agree with them in sentiment and practice."[90]

Although Episcopalians were less affected by this trend than other historic Protestant churches, Evangelical Episcopalians expressed private dismay over the inadequacies of their baptismal service for missionary and evangelistic purposes. The PESPEK published a pamphlet urging parents to baptize their children and refuted Baptist claims to the necessity of immersion.[91] In spite of their elaborate (and sometimes tortured) explanations of the language of regeneration, they admitted that the simple sense of the words implied that infants were born again through baptism. Bemoaned William Meade as early as 1827: "Why could not another prayer . . . be introduced into the Baptismal Service, and allowed to be used in the place of the one which we now must use, but which I never do without pain, because its plain, literal meaning contradicts my belief?"[92] Thirty years later, when asked to respond to Muhlenberg's Memorial, Meade made the same point and requested that ministers be allowed to omit the declaration of regeneration in the baptismal service. Meade wrote; "Many parents I believe are prejudiced against the baptism of their children, and put it off, on account of these words, and their supposed meaning. I believe nothing stands more in the way of converts from other denominations . . . than the required use of these words in our Baptismal service."[93]

Meade's 1857 suggestion for revision indicated the beginning of a shift in the views of Evangelical Episcopalians. The downturn in Protestant infant baptisms happened to coincide with new research on the history and theology of the Reformation. The work of these European scholars began to be widely read in

America in the 1850s and 1860s, and some American theologians were beginning to rethink baptism as a result.[94] Until then, Evangelical Episcopalians assumed that their doctrine of baptism, heavily influenced by American Reformed thought as it was, was exactly the same as that of the English Reformers: evangelical theology was identical to Reformation theology. The new scholarship undermined this assumption, however. For example, Karl R. Hagenbach, the German historical theologian whose *History of Doctrines* was widely read, claimed that "among the doctrines in which Roman Catholics and Protestants preserved a certain agreement . . . was that concerning baptism" and that "Protestants and Catholics entertained essentially the same view of the nature of baptism." As if to aggravate Evangelical Episcopalians, he also asserted that "the divines of the Church of England taught the doctrine of baptismal regeneration, yet with cautions."[95]

In 1860, Maryland's High Church Bishop William Whittingham published a pamphlet on baptismal regeneration (a series of letters that had appeared in the *Southern Churchman*), which used the arguments of historical theology to prove that the English Reformers believed in baptismal regeneration.[96] For decades, Evangelical Episcopalians used the English Reformers to support their position. Whittingham now appropriated "their side," so to speak, to disprove Evangelical baptismal theology and argue for the High Church position. The argument Whittingham put forth was secondary to the symbolism of the attack.

McIlvaine was quick to see the danger in this. With an evident haste, he wrote a pamphlet in reply, entitled *Some Thoughts on Baptismal Regeneration*:

> The doctrine of Regeneration, with that of Justification, constitutes the substance of the teaching of the Scriptures concerning the spiritual life in fallen man. "Except a man be born again, he can not see the Kingdom of God." What that great spiritual change import; by what means it is wrought; . . . what relation its sacramental *sign* [Baptism] bears to that "inward and spiritual grace;" in other words, what relation sacramental Baptism bears to real Baptism, the sign to the thing signified . . . these are certainly questions of very momentous importance; . . . Nothing draws a wider line between different classes of our people and clergy than the pro and con of these questions. The whole character of our theology, and of our experimental religion, as being *evangelical* or *unevangelical*, depends on it.[97]

McIlvaine's argument, like Whittingham's, was in some sense less important than the way in which he argued: McIlvaine used the theology of John Henry Hobart to support his own views! Even Hobart, argued McIlvaine, did not believe that spiritual regeneration (which Hobart called "renovation") occurred in baptism. Thus, even the old-fashioned High Church party separated baptism from spiritual regeneration. Wrote McIlvaine:

> Baptismal Regeneration is distinguished from Regeneration, just as the sacramental sign is distinguished from the inward grace. All baptized are spoken of as having "Baptismal Regeneration," while some of them are spoken of as still "unregenerate." From the very nature of a covenant, the assurance mentioned is *conditional*. The condition is the very repentance and faith which the infant promises, as our Catechism says, by his sureties, and on which promise he is

baptized. We think the Westminster Assembly would have had no objection to such Baptismal Regeneration. As for us, we believe in it. It is the doctrine of our Church.[98]

To finish his argument, McIlvaine dismissed Whittingham's claim that Latimer was the best representative of the English Reformation and accused Whittingham of using Latimer selectively. McIlvaine remained convinced that theology of the English Reformation was the same as nineteenth-century evangelical theology.

Not all Evangelical Episcopalians agreed with him. After the publication of Hopkins's *Law of Ritualism*, which pointed out, in part, that some Ritualistic practices were supported in the first prayer book of Edward VI, the debate over the baptismal theology of the Reformation began to focus on the prayer book itself. In 1868, the Rev. Franklin S. Rising published a pamphlet that became a rallying point for discontented Evangelical Episcopalians. In *Are There Romanizing Germs in the Prayer Book?*, Rising argued that the English Reformation was "political rather than spiritual in its origin." As such, it embodied "the spirit of compromise." The Edwardian Reformers had not even gone far enough in a Protestant direction, he argued; had they lived longer, they would produce a third, and thoroughly Reformed, prayer book. But, as it stood, their second prayer book was a "nobly conceived but half-wrought statue. . . . The Liturgy," Rising stated, "is Romish"; only the Thirty-nine Articles were completely Protestant.[99]

The most offensive part of the prayer book was the baptismal liturgy. Here, Rising believed, was the greatest failure of the Reformation. To support his point, he summoned Cranmer, Bucer, and Jewel. "Baptismal regeneration," he argued, "was the prevailing belief among all classes of theologians for years after the Reformation." He rejected William Goode's Evangelical and Reformed interpretation of the English Reformation and, instead, accepted Hagenbach's. The un-Reformed prayer book, according to Rising, was the source of all the "Romanizing germs" in the Protestant Episcopal Church. He urged fellow Evangelicals that it rested upon them "to take up that Reformation where it was interrupted by Mary, and to present to the world the precious gift of a purely evangelical Liturgy." The only hope to eliminate all Roman Catholic tendencies in the church would be to revise the prayer book and purge it of all its nonevangelical doctrines. To that end, Rising exclaimed, "Let us *agitate*, AGITATE, and AGITATE!"[100]

Rising focused Evangelical anxiety on a single issue: prayer book revision. Since the 1850s, the party had experienced a general lack of confidence in the church's institutions. In the years following the Civil War, that general discontent centered on the prayer book. This was a surprising change: the prayer book, like the Reformation, had always been used to support the Evangelical position in the church. Sounding a bit like Stephen or Dudley Tyng from the 1850s, Rising now argued, "We cannot use or give a Prayer-Book without, in some sense, becoming a party to its errors."[101] The Evangelical quest for purity extended from the church in general to its liturgies—its baptismal liturgy in particular.

Rising was not alone. In 1869, the Rev. Benjamin B. Leacock of Harrisburg, Pennsylvania, argued that in the Reformation "error was not wholly extirpated." "The Anglican Reformation," he stated, "*is incomplete*. . . . The mind of the

Reformers was still developing towards Protestantism." As a result, *"the Book of Common Prayer is inconsistent with, if not contradictory to, itself."*[102] Following much of Rising's argument, Leacock believed that the prayer book—as it existed—was essentially un-Protestant while the Thirty-nine Articles were Reformed. Echoing the rhetoric once used by McIlvaine about Tractarianism, Leacock stated:

> How can two systems, so diametrically opposed, find a home under the same roof, draw their inspiration from the same source, and strengthen and establish themselves by citations from the same book? . . . We have every reason to anticipate that the antagonism existing between these two systems, must be found in the Prayer Book also.[103]

Some Evangelical Episcopalians, so perplexed by the growth of Ritualism, began to blame both the Reformation and the prayer book for present-day troubles. Argued Leacock:

> The Prayer Book is the friend of both parties. It contains within its covers both systems—Protestantism and Sacerdotalism. . . . *The only remedy for the evil, that is overwhelming our beloved Church, and that therefore, there must be a revision of the Prayer Book.* The whole body, as one man, must rise up, and *demand that words and expressions, and usages, that give a coloring to sarcedotalism, or to any other error, must be expunged from the Service Book.* . . . Nothing less than this will save us, either as a party, or as a Church.[104]

McIlvaine was not pleased by this development. He hated Rising's pamphlet, and he wrote to Judge Conyngham, president of the American Church Missions Society, demanding that Rising be removed from his position as the society's secretary. He called Rising's views "extreme" and accused him of using his position to zealously propagate them. "In these days," McIlvaine argued, "our Evangelical ranks should be as much as possible undivided."[105] Leacock pointed out that some (implicating McIlvaine, Lee, and Eastburn) Evangelicals were among those most resistant to prayer book revision. In January 1867, McIlvaine signed a declaration with twenty-three other bishops (High Church bishops included) that condemned Ritualism as an innovation from Anglican practice. They rejected the argument that Hopkins made from the Edwardian prayer book. McIlvaine evidently thought this declaration was sufficient and that measured action would eliminate Ritualism; the prayer book revision scheme seemed unnecessary. Rising, Leacock, and those following them disagreed.

In November 1867, at the Evangelical societies meetings in Philadelphia, a sizable group of clergy and laypeople called for a revision of the prayer book. Dozens of important Evangelical leaders attended these meetings—including bishops McIlvaine, Lee, and Eastburn, and the Tyngs. "I can remember now," wrote one participant, "the impassioned earnestness with that peculiar inflection of the Tyng tone, in the young rector . . . spoke for absolute secession from the sacramental system of the church."[106] Although he was present at these meetings, McIlvaine abstained from signing their declarations. "The three evangelical bishops present," wrote one historian, "McIlvaine, Lee, and Eastburn, saved the meeting from radical legislation."[107] A participant put it more bluntly: "The three evangelical bishops who were present, Bishops McIlvaine, Lee and Eastburn, put down their six episcopal feet upon the movement."[108]

McIlvaine was distressed by the talk of schism and believed it part of his episcopal duty to hold the church together. Younger priests and layman looked to him for leadership, and his sermons and writings on Romanism clearly influenced their thinking. He had alerted them to the dangers of the Ritual movement; they felt they were following his lead. As they built on his ideas and threatened schism, McIlvaine tried to hold the Evangelical party together—and to keep it in the church. McIlvaine confided to William Carus:

> We are in much trouble in our American Episcopal Church. The growth of Romish doctrine, and of ritualistic extravagance, has quickened the long-felt grievance of certain things in the Prayer Book—especially the words of the Baptismal Office ("regenerated by the Holy Spirit," etc.), into such revolt, that there is a considerable body of clergy and laity determined on having a change, or making a separation. . . . It will ripen into a schism unless some relief is given.[109]

Not until the talk of schism did McIlvaine reluctantly support some sort of "relief"—not necessarily revision. "My position is trying," he wrote, "I am looked to to take the lead in emergencies of this sort—*on one side*—and I feel very, *very* incompetent."[110]

McIlvaine was plagued with personal problems, as well: many of his dearest friends had passed away; his invalid son was worsening; his grandson-namesake had died; his anxiety illness had returned; and his own fears of death increased. His diary during this period is full of exhaustion, prayers for strength and power, and a desire for release from life:

> Let me not be weary! Let me not be afraid what men can do unto me. Let not the faith and constancy of any of my dear children be ever shaken—though all should forsake thee, Lord, let not this poor heart go away. Make all thy truth in all its simplicity, more & more dear to my soul.[111]

He was worried about his health, his family, old age, and dying. There is scattered evidence that some sort of breach existed between him and his only surviving son, the Rev. Charles E. McIlvaine, who lacked his father's charismatic gifts and seemed relatively unconcerned about the Evangelical cause. Struggling with the pain of personal burdens, McIlvaine was forced to lead the Evangelical party through its greatest crisis.

By 1869, when McIlvaine wrote to Carus about feeling incompetent, the situation was nearly out of control. At the 1868 General Convention, L. W. Bancroft, professor of church history at Bexley Hall, Rising, Leacock, and Richard Newton presented a memorial to the House of Bishops requesting permission to omit "such words, expressions, or passages, of said Book which he conscientiously believes to be contrary to Holy Scriptures." They argued for "relief" on the "broad ground of Christian liberty and brotherly toleration."[112] The House of Bishops denied this petition for greater liturgical latitude and postponed the issue of liturgical revision until 1871. Their inaction gave the Evangelicals three more years to organize, agitate, and, sadly, bicker among themselves. In 1867, McIlvaine, along with Lee and Eastburn, had been barely able to control their followers; after the 1868 convention, their leadership of the Evangelical party would be seriously tested.

Catholicism at Kenyon: The Case of James Kent Stone

While the Evangelical party was pulling itself apart over its response to Ritualism, McIlvaine faced a serious and disturbing problem in Ohio. Kenyon College and Bexley Hall survived the war in good shape. Since the Theological Seminary at Alexandria was closed during the war, many young Evangelicals went to Gambier instead for their education. In 1865, both institutions were strong in terms of faculty and students. The president of Bexley was S. A. Bronson; his faculty included systematic theology professor John J. McElhinney, church historian L. W. Bancroft, and biblical studies professor Frederic Gardiner. Kenyon's president was Charles Short, a Harvard graduate and linguist whose faculty included William Newton, known for his millennial theology, and James Kent Stone, son of the well-known Evangelical leader, John Seeley Stone.

In April 1867, Bexley experienced a mild uproar when Gardiner protested to the Board of Trustees that Bancroft and McElhinney were teaching unsound doctrine. McElhinney had seen this coming: in January he had written to McIlvaine complaining that "Prof. Gardiner is entirely out of sympathy with the spirit and teaching which have heretofore prevailed here."[113] It appeared he was some sort of rationalist. McElhinney reported to the bishop that Prof. Gardiner had four major objections to Bexley's theology: first, it was too "subjective" with all "aids of science" ignored or dismissed; second, it was antinominian; third, it was "ultra-millenarian"; and fourth, it was "Baptist" and "Calvinist" in sacramental theology. Bancroft and McElhinney were indeed millennialists (as were Bronson and Newton), were skeptical about rationalistic biblical interpretation, and held standard evangelical views on works and sacraments. In other words, although McElhinney objected to Gardiner's characterization of "antinomian" and "Baptist" (but not to "Calvinist"), the charges were true. After an investigation, the board declared that Gardiner's charge – that these doctrines were "unsound doctrine" – was unproved; the evangelical theology taught by Bancroft and McElhinney was perfectly orthodox. Gardiner resigned. Bancroft, tired of the controversy, decided to leave the seminary. McElhinney, however, stayed on with the full blessing of President Bronson and the Board of Trustees. Bexley's evangelical course was set.

In that same year, the college faced a public controversy. President Short was unable to properly discipline the young men, and some rumors of "defects of a serious character" at the college circulated in the diocese. Short was forced to resign. The trustees elected James Kent Stone, another Harvard graduate and professor of Latin, to succeed him. Stone was quite young – only twenty-eight – and the son of an old friend of bishops McIlvaine and Bedell, John Seeley Stone, who had served evangelical parishes in Brooklyn and Boston and was then dean and theology professor at the new Evangelical Episcopal seminary in Cambridge, Massachusetts.[114] He vigorously opposed Tractarianism, was quite learned in Reformation theology, and wrote two capable books on evangelical positions on sacraments and the church, *The Mysteries Opened* (1844) and *The Church Universal* (1846).[115] Both works were anti-Tractarian treatises, republished in 1866 to combat the new Ritualism. The Kenyon trustees were happy to have Stone's son as their new president.

James Kent Stone was not entirely what was expected: he defended McElhinney and Bancroft against Gardiner's attack in a sermon preached in Rosse Chapel on February 24, 1867. Stone defended them, however, on the basis of the right to liberty in judgment—not because he agreed with them. He argued for "moderation and toleration" in theology because certain doctrines, such as millennialism and the tension between justification by faith and justification by works, were outside the realm of human speculative ability. "Truth," he proclaimed, "is many sided." The differences between "High Church and Low Church, Ritualist and Evangelical, Millennarian and old-fashioned Churchman" were less important than Christian charity.[116] The college faculty enthusiastically endorsed Stone's sermon; the seminary faculty did not. Ostensibly a defense of their rights, the seminary community considered it an attack on Evangelical beliefs.

To make matters worse, at the beginning of the next term, Stone bowed—in Ritualist fashion—during recitation of the Apostles' Creed. "A custom," complained Bronson to Stone, "not in accordance with the practice of our Bishop and new to you. It had the appearance of an attempt to identify yourself with a party in the Church, and that too, opposed to our Bishop."[117] After this curt reprimand, Stone temporarily stopped the practice.

Not long thereafter, Bishop Bedell gave a series of lectures at the college against the dangers of Ritualism and Roman Catholicism. On the Sunday following the bishop's address, President Stone preached on "making the Incarnation the central doctrine of Christianity and extolling the mystery of sacramental grace, but without a word upon the qualifications needed to receive that grace."[118] This sermon, delivered in February 1868, served notice that Stone had "gone over" to Tractarianism. Evangelicals, such as McIlvaine, had long insisted that the atonement was the central doctrine of Christian faith; Tractarians, on the other hand, emphasized the incarnation as the starting point for Christian theology. "Incarnation" had been a buzz word for evangelicals since publication of Robert Isaac Wilberforce's (the High Church son of William Wilberforce) 1848 *The Doctrine of the Incarnation*, which emphasized the church as the incarnation of Christ and the sacraments as the means of union with Christ.[119] Wilberforce's subsequent conversion to Roman Catholicism did little to promote incarnational theology among Evangelicals.[120] What little can be gathered of Stone's position at the time implies that he followed Wilberforce's argument.

After the sermon of February 1868, the Evangelical professors at Bexley were convinced that Stone was a Ritualist. Reported Bronson to McIlvaine: "The College Faculty have now avowedly placed themselves in antagonism to the doctrines you and Bishop Bedell are so nobly upholding." On February 6, Stone confessed to Bronson that the two men's "Church views differed." Bronson was convinced, and did not hesitate to tell McIlvaine, "that he was doing his best to indoctrinate the students with mediaeval Catholicism and sacramentalism." Bronson reported that Stone had confessed to this charge as well.[121] "Our beloved

College," wrote J. W. Cracraft, a minister residing in Gambier, "is now in the hands of her old enemies and has for her President, a man who is in entire sympathy with the worst errors of Ritualism."[122]

It is not entirely clear what happened to James Kent Stone. How had he become a Tractarian? In his apologetic, Stone indicated that he was frustrated over liberalism in the church and believed that even "the most conservative Protestant" was influenced by rationalism, as indicated by the evangelical rejection of modern miracles. "Those who in effect deny the possibility of miracles in the nineteenth century," wrote Stone, "must end by denying their possibility in the first." This inconsistency, the "illogical" basis of Protestantism "must end inevitably – there is no possibility of escape – in logical rationalism."[123] Protestantism, he became convinced, would always result in theological liberalism. Neither Gambier's, nor his father's, earnest and committed evangelicalism could stop Protestantism's tendency toward rationalism. Only Roman Catholicism had correctly preserved the supernatural elements of Christianity.

Bronson was unaware of Stone's increasing skepticism about the Protestantism of the Episcopal Church. He believed that Stone had "become giddy" over his elevation to the presidency and was using his newfound power and influence to wrest control of the diocesan newspaper, the *Western Episcopalian*, and the college from Bishop McIlvaine.[124] For himself, Stone continued to insist that McIlvaine would not see anything objectionable in his views and interpreted the whole affair as a personal attack by Bronson.[125] Tensions were running high between the college and the seminary.

Bronson kept up an almost daily correspondence with McIlvaine. "But in the College Faculty," he insisted, "there is evident very bitter hostility to what you and I call Gospel preaching." By March, McIlvaine had corresponded with Stone as to his views of the sacraments. Stone, McIlvaine believed, was in error. The bishop requested that Stone read evangelical William Goode's work on the real presence in the eucharist – an Anglican attack on Wilberforce's views of the sacrament. This reading, McIlvaine hoped, would "enable him to measure and define his own views" to clarify terms.[126] Stone's position sounded like Wilberforce's, but McIlvaine wanted to give the young man every opportunity to prove himself within the evangelical camp.

The Board of Trustees met in a special session with Stone and the two bishops and decided that because Stone had *intended* no harm, the college should consider itself at peace. If he had wanted to keep his job, Stone should have left the situation alone; just a few weeks later, however, as preacher of the baccalaureate sermon, he aggravated the Evangelicals again. The next day, when the student valedictorian defended Stone as a "victim of those who, while professing to be advocates of religious toleration, were unwilling that it should apply to any except those whose opinions agreed with their own," it was clear that Stone's presence would be a continuing source of tension and agitation. He had to go.[127] In April 1868, under pressure, he resigned.

A short time later, James Kent Stone accepted the presidency of Hobart College, an Episcopal High Church school, in Geneva, New York. A year after his resignation from Kenyon, he wrote to McIlvaine: "I honestly thought my theological opinions to be identical with those of Ridley, of Cranmer, of Jewel, and of Hooker, not with those of the Oxford School of our own day."[128] That opinion proved wrong; he was a High Churchman. Hobart College's High Churchmanship, however, provided a temporary respite for Stone. After only a year at the college, Stone was received into the Roman Catholic Church.[129]

The James Kent Stone case troubled Evangelicals. Many Roman Catholic converts from the Episcopal Church had been, at some time in their careers, Evangelicals. Episcopalians regarded as such converts as mentally unstable, and Evangelicals tried to dismiss, or ignore, their actions. But someone from a leading Evangelical family and president of a leading Evangelical institution? It was difficult to explain away, or cover up, Stone's departure to Rome. Dr. Bronson pictured it in millennial terms: "Now, about the the great struggle that is coming. It is upon us. This is no side issue. Kenyon is one of our outposts. It was besieged and perhaps taken."[130] Ritualism had, in a very public way, arrived in the center of the Evangelical Episcopal world. If "popery" could almost succeed there, it could succeed anywhere.

In addition, Stone had raised a disturbing issue about the limits of toleration. He defended his actions on the basis of "moderation and toleration" in theology and asked for liberty on issues of conscience. In short, he made the exact same argument to defend his growing Ritualistic tendencies as did the Evangelicals who opposed baptismal regeneration. When he pointed this out, as he did in his baccalaureate sermon, he was dismissed from his post. Liberty, moderation, and toleration, he argued, worked two ways. The Kenyon Evangelicals disagreed. They were glad to see Stone depart. But, unlike the conversion of Levi Ives years earlier, James Kent Stone's conversion gave Evangelicals little cause for triumph or rejoicing.

The Problem That Would Not Go Away: The Baptismal Controversy, 1869–1871

In an effort to stop the possible schism of a significant number of Evangelical clergy, nine bishops—with McIlvaine at the head of the list—issued a circular that proposed allowing some "alternate phrases or some equivalent modification" in the baptismal liturgy. The bishops, however, still believed that the more radical Evangelicals were wrong in their interpretation of the prayer book. "We have always been fully persuaded," they inserted in one clause, "that our Formularies of faith and worship, in the just interpretation, embody the truth of Christ, are warranted by the teaching of Holy Scripture, and are a faithful following of the doctrines professed and defended by our Anglican Reformers."[131] The bishops urged "brotherly kindness and charity" toward those men of conscience who felt they could no longer use the service, and the bishops blamed the change toward the prayer book on the Ritualists whose "bold innovations in doctrine and usage" had cast reproach upon the Protestant character of their liturgy.

In May 1869, McIlvaine made his clearest public statement on the problem of the prayer book. This statement was made in the form of a letter to a clergyman who suffered a difficulty of conscience with the prayer book and contemplated leaving the church. "I sympathize with your trouble," began McIlvaine, "but not in the cause as I have never experienced the difficulties you speak of." McIlvaine stated that he had never "known dissatisfaction" with the prayer book and "ever regarded" it "as consistent with Scriptural truth." He admitted to being amazed by the change in certain quarters of the Evangelical party regarding the liturgy and accounted for it as a reaction against Ritualism. "Extravagant churchmanship," he believed, "has created in brethren to whom the Gospel in its simplicity is dearer than life, an extreme dissatisfaction" with some parts of the prayer book. This reaction had led to the call for revision. Revision, McIlvaine argued, was acceptable if the meaning of words had actually changed. For example, he believed, *priest* had been used by the Reformers interchangeably with *presbyter*; in the nineteenth century, however, in the popular mind, priest had become associated with sacrifice. To replace "misunderstood expressions" constituted a legitimate revision of the prayer book.[132]

This kind of revision differed completely "from Revision sought on the allegation that there are parts of the Prayer Book not susceptible of fair vindication consistently with Evangelical truth–parts which not only *seem*, according to present use of words, to teach false doctrine but do teach it, when interpreted in the sense of the writers." In short, McIlvaine rejected the argument that the prayer book was incomplete or unreformed. It was, as it stood, "scriptural, evangelical, protestant [and] eminently devotional." He argued that Rising and others were interpreting the language too literally. The Bible itself had such problems: it seemed to teach that Christ was bodily present in the eucharist, that Peter was the "rock" of the church, and that Abraham had been justified by works. He argued that the prayer book had to be interpreted by comparison with other parts of the liturgy, Anglican theology, and Scripture. "Should you treat the Scriptures," he warned, "as you do the Prayer Book, your difficulties would be much increased."[133]

There is a tension in McIlvaine's principles of interpretation when this argument is compared to his argument for Scripture. In his debates with rationalists, McIlvaine argued that Scripture should be taken at its simple, literal meaning, and he rejected all attempts of higher critics to analyze the meaning of the text by placing it in historical context. Just the opposite was true when he approached the prayer book: the literal meaning of the language could not possibly be "true." Therefore, it had to be placed within its historical context and understood from the point of view of the framers. Educated Evangelical leaders had been applying a kind of historical criticism to the liturgy for years and had been relatively comfortable with it. In the 1860s, however, when new Reformation historiography questioned the old Evangelical interpretation, some Evangelicals felt the need to reject the prayer book completely; others, such as McIlvaine, rejected only the findings of the newer criticism, but not the need for an historical interpretation of the liturgy. Those who accepted the newer criticism, saw that it was clearly out of line with Evangelical belief and wanted to make liturgical language simpler, more literal, and in line with their doctrine. The call for revision fits within a general evangelical pattern of the time: language and meaning must be identical–simple, clear, and precise. All evangelicals argued for simplicity and clarity in biblical interpretation; almost all Evangelical Episcopalians argued for at least some liturgical revision on these principles. They were, in a word, prayer book literalists. But there were disagreements within the party as to what should be revised and why. They were divided on the issue of whether or not the prayer book was faithful to the theology of the Protestant Reformation.

Even McIlvaine, who approached the prayer book in a less literal fashion, admitted to the need for more precise language to fellow bishop George Cummins in a private letter. In spite of his continued belief that the prayer book was reformed enough, he also said that the baptismal service was a "stumbling block, not for what it does teach according to the meaning of the framers, but for what it *does* and *will* and *must* be understood to teach according to the apparent and contrary use of terms. . . . *In some sense or other*, it teaches Baptismal Regeneration."[134] This was a constant cry in the antibaptismal literature. We are satisfied, wrote the Rev. Charles Wesley Andrews, "that their authors intended nothing incompatible with the evangelical faith as now received, but at the same time we are just as fully satisfied that their *manner* of writing figurative and otherwise was the great practical blunder of the Reformation."[135] Regeneration was understood to mean "a change of character, not a change of state . . . a radical change, a spiritual change"; the "*apparent*, not the *real* meaning" disturbed even moderated Evangelicals.[136] Only the apparent meaning, according to the Evangelicals, was wrong. It was not enough to understand the liturgy historically, theologically, or poetically. The language, therefore, should be changed.

Evangelicals were at a loss as to what to do in regard to the liturgy while they waited for the 1871 General Convention to take up the issue. In July 1869, the Rev. Charles Cheney of Chicago, following the practice of other Evangelicals, was brought to trial for omitting the word *regeneration* from the baptismal service. His case became a *cause célèbre* among Evangelicals, and when he was deposed in 1871, a large number of Evangelicals rallied to show their sympathy for his plight and to express their belief that he had acted out of conscience.[137]

The 1871 General Convention arrived with hopes that the problems would be solved and the schism averted. After four days of deliberation, the bishops concluded that revision was not in order but that a declaration of the position of the church would be sufficient to clarify the baptismal liturgy: "The word 'regenerate' is not there so used as to determine that a moral change in the subject of baptism is wrought in the recipient."[138] In other words, the language of the liturgy shall not be used to determine a doctrine of moral change in baptismal regeneration. All the bishops, with only one exception, signed this declaration. McIlvaine took it as a triumph for the Evangelicals:

> Of course we do not support that under that negative declaration there are not diversities of views, but the whole Tractarian and Romish *opus operatum* is denied, the inseparableness of the sign and the grace signified is denied, and the utmost latitude for the evangelical views of the efficacy of baptism is acknowledged.[139]

Writing to William Carus, McIlvaine acknowledged that the declaration still allowed "divergent views as to the meaning of the word regenerate." He was convinced, however, that the bishops, by denying a theological interpretation of moral change during baptism, had reaffirmed the Protestant doctrine of baptism in the articles and rejected any possible Roman Catholic interpretation.[140] The nine bishops, as a follow-up on their proposal, issued a letter appealing to other Evangelicals to be content with the action of the church.

Some were satisfied. "I sympathized with those," wrote Heman Dyer, "who sought a change; and wrote and worked for it: but I accepted what was done."[141] Others, like Bishop Cummins, "came away from the General Convention of 1871 sad and dispirited."[142] He felt that the declaration allowed for two differing interpretations of baptism and was distressed that other Evangelicals found this situation satisfactory. As for himself, McIlvaine confessed, "I feel greatly more hopeful than I did before."[143]

In this case, Cummins may have read the situation better. Within a matter of weeks, McIlvaine's hope for unity and the defeat of Ritualism was dashed. "When I got home," he wrote to a friend, "I had to plunge right into a matter of great anxiety and trouble connected with Kenyon College, and our Theological Seminary; in the latter, indications of views [from the Evangelical side] as to the offices of Baptism, and dissatisfaction with them in spite of the Declaration of the Bishops."[144] McElhinney had published a pamphlet, *Regeneration in Baptism*, which argued that the literal meaning of the liturgy was the Roman Catholic meaning and concluded that the baptismal liturgy was "framed upon a theory of sacramental grace inconsistent with the thoroughly evangelical tenor of our Liturgy and Articles of Religion."[145]

McIlvaine was furious. He wrote to McElhinney:

> I have no words, to express the surprise and pain—the shock indeed with which I have read your pamphlet on Regeneration in Baptism. I hardly dare to think of its consequences to our Theological Seminary and otherwise. Or of the storm it will bring upon us, or of the triumphant greeting it will receive from Romanist and all Romanizers—more especially as coming out after the happy and remarkably united declaration of the Bishops. . . . I need not say how far I am from agreeing with the conclusions which your pamphlet, apparently with so much zeal, proclaims."[146]

McIlvaine responded with a quick letter to the *Standard of the Cross* defending the bishops' declaration. "I add," he proclaimed, "that I am perfectly convinced that the Anglican Reformers held and taught no doctrine of Sacramental grace." He condemned the "literal interpretation" of the prayer book and argued that the "Reformers constantly spoke of both Sacraments in the same figurative sense." To defend his position, he appealed to Augustine, Cranmer, Cartwright, and the recent Gorham case. McElhinney, he insisted, was wrong. Neither the baptismal service nor the Anglican Reformers "contain the doctrine of *spiritual* Regeneration . . . in the Sacrament of Baptism."[147]

McElhinney responded that, within his capacity as professor, he was obligated to publish these views after a long and serious historical study of the baptismal rite:

> I was profoundly convinced *that the one sole stronghold of Anglo-Catholicism, Ritualism, or Romanism in our communion is formed in our Baptismal Services.* As long as this part of our Ritual remains unreformed or unmodified, the Evangelical interest in our communion must necessarily continue to lose ground.[148]

He argued that Evangelicals were forced to use a "non-natural interpretation" of the words. This had forced them to argue for liberty in usage in interpretation. Here McElhinney saw a danger: "We cannot with any show of consistency, deny to our Romanizing adversaries a like liberty or license, in the interpretation of the Communion office in accommodation to their own views; there finding ourselves compelled, by the exigencies of our position, to become tributary to our foes." Liberty of usage, or continued ambiguity from the bishops, would allow Ritualism to continue without any possible check. Evangelicals could not argue for their own consciences while denying the exercise of the same to Ritualists. McElhinney was convinced that only a confrontation "with the facts of history" could solve the problem: admit that the baptismal office (and McElhinney believed that it was the only un-Protestant part of the prayer book) was flawed and change it.[149]

For his defense of historical inquiry, McElhinney, along with his colleague, S. A. Bronson, was fired. Bronson, who agreed with McElhinney, wrote a pained letter to McIlvaine explaining his fidelity to the church but argued that the bishops had made a mistake in issuing the declaration:

> My difficulty with the Declaration of the Bishops is, that it does not say what the words *do* mean. And I hesitate to come before God in a solemn thanksgiving with words of which I do not know the meaning; and which may mean one thing to one person and another to another. What shall I do then? Shall I leave the Church because of one little defect?[150]

Even his assistant, Bishop Bedell, questioned the wisdom of the declaration, but McIlvaine persisted in defending the action. The bishops, he asserted, had purposefully avoided the question of the *meaning* of regeneration. The declaration asserted that the liturgy should not be used to teach a doctrine of baptismal regeneration.[151]

By this time, however, it must have been clear to McIlvaine that the 1871 declaration had not solved the problem. If two of Bexley's professors, and his own assistant, disagreed as to the nature and effect of the declaration, how could such a poorly worded and confusing document stop like-minded Evangelicals from leaving the church? McIlvaine, once so full of hope for unity, had badly misjudged the reaction of even some of his closest associates.

Evangelical Unity or Evangelical Schism?

In the 1867 meeting, discontented Evangelicals expressed their displeasure over two issues: the problem of the prayer book and the baptismal liturgy and the problem of Episcopal "exclusiveness." Because of the "subversion of the Protestant and Evangelical character," that is, Ritualism, of the Episcopal Church, the signers of the Philadelphia declaration believed that

> the present crisis of Protestantism demands a higher degree of sympathy and co-operation among the various evangelical bodies into which we are divided. An exclusive position in this respect we hold to be injurious to our own Church, and inconsistent with our history and standards, as well as with the spirit of the Gospel.[152]

The signers maintained that the Episcopal Church could no longer withhold recognition of other Protestant ministers "without imperiling the interest of evangelical religion."[153] Greater evangelical unity was the only thing that could effectively block the advance of all forms of Ritualism.

High Churchmen viewed this development with suspicion. Bishop Whittingham called the declaration "an open avowal of party warfare in the church." He blamed the current discontent on the growth and influence of the radical elements in the Evangelical Knowledge Society (EKS), "a movement which was sure to recoil in mischief." Since the EKS's inception in 1853, Whittingham believed that the society would polarize the church and argued that their "church within the church" strategy could only result in schism. The result of the EKS's work, he stated, "has been to startle men otherwise indifferent to the questions agitated within the Church into active opposition."[154] Bemoaning the amount of energy, time and money wasted in party warfare, Whittingham eloquently pleaded for the old truce:

> Are the old paths closed? . . . "Declarations" and "associations" may have their temporary influence and effect; but when employed in the Church of GOD, they are as waters of bitterness poured out, which may at the first sweep away much before them, but must quickly pass away, and leave their traces only in desolation and deformity.[155]

McIlvaine, it seemed, agreed with him. In spite of his sympathy for the cause, he refused to sign the Philadelphia declaration.

Many evangelical clergy, however, could no longer be swayed by such arguments. The immediate cause for their discontent over the exclusive nature of the Episcopal ministry was the censure of Stephen Tyng, Jr. During the summer of 1867, Tyng visited one of his parishioners, at the family's summer residence in New Brunswick, New Jersey. The family, quite evangelical in their convictions, attended the local Methodist Church in the summer because New Brunswick's two Episcopal churches were not to their liking. They invited Tyng to preach at this Methodist Church. Tyng accepted and, as a result, was prohibited by the local Episcopal clergy to preach in the city, the geographical limit of their parishes. Tyng believed they had no jurisdiction to forbid him from preaching in a *city* and went ahead and officiated at the Methodist Church the following Sunday. Because of this, he was presented for trial for preaching without the consent of the parish ministers. In 1868, Tyng was officially—and publicly—admonished for his action.[156]

The Evangelicals considered this action an infringement on their liberty and evidence for the sectarian spirit of the Episcopal Church. The elder Tyng accused the presenters: "You have chosen to initiate this authoritative persecution, and to prohibit a liberty which was never challenged by authority before."[157] The Evangelicals, he argued, wanted a "fair and comprehensive liberty," which, if it allowed Ritualistic practices to advance unchecked, must also allow Evangelicals to preach whereever they wished. High Churchmen argued that the Tyng case was a matter of church order and not of freedom. The Evangelicals argued that the authority to preach the gospel throughout the world came from God—not a bishop or church. "That organization," protested young Tyng, "which presumes to interpose its man-made law between the burden of the salvation of the world and the full liberty of preaching must either prove itself infallible or confess itself impertinent."[158]

It is doubtful that the New Brunswick Methodists were so removed from the "the salvation of the world" that Stephen Tyng was God's sole instrument to preach the gospel to them. But the incident became a symbol of the restrictions that the Episcopal Church, at any time, could place on the evangelical message. To deny the freedom of preaching, which Tyng likened to a denial of his constitutional rights, aligned the Episcopal Church with other "repressive" organizations – such as the Roman Catholic Church. He believed that his case was tied to the Ritualists' agenda and would lead to a "selfish and worldly type religion" directly in conflict with both evangelical and American values.[159] The Tyng case ended quickly, but the Evangelical party did not forget the threat to their "gospel liberty" and their right to associate with like-minded evangelicals. To Evangelicals, the public admonition of Stephen Tyng, Jr., was an ominous victory for the Romanists.

In light of the encroaching Romanism, and the threat felt by Evangelicals, the need for Christian unity took on new urgency. In 1871, McIlvaine was invited, by Philip Schaff on behalf of the Evangelical Alliance, to join a delegation to discuss Christian unity with the Russian Czar and the Orthodox church.[160] Their meeting was not very successful, but it showed how anxious evangelicals were to stop the advance of the Roman Catholic Church. Indeed, common fear and hatred of Roman Catholicism was one of the forces holding the Evangelical Alliance together. In the last few years of his life, McIlvaine directed his energies in the alliance toward the world assembly of the body, which was to be held in New York in 1873.

Evangelical Episcopalians looked to the alliance as the single organization through which, as a united body with other Protestants, they could resist both rationalism and Romanism. As McIlvaine warned, evangelicals needed "to be *united* in their warfare . . . against Popery and Infidelity."[161] When the conference finally met in October 1873, William Dodge, president of the alliance, proclaimed that the organization was "a victorious standard in the face of modern skepticism, rationalism, the claims of Popery, and every other false system."[162] On the first night, the Rev. Noah Hunt Schenk, known in Episcopal circles for leading the 1858 revival at Kenyon College, conducted the evening prayer exercises and benediction.

During the ten-day conference, participants listened to orations, papers, and lectures on the state of evangelical churches throughout the world; the possibility of Christian union; the theological and philosophical problems facing the church; and spirituality and politics, missions and social reform. One entire day was devoted to "Modern Romanism and Protestantism." On that day, Bishop Cummins delivered the address, "Roman and Reformed Doctrines of Justification Contrasted," which in a clear and decided tribute to Bishop McIlvaine summarized the arguments of his *Oxford Divinity Compared*. Proclaimed Cummins:

Fellow Protestants of every name and nationality! Children of the Reformation! This is the very citadel of our faith, the very heart of the Gospel. This truth made the Reformation. And, under God, this truth alone can preserve it; revive it where it has become sickly and feeble, purify it where it has fallen from its first estate. In the reception, maintenance, and personal experience of this "truth as it is in Jesus," we are to find the real unity of all Protestant Christendom. United to Christ by a saving faith, I am one with every other believer.[163]

To demonstrate their unity, evangelicals of various denominations conducted nonofficial prayer and communion services throughout the conference.

One of those services caught the attention of Bishop Potter of New York. On October 5, the Very Rev. R. Payne Smith, dean of Canterbury, assisted in a united communion service in a Presbyterian church. Bishop William Tozer of Zanzibar wrote to Potter, pointing out that it would have been "more courageous" if Smith had "inaugurated this irregular venture for the promotion of Christian unity in his own cathedral city . . . where it could not have escaped the notice of those under whose authority even cathedral dignitaries are placed."[164] Having been alerted by Tozer of this action in his diocese, Potter censured Smith using the same canon that had been used six years earlier against Stephen Tyng, Jr.

This outraged Bishop Cummins of Kentucky, who, on October 12, had participated in a similar service. Wrote Cummins to protest Smith's censure:

> I deny most emphatically that the Dean of Canterbury or myself have violated "the ecclesiastical order" or "discipline" of the Church of England, or of the Protestant Episcopal Church. There is nothing . . . forbidding such an act of inter-communion among Christian people who are one in faith and love, one in Christ their great Head. The Church of England does not deny the validity of the orders of ministers of non-Episcopal churches.[165]

Cummins's letter to Potter let loose a storm of controversy. Smith thanked him for his defense. Non-Episcopal evangelicals, like Presbyterian author Susan Warner, praised Cummins for his action and urged him to rejoice in persecution.[166] Presbyterian minister William Adams invited Cummins to preach in his New York church. Evangelical Episcopalians were upset by Potter's action, as they had been angered by his treatment of Stephen Tyng, Jr., but Cummins's next action stunned them: just a month after the great meeting on Evangelical unity, Cummins left the Protestant Episcopal Church.[167]

In his letter to Kentucky's senior bishop, fellow evangelical B. B. Smith, Cummins identified three reasons for leaving the Episcopal Church: first, his conscience had been troubled by having to preside in Ritualistic churches in Kentucky; second, he had "lost all hope" that Ritualism could, or would, be eradicated by the national church; and third, the communion controversy caused him to see that his real unity was with other like-minded evangelicals—not with Episcopalians.

> As I cannot surrender the right and privilege to meet my fellow-Christians of other Churches around the table of our dear Lord, I must take my place where I can do so without alienation those of my own household of faith. . . . I have an earnest hope and confidence that a basis for the union of all Evangelical Christendom can be found in a communion which shall retain or restore a primitive

Episcopacy and a pure Scriptural Liturgy, with a fidelity to the doctrine of justification by faith only.[168]

On December 2, 1873, a group of eight clergymen and nineteen laymen organized the Reformed Episcopal Church as a protest against the Romanizing tendencies of the Protestant Episcopal Church and as a guardian of the Protestant and evangelical doctrines of the Anglican tradition.

Scattered evidence indicates that Cummins only used Potter's censure to do what was already on his mind. The Ritualistic controversy had unsettled him, and he was unhappy with the bishops' declaration from the 1871 convention. Annie Darling Price, a Reformed Episcopal historian, indicated that Cummins had come into possession of 1785 prayer book in October 1873 and became convinced that its liturgy was more Protestant than the current book.[169] Although Price denied it, it is probable that Cummins was formulating the basis for a more reformed Episcopal church even then. He was extremely discontented before the alliance incident; the speed at which he called a meeting and drew up a constitution for a new church indicate that he might have been planning his exodus for quite some time. Since some Evangelicals had been considering leaving the church in 1868, it seems likely that Cummins was ready to do so if the opportunity arose. The Evangelical Alliance communion service provided such an opportunity.

Most Evangelical Episcopalians condemned Cummins's action. Of those to join Cummins at an early stage were ministers deposed or censured by their own bishops.[170] By 1874, the mainstream of the Evangelical party was relatively content with the settlement and declaration worked out at the 1871 convention. The Cummins succession brought back all the old charges from other Episcopalians: Evangelical religion would always lead to schism. The Evangelicals, therefore, had to prove their loyalty and distance themselves from Cummins. All the Evangelical bishops expressed pain, dismay, and sadness over Cummins's withdrawal. The editor of the *Standard of the Cross* proclaimed the Cummins secession a mistake and for weeks published articles condemning the action.[171] "The radical Reformer," the editor argued, "works always at a disadvantage; he strikes the axe at the root of evil, and often in his rudeness rends and withers delicate interlacings which ought to live."[172]

The Reformed Episcopalians argued that they were merely "Old Evangelicals who carried the Evangelical banner so nobly."[173] They believed that they were the guardians of the faith as it had been delivered to their evangelical forebears. They did not see how much their party had been changed by new theological trends, however, nor did they see how these trends affected the way in which they conceived of being both evangelical and Episcopal.

By the time of the schism, the Evangelical party of the Episcopal Church was moving toward what would later be called fundamentalism. Stemming from the 1850s, and their loss of confidence in the church, Evangelical Episcopal identity had become more evangelical than Episcopal. As a group, they exhibited all the characteristics of early fundamentalism: a more defined idea of biblical language; premillennialism and, occasionally, full-blown dispensationalism; holiness and an interest in the power of the Holy Spirit; and evangelical ecumenism. They shared concerns about skepticism, rationalism, liberalism, and Roman Catholicism with other conservative Protestants, and they became increasingly pessimistic about social change.[174]

The 1873 schism of the Cummins group stopped some of this development. Although the schism was quite small, it jolted Evangelical Episcopalians back into some concern for the "Episcopal" part of their dual identity. They reacted against the schism by returning to the themes of the 1830s, the time when they reacted against radical evangelicalism. For example, McIlvaine's "Apostolic Succession," the sermon that had gotten him into trouble with Charles Hodge, was reprinted in two editions in the 1870s.[175] Evangelical Episcopalians rushed to prove their fidelity to the prayer book and the church. The Cummins schism affected them by redirecting their energies toward what it meant to be Episcopal.

Some of those who stayed in the church, however, did not cease to be proto-fundamentalists. For example, even the militant Tyngs, who were strong millennarians and defenders of a conservative view of Scripture, remained in the church. Richard Newton, premillennialist writer and agitator for prayer book revision, defended the institutions of the church. Isaac Labagh, also a dedicated premillennialist, wrote a book defending the apostolic succession of the Episcopal Church against the claims of Protestant denominationalism.[176] Being an early fundamentalist, or millennarian, was not the determining factor in whether one left the Protestant Episcopal Church; the determining factors seem to have been one's interpretation of the prayer book and one's personal degree of institutional loyalty. Those who believed that the Episcopal Church had been incompletely reformed left; those who still believed that the Anglican Reformation was true to the spirit of Evangelical religion, stayed. Even the radical Tyngs, who had been talking schism for twenty years, still believed the Episcopal Church was a vehicle for evangelical religion and resisted the urge to leave.

The Episcopal schism of 1873, therefore, was not entirely an early quarrel between fundamentalists and modernists; instead, it was an internal Evangelical Episcopal quarrel as to whether or not "evangelical" and "Episcopal" were compatible categories. The argument did have a profound effect on the development of fundamentalism in the Episcopal Church, however. A number of early fundamentalists left, but some stayed. The fundamentalists who stayed in the Episcopal Church had a high degree of institutional commitment and, with the exception of the Tyngs, were less prone to militancy than those who left. They felt a need to reassert their Episcopal-ness and, in some ways, drew back from some of their activities with other American evangelicals. In trying to prove their loyalty, they may have unwittingly been swallowed up by the very rationalism and Ritualism that had once been their sworn enemies.

Conclusion: The Contested Legacy of Charles P. McIlvaine

In late 1872, Bishop McIlvaine, troubled by the baptismal controversy and suffering from nervous exhaustion, went to England to visit old friends and escape some of the ecclesiastical pressure. At 74, his health and strength were worn. After several months in England, he felt considerably better and decided to tour Italy with some friends. When they reached Florence in February 1873, he suddenly became quite ill. For nearly a month, he weakened, and on March 13 he died.

In his last days, McIlvaine was relieved of the great fears that had plagued his life. To his friends he confessed, "I don't see any cause for care or apprehension; I know I am dying, but I have no care." He finally realized "It is a dishonour to Christ to be afraid." In characteristic fashion, however, the burden of his evangelical call was upon him: "Oh that I had served Him better! What I have left undone most troubles me. Every enlightened conscience has, I suppose, an exceeding sense of shortcomings." He sent his love to his wife, but no message to his son—only his daughter, "Tell her my peace is perfect."[177] In remarkable contrast to his life, spent in turmoil and controversy, Charles McIlvaine died quietly in his sleep. His body was sent back to England, where an impressive funeral was held in Westminster Abbey. He was buried near his home in Clifton, Ohio. He did not live to participate in the great New York meeting of the Evangelical Alliance nor did he witness the birth of the Reformed Episcopal Church as a separate, evangelical Episcopal church.

Both sides of the schism, however, claimed McIlvaine for their own. Cummins related an incident that had occurred several years before McIlvaine's death. According to Cummins, he visited McIlvaine at his home in Cincinnati, and the two men discussed the upcoming (1871) convention. "We are looking to you," Cummins urged, "my dear bishop, to lead us, like another Moses, out of our present state of bondage to freedom and liberty." McIlvaine responded, in the account, by laying his hand on Cummins's shoulder and saying, "Ah! I am too old for any such contest, and too feeble. The younger Bishops, such as you, must fight the battle which is inevitable."[178] Cummins interpreted this incident as McIlvaine appointing him the Joshua of Evangelical Episcopalians. The implication was clear: had McIlvaine been younger, and healthier, he would have led the schismatic group into the promised land.

The editor of the *Standard of the Cross* had a different perspective. A year after McIlvaine's death, he speculated how the former bishop would have "met the issue" of Cummins's schism. "Are we ready to believe," the editor wrote, "as he taught us, that we can rightfully proclaim [Evangelical doctrines] in the Church; and that loyalty in our attachment to the Church is involved in the higher loyalty to Christ?" The great legacy of Bishop McIlvaine, stated the paper, was his unwavering evangelicalism "without casting even a shadow of disloyalty across the Church's path." McIlvaine's greatest memorial would be the Episcopal Church in Ohio guarding and keeping evangelical doctrine there "forever conspicuous."[179]

The editor of the *Standard of the Cross* was right. It would have been completely out of the character of his fifty-year ministry to leave the Episcopal Church under any circumstances. But, had he lived, could he have prevented the schism? Probably not. In the last five years of his life, McIlvaine did everything he could to prevent it. His presence in the last months of conflict probably would have mattered little. In spite of McIlvaine's greatest efforts, Cummins and other believed the Episcopal Church had lost its Protestant moorings—its soul—and nothing except schism remained. McIlvaine could not have prevented the fringe of his party from leaving the church. He had given them a vision to resist Romanism at all cost, and the cost became the unity of the Episcopal Church. In the end, McIlvaine's battle for evangelical truth came in conflict with his love and loyalty for his church. It was a terrible and bitter irony. Even though he did not live to see it, he surely knew it was coming. It was easier to escape to Europe than to watch his life's work be destroyed.

To justify their schism, the Reformed Episcopalians republished Albert Barnes's 1844 attack on their party. In this small volume, they included Barnes's original pamphlet, the *Episcopal Recorder*'s response, and Barnes's reply. The Reformed Episcopal editor clearly thought the *Recorder*'s reply inadequate. Their new church, he argued in the preface, finally answered Barnes's main argument: that Evangelicalism had been grafted onto the Episcopal Church and without some sort of radical change could never permanently survive. "The Reformed Episcopal Church," argued the compiler, "has aimed at, and has, as far as possible, adopted all the reforms which thoughtful men in the Protestant Episcopal Church, and outside of it, have long agreed to be desirable."[180] It was telling, however, that the Reformed Episcopal editor did not include that much better argued and more nuanced response to Barnes published by G. W. Ridgeley, which dealt directly with both the problems of the liturgy and the ministries of other churches.

Most Evangelical Episcopalians, however, still refused to believe that Barnes had been right. They argued hard against the schism, loudly proclaiming their loyalty to the Church and protesting any comparison of their position to Cummins's. One writer to the *Standard of the Cross* recalled a similar incident some sixty years earlier:

> Bearing on this point, might be mentioned a fact in the early history of the Church in Maryland; a fact not generally known, but which may be within the recollection of a few still living. In 1814, when Bishop KEMP was elected to the Episcopate, the defeated candidate of the party opposed to the Bishop, the Rev. Mr. DASHIELL, with a few other disaffected persons, withdrew from the Church.[181]

They started their own "society" and rewrote the prayer book "to suit their views." What happened to these disgruntled Evangelical Episcopalians? "The organization soon ceased to exist, and it is now scarcely remembered even in name." The same, the writer confidently expected, would happen to the new Reformed Episcopal Church.[182] As George Dashiell had disappeared from memory, so would George Cummins.

In spite of all that had happened, and all the changes they had undergone, most Evangelical Episcopalians persisted in the belief that the two elements of their dual identity—being both Evangelical and Episcopal—were compatible. They refused to admit that Cummins's succession made any difference to their vision for a liturgical, orderly, Protestant, and evangelical Episcopal Church. One wonders if they were blind.

Notes

1. One historian has described the post–Civil War decades as "years in search of a style." See Howard Mumford Jones, *The Age of Energy: Varieties of American Experience* (1970; reprint New York, 1973), 11. On the difficulties facing postwar Christianity, see Francis P.

Weisenberger, *Ordeal of Faith: The Crisis of Church-Going America, 1865–1900* (New York, 1959).

2. McIlvaine to Gregory Bedell, January 20, 1870, in McI, Dio. Ohio Arch.

3. McIlvaine to Carus, February 1, 1865, in Carus, *Memorials of McIlvaine*, 251.

4. McIlvaine, personal journal, December 21, 1865, in McI, Kenyon College.

5. McIlvaine to Carus, November 17, 1865, in Carus, *Memorials of McIlvaine*, 257. For the confidence of northern Protestants following the war, see Henry F. May, *Protestant Churches in Industrial America* (New York, 1949), 39–50.

6. Preceding quotes from McIlvaine, personal journal, August 6, 1865, in McI, Kenyon College.

7. Evangelical Episcopalians generally did not refer to this movement as *liberal*. They considered themselves liberal because they were open to other Christian traditions—even though they were traditional and conservative in their theology. In this chapter, I have tried to retain the spirit of their worldview by calling Protestant liberalism *rationalism*. To them, rationalism is the use of secular methodologies in biblical studies and theology; it was the spirit of "worldly" thought intruding on and interpreting spiritual matters. Occasionally, however, I will refer to liberalism in the sense in which it is used by modern historians and theologians.

8. For the fascination of late nineteenth-century Americans with the medieval, see T. Jackson Lears, *No Place of Grace* (New York, 1981). Lears's discussion includes a chapter on the growth of Anglo-Catholicism in the Episcopal Church.

9. Preface, *Essays and Reviews*, 7th ed. (London, 1861).

10. Chadwick, *Victorian Church*, II: 76–77.

11. Davies, *Worship and Theology in England, From Newman to Martineau, 1850–1900*, 181–182.

12. For a summary of Evangelical reaction to liberalism in the 1860s, see Hylson-Smythe, *Evangelicals in the Church of England*, 137–141. See also Reginald Fuller, "Historical Criticism and the Bible," in *Anglicanism and the Bible*, ed. Frederick H. Borsch (Wilton, Conn., 1984), 146–149.

13. The best survey of the controversy is Ieuan Ellis, *Seven Against Christ: A Study of "Essays and Reviews"* (London, 1980). See also, Chadwick, *Victorian Church*, II: 75–97.

14. McIlvaine to Carus, December 30, 1862, in Carus, *Memorials of McIlvaine*, 238.

15. Charles P. McIlvaine, *Righteousness by Faith, or the Nature and Means of Our Justification Before God*, 2nd ed. (Philadelphia, 1864), v. A linkage between Tractarianism and rationalism—imagined or otherwise—had already been established by the English evangelical paper, *The Record* (January 10, 1849): 6. See Ellis, *Seven Against Christ*, 28–29.

16. McIlvaine, *Righteousness by Faith*, xiv. McIlvaine makes a similar argument in his *Inaugural Address Delivered at the Opening of Huron College*, 24–34.

17. I have not been able to discover any substantial historical work on the reaction of American evangelicals to *Essays and Reviews*. There is a thoughtful inclusion of it very briefly in Mark A. Noll, *Between Faith and Criticism: Evangelicals, Scholarship and the Bible in America* (San Francisco, 1986), 64–67. Historians of liberalism have often noted that the Episcopal Church was particularly hospitable to liberal theology, but none have speculated that the English theological debate prepared the American Episcopal Church for liberal theological ideas. The debate over liberalism in the Episcopal Church certainly began at an earlier date than in other American denominations. It seems to me that McIlvaine's antiliberal works are a relatively early defense of traditional evangelicalism against the new theology.

Although British liberalism provided American theologians with an *English-language* liberal theology, with the exception of the influence of Samuel Coleridge on Bushnell and transcendentalism, English transmission of liberalism is little-studied—especially when compared to German influences on American theology. See, for example, Jerry W. Brown, *The Rise of Biblical Criticism in America, 1800–1870* (Middletown, Conn., 1969). Although it is a very helpful and thorough work, even William Hutchison's *The Modernist Impulse in American Protestantism* (Cambridge, Mass., 1976) largely ignores English liberalism.

18. All quotes this paragraph from Charles P. McIlvaine, *Rationalism, as Exhibited in the Writings of Certain Clergyman of the Church of England. A Letter . . . Set Forth by Direction of the House of Bishops* (Cincinnati, 1865), 9, 20–21.

19. Ibid., 22.

20. Ibid., 24–25.

21. Ibid., 28.

22. For the views of many American evangelicals at the time, see Randall Balmer, "The Princetonians and Scripture: A Reconsideration," *Westminster Theological Journal* 44 (1982): 352–365, and John D. Woodbridge, *Biblical Authority: A Critique of the Rogers/McKim Proposal* (Grand Rapids, Mich., 1982), 119–140.

23. See Charles Hodge, "Inspiration," *Biblical Repertory and Princeton Review* 29 (1857): 660–698. A modern reprint is in Mark A. Noll, ed., *The Princeton Defense of Plenary Verbal Inspiration* (New York and London, 1988), along with Noll's thoughtful introduction to Hodge's views on Scripture. About Hodge's theology, McIlvaine wrote: "As to a course of divinity . . . I could not do better if I were present to teach then choose the late publication of Dr. Hodge's Lectures (the elder Hodge, very old friend) for a text book." McIlvaine to Bedell, August 1872, in McI, Dio. Ohio Arch.

24. McIlvaine, *Rationalism Exhibited*, 7–8.

25. [Charles P. McIlvaine,] *The Washington Miracle Refuted: or, a Review of the Rev. Mr. Matthews's Pamphlet* (Washington, D.C., 1824). His argument is an interesting blend of evangelical Protestant theology and Enlightenment thought – much indebted to the teaching he received at Princeton. It shows clear dependence on David Hume's argument against miracles. For early Princeton's blending of the Enlightenment and Evangelicalism, see Noll, *Princeton and the Republic*.

26. Gregory T. Bedell, *Personal Presence of God the Holy Ghost: Primary Charge . . .* (Cleveland, 1874).

27. Chorley, *Men and Movements*, 305–310.

28. *Episcopal Recorder* (January 20, 1866).

29. Croley, *Apocalypse of St. John*, 3. The fall of both Roman Catholicism and liberalism is the thesis of Edward Irving's *Babylon and Infidelity Foredoomed of God: A Discourse on the Prophecies of Daniel and the Apocalypse* (Philadelphia, 1828).

30. Irving, *Babylon and Infidelity*, 316.

31. McIlvaine to Carus, March 9, 1866, in Carus, *Memorials of McIlvaine*, 260.

32. See also William Newton, *Lectures on the First Two Visions of the Book of Daniel* (Philadelphia, 1859), 194. The year 1866 was the end of "the twelve hundred and sixty days of the dominion . . . of Papal Apostasy," and it seems to have been promoted by George Stanley Faber. Stephen Tyng, however, seemed to believe that the great year would be 1868. See quote from Tyng in "The Days in Which We Live," *Prophetic Times* 1 (1863): 2.

33. On the development of dispensational premillennialism in this period, see Weber, *Living in the Shadow of the Second Coming*. See also C. Norman Kraus, *Dispensationalism in America: Its Rise and Development* (Richmond, Va., 1958), and Clarence B. Bass, *Backgrounds to Dispensationalism: Its Historical Genesis and Ecclesiastical Implication* (Grand Rapids, Mich., 1960). An example of this is Richard C. Shimeall's *Post-Millenarianism Only 150 Years Old. Scripturally and Historically Demonstrated* (New York, 1867), and idem; *Christ's Second Coming: Is It Pre-Millennial or Post-Millennial? The Great Question of the Day* (New York,

1865). Shimeall had been an Episcopalian who converted to Presbyterianism during the Oxford Movement crisis around 1850.

34. S. A. Bronson to McIlvaine, March 12, 1867, in McI, Dio. Ohio Arch.

35. See Richard Newton, *The Study of Prophecy, A Commanded Duty* (Philadelphia, 1848). Newton rearticulated this theme in a more general evangelical article, "The Duty of Studying Prophecy," *Prophetic Times* 1 (1863): 15–16.

36. "The Advent, and the Denominational Religious Press," *Prophetic Times* 1 (1863): 173. Through the next several years, the *Times* continued to excerpt articles on premillennialism from the *Western Episcopalian*.

37. Richard Newton, *A Voice from Olivet: or The Warning Sign* (Philadelphia, 1869), 29–30.

38. Shimeall, *Christ's Second Coming*, xxiii. Shimeall also identified High Church Bishop Hopkins of Vermont as agreeing with McIlvaine and Tyng on this issue. In spite of general distaste of the High Church party for evangelical millennial schemes, there were usually a few who were interested in prophecy. Shimeall might have based this assessment of Hopkins's views on the bishop's *Two Discourses on the Second Advent of the Redeemer* (Burlington, Vt., 1843), which refutes Millerite claims to date the advent in 1843 but accepts a general millennial framework.

39. Shimeall's *Our Bible Chronology, Historic and Prophetic, Critically Examined and Demonstrated* (London, 1860), for example, was pronounced a "standard work" by the Rev. Samuel R. Johnson, dean of the General Theological Seminary, and the Rev. Francis L. Hawks, Episcopal Church historian, in a flyleaf advertising the work. *Our Bible Chronology* was a complete chart of biblical history to the nineteenth century, outlining prophetic events.

40. Wilson Waters, *The History of St. Luke's Church, Marietta, Ohio* (Marietta, 1884). Waters's history is an extremely detailed account of an Evangelical Episcopal parish throughout the nineteenth century.

41. The New Year's address appeared in the *Standard of the Cross* and is reprinted in full in Carus, *Memorials of McIlvaine*, 304

42. McIlvaine, personal journal, January 18, 1871, in McI, Kenyon College; also printed in Carus, *Memorials of McIlvaine*, 308–309.

43. Stephen H. Tyng, Jr. *He Will Come; or, Meditations upon the Return of the Lord Jesus Christ to Reign over the Earth* (New York, 1877), 91.

44. Newton, *Lectures on Daniel*, 201.

45. In an article on Episcopal missions to the Jews, James Warnock argues that millennialism provided little or no motivation to late nineteenth-century ministries in the Episcopal Church. That may be true of the Church Society for Promoting Christianity Amongst the Jews (CSPCJ) in the 1880s and 1890s. It was not true among earlier efforts started by Evangelicals, however. I suspect that even some of the founders of the CSPCJ held millennial views as well—such as the Rev. Noah Hunt Schenck quoted in the article— but resisted publication of those views in the platform of the society in order to increase their support from the Episcopal Church at large. Postmillennialism was clearly a factor in Evangelical calls for the evangelization of the Jews–a heritage Warnock was clearly unaware of in the construction of his argument. See Warnock, " 'This Year They More Nearly Approached Us Than Ever': A Response of the Protestant Episcopal Church to Jewish Immigration," *Fides et Historia* 22 (1990): 35–48.

46. Ibid., 202.

47. McIlvaine, personal journal, February 24, 1867, in McI, Kenyon College; also in Carus, *Memorials of McIlvaine*, 265–267.

48. McIlvaine, personal journal, ibid.

49. Carus, *Memorials of McIlvaine*, 309.

50. The quest for Christian unity parallelled a more general American cultural quest for unity. Jones, *Age of Energy*, identified the search for unity as one of the major themes of this period of American history.

51. Preceding quotes from Benjamin Aycrigg, *Memoirs of the Reformed Episcopal Church, and of the Protestant Episcopal Church* (New York, 1880), 169.

52. Hodge, *Life of Charles Hodge*, 505.

53. McIlvaine to Carus, Christmas Day, 1867, in Carus, *Memorials of McIlvaine*, 273.

54. Hodge, *Life of Charles Hodge*, 507.

55. McIlvaine to Carus, note 53.

56. Preceding quotes from Elizabeth L. Smith, *Henry Boynton Smith. His Life and Work* (New York, 1881), 280, 281.

57. Hodge, *Life of Charles Hodge*, 505; also Aycrigg, *Memoirs*, 171.

58. For this conference, see William R. Curtis, *The Lambeth Conferences: The Solution for Pan-Anglican Organization* (New York, 1942), and Alan M. G. Stephenson, *The First Lambeth Conference, 1867* (London, 1967).

59. For Hopkins's involvement in the Lambeth proposal, see John Henry Hopkins, Jr., *The Life of the Late Rt. Rev. John Henry Hopkins, First Bishop of Vermont and Seventh Presiding Bishop* (New York, 1873), 392–393.

60. McIlvaine to Carus, April 18, 1867, in Carus, *Memorials of McIlvaine*, 278.

61. McIlvaine to Carus, September 13, 1867, in ibid., 281.

62. Ibid., 280.

63. Ibid., 280–281.

64. Stephenson, *First Lambeth Conference*, 254.

65. McIlvaine to Carus, September 30, 1867, in Carus, *Memorials of McIlvaine*, 283.

66. For British Evangelical reaction to Lambeth, see Stephenson, *First Lambeth Conference*, 295–302.

67. The most complete work on this topic is Jordan, *Evangelical Alliance*.

68. Gregory T. Bedell, "Spiritual Unity Not Organic Union," in *History, Essays, Orations and Other Documents of the Sixth General Conference of the Evangelical Alliance, Held in New York, October 2–12 , 1873*, ed. Philip Schaff and S. I. Prime (New York, 1874), 150.

69. For Smith's report to the World Conference, see Evangelical Alliance of the United States of America, *Document Number One, Constitution and Officers . . .* (New York, 1868).

70. Quoted in Jordan, *Evangelical Alliance*, 88, from McIlvaine, Letter to the Conference, Evangelical Alliance, *Document Number Three* (1869), 4.

71. For some of the religious and theological issues surrounding these developments, see Jane Rasmussen, *Musical Taste as a Religious Question in Nineteenth Century America* (Lewiston, N.Y., 1986). Her work continues a number of references to McIlvaine in particular. See also McIlvaine, *Pastoral Letter to the Clergy and Laity in Ohio*, and idem, *Processional Singing by Surpliced Choirs an Unauthorized Innovation in the Public Worship of the Protestant Episcopal Church* (Columbus, 1868).

72. McIlvaine to Carus, January 17, 1866, in Carus, *Memorials of McIlvaine*, 259.

73. Chadwick, *Victorian Church* I: 491–501; quote on 501.

74. All quotes this paragraph from John Henry Hopkins, *The Law of Ritualism Examined in Its Relation to the Word of God . . .* (New York, 1866), 75–76. See also Robert Bruce Mullin, "Ritualism, Anti-Romanism, and the Law in John Henry Hopkins," *Historical Magazine of the Protestant Episcopal Church* 50 (1981): 377–390.

75. McIlvaine, *Righteousness by Faith*, xii.

76. Ibid., viii–ix.

77. Ibid.

78. In addition to the chapter on baptism in McIlvaine, *Oxford Divinity Compared*, see John Seeley Stone's *The Mysteries Opened, or Scriptural Views of Preaching and the Sacraments, as Distinguished from Certain Theories Concerning Baptismal Regeneration and the Real Presence* (New York, 1844), particularly pages 123–139, on the role of the Holy Spirit in baptism.

79. This position had been articulated early in the nineteenth century by William Wilmer in his *Episcopal Manual* (1815).

80. Stone, *Mysteries Opened*, 243.

81. On the Reformed basis of Episcopal theology of Baptism, and the interpretation of baptism by Bishop White, see Pritchard, "Theological Consensus," 103–123.

82. Stone, *Mysteries Opened*, 244.

83. [Benjamin B. Leacock,] *Prayer Book versus Prayer Book* (Philadelphia, 1869), 24.

84. For a full explanation of the "hypothetical theory," see Charles Wesley Andrews, *Review of the Baptismal Controversy* (Philadelphia, 1869), 10–11.

85. Because of the Erastian implications of the judgment, a number of prominent Tractarians left the Church of England and became Roman Catholics.

86. For the variety of Evangelical views on baptism, see Toon, *Evangelical Theology*, 188–192.

87. "Preface to the American Edition," in William Goode, *The Doctrine of the Church of England as to the Effects of Baptism in the Case of Infants* (New York, 1850), vii.

88. Charles P. McIlvaine, *Some Thoughts upon the Subject of Baptismal Regeneration* (New York, 1861), 29.

89. See Charles Hodge, *Biblical Repertory and Princeton Review* (1857): 73–101.

90. James H. Nichols, *Romanticism in American Theology: Nevin and Schaff at Mercersburg* (Chicago, 1961), 238–239.

91. D. F. Sprigg, *A Plea for the Baptism of Infants with Additional Remarks upon Immersion* (Alexandria, Va., 1859).

92. William Meade to John Henry Hobart, February 10, 1827, in Johns, *Memoir of Meade*, 162.

93. *Memorial Papers: The Memorial with Circular and Questions of the Episcopal Commission* (Philadelphia, 1857), 155–156.

94. For an example of a Reformed controversy over baptismal regeneration theology, see Nichols, *Romanticism in Theology*, 236–258.

95. Preceding quotes from Karl R. Hagenbach, *A Textbook on the History of Doctrines*, ed. Henry B. Smith from the Edinburgh translation of the fourth German edition (New York, 1861), II: 364, 366.

96. William Whittingham, *Baptismal Regeneration: Held After Luther and Melancthon, by Cranmer, Ridley and Latimer* (Baltimore, 1860).

97. McIlvaine, *Some Thoughts on Regeneration*, 3–5.

98. Ibid., 12.

99. Franklin S. Rising, *Are There Romanizing Germs in the Prayer Book?* 2nd ed. (n.p., n.d.), 10–13. The first edition was published in 1868.

100. All quotes this paragraph from Ibid., 43, 64.

101. Ibid., 66.

102. Preceding quotes from [Leacock,] *Prayer Book versus Prayer Book*, 3, 4.

103. Ibid., 6.

104. Ibid., 30. Other examples of radical evangelical statements against the prayer book include *Revidenda; or a Brief Statement of Those Things in the Liturgy Which Should Be Revised and Altered, Together with a Short History of the Prayer-Book and the Revisions It Has Already*

Undergone (Philadelphia, 1868), and *The Book of Common Prayer as It is. A Catechetical Examination of Certain Portions of the Prayer Book* (New York, 1871).

105. McIlvaine to Judge Conyngham, October 21, 1868, in Gratz Collection, Historical Society of Pennsylvania, Philadelphia. [Hereafter cited as Gratz, Hist. Soc. Pa.] The letter, in McIlvaine's handwriting, is also signed by Lee, Eastburn, Bedell, and Vail. Forces greater than McIlvaine, however, removed Rising from office: he died in a gruesome steamboat accident on the Ohio River on December 4, 1868.

106. William Wilberforce Newton, *Yesterday with the Fathers* (New York, 1910), 59.

107. Albright, *History of the Protestant Episcopal Church*, 276–277.

108. Newton, *Yesterday with the Fathers*, 59.

109. McIlvaine to Carus, September 4, 1869, in Carus, *Memorials of McIlvaine*, 297.

110. Ibid.

111. McIlvaine, personal journal, February 24, 1867, in McI, Kenyon College.

112. Bancroft et al, "Memorial from Sundry Presbyters of the Protestant Episcopal Church," *Journal of the General Convention* (1868): Appendix, 423–424.

113. McElhinney to McIlvaine, January 8, 1867, in McI, Dio. Ohio Arch.

114. On the evangelical origins of Episcopal Theological School, see James A. Muller, *The Episcopal Theological School, 1867–1943* (Cambridge, Mass., 1943).

115. Stone, *Mysteries Opened*, and idem, *The Church Universal: A Series of Discourses . . .* (New York, 1846).

116. Preceding quotes from James Kent Stone, *Moderation and Toleration in Theology. A Sermon Preached in Rosse Chapel* (Gambier, Ohio, 1867), 20.

117. Bronson to Stone, February 24, 1868, in McI, Dio. Ohio Arch.

118. Bronson to McIlvaine, February 11, 1868, in McI, Dio. Ohio Arch.

119. Robert Isaac Wilberforce, *The Doctrine of the Incarnation of Our Lord Jesus Christ in Its Relation to Mankind and to the Church* (London, 1848).

120. David Newsome's study *The Parting of Friends: The Wilberforces and Henry Manning* (London, 1966) is a fine, well-researched volume on the impact of Tractarianism on one Evangelical family: the Wilberforces and their relations. It has a good deal on Robert Wilberforce and his conversion.

121. Preceding quotes from Bronson to McIlvaine, note 118.

122. J. W. Cracraft to McIlvaine, February 18, 1868, in McI, Dio. Ohio Arch.

123. James Kent Stone, *The Invitation Heeded: Reasons for a Return to Catholic Unity* (New York, 1870), 72–79

124. Bronson to Stone, note 117.

125. Stone to Bronson, February 21, 1868, in ibid.

126. McIlvaine to Bedell, March 12, 1868, in McI, Kenyon College.

127. Smythe, *Kenyon College*, 197. The Smythe account of the James Kent Stone case was borrowed—almost in its entirety, uncritically, and without reference—by the hagiographic biography of Stone by Walter George and Helen Grace Smith, *Fidelis of the Cross: James Kent Stone* (New York and London, 1926), 116–121.

128. Stone to McIlvaine, in McI, Kenyon College.

129. *The Invitation Heeded* is Stone's *Apologia Pro Vita Sua*. Stone eventually became a Passionist missionary to South America and served in high positions in the order in South America, the United States, and Rome. He died in California in 1921.

130. Bronson to McIlvaine, February 14, 1868, in McI, Dio. Ohio Arch.

131. This circular became known as the Proposition of the Nine Bishops and was reproduced in numerous sources. It created a great deal of discussion in the church. See, for example, *Papers on the Proposition of "The Nine Bishops"* (Philadelphia, 1871). Also, Thomas Vail, *Suggestions on Church Comprehensiveness, and the Request of the Nine Bishops* (Lawrence,

Kan., 1870) and idem, *Further Suggestions on Church Comprehensiveness and the Request of the Nine Bishops* (Lawrence, Kan., 1871).

132. All quotes this paragraph from "Letter of Bishop McIlvaine on the Prayer Book," *Standard of the Cross*, (May 15, 1869): 4–6.

133. All quotes this paragraph from ibid.

134. McIlvaine to Cummins, June 7, 1869, in McI, Dio. Ohio Arch.

135. Andrews, *Review*, 17.

136. Cummins to Bedell, May 14, 1869, in A. M. Cummins, *Memoir of George David Cummins, D.D., First Bishop of the Reformed Evangelical Church* (Philadelphia, 1878), 338, 332.

137. For more on the Cheney case, see Chorley, *Men and Movements*, 405–408; Albright, *History of the Protestant Episcopal Church*, 280–281; and Percy V. Norwood, "Bishop Whitehouse and the Church in Illinois," *Historical Magazine of the Protestant Episcopal Church* 16: 2 (June 1947): 175–179.

138. Quoted in Chorley, *Men and Movements*, 409.

139. Charles P. McIlvaine, "Bishop McIlvaine on the Late General Convention," *Standard of the Cross* (January 27, 1872): 2.

140. McIlvaine to Carus, October 15, 1871, in Carus, *Memorials of McIlvaine*, 315.

141. Dyer, *Records of an Active Life*, 335.

142. Cummins, *Memoir of Cummins*, 402.

143. McIlvaine to Carus, October 29, 1871, in Carus, *Memorials of McIlvaine*, 318.

144. McIlvaine to Carus, February 1872, in ibid., 322–323.

145. J. J. McElhinney, *Regeneration in Baptism: A Paper Read at a Conference Held at Columbus, O., September 13, 1871* (Columbus, 1871), 23. See also two letters from McElhinney which appeared in the *Standard of the Cross* in early 1872; clippings in McI, Dio. Ohio Arch.

146. McIlvaine to McElhinney, December 15, 1871, in McI, Dio. Ohio Arch.

147. All quotations this paragraph from Charles P. McIlvaine, "Letter from Bishop McIlvaine," *Standard of the Cross* (January 27, 1872): 1.

148. McElhinney to McIlvaine, December 19, 1871, in McI, Dio. Ohio Arch.

149. All quotes this paragraph from ibid.

150. Bronson to McIlvaine, January 20, 1872, in ibid.

151. McIlvaine to Bedell, June 21, 1872, in ibid.

152. "The Philadelphia Declaration," quoted from the *Protestant Churchman*, (December 12, 1867), in Aycrigg, *Memoirs of the Church*, 125. The declaration was signed by nearly 100 clergymen and an interdeterminable number of laypeople. The total number of Episcopal bishops and clergy in 1868 was 2,662. The signers represented slightly less than 5 percent of that number. When one accounts for the clergy who did not attend the Philadelphia meetings due to travel and expense, and those who, like McIlvaine, thought the declaration too extreme, this number is a good indication that at least (a conservative estimate) 10 percent of the Episcopal clergy were committed, active, and ideological Evangelicals. Among the prominent clergy were Richard Newton, Stephen Tyng, Sr. and Jr., John S. Stone, Heman Dyer, and Charles Cheney. Of the fifty-two bishops, fifteen were active leaders of the Evangelical party.

153. Ibid., 125–126.

154. All quotes this paragraph from William R. Whittingham, *A Letter to the Rev. Richard Newton* (n.p., 1868), 1, 4, 5.

155. Ibid., 8.

156. For the Tyng case, see *The Tyng Case: A Narrative, Together with the Judgement of the Court and the Admonition by the Bishop of New York.* (New York, 1868), and Tyng, *Life and Work of Stephen Tyng*, 468–479.

157. Tyng, *Life and Work of Stephen Tyng*, 476.

158. Stephen H. Tyng, Jr. *The Liberty of Preaching: Its Warrant and Relations*. (New York, 1867), 8.

159. Ibid., 30.

160. For McIlvaine's participation in this delegation, see Carus, *Memorials of McIlvaine*, 309–314.

161. Jordan, *Evangelical Alliance*, 88.

162. Schaff and Prime, *History, Essays, Orations, and Other Documents of the Sixth General Conference of the Evangelical Alliance*, 14.

163. George D. Cummins, "Roman and Reformed Doctrines of Justification Contrasted," in ibid., 474.

164. Quoted from *New York Tribune* (October 6, 1873), in Chorley, *Men and Movements*, 412.

165. Quoted from *New York Tribune* (October 13, 1873), in Cummins, *Memoir of Cummins*, 413.

166. Warner to Cummins, n.d., in ibid., 427.

167. The only two modern interpretations of the Cummins schism are Warren C. Platt, "The Reformed Episcopal Church: The Origins and Early Development of Its Ideological Expression," *Historical Magazine of the Protestant Episcopal Church* 52 (1983): 245–273, and Paul A. Carter, *The Spiritual Crisis of the Gilded Age* (DeKalb, Ill., 1971), 177–198. Carter's account is suggestive for noting the tensions between ecumenism and schism, but it was not exhaustively researched. Platt's article is better researched, but he treats the Cummins schism as if it was totally disconnected from the history of the Evangelical party in the Episcopal Church. Platt's conclusions, therefore, which he made out to be totally unique to the Reformed Episcopal Church, are wrong. The same set of characteristics and commitments were held by Evangelicals who did not leave the Episcopal Church. The issue between the two groups was how to interpret those commitments in the face of Ritualism and modern theological thought. The Evangelical vision and the Reformed Episcopal vision were essentially the same; the Reformed Episcopalians, however, lost hope that that vision could ever be carried out within the context of the Episcopal Church. Many Evangelicals resisted this conclusion.

168. Cummins to Smith, November 10, 1873, in Cummins, *Memoir of Cummins*, 418–420.

169. Annie Darling Price, *A History of the Formation and Growth of the Reformed Episcopal Church, 1873–1902* (Philadelphia, 1902), 89. That Cummins would approve of the 1785 book is more than a little ironic. That book, influenced so strongly by William White, was more latitudinarian than anything else.

170. Chorley, *Men and Movements*, 418. Stephen Tyng, Jr., resisted this temptation.

171. "Bishop Cummins," *Standard of the Cross* (November 22, 1873): 4ff.

172. "The New Movement – The Cause," *Standard of the Cross* (December 13, 1873): 4.

173. This is a recurring theme in Reformed Episcopal Church apologetic literature. This particular quote is from Aycrigg, *Memoirs of the Church*, 158. Other examples are W. R. Nicholson, *Reasons Why I Became a Reformed Episcopalian* (Philadelphia, 1875), and Charles Edward Cheney, *A Word to Old-Fashioned Episcopalians. A Tract for the Times* (Philadelphia, 1889).

174. This set of characteristics is described by George Marsden, *Fundamentalism and American Culture: The Shaping of Twentieth-Century Evangelicalism, 1870–1925* (New York, 1980).

175. Charles P. McIlvaine, *The Apostolic Succession* (Hartford, Conn., 1872).

176. Isaac Labagh, *Theoklesia: or the Organization and Perpetuity, Conflicts and Triumphs of the One Holy Catholic and Apostolic Church* (New York, 1869).

177. Preceding quotes from Carus, *Memorials of McIlvaine*, 346, 349.

178. Preceding quotes from Cummins, *Memoir of Cummins*, 400–401.

179. Preceding quotes from "In Memoriam," *Standard of the Cross* (March 21, 1874): 292.

180. "Preface," in Albert Barnes, *The Position of the Evangelical Party in the Episcopal Church*, 5th ed. (Philadelphia, 1875), xi.

181. "A Fact in the History of Our Church," *Standard of the Cross* (February 21, 1874): 245.

182. Ibid.

7

Conclusion: Whither Evangelicalism?

Nearly every history of the Episcopal Church ends the story of the Evangelical party with the baptismal crisis and the Reformed Episcopal schism, as if the Evangelicals disappeared overnight. "As a great party struggling hopefully for the mastery within the Church," pronounced John Henry Hopkins, Jr., in 1872, "the old Evangelical party is dead, dead, dead."[1] Hopkins's announcement may have been premature: the Evangelical party did not simply die at the 1871 General Convention. It was, however, wounded and seriously divided. Although most Evangelicals agreed on issues of the new birth, spirituality, millennialism, and Scripture, their party splintered along very deep, old lines: their view of and relationship to the Episcopal Church.

As far back as the eighteenth-century Methodist revivals, some evangelicals stayed within the church and some felt the necessity to leave. In the nineteenth-century American church, the Evangelical party managed to maintain a unified front for nearly fifty years in spite of the fissures that existed within it. Radical and moderate evangelicals had always been somewhat at odds in their commitment to Episcopal forms and polity. The radicals tended to regard the episcopacy as little more than their particular church-form and were flexible in using the Book of Common Prayer. They identified more strongly with other Protestant evangelicals than with fellow Episcopalians, and they tended to be further from the centers of church power and authority. Moderates shared some of these sentiments, yet they generally regarded church order more highly and valued the episcopacy as necessary to the well-being of the church. The moderates tried to hold together their commitments to both other evangelicals and to their own Protestant Episcopal Church. They often held important ecclesiastical offices and controlled influential parishes. By 1872, these long-existing divisions in the Evangelical party were clear to all, and they could no longer present a united front for church reform. Thus, when he stated that the Evangelicals—as a party—were dead, John Henry Hopkins, Jr., was, in a limited sense, right. The Evangelical argument over the prayer book and the baptismal liturgy made a public spectacle of the party. Their influence and their ability to work for change in the whole institution was severely damaged by internal disagreements.

It was not this struggle that fatally wounded the Evangelical party, however. Most Evangelicals resisted radical tendencies and successfully recommitted themselves to the mainline church. A puzzling question arises: What then happened to those Evangelicals who stayed within the church?

224

In the years following 1875, the party faced two difficult problems, which changed it in some truly significant ways: the problem of evangelical succession and the problem of continuity of vision in a new cultural setting. The resulting changes were so powerful that they effectively destroyed old-style evangelicalism within the Episcopal Church. The new generation of leaders, initially Evangelicals, slowly abandoned old party loyalty in favor of the Broad Church whose new emphasis on critical theology and social ministry seemed to better address the problems of post–Civil War America.

The problem of succession became acute in the 1870s. In the years following the Cummins schism, all the most powerful and influential Evangelicals died.[2] The few remaining leaders of McIlvaine's generation, like Stephen Tyng, became proto-fundamentalists and maintained a conservative doctrine of Scripture, resisting Darwinism.[3] Admitted George Cummins in 1876:

> "Faithful and true men, among our old teachers and co-workers," men like [Charles Wesley] Andrews and [William] Sparrow, lift up a trumpet note of warning and alarm, but they fall at their posts, fighting in a most unequal and hopeless struggle, and there are no successors like minded to prolong the conflict. . . . These men are rapidly diminishing, and in another generation will scarcely be found in the old Church.[4]

The Cummins schism, though initially small, probably did work to drain off some of the more disillusioned Evangelicals.[5] In the twenty-five years following 1873, the Reformed Episcopal Church grew from 17 to over 10,000 communicants. Cummins's prophecy had somewhat of a self-fulfilling aspect: the breakaway church did attract at least a few of those who might have been most capable of maintaining traditional evangelicalism in the mainline church.

The problem of replacing the dying generation was compounded by a problem of intellectual and visionary succession as well. This was most pointed in the children of the old Evangelicals. Like their parents, they were sensitive to cultural change and they believed that the Evangelical party needed to change to address the times. With the rare exception of someone like Stephen Tyng, Jr., however, they rejected the fundamentalist answer to modern changes. They also rejected some key doctrines of the old Evangelical tradition. Phillips Brooks, a graduate of the Evangelical seminary in Virginia, for example, deemphasized the uniqueness of Christ's atonement and stated, quite openly, "I don't believe in total depravity."[6] In the 1880s, an aging Bishop Bedell paid little attention to the progress of liberal theology at Kenyon College. Kenyon's new president, William Bodine, rejected old-style evangelical religion. "We wonder, indeed," mocked Bodine, "that 'Hodge's Outlines of Theology' could ever have been a leading text-book in a Church training-school, and that the literature of the Plymouth Brethren could have been commended as the most valuable of Christian literature."[7] A similar process occurred at Evangelical Episcopal seminaries in Virginia and Cambridge as younger faculty members embraced Protestant liberalism, scientific Darwinism, and higher criticism with little opposition. By the end of the century, all the Evangelical educational institutions had become liberal.[8]

Why younger Evangelical Episcopalians were so completely won over by liberal theology is not entirely clear. The new generation clearly rejected Evangelical theology, but there were two significant continuities between the two movements: the rhetoric of liberality and the centrality of experience. These two continuities, when combined with the younger generation's rejection of traditional evangelical theology, formed a sort of bridge between evangelicalism and liberalism. The younger generation of Evangelicals, those of more moderate sympathies and the ones who stayed within the church, willingly crossed the bridge their parents had unwittingly built.

Rhetoric of Liberality

Throughout the nineteenth century, Evangelicals vigorously argued for the "liberty" to be flexible using the liturgy and associating with other non-Episcopal ministers. In the years between 1868 and 1873, this argument was particularly prominent as Evangelicals defended the practice of preaching in non-Episcopal churches (the Tyng case) and argued for latitude in using the Prayer Book. In 1868, Richard Newton declared "there have been different views held among us in regard to various things." Episcopal liberality, he believed, was at the very heart of the church's tradition. "The spirit of our Church," he proclaimed, "is not an exclusive but a liberal spirit."[9]

During the baptismal crisis, some Evangelicals, such as Prof. J. McElhinney at Kenyon, recognized that this strategy had backfired on the party. He wrote to Bishop McIlvaine; "We cannot, with any show of consistency, deny to our Romanizing adversaries a like liberty or license . . . thus finding ourselves compelled, by the exigencies of our position to become tributary to our foes."[10] He clearly saw that the Evangelical argument for liberty of usage and association, so long at the center of Evangelical strategy and identity, was now working in favor of the Ritualists. McElhinney saw no way out of this corner—short of revising the prayer book and enforcing uniformity.

What McElhinney did not see quite as clearly was that the Ritualist crisis had forged an alliance between Evangelicals and Broad Churchmen on the issue of "liberality." The Broad Church party willingly supported the Evangelicals against Ritualistic, or Romanizing, tendencies. Liberals feared Anglo-Catholic uniformity nearly as much as the Evangelicals. Once they were allies on the issue of "liberality," however, it would be nearly impossible for Evangelicals to ever use exclusionary rhetoric against the liberals. Blinded by their anti-Ritualism, Evangelicals had difficulty seeing the dangers in the Broad Church movement. The baptismal crises diverted Evangelical attention from the steady development of liberalism. When the non-Evangelical compromise candidate, Benjamin Paddock, replaced Manton Eastburn as bishop of Massachusetts, the older Evangelicals were not overly concerned. "I have seen the result of the election in Massachusetts," confided McIlvaine to Bedell; "it might have been much less acceptable."[11]

Some Evangelical leaders believed that the Cummins schism would force the church to adopt more latitudinarian policies toward particular canons and rubrics.

"His success," wrote William Sparrow, "might liberalize *us*, and bring us together again." Indeed, such freedom was considered essential to the mission of the Evangelicals. "The Protestant Episcopal Church needs only to be liberalized," Sparrow stated, "and rid of Romish germs, to overspread this Continent, at least in the upper and middle state of society."[12] His wish echoed Evangelical hopes surrounding the proposed Muhlenberg memorial from the early 1850s. Long part of their program, Evangelicals allied themselves with calls for greater liturgical and canonical flexibility—freedoms that would support their practices of extemporaneous prayer, revival meetings, and evangelistic strategies.

The rising generation of ministers and theologians, many trained in Evangelical institutions or from Evangelical families, coopted the "liberality" argument to introduce liberal theology and biblical criticism into the Episcopal Church. Not content with only liturgical freedom, these younger leaders argued for creedal liberalization as well. The "common motto" of the Broad Churchmen became "where the Spirit of the Lord is, there is liberty,"[13] and theological liberals took advantage of the Evangelical call for greater "church comprehensiveness" to forward their own position. An example of this was Alexander Viets Griswold Allen's *Freedom in the Church*. Allen, son of the Rev. Ethan Allen, an Evangelical in McIlvaine's circle and named after Bishop Griswold, used the argument for freedom to guard his right of theological inquiry. As a result of his own inquiry, Allen rejected the doctrine of the virgin birth as essential to matters of salvation.[14] Evangelicals themselves were denied liberty of usage by the General Convention in 1871, but their rhetoric was picked up by their opposition. Although the Evangelical Episcopal call for freedom failed to secure their own place within the church, it was successfully employed by liberals. Theological liberals also carried the Evangelical tradition of freedom to associate with non-Episcopal ministers in the twentieth-century ecumenical movement.

Centrality of Experience

The centrality of religious experience formed a second continuity between the Evangelical and the Broad Church traditions. Although Broad Churchmen rejected Evangelical views of theology, the Bible, and conversion, they retained the idea that human beings must know and feel God experientially. In 1938, one Episcopal priest identified the core of Evangelicalism as "one, eternal unchanging Spirit moving through all the outward forms of change." This spirit, he believed, "meant direct access to a living, loving, personal Father and a personal relationship with all the members of His human family."[15]

This emphasis on the internal, personal, and spiritual nature of religious knowledge is everywhere evident in Episcopal liberalism. While defending higher criticism of the Bible, the Rev. R. Heber Newton, one of Richard Newton's sons, stated:

> If, then, any one asks me how he may know that there is a revelation in the Bible, I tell him to walk in its light, and see what it reveals. If any one asks me how I know

that the Bible is inspired, I answer him in Mr. Moody's words: "I know that the
Bible is inspired, because it 'inspires me.' "[16]

Phillips Brooks rejected the "crude, hard, and untrue statements" of the Evangelicals and resigned his position in the Evangelical Education Society when he refused
to sign a statement of faith, but even he admired the fact that the Evangelicals
"created most profound experiences."[17] Well into the twentieth century, a movement of "liberal Evangelicals" believed they were the heirs of the old Evangelical
tradition because they continued to emphasize the inward, emotional, and spiritual aspects of Christian faith.[18]

Rejection of Evangelical Theology

The Broad Church party kept the Evangelical strategy of "freedom" and maintained their emphasis on internal and spiritual religion. They bitterly attacked
Evangelical theology, however, and it was that theology which crumbled before
the Broad Church advance. William Wilberforce Newton, another of Richard
Newton's sons, mused:

> It would seem as if it were a foregone conclusion, that if anything remained after
> the Evangelical party had done its work, it would be its radical, and yet in a
> certain sense, its strong theology. . . . The "simple gospel," the "clear views,"
> justification by faith, the commercial conception of the covenant, of the blood
> of reconciliation, of the Anselmic atonement, of the Calvinistic election, and
> of a stronger than Tridentine theory of future punishment, hell and retribu-
> tion, stronger than the statement of Trent . . . were doctrines which could
> not last beyond the strength of the individual convictions which maintained
> them. . . . This structure of thought was the fashion of the religious mind of that
> day; but this theological mould could not produce the form of thought for the
> age which was to come after it.[19]

Newton did not realize that Evangelical theology had changed its emphases
throughout the century. He did recognize, however, that the theological core had
not substantially changed, and it was this core that liberals rejected. Other Broad
Churchmen agreed. "Puritan evangelicalism did a great and good work," declared
the Rev. William S. Rainsford. "Perhaps it made our own type of Anglo-Saxon
democracy possible; but it proclaimed a divine partiality that is now unthinkable.
It is time to face the truth about ourselves and God."[20]

This rejection points to a major failure of the Evangelical party: they failed to
adapt the presentation of their core message in a way that engaged modern
thought and maintained traditional Protestant theology at the same time. In the
Episcopal Church, a highly educated, elite, urban church, this was a critical failure.
When the old Evangelical party failed to think—or failed to train a new generation
to think—of a new way to talk about Christ's satisfactory atonement and human
sin, young Episcopal leaders abandoned the party of their forebears, rejected the
distinctive doctrines of the movement, and embraced liberalism. When the Evangelical party most desperately needed to reassert its theology in a new way, it failed

to meet the challenge. Its genius, throughout the century, had been its ability to maintain its theological *and* experiential core in the face of successive changes.

The younger Evangelicals-turned-liberals did attempt to modify evangelical theology for the new generation. They modified it so much, however, that it bore little resemblance to traditional orthodoxy. Some of them recognized that, in essence, they had rejected the faith of their forebears. Some of the younger leaders, such as Rainsford, argued that this liberal modification was a legitimate offspring of older Evangelicalism. Rainsford praised Wesley and Whitefield as preachers of pardon for sinners and as "new strength and hope for reborn man." He claimed his message the same as theirs and declared, "*I am convinced it ever will remain the central core, the living, growing seed core, of the Gospel of the Universal Jesus.*"[21] Although Rainsford claimed continuity, it is difficult to imagine Wesley or Whitefield recognizing a "universal Jesus" or believing that the message of pardon for sinners could be delivered without a classical Protestant understanding of the atonement. The liberals modified, but they modified Evangelicalism completely on the basis of modernity, thus losing an important component of the evangelical tradition: the doctrinal core. They reasserted evangelical theology in a new way, but in doing so made it something almost completely different from what it had been. Against the whirlwind of liberalism, old Evangelicalism lost its theological footing. That gone, all that was left of the old synthesis of the Reformation mind and the transformed heart was the internal and experiential. The liberals gleefully disassembled the evangelical mind, while keeping what they considered the "spirit" of the evangelical heart. Without evangelicalism's theology, liberals transformed the evangelical "spirit" into something that bore little resemblance to old-fashioned evangelical religion and piety.

Coupled with the intellectual failure of the Evangelical party was an institutional failure. Some Evangelicals had worked out a proto-fundamentalist intellectual response to late nineteenth-century problems; Evangelical institutions failed to successfully promote this response, however. As the institutions rejected fundamentalism, nineteenth-century evangelicalism eventually came to be seen as "outside" Episcopal tradition. In reality, there had been a kind of incipient fundamentalism in the nineteenth-century Episcopal Church. By the twentieth century, however, there were neither leaders nor institutions to pass on Episcopal fundamentalism. The most likely candidates to do so had, by that time, abandoned the Protestant Episcopal Church and joined the Reformed Episcopal Church.

After 1875, Evangelicals failed to present an intellectual, spiritual, and moral vision to excite and energize their own children. The children, therefore, became attracted to new ways of thinking about religious experience. Ironically, the Evangelicals lost their battle to gain liturgical liberalization, while maintaining old-fashioned creedal orthodoxy at the same time that the Broad Church party, who more strictly obeyed the canons, rubrics, and liturgy, increasingly liberalized traditional theology. Due to lack of new leadership, the loss of evangelical commitment at their seminaries, and the slow abandonment of Evangelical theology, the old Evangelical party died a long death in the two decades following the Cummins schism.

Transformation of Old Evangelicalism and St. George's, New York

"Death" may be too strong a word. The nineteenth-century Evangelical party had two impulses: a moderate, churchly impulse and a radical, more sectarian one. By 1875, due to new cultural forces, and the internal pressures of the Episcopal church, these two impulses had divided into two different forms of evangelical Protestantism: the first, most of the moderates, now reasserting their institutional loyalty, became *liberal evangelicals* in an attempt to stay relevant; the second, the radicals, a group I call the *proto-fundamentalists*, continued to align themselves primarily with interdenominational evangelicalism. As tensions increased at the end of the century, the gulf between these two groups widened. Liberal evangelicals became full-blown liberals; proto-fundamentalists left the Protestant Episcopal Church for the Reformed Episcopal Church in larger numbers. By 1900, old-style Evangelicals, like Bishop McIlvaine, who successfully combined both impulses, seemed no longer to exist. If they did, there was little institutional space for them to remain Evangelical: either join with the church's liberal program, or leave for the Reformed Episcopal Church. Larger issues in American religion were slowly driving a wedge between liberal and fundamentalist evangelicals in the Episcopal Church as they were in every Protestant church.

The divergence between conservative and liberal evangelicals in the Episcopal Church did not occur immediately;[22] it was a slow process over a number of years. St. George's Church in New York serves as a sort of paradigm for the larger Evangelical party. The elder Stephen Tyng had been rector of St. George's for more than thirty-five years; under him, the church had been a center for the most committed, even extreme, forms of old-fashioned evangelicalism, which he insisted was the same in his day as during the times of the apostles and the British Reformation. In a sermon during the last year of his ministry, Tyng preached: "I profess, myself . . . to be one of these narrow-minded men, holding with unshrinking grasp the inspired word of God; adhering to the old paths and walking in them."[23] After securing an evangelical succession for his pulpit, the venerable Tyng retired in 1878.

The Evangelical heir, Walter Williams, a weak leader and ineffective preacher, resigned after only five years. His successor was the Rev. William S. Rainsford, who is remembered in Episcopal history as a heroic liberal and social gospel leader. In reality, his story is not so clear. St. George's believed that Rainsford would continue the Tyng Evangelical tradition in their parish. There was good reason for them to believe this: Rainsford, the Irish-born son of an Evangelical Anglican revivalist, was himself an evangelical. One biographer notes:

> On Saturdays when people gathered in the market square he stood there ringing a great bell and when he got a crowd around him preached. He sought co-operation from young men in this street preaching, assigning districts to them, and they all preached in the old style of evangelical address, urging upon their hearers personal conviction of sin, conscious conversion to God which they called the new birth, the love of Jesus, and salvation as deliverance from hell-fire.[24]

After arriving in New York in 1876, Rainsford assisted Stephen Tyng, Jr., at Holy Trinity and became a successful tent evangelist. He conducted revivals in Baltimore, Philadelphia, Washington, Richmond, New Orleans, and Louisville. His most spectacular success was in London, Canada, and a subsequent mission in Toronto where "crowds thronged the church, many could not get in. Hundreds remained for counsel on the all-absorbing theme of personal religion."[25]

In spite of such success, Rainsford was troubled by issues facing the Evangelical party. His "first growing pain" came while studying baptism in the New Testament. "The stock arguments," he confessed, "with which the Evangelical party sought to compromise between the plain teaching of our service and their preaching, I could not swallow."[26] He became intrigued by Phillips Brooks. He discovered the works of Frederick Robertson, an Anglican preacher who had abandoned Evangelicalism for Broad Church liberalism. "He studied Robertson, and drank in his teaching as only a man parched with thirst can drink. Old truths took on new forms, new life."[27] While serving a parish in Toronto, he distanced himself from Evangelical arguments. "To the old Evangelicals," he recalled, "I smelt of heresy."[28] He doubted the satisfaction theory of the atonement, the verbal inspiration of Scripture, and the doctrine of eternal punishment. On pragmatic matters, however—such as the messages he preached, drawing large numbers of people to church, leading exciting Bible classes, and balancing the church budget with generous collections—Rainsford continued to please his Evangelical constituents. Although he was slowly abandoning Evangelical doctrine, Rainsford still embodied Evangelical style. In January 1883, he was called to St. George's in New York—a congregation suffering from five years of neglect and a shadow of its former self under Stephen Tyng.

The congregation, it seems, was attracted chiefly to two qualities in Rainsford: his Evangelical message and his leadership abilities. He reenergized St. George's Sunday school, abolished pew rents, encouraged congregational singing, and launched an urban ministry program into the surrounding community. All these projects and programs were continuous with earlier Evangelical commitments. In spite of his intellectual attraction to Robertson, Rainsford himself had not made a clear break with his own Evangelical past. As late as November 1885, he held a massive revival at St. George's which included Evangelical luminaries such as Bishop Bedell and Ira Sankey. He actively supported the Evangelical Education Society. And he built St. George's into one of the great institutional churches of the 1890s.

Nevertheless, in 1895, Bishop Thomas Clark of Kansas, an Evangelical leader active since the 1870s, observed a shift in evangelical interests at St. George's.

> We have extended the range of our work and are now adjusting the mechanism of the Church in order to meet the emergency. We are beginning to recognize the fact the Gospel must be brought to bear directly upon *society* as well as the individual. . . . I have this moment taken up the Year-book of St. George's Church, New York, and nothing could more strikingly illustrate the change of which I am speaking. The contents of this book would have been a puzzle to the members of old St. George's . . . and I am afraid that good Dr. Milnor would have shaken his head somewhat ominously if it had fallen under his inspection.[29]

After describing the numerous athletic, literary, and social service clubs at the church, Clark finished by explaining how this evangelical parish had so changed:

> We believe that in recognizing these things as pertaining to the kingdom of God,
> we are not only following the example of Christ and obeying His precepts, but we
> are breaking down the old distinction between the secular and the religious – not
> by making our religion secular, but by trying to bring all things into conformity
> with the mind of God.[30]

Clark did not see the change as a complete abandonment of Evangelical principles. Rather, those principles had been extended from the individual to the corporate sphere. One wonders if the secularizing forces of the Civil War, such as McIlvaine's diplomatic mission to England and the nationalism of the church, helped contribute to the need to break down "the old distinction between the secular and the religious." In spite of their opposition to rationalism, here, too, Evangelicals ironically contributed to the modernization of theology that would eventually make their own views obsolete.

For Rainsford, the change was complete by the turn of the century. In 1903, eleven Philadelphia clergymen (who called themselves "members of both the great historic schools of the Church" – High Church and Evangelical) accused him of heresy. In 1905, he openly declared:

> I am confident that unless our creeds are treated as symbols of divine truth,
> beautiful and necessary if you will – but still as symbols and not as complete and
> final expressions of divine truth – these creeds that we have been brought up to
> love and reverence, will seem to our fellow-men as bandages we insist on binding
> on their eyes – not as lamps we would if we might place in their hands.[31]

If Rainsford's story, and the transformation of Stephen Tyng's beloved St. George's, is any indication, it is apparent what happened to the Evangelicals who remained in the Episcopal Church: they became liberals. The generation that came of age shortly before the Civil War found old-fashioned evangelicalism inadequate to meet the needs of contemporary society. In some ways, the groundwork laid by the older Evangelicals contributed to the success of liberalism. Their stresses on liberality and religious experience dovetailed with new liberal theology. Their flexibility and adaptability to cultural changes placed them in a vulnerable position: How far could one adjust to the contemporary milieu? During the antebellum period, the older Evangelicals had successfully accommodated Anglicanism to American evangelicalism. By adapting that tradition to post–Civil War realities, younger Evangelicals recognized a certain continuity between their vision and that of their parents. In a very real sense, Bishop McIlvaine had two heirs: the younger liberal evangelical generation, ever ready to experiment with new ideas to keep the gospel relevant, and the fundamentalistic Reformed Episcopalians. Neither group retained the full heritage of McIlvaine's Evangelical Episcopalianism. Nor was either group completely comfortable with their lineage.

The Reformed Episcopal schism, a proto-fundamentalist schism, mitigated any full-fledged conservative response against liberalism within the context of the church. Unlike other American Protestant denominations, in which fundamentalism and liberalism continued to grow together within the context of the institutions, and then suffered schism in the twentieth century, the Episcopal Church went through this process – in a modified form – a half century earlier. Thus, when the fundamentalist/modernist controversy occurred in the 1920s, the Episcopal Church was relatively untouched—with the exception of some arguments over the creeds.[32] The lack of a fundamentalist/modernist argument does not mean Episcopalians were less likely to fight about church identity; it only means they did it *earlier*. The results of that long, bitter argument affected the later one. Had the Reformed Episcopalians not split off in 1874, there might have been a more vigorous fundamentalism in the Episcopal Church and the story of early twentieth-century Episcopalianism might have been more like that of other American Protestants.

The Evangelical party did not die, as Hopkins stated, in 1871, but it was being transformed. Its leaders lacked the foresight they needed to shape that transformation in a way that would hold two evangelical impulses together. Evangelicals, in short, were unable to articulate an *evangelical* theological identity that was clearly committed to the mainline church. Because of this failure, by 1900 Broad Church liberalism and Ritualism—the two great enemies of evangelicalism in the 1870s—won the battle for the Episcopal soul.

Looking Southward: Divided Evangelical Episcopalians

Evangelical Episcopalianism was transformed by another significant factor as well: the Civil War. Throughout the nineteenth century, Evangelical strength was geographically even, north and south. The major Evangelical institutions were in Ohio and Virginia. The movement's most dynamic leaders came from both sides of the Mason-Dixon line. McIlvaine and Meade's growing divergence in the 1850s illustrates the regional tensions that slowly rent party unity. By the Civil War, when the southerners formed a separate Episcopal Church in the Confederate States, the division was complete. One historian notes: "While much of the high church strength had been concentrated in the North, evangelical leadership had come from both North and South. The war divided and, therefore, weakened the [evangelical] movement."[33]

When the war ended, bitter feelings prevailed among Evangelical factions. McIlvaine, long-time champion of evangelical unity, steadfastly resisted the readmission of Confederate supporters into the Protestant Episcopal Church. While professing his "kindest feelings toward our Southern brethren in general and am affectionate desire that we should all be united again," he nevertheless protested to Bishop Hopkins the church's invitation asking the southerners to attend the 1865 General Convention. He cited a sermon preached at the funeral of the late Bishop Polk which criticized the United States government and the Union—an action that displayed flagrant disloyalty:

> Nor can I say that I could welcome all whom Southern Dioceses might send as Delegates to that body. A clergyman, for example, who voluntarily assumed the place of a military commander and actively participated in the bloody struggle of the late terrible war against the Government and the Union, I could not welcome.[34]

For McIlvaine, principle, justice, and integrity demanded that the northern church not welcome the Confederates back on the basis of sentiment. Although earlier in his career he resisted the intertwining of politics and religion, by 1865 the division between the two had broken down. During the war, Union politics, particularly once Lincoln issued the Emancipation Proclamation, became an expression of evangelical theology. Northern nationalism and the gospel merged.

Ironically, the same process occurred among southern Evangelical Episcopalians as well. However, to McIlvaine the merger of the southern cause with the gospel was abominable. Evangelical Episcopalianism had been the religion of many of the great southern leaders: Polk, Lee, and Davis among them. When ordered to replace the prayer for the Confederate president with one for the president of the United States, evangelical stalwart Bishop Richard Wilmer of Alabama recommended his clergy omit such prayers altogether.[35] After the war, however, southern Evangelical Episcopalianism buttressed the religion of the Lost Cause. Wrote one historian:

> The Episcopalians played an especially prominent role in the Southern civil religion, particularly in its rituals. This stemmed partly from their position in Southern society: The Episcopal Church was the church of the antebellum planter class, and after the war the Episcopalians helped make the Lost Cause a defense of aristocratic values. The role played by the Episcopalians in the Lost Cause also came from their leadership role in the Confederate cause.[36]

In addition to Lee, Davis, and Polk, Capers, Hardee, Hood, and Johnston were Episcopalians. The Episcopal church provided a significantly disproportionate number of chaplains for the Confederate army—four of whom later became bishops.[37] McIlvaine's West Point convert Leonidas Polk, the Fighting Bishop exalted in southern civil religion, best illustrates the interrelatedness of Evangelical Episcopalianism and the Confederacy. Resigning his position as bishop to take up a military commission, Polk believed that Christ had called him to defend the gospel and the south. Polk died in battle, and "when the fatal shot cut him down, a blood stained prayer-book was found next [to] his heart."[38]

McIlvaine, Union agent and bishop for Lincoln, and Polk, the bishop-general of the Confederacy, illuminate two sides of the same problem: the adaptability and malleability of evangelical religion to the prevailing culture. Throughout the nineteenth century, evangelical religion served as a way to Americanize Anglicanism. By mid-century, however, political concerns usurped a distinctive evangelical identity and created two different forms of evangelical Episcopalianism, each of which reflected its regional culture. Until the war, the divergences within the party were kept to a minimum. But the Civil War ultimately ruptured remaining party unity. In the north, Evangelical Episcopalians followed a course much like other evangelical Protestants: postwar problems transformed the Evangelical party into two distinct groups—one that claimed to be "old-fashioned" evangelicalism yet modified by embracing dispensational premillennialism and a strict form of biblical inerrancy; another that retained evangelical postmillennialism but expanded their vision of reform to include secular as well as religious concerns.[39] So, in the north, the evangelical party slowly diverged into proto-fundamentalist and evangelical liberal camps. In the south, Evangelical Episcopalians, still identified with the upper class, preserved antebellum values through ritual and institutions (such as the University of the South) and retained, overall, a more traditional, Low

Church evangelicalism than did the northern party, especially after the Reformed Episcopal schism. As the religion of the establishment, southern Evangelical Episcopalianism mitigated against extremism and prevented both the development of the sectarian Reformed Episcopal church and northern theological liberalism. So, in an ironic twist of history, southern—not northern—Evangelical Episcopalianism managed to maintain the moderation of the McIlvaine synthesis but interpreted it through the lens of the Lost Cause.

The Irony of Forms

When the younger Evangelicals abandoned the theology that empowered revivalism, the born-again experience, personal holiness, and the "preaching of Christ crucified," they emptied their tradition of its life blood. Ironically, they kept many the forms of their parents' evangelicalism: plainer churches, limited ritualism, tables instead of altars, seldom-celebrated communion, minimal choral singing, and read psalms.[40] This plain piety had once symbolized the theology of the Reformation and the experience of a heart moved by God alone. Liberalism emptied it of these meanings and replaced them with its own vision of theology, piety, Christian nurture, and morality. The remnants of Evangelical antiformalism became a new kind of form. Well into the twentieth century, many Episcopal churches still resisted Ritualism and greater ceremonialism because Evangelical "forms" had become a kind of antiformal traditionalism. The original meaning of Evangelical religion was gone; only the forms remained.

Nothing was further from the intention or spirit of nineteenth-century Evangelicalism. Charles McIlvaine and his colleagues poured their energy into a vision of Episcopalianism that enlivened forms with the spirit of biblical, Protestant, and evangelical Christianity. For many years, they offered a theology and an identity that invigorated the young Episcopal Church, giving it a vision for saving the souls of nineteenth-century Americans. In the last years of the century, the vision of the old Evangelicals, so carefully crafted by McIlvaine and his clerical friends, failed to inspire the imaginations of young Episcopalians. The progeny departed from the ways of their parents, forged a different vision of Episcopal identity, buried the memory of Bishop McIlvaine and the Evangelical party, and offered a new theology for what they believed would be a new world.

Notes

1. John Henry Hopkins, Jr., "Decline and Fall of the Low Church Party," originally appeared in the *Church and the World* (April and July, 1872); reprinted in full in Charles F. Sweet, *A Champion of the Cross, Being the Life of John Henry Hopkins, S.T.D.* (New York, 1894), 295–358.
2. Almost all of the most visionary, influential, and intellectually capable Evangelical leaders died before 1890: McIlvaine, 1873; Alfred Lee, 1887; William Sparrow, 1874; Manton Eastburn, 1872; Stephen Tyng, 1885; William Meade, 1862; John Seeley Stone, 1882; Richard Newton, 1887; J.P.K. Henshaw, 1852; Benjamin Clark Cutler, 1863;

B.B. Smith, 1884; and John Johns, 1876. Living into the 1890s were Stephen Tyng, Jr. (1898), and Gregory Bedell (1892). Of all the Evangelical leaders of the 1870s, only Thomas M. Clark lived into the twentieth century. By that time, Clark had become a Broad Churchman.

3. See, for example, Tyng's sermons on Scripture and Darwinism, in Tyng, *Life and Work of Stephen Tyng*, and Richard Newton's *Bible Bulwarks: or a Sevenfold Argument in Defence of the Scriptures* (Philadelphia, 1875).

4. George D. Cummins, *Following the Light: A Statement of the Author's Experiences* (Philadelphia, 1876), 14.

5. Tracts like Cheney's *A Word to Old-Fashioned Episcopalians* illustrate Reformed Episcopal evangelistic efforts directed at the mainline Episcopal Church.

6. Alexander V.G. Allen, *Life and Letters of Phillips Brooks* (New York, 1900), II: 15. Boston Unitarians flocked to hear Brooks—whose message they recognized as being the same as their own.

7. "Some Words Concerning Gambier—Past, Present and Future," in Bodine, *Kenyon Book*, 378.

8. For the liberalization of the Evangelical Episcopal seminaries, see Smythe, *Kenyon College*, 213ff, and Muller, *Episcopal Theological School*. Virginia remained evangelical the longest, but by the late 1880s, liberal influences were evident there as well. See W.A.R. Goodwin, *History of the Theological Seminary in Virginia and Its Historical Background* (New York, 1923), I: 262–316.

9. Preceding quotes from Richard Newton, *Liberal Views of the Ministry in Harmony with the Bible, the Prayer Book, and the Canons* (Philadelphia, 1868), 35.

10. McElhinney to McIlvaine, December 19, 1871, in McI, Dio. Ohio Arch.

11. McIlvaine to Bedell, December 29, 1872, in ibid.

12. All quotes this paragraph from Walker, *Life and Correspondence of Sparrow*, 352.

13. Allen, *Life and Letters of Brooks*, I: 447–448.

14. Alexander V. G. Allen, *Freedom in the Church, or the Doctrine of Christ* (New York, 1907).

15. R.O. Kevin, Jr. "Evangelicalism and the Bible," in *Abiding Values of Evangelicalism: Papers and Addresses Read at the Seventy-fifth Anniversary of the Evangelical Education Society of the Protestant Episcopal Church* (Philadelphia, 1938), 79.

16. R. Heber Newton, *The Right and Wrong Uses of the Bible* (New York: Putnam, 1883), 78.

17. Allen, *Life and Letters of Brooks*, II: 76.

18. For "liberal Evangelicalism" as a movement in the American Episcopal Church, see Chorley, *Men and Movements*, 435–439; Raymond W. Albright, *A History of the Protestant Episcopal Church* (New York, 1964), 317; and *Abiding Values of Evangelicalism*. "Liberal Evangelicalism" in the early twentieth century had its roots in nineteenth-century tradition and was influenced by a similar movement in the Church of England. See Hylson-Smith, *Evangelicals in the Church*, 250–252; *Liberal Evangelicalism: An Interpretation* (London, 1923); and *The Inner Life: Essays in Liberal Evangelicalism* (London, 1924). The difference between liberal Evangelicalism in the Church of England and the Protestant Episcopal Church was that in the American church, the liberal Evangelical voice was the *only* evangelical voice. In the Church of England, traditionalist Evangelicals opposed the development of liberal Evangelicalism.

19. Newton, *Yesterday with the Fathers*, 189–191.

20. William S. Rainsford, *The Story of a Varied Life: An Autobiography* (1922; reprint, New York, 1970), 377.

21. Ibid., 134.

22. Nor did it occur immediately in American Protestantism generally. For the continued intertwining of liberalism and conservative evangelicalism, see Grant Wacker, "The Holy Spirit and the Spirit of the Age in American Protestantism, 1880–1910," *Journal of American History* 72 (1985): 45–62.

23. Preceding discussion and quotes from Tyng, *Life and Work of Stephen Tyng*, 508, 561.

24. Henry Anstice, *History of St. George's Church in the City of New York, 1752–1811–1911* (New York, 1911), 425.

25. Ibid., 426–427.

26. Rainsford, *Story of a Varied Life*, 137–139.

27. Anstice, *History of St. George's*, 426–427.

28. Rainsford, *Story of a Varied Life*, 191.

29. Anstice, *History of St. George's*, 327.

30. Ibid.

31. Ibid., 360.

32. For fundamentalism in the Episcopal Church, see Norman F. Furniss, *The Fundamentalist Controversy, 1918–1931* (Hamden, Conn., 1963), 162–169, and Prichard, *History of the Church*, 205–213. Fundementalism in the Episcopal Church has not been well researched at all. For example, when the bishops tried to remove the Thirty-nine Articles from the 1928 prayer book, more than 300,000 people protested. This seems to indicate that, in spite of the liberalization of the clergy and institutions, some sort of Episcopal traditionalism persisted. I have concluded that parish studies might prove the best route to understanding the extent and nature of Episcopal fundamentalism. Much of this part of my own argument is speculative because of the lack of solid research done on this period and subject.

33. Prichard, *History of the Church*, 147.

34. McIlvaine to Hopkins, July 1, 1865, in McI, Dio. Ohio Arch.

35. See Edwin S. Gaustad, ed., *A Documentary History of Religion in America Since 1865* (Grand Rapids, Mich., 1983), 6–8; Richard H. Wilmer, *The Recent Past from a Southern Standpoint: Reminiscences of a Grandfather* (New York, 1887); and Charles Reagan Wilson, *Baptized in Blood: The Religion of the Lost Cause, 1865–1920* (Athens, Ga., 1980), 42. Wilson's work shows the extent to which Episcopalians—almost all of Evangelical sympathies—undergirded the religion of the Confederacy and the Lost Cause.

36. Wilson, *Baptized in Blood*, 35–36.

37. Ibid.

38. Quoted in ibid., 55. On Polk, see Polk, *Leonidas Polk*.

39. Although it was not evident in the McIlvaine-Tyng generation, in the postbellum period premillennialism seemed to make its adherents less nationalistic. If one believed that history must end before the kingdom arrived, there might be less of a temptation to identify the kingdom with American culture or destiny. After the war, postmillennialism became more "secular" as the kingdom was redefined in terms of the social gospel. Thus, it seems that postmillennialists, often social gospel liberals, were also highly nationalistic, confusing the kingdom with "Anglo-Saxon" culture.

40. Even in many rigorously evangelical dioceses, like Ohio, some Ritualistic practices—such as using flowers in churches and the limited use of candles—became acceptable.

Selected Bibliography

Primary Sources

Collections

Charles P. McIlvaine Collection. Thomas Greenslade Manuscripts and Archives, Olin Library, Kenyon College, Gambier, Ohio. [McI, Kenyon College]

Charles P. McIlvaine papers, Diocese of Ohio Archives, Cleveland, Ohio. (McI, Dio. Ohio Arch.]

Ethan Allan Collection. Maryland Diocesan Archives, Episcopal Diocesan House, Baltimore, Md. (EA, MD Dio. Arch.]

Ethan Allen Collection. Thomas Greenslade Manuscripts and Archives, Olin Library, Kenyon College, Gambier, Ohio.

Gratz Collection. Historical Society of Pennsylvania, Philadelphia, Pa. [Gratz, Hist. Soc. Pa.]

Philander Chase Collections. Thomas Greenslade Manuscripts and Archives, Olin Library, Kenyon College, Gambier, Ohio.

Protestant Episcopal Bishops Collection. Yale University Library, New Haven, Conn.

Salmon P. Chase papers. Historical Society of Pennsylvania, Philadelphia, Pa. [Chase, Hist. Soc. Pa.]

William Lane papers. Yale University Library, New Haven, Conn.

Newspapers, Magazines, and Journals

Annual Report, American Tract Society
Biblical Repertory and Princeton Review
Christian Lady's Magazine
Christian Observer
Churchman
Church Review and Register
Episcopal Recorder
Gambier Observer
Journal of the Diocese of Maryland
Journal of the Diocese of Ohio
Journal of the Diocese of Pennsylvania
Journal of the General Convention, Protestant Episcopal Church
New York Observer

Prophetic Times
Southern Churchman
Standard of the Cross
Washington Theological Review
Western Episcopalian

Books and Pamphlets

Allen, Alexander V.G. *Freedom in the Church, of the Doctrine of Christ*. New York: Macmillan, 1907.

[Andrews, Charles Wesley.] *An Apology. The Protestant Episcopal Society for the Promotion of Evangelical Knowledge: Its Origin, Constitution, Tendencies and Work*. New York: Gray, 1854.

Aycrigg, Benjamin. *Memoirs of the Reformed Episcopal Church, and of the Protestant Episcopal Church. . . .* New York: Edward Jenkins, 1880.

Baird, Robert. *Religion in America; or an Account of the Origin, Relation to the State, and Present Condition of the Evangelical Churches in the United States*. New York: Harper and Bros., 1856.

Barnes, Albert. *Reply to a Review of the Tract on the Position of the Evangelical Party in the Episcopal Church*. 1844, Reprint. Philadelphia: Moore, 1875.

——. *The Position of the Evangelical Party in the Episcopal Church*. 5th ed. Philadelphia: Moore, 1875.

——. *The Scriptural Argument for Episcopacy Examined*. New York, 1835.

Bedell, Gregory T. *Personal Presence of God the Holy Ghost*. Cleveland: Office of the Standard of the Cross, 1874.

Beecher, Lyman. *A Plea for the West*. 2nd ed. Cincinnati: Truman and Smith, 1835.

The Book of Common Prayer as It Is. A Critical Examination of Certain Portions of the Prayer Book. New York, 1871.

Brooke, J. T. *Decision: A Plain Sermon for the Times*. Cincinnati: H. W. Derby, 1850.

——. *The Law of Liberality Between Christian Denominations Applied to the Episcopal Church*. Cincinnati: McKay, 1856.

——. *Union: How Far Consistent or Justifiable in View of the Present Differences Between Churchmen: An Address*. Cincinnati: Moore, Wilstack, Kerp, 1859.

Calvary Pastoral, with Comments: A Tract for the Times. New York, 1849.

Caswall, Henry. *America and the American Church*. London: Rivington, 1839.

——. *America and the American Church*. 2nd ed. London: Mozley, 1851.

"Catholicus." *Letter to the Rt. Rev. Alonzo Potter, D.D. in Vindication of the Principle of Christian Union for the Propagation of the Gospel*. Philadelphia: Moore, 1850.

Cheney, Charles Edward. *A Word to Old-Fashioned Episcopalians. A Tract for the Times*. Philadelphia: Reformed Episcopal Publishing Society, 1889.

——. *The Evangelical Ideal of a Visible Church. A Sermon Preached Before the Second General Council of the Reformed Episcopal Church, in the City of New York*. Philadelphia: Moore, 1874.

Clark, John A. *Letters on the Church*. Philadelphia: William Stavely, 1839.

Colton, Calvin. *Genius and Mission of the Protestant Episcopal Church in the United States*. New York: Stanford, 1853.

——. *History and Character of American Revivals of Religion*. London: Westly and Davis, 1832.

——. *Protestant Jesuitism*. New York: Harper and Bros., 1836.

——. *Thoughts on the Religious State of the Country with Reasons for Preferring Episcopacy*. New York: Harper and Bros., 1836.

Conant, William C. *Narratives of Remarkable Conversions and Revival Incidents. . . . An Account of the Rise and Progress of the Great Awakening of 1857–1858.* New York: Derby and Jackson, 1858.

Correspondence Between the Rt. Rev. George Washington Doane and the Rev. S. Wilmer on the Subject of Associations. Philadelphia: Whethan, 1835.

[Coxe, A. C.] *Fixed Principles: The Laws of Christian Unity Compared with Schemes of Sectarian Union.* Baltimore: J. Robinson, 1859.

Cracraft, J. W. *Judiaizing Teachers, Ancient and Modern, or Sacramental Error Refuted by the Teaching of Scripture, and the Authorities of the Episcopal Church.* Chicago, 1858.

Cranmer, Thomas. "An Homily or Sermon of Good Good Works Annexed unto Faith." In *Miscellaneous Writings and Letters of Thomas Cranmer, Archbishop of Canterbury, Martyr, 1556,* edited by John E. Cox. Cambridge: Cambridge University Press, 1846.

——. "The Council's Letter to Bp. Ridley to Take Down Altars and Place Communion Tables in Their Stead." In *Miscellaneous Writings and Letter of Thomas Cranmer, Archbishop of Canterbury, Martyr, 1556,* edited by John E. Cox. Cambridge: Cambridge University Press, 1846.

——. "Reasons Why the Lord's Board Should Rather be After the Form of a Table Than of an Altar." In *Miscellaneous Writings and Letters of Thomas Cranmer, Archbishop of Canterbury, Martyr, 1556,* edited by John E. Cox. Cambridge: Cambridge University Press, 1846.

Croley, George. *The Apocalypse of St. John, or Prophecies of the Rise, Progress and Fall of the Church of Rome . . . and the Final Triumph of Christianity.* London, 1838.

Cummins, George D. *Following the Light: A Statement of the Author's Experiences.* Philadelphia: Moore, 1876.

Dashiell, George. *An Address to the Protestant Episcopal Church in Maryland.* N. p., [1814].

——. *An Ordination Sermon Delivered on the 30th of April 1821 in St. John's Church, Baltimore.* Baltimore, 1821.

A Debate on the Roman Catholic Religion: Held in the Sycamore-Street Meeting House. Cincinnati . . . Between Alexander Campbell and the Rt. Rev. John B. Purcell. Cincinnati, 1873.

Edwards, Jonathan. *The Great Awakening.* Edited by C. C. Goen. New Haven and London: Yale University Press, 1972.

——. *Religious Affections.* Edited by John E. Smith. New Haven and London: Yale University Press, 1959.

Evangelical Alliance of the United States. *Document Number One, Constitution and Officers.* New York: Carter and Bros., 1868.

——. *Document Number Three,* 1869.

Evangelical Religion in Its Historical Connection with the Church of England and the Protestant Episcopal Church: A Letter to a Friend. New York: PESPEK, 1857.

Faber, George Stanley. *The Primitive Doctrine of Justification Investigated Relatively to the Several Definitions of the Church of Rome and the Church of England.* London: Seeley and Burnside, 1837.

Few Earnest Words to the Laity of the Protestant Episcopal Church. 2nd ed. Philadelphia: McCauley, 1868.

A Few Words in Answer to the Attack Made by Bishop Doane on Three Bishops and Four Laymen, in His "Protest, Appeal and Reply." Trenton, N.J.: N.p., n.d.

Fish, F. G. *St. Ann's Church, Brooklyn, New York from the Years 1784–1845 with a Memorial of the Sunday Schools.* New York, 1845.

Full and True Statement of the Examination and Ordination of Mr. Arthur Carey Taken from the Churchman. New York: Sparks, 1843.

Garden, Alexander. *Regeneration and the Testimony of the Spirit. Being the Substance of Two Sermons . . . Occasioned by Some Erroneous Notions of Certain Men Who Call Themselves Methodists.* Charleston, S.C., 1740.

Goode, William. *The Doctrine of the Church of England as to the Effects of Baptism in the Case of Infants.* New York: Stanford and Swords, 1850.

Green, Ashbel. *A Report to the Trustees of the College of New Jersey: Relative to a Revival of Religion Among the Students of Said College, in the Winter and Spring of the Year 1815.* Philadelphia, 1815.

Griswold, Alexander Viets. *The Reformation: A Brief Exposition of Some of the Errors and Corruptions of the Church of Rome.* N.p., 1843.

——. *Remarks on Social Prayer-Meetings.* Boston: Gould and Lincoln, 1858.

Hagenbach, Karl R. *A Textbook on the History of Doctrines.* Edited by Henry B. Smith from the Edinburgh translation of the fourth German edition. New York: Sheldon and Co., 1861.

Hare, George Emlen. *Christ to Return: A Practical Exposition of the Prophecy Recorded in the 24th and 25th Chapters of the Gospel According to St. Matthew.* Philadelphia, 1840.

Henshaw, J. P. K. *An Inquiry into the Meaning of the Prophecies Relating to the Second Advent of Our Lord Jesus Christ.* Baltimore, 1842.

Hobart, John Henry. *The Candidate for Confirmation Instructed.* New York, 1819.

——. *A Catechism for Confirmation.* New York, 1819.

——. *A Reply to a Letter to the Rt. Rev. Bishop Hobart Occasioned by the Strictures on Bible Societies, Contained in His Late Address to the Convention of New York.* New York: T. & J. Swords, 1823.

Hodge, Charles. "Inspiration," *Biblical Repertory and Princeton Review* 29 (1857): 660–698.

Hopkins, John Henry. *Bible View of Slavery.* N.p., 1863.

——. "Decline and Fall of the Low Church Party." In Charles F. Sweet, *A Champion of the Cross, Being the Life of John Henry Hopkins, S.T.D.* New York: J. Pott and Co., 1894.

——. *The Law of Ritualism Examined in Its Relation to the Word of God, to the Primitive Church, to the Church of England and to the Protestant Episcopal Church.* New York, 1866.

——. *The Novelties Which Disturb Our Peace: A Fourth Letter Addressed to the Bishops, Clergy, and Laity of the Protestant Episcopal Church in the United States.* Philadelphia: Hooker, 1844.

——. *A Scriptural, Ecclesiastical and Historical View of Slavery.* New York: W.I. Pooley, 1864.

——. *Two Discourses on the Second Advent of the Redeemer.* Burlington, Vt.: C. Goodrich, 1843.

Irving, Edward. *Babylon and Infidelity Foredoomed of God: A Discourse on the Prophecies of Daniel and the Apocalypse.* Philadelphia, 1828.

Jay, John. *Facts Connected with the Presentment of Bishop Onderdonk: A Reply to Parts of the Bishop's Statement.* New York: Stanford and Swords, 1845.

Jay, William. *A Letter to the Rt. Rev. Bishop Hobart in Reply to the Pamphlet Addressed by Him to the Author, Under the Signature of Corrector.* New York: J. P. Haven, 1823.

——. *A Letter to the Rt. Rev. Bishop Hobart Occasioned by the Strictures on Bible Societies Contained in His Late Charge.* New York: J. P. Haven, 1823.

——. *Miscellaneous Writings on Slavery.* Boston and Cleveland: Jewett, 1853.

——. *A Reply to a Second Letter to the Author from the Rt. Rev. Bishop Hobart with Remarks on His Hostility to Bible Societies.* New York: J. P. Haven, 1823.

Labagh, Isaac. *Theoklesia; or the Organization and Perpetuity, Conflicts and Triumphs of the One Holy Catholic and Apostolic Church.* New York, 1869.

——. *Twelve Lectures on the Great Events of Unfulfilled Prophecy, Which Still Await Their Accomplishments and Are Approaching Their Fulfillment.* New York, 1859.

Laurence, Richard. *An Attempt to Illustrate Those Articles of the Church of England Which the Calvinists Improperly Consider as Calvinsitical.* Oxford, 1805.

[Leacock, Benjamin B.] *Prayer Book vs. Prayer Book.* Philadelphia, 1869.

Lee, Alfred. *In Memoriam. Charles Pettit McIlvaine, A Sermon.* Cleveland, 1873.

——. *The Sermon Delivered at the Opening of the General Convention of the Protestant Episcopal Church in the United States of America in Trinity Church.* New York, 1808.

Luther, Martin. *The Freedom of a Christian.* In *Martin Luther: Selections from His Writings,* edited by John Dillenberger. New York: Doubleday, 1961.

Massie, J. W. *The Evangelical Alliance: Its Origin and Development.* London, 1847.

McElhinney, J.J. *Regeneration in Baptism: A Paper Read at a Conference Held at Columbus, O., September 13, 1871.* Columbus, Ohio, 1871.

McIlvaine, Charles P. "Address to the American Tract Society." In *First Annual Report, American Tract Society,* 35–38. New York: American Tract Society, 1826.

——. "Address to the American Tract Society." In *Thirty-third Annual Report, American Tract Society,* 7–10, 199–201. New York: American Tract Society, 1858.

——. *Address to the Young Men of the United States on Temperance.* New York: American Tract Society, n.d.

——. *The Apolistic Succession.* Hartford, Conn.: Mallory and Co., 1872.

——. *The Apostolical Commission. The Sermon Preached at the Consecration of the Rt. Rev. Leonidas Polk, D.D., Missionary Bishop for Arkansas in Christ Church, Cincinnati, December 9, 1838.* Gambier, Ohio: Myers, 1838.

——. *Appeal on Behalf of Kenyon College, Ohio, United States.* London, 1835.

——. *Baccalaureate Discourse Delivered in Rosse Chapel, Gambier to the Senior Class of Kenyon College.* Gambier, Ohio: Myers, 1837.

——. *Bishop McIlvaine on Confirmation.* N.p., [1840].

——. *Bishop McIlvaine's Address to the Convention of the Diocese of Ohio, on the Revival of Religion.* Cincinnati: Bradley, 1858.

——. *A Charge to the Clergy of the Protestant Episcopal Church in the State of Ohio on the Preaching of Christ Crucified, September 5, 1834.* Gambier, Ohio: Acland, 1834.

——. *The Chief Danger of the Church in These Times: A Charge Delivered to the Clergy of the Diocese of Ohio.* New York: Harper and Bros., 1843.

——. *The Christian Minister's Great Work: The Sermon at the Consecration of the Rt. Rev. George Upford, D.D..* Cincinnati: Derby, 1850.

——. *The Christian's Duty in the Present Crisis.* Cincinnati, 1861.

——. *The Church in Its Final Unity and Glory, or the Whole Family in Heaven and Earth.* New York: PESPEK, 1861.

——. *The Church of Christ in Its Being, and in its Relation to Divinely Appointed Ordinances. The Sermon Before the Directors of the PESPEK.* Philadelphia: King and Baird, 1848.

——. *Contrasted Hopes.* New York: American Tract Society, n.d.

——. *Correspondence Between Bishops Chase and McIlvaine.* Detroit: Whitney, 1834.

——. *Correspondence Between the Rt. Rev. Charles P. McIlvaine and the Rev. James A. Bolles with an Explanatory Pastoral.* Cleveland: Harris, Fairbanks, 1857.

——. *An Earnest Word from Bishop McIlvaine in Behalf of the Church Institutions at Gambier, Ohio.* New York: Osborn, 1843.

——. *Farewell Discourse Preached in St. Ann's Church, Brooklyn, New York on the 29th of April, 1833.* New York: Morgan and Burger, 1833.

——. *The Form and the Power of Godliness: A Sermon Preached at the Opening Services of the New St. Ann's on the Heights, Brooklyn, New York on Wednesday, October 20, 1869*. New York: Gardner, 1869.

——. *The Harvest and the Labourers. The Sermon Before the General Convention of the Protestant Episcopal Church in the U.S.A. in Trinity Church*. New York: Billin and Bros., 1853.

——. *The Holy Catholic Church, or the Communion of Saints in the Mystical Body of Christ: A Sermon*. Philadelphia: Hooker, 1844.

——. *The House of Prayer: A Sermon Preached at the Consecration of Calvary Church, Clifton, Ohio*. Cincinnati: Clarke, 1868.

——. *How a Minister of Christ May Both Save Himself and Them That Hear Him. A Sermon Delivered at the Consecration of the Rt. Rev. Alfred Lee*. Philadelphia: Gaskill, 1850.

——. *The Importance of Consideration*. New York: American Tract Society, n.d.

——. *The Inaugural Address Delivered at the Opening of Huron College, London, Canada West on the 2nd of December, 1863*. London: Dawson, 1864.

——. *Justification by Faith: A Charge Delivered Before the Clergy of the Protestant Episcopal Church in the Diocese of Ohio . . . September 13, 1839*. Columbus, Ohio: I. N. Whiting, 1840.

——. "A Letter on Revivals." In *Lectures on Revivals of Religion*, edited by William B. Sprague. Albany, Philadelphia, and Boston, 1832.

——. "The Missionary Character and Duty of the Church." In *Select Family and Parish Sermons*. Vol. 2, 309–328. Columbus, Ohio: Whiting, n.d.

——. *National Thanksgiving Day*. N. p., 1863.

——. *The Necessity of Religion to the Prosperity of the Nation: A Sermon*. Gambier, Ohio: Myers, 1838.

——. *No Priest, No Sacrifice, No Altar but Christ*. New York: PESPEK, 1854.

——. *The Office of the Church of Christ: The Sermon Preached at the Consecration of St. John's Church, in the City of Cincinnati on Thursday, February 9, 1854*. Cincinnati: Derby, 1854.

——. *Opinion of the Rt. Rev. Charles P. McIlvaine in Answer to Certain Questions Regarding the Official Position of the Clergy of Grace Church, Cleveland*. Cleveland, 1856.

——. *Origin and Design of the Christian Ministry: A Sermon*. Gambier, Ohio, 1839.

——. *Oxford Divinity Compared with That of the Romish and Anglican Churches with a Special View to the Illustration of the Doctrine of Justification*. Philadelphia: Whethan and Son, 1841.

——. *Pastoral Letter Addressed to the Members of the Protestant Episcopal Church in the Diocese of Ohio*. Columbus, Ohio: Thrall, 1848.

——. *Pastoral Letter of the Bishops of the Protestant Episcopal Church in the U.S.A. to the Clergy and Laity of the Same, Delivered Before the General Convention . . . October 17, 1862*. New York: Baker and Goodwin, 1862.

——. *Pastoral Letter to the Clergy and Laity of the Protestant Episcopal Church in the Diocese of Ohio on the Subjects of Confirmation and Church Music*. Columbus: Ohio State Journal Co., 1855.

——. *The Pastor's Address to a Candidate for Confirmation in St. Ann's Church, Brooklyn*. New York, 1831.

——. *The Present Condition and Chief Want of the Church: A Charge to the Clergy of the Protestant Episcopal Church of Ohio*. Gambier, Ohio: Western Protestant Episcopal Press, 1836.

——. *Processional Singing by Surpliced Choirs an Unauthorized Innovation in the Public Worship of the Protestant Episcopal Church*. Columbus, Ohio: Nevins and Myers, 1868.

——. *Rationalism, as Exhibited in the Writings of Certain Clergymen of the Church of England. A Letter to the Clergy and Candidates for Holy Orders of the Protestant Episcopal Church in the United States: Set Forth by Direction of the House of Bishops.* Cincinnati: Bradley, 1865.

——. *Reasons for Refusing to Consecrate a Church Having an Altar Instead of a Communion Table.* Mt. Vernon, Ohio: Cochran, 1846.

——. *The Respectful Address of Charles P. McIlvaine . . . to All Who Would Promote the Progress of Learning and Religion in the Western States.* New York: Sleight and Van Norden, 1833.

——. *Rev. Mr. McIlvaine in Answer to the Rev. Henry U. Onderdonk, D.D.* Philadelphia: William Stavely, 1827.

——. *Righteousness by Faith, or the Nature and Means of Our Justification Before God.* 2nd ed. Philadelphia: Protestant Episcopal Book Society, 1864.

——. *Rome and Geneva, or False Protestantism Exposed.* New York: PESPEK, 1841.

——, ed. *Select Family and Parish Sermons. A Series of Evangelical Discourses.* 2 vols. Columbus, Ohio: Whiting, 1838.

——. *The Sermon Before the Bishops, Clergy and Laity of the Protestant Episcopal Church in the U.S.A. in General Convention, at the Consecration of the Rev. Alfred Lee, D.D. . . . October 12, 1841.* New York: Swords and Stanford, 1842.

——. *Sermon Preached at the Ordination Held at St. Paul's Church, Chilicothe on Sunday, September 12, 1841.* Cincinnati: Western Church Press, 1841.

——, ed. *Sermons by Henry Melvill, B.D.* New York: Swords and Stanford, 1839.

——. *The Sinner's Justification Before God: Its Nature and Means.* New York: PESPEK, 1860.

——. *Some Thoughts Upon the Subject of Baptismal Regeneration.* New York: Bible House, 1861.

——. *Spiritual Declension.* New York: American Tract Society, n.d.

——. *Spiritual Regeneration with Reference to the Present Times: A Charge Delivered to the Clergy of the Diocese of Ohio.* New York: Harper and Bros., 1851.

——. *The Temple of God, or the Holy Catholic Church and Communion of Saints in Its Nature, Structure and Unity.* Philadelphia: Protestant Episcopal Book Society, 1860.

——. *The Truth and the Life: Twenty-two Sermons.* New York: Robert Carter and Bros., 1854.

——. *A Valedictory Offering: Five Sermons in Token of Christian Love and Remembrance Towards His Brethren in England.* London: Seeleys, 1853.

[——.] *The Washington Miracle Refuted; or, a Review of the Rev. Mr. Matthew's Pamphlet.* Washington, D.C.: Dunn, 1824.

——. *A Word in Season to Candidates for Confirmation.* New York: PESPEK, n.d.

——. *The Work of Preaching Christ.* Boston: Gospel Books, 1871.

——. *The Worth of the Soul.* New York: American Tract Society, n.d.

——, with William Hawley and Stephen Tyng. *Letter to the Rt. Rev. James Kemp, D.D. in Defense of the Clergy of the District of Columbia Against Certain Charges Preferred Against Them in His Late Pastoral Letter.* Washington, D.C.: Duncan, 1822.

Meade, William. *Reasons for Loving the Episcopal Church.* New York: PESPEK, 1854.

Memorial Papers: The Memorial with Circular and Questions of the Episcopal Commission. Philadelphia, 1857.

Newman, John Henry. *Lectures on the Doctrine of Justification.* London: Rivington, [1838], 1885. Green, 1892.

——. *Remarks on Certain Passages in the Thirty-Nine Articles.* Tract 90. London: Rivington, 1841.

Newton, R. Heber. *The Right and Wrong Uses of the Bible.* New York: Putnam, 1883.

Newton, Richard. *Bible Bulwarks: or a Sevenfold Argument in Defence of the Scriptures.* Philadelphia, 1875.

——. *Liberal Views of the Ministry in Harmony with the Bible, the Prayer Book, and the Canons.* Philadelphia: Ashmed, Book and Job, 1868.

——. *The Study of Prophecy, a Commanded Duty.* Philadelphia: R.S.H. George, 1848.

——. *A Voice from Olivet: or The Warning Sign.* Philadelphia, 1869.

Newton, William. *Israel Jehovah's Witnessing People: A Sermon.* Philadelphia: Moore, 1872.

——. *Lectures on the First Two Visions of the Book of Daniel.* Philadelphia, 1859.

——. *The Catholicity of the Protestant Episcopal Church: A Sermon, Sunday, January 3, 1869.* Norwalk, Ohio, 1869.

Newton, William Wilberforce. *Yesterday with the Fathers.* New York: Cochrance, 1910.

Nicholson, W. R. *Reasons Why I Became a Reformed Episcopalian.* Philadelphia: Moore, 1875.

No Church Without a Bishop, or, a Peep into the Sanctuary! . . . by a High Churchman. Boston, 1845.

Office of Infant Baptism Explained and Defended. Philadelphia, n.d.

Onderdonk, Benjamin T. *A Statement of Facts and Circumstances Connected with the Recent Trial of the Bishop of New York.* New York, 1845.

"One Faith": or Bishop Doane vs. Bishop McIlvaine on Oxford Theology: Exhibited in Extracts from Their Writings . . . by a Presbyterian. 2nd ed. Burlington, N.J.: J. L. Powell, 1843.

Papers on the Proposition of "The Nine Bishops." Philadelphia, 1871.

Pentecost; or the Work of God in Philadelphia, A.D. 1858. Philadelphia, 1859.

Proceedings of the Court Convened for the Trial of the Rt. Rev. Benjamin T. Onderdonk. New York: Appleton, 1845.

Pusey, E.B. *Scriptural Views of Holy Baptism.* London: J.G. & F. Rivington, 1836.

Revidenda; or a Brief Statement of Those Things in the Liturgy Which Should Be Revised and Altered, Together with a Short History of the Prayer-Book and the Revisions It Has Already Undergone. Philadelphia: The Episcopalian, 1868.

Reply of Bishops Meade, McIlvaine, and Burgess to the Arguements Presented by the Committee of the Convention of the Diocese of New Jersey, to the Court of Bishops, in Session at Burlington for the Trial of Bishop Doane. Philadelphia: T. K. and P. G. Collins, 1852.

Richmond, James. *The Conspiracy Against the Late Bishop of New York Unravelled.* N.p., n.d.

[Ridgely, G. W.] *An Examination of Mr. Barnes' Reply to the Episcopal Recorder by One of the Editors.* Philadelphia, 1844.

Rising, Franklin S. *Are There Romanizing Germs in the Prayer Book?* 2nd ed. N.p., n.d.

Schaff, Philip and Irenaeus Prime, eds. *History, Essays, Orations and Other Documents of the Sixth General Conference of the Evangelical Alliance, Held in New York, October 2–12, 1873.* New York: Harper and Brothers, 1874.

Schenck, Noah Hunt. *Christ Our Helper: An Anniversary Discourse.* Gambier, Ohio: Edmonds, 1857.

[Seabury, Samuel]. *A Full and True Statement of the Examination and Ordination of Mr. Arthur Carey.* New York, 1843.

[Shanklin, J. A.] *Some Objections to the Episcopal Church Considered and Answered.* New York: PESPEK, 1858.

Shimeall, Richard C. *Christ's Second Coming: Is It Pre-Millennial or Post-Millennial? The Great Question of the Day.* New York, 1865.

——. *Our Bible Chronology, Historic and Prophetic, Critically Examined and Demonstrated.* London: Sampson, Low, Son, and Co., 1860.

——. *The Political Economy of Prophecy.* New York: Trow, 1866.

——. *Post-Millenarianism Only 150 Years Old. Scripturally and Historically Demonstrated*. New York: Shepherd, 1867.

Smith, B. B. *Position of Episcopalians in Relation to Christians of Other Names*. Louisville, Ky. Morton and Griswold, 1850.

——. *Special Vocation of the Protestant Episcopal Church in These United States*. Philadelphia: King and Baird, 1850.

Smith, Hugh, and Henry Anthon. *The True Issue for the True Churchman*. New York: Harper and Bros., 1843.

Some Remarks on a Pamphlet Entitled, Rev. Mr. McIlvaine: In Answer to the Rt. Rev. Henry U. Onderdonk by an Episcopalian of Maryland. Baltimore, 1829.

Sparrow, William. *A Reply to the Charges and Accusations of the Rt. Rev. Philander Chase, D.D.* Gambier, Ohio, 1832.

Sprague, William B. *Annals of the American Pulpit*. Vol. 5, *The Episcopal Church*. New York: Robert Carter, 1857.

——. *Lectures on Revivals of Religion*. Albany, New York, Philadelphia, and Boston, 1832.

[Sprigg, D. F.] *The Doctrine of Baptismal Regeneration as Held by Cranmer, Latimer and Ridley. A Discussion Between Bishop Whittingham and the Southern Churchman*. New York: John Gray, 1860.

Sprigg, D.F. *A Plea for the Baptism of Infants with Additional Remarks upon Immersion*. Alexandria, Va.: 1859.

Stand Up for Jesus! A Christian Ballad: with Notes, Illustrations and Music. Philadelphia, 1858.

"Stand Up for Jesus." Last Hours and Funeral Services of the Rev. Dudley A. Tyng. Philadelphia, 1858.

Stanton, R.L. *The Church and the Rebellion*. New York, 1864.

Statement of the Distinctive Principles of the Protestant Episcopal Society for the Promotion of Evangelical Knowledge. New York: PESPEK, 1850.

Statement to the Congregation of the Church of the Epiphany, Philadelphia, of Facts Bearing on the Resignation of the Rector. N.p., 1856.

Stone, James Kent. *Moderation and Toleration in Theology. A Sermon Preached in Rosse Chapel*. Gambier, Ohio, 1867.

Stone, John Seeley. *Christian Toleration: A Sermon Before the New York Auxiliary to the PESPEK*. New York: Swords and Stanford, 1849.

——. *The Invitation Heeded: Reasons for a Return to Catholic Unity*. New York: Catholic Publishing Society, 1870.

——. *The Mysteries Opened, or Scriptural Views of Preaching and the Sacraments, as Distinguished from Certain Theories Concerning Baptismal Regeneration and the Real Presence*. New York: Harper Bros., 1844.

[Taylor, J. H.] *Sketches of the Religious Experiences and Labors of a Layman with an Appendix*. Hartford, Conn.: Case, Lockwood, 1867.

Two Views of Episcopacy: Old and New. Philadelphia: Stavely and McCalla, 1854.

The Tyng Case: A Narrative, Together with the Judgement of the Court and the Admonition by the Bishop of New York. New York: Pott and Amery, 1868.

Tyng, Dudley. *An Address on the Legal Prohibition of the Traffic in Intoxicating Liquors. February 1, 1853*. Columbus: Scott and Bascom, 1853.

——. *Our Country's Troubles: A Sermon Preached in the Church of the Epiphany, Philadelphia, June 29, 1856*. Boston: Jewett, 1856.

——. *Our Country's Troubles, No. II, or, National Sins and National Retribution. A Sermon Preached in the Church of the Covenant, Philadelphia, July 5, 1857*. Philadelphia: Martien, 1864.

——. *The State and Prospects of Our Church, as Indicated by Her Last General Convention: A Sermon in Christ Church, Cincinnati*. Cincinnati: Bradley, 1854.

[——]. *Vital Truth and Deadly Error*. Cincinnati: Derby, 1853.

Tyng, Stephen H. *The American Sunday School Union and the "Union Principle" in Reply to A. in the Episcopal Recorder*. New York: Gray, 1855.

——. *Christ Is All*. New York: PESPEK, 1872.

——. *The Connexion Between Early Religious Instruction and Mature Piety. A Sermon, May 22, 1837*. Philadelphia: American Sunday School Union, 1837.

——. *The Duty and Responsibility of Private Judgement in Religion: A Sermon*. New York: PESPEK, 1853.

——. *The Feast Enjoyed: Illustrative of the Lord's Supper*. New York: PESPEK, n.d.

——. *Fellowship with Christ: A Guide to the Sacraments*. New York: PESPEK, 1856.

——. *Forty Years Experience in Sunday School*. New York, 1860.

——. *Guide to Confirmation*. Philadelphia: George, Latimer, 1833.

——. *The Israel of God: A Series of Practical Sermons*. New York, 1845.

——. *A Letter Sustaining the Recent Ordination of Mr. Arthur Carey*. New York: Appleton, 1843.

——. *Statement to the Congregation of the Church of the Epiphany, Philadelphia, of Facts Bearing on the Action of the Vestry in Requesting the Resignation of the Rector*. Philadelphia, 1856.

——. *The Trial of American Principles*. Philadelphia, 1839.

Tyng, Stephen H., Jr. *He Will Come: or, Meditations Upon the Return of the Lord Jesus Christ to Reign over the Earth*. New York, 1877.

——. *The Liberty of Preaching: Its Warrant and Relations*. New York: Gray and Green, 1867.

Vail, Thomas. *Suggestions on Church Comprehensiveness and the Request of the Nine Bishops*. Lawrence, Kan.: Journal, Book and Job, 1870.

——. *Further Suggestions on Church Comprehensiveness and the Request of the Nine Bishops*. Lawrence, Kan.: Journal, Book and Job, 1871.

The Voice of Experience, or Thoughts on the Best Method of Conducting Missions in the Protestant Episcopal Church in Its Present State. Philadelphia and New York, 1852.

Voluntary Principle in Missions. N.p., n.d.

Waylen, Edward. *Ecclesiastical Reminiscences of the United States*. London: Straker, 1846.

White, William. *The Case of the Episcopal Churches in the United States Considered*. N.p., 1782.

Whittingham, William. *Baptismal Regeneration: Held, After Luther and Melancthon, by Cranmer, Ridley and Latimer*. Baltimore: Robinson, 1860.

——. *A Letter to the Rev. Richard Newton*. N.p., 1868.

Wilberforce, Robert Isaac. *The Doctrine of the Incarnation of Our Lord Jesus Christ in Its Relation to Mankind and to the Church*. London: J. Murray, 1848.

Wilberforce, Samuel. *A History of the Protestant Episcopal Church in America*. New York: Stanford and Swords, 1849.

Williams, Isaac. *On Reserve in Communicating Religious Knowledge*. Tract 87, 2nd ed. London: Rivington, 1840.

Wilmer, William. *Episcopal Manual*. N.p., 1815.

Winthrop, Edward. *Lectures on the Second Advent of the Messiah*. Cincinnati, 1843.

——. *Letters on the Prophetic Scriptures*. New York: Franklin Knight, 1850.

Memoirs and Collections of Correspondence

Alexander, James, *The Life of Archibald Alexander, D.D.* New York: Scribner, 1854.

Allen, Alexander V. G. *Life and Letters of Phillips Brooks*. 2 vols. New York: Dutton, 1900.

Allen, Thomas G. *Memoir of the Rev. Benjamin Allen, Late Rector of St. Paul's Church, Philadelphia, Pennsylvania*. Philadelphia: Latimer, 1832.

Ayers, Anne. *The Life and Work of William Augustus Muhlenberg*. New York: Harper Books, 1880.

Brandt, William Francis. *Life of William Rollinson Whittingham, Fourth Bishop of Maryland*. 2 vols. London: Gardener and Darton, 1883.

Burglas, Alexander. *Memoirs of the Life of the Rt. Rev. George Burgess, D.D., First Bishop of Maine*. Philadelphia: Claxton, Remsen and Hoffelfinger, 1869.

Carus, William, ed. *Memoirs of the Life of the Rev. Charles Simeon, M.A.* The American Edition by the Rt. Rev. Charles P. McIlvaine. New York: Robert Carter, 1847.

——, ed. *Memorials of the Rt. Rev. Charles Pettit McIlvaine, D.D., D.C.L.* New York: Whittaker, 1882.

Chase, Philander. *Reminiscences: An Autobiography*. 2 vols. Boston: Dow, 1848.

Cummins, A. M. *Memoir of George David Cummins, D.D., First Bishop of the Reformed Episcopal Church*. Philadelphia: Claxton, 1878.

Dyer, Heman. *Records of an Active Life*. New York: Whittaker, 1886.

Hall, John, ed. *Forty Years' Familiar Letters of James W. Alexander, D.D., Constituting with the Notes, a Memoir of His Life*. New York: Scribner, 1860.

Hemphill, W. Edwin. *The Papers of John C. Calhoun*. Charleston: University of South Carolina Press, 1948.

Henshaw, J. P. K. *Memoir of the Life of the Rt. Rev. Richard Channing Moore, D.D.* Philadelphia: William Stavely, 1842.

Hodge, A. A. *The Life of Charles Hodge, D.D., LL.D. Professor in the Theological Seminary, Princeton, N.J.* New York, 1880.

Hopkins, John Henry, Jr. *The Life of the Late Rt. Rev. John Henry Hopkins, First Bishop of Vermont and Seventh Presiding Bishop*. New York: Huntington, 1873.

Jarratt, Devereux. *The Life of the Reverend Devereux Jarrett*. Baltimore, 1806.

Jay, John. *The Correspondence and Public Papers of John Jay*. 4 vols. Edited by H. P. Johnston. New York: Putnam, 1890–1893.

Johns, John. *A Memoir of the Life of the Rt. Rev. William Meade, D.D.* Baltimore, 1867.

Memorabilia of George B. Cheever, D.D., Late Pastor of the Church of the Puritans, and of His Wife, Elizabeth Wetmore Cheever. New York, 1890.

Newton, William Wilberforce. *American Religious Leaders: Dr. Muhlenberg*. Boston and New York, 1890.

Polk, William M. *Leonidas Polk, Bishop and General*, 2nd ed. 2 vols. New York: Longmans, Green, 1915.

Rainsford, William S. *The Story of a Varied Life: An Autobiography*. [1922]. New York: Books for Libraries Press, 1970.

Smith, Elizabeth L. *Henry Boynton Smith. His Life and Work*. New York: A.C. Armstrong and Son, 1881.

Stone, John S. *A Memoir of the Life of James Milnor, D.D.* New York: American Tract Society, 1848.

——. *Memoir of the Life of the Rt. Rev. Alexander Viets Griswold, D.D., Bishop For the Protestant Episcopal Church in The Eastern Diocese*, abridged edition. New York: PESPEK, 1845.

Sumner, George H. *Life of Charles Richard Sumner, D.D., Bishop of Winchester*. London: Murray, 1876.

Tyng, Charles Rockland. *Record of the Life and Work of the Rev. Stephen Higginson Tyng, D.D. and History of St. George's Church, New York*. New York: Dutton, 1890.

Tyng, Stephen H. *Memoir of the Rev. Gregory T. Bedell, D.D.* 2nd ed. Philadelphia: Perkins, 1836.

Walker, Cornelius. *The Life and Correspondence of the Rev. William Sparrow, D.D., late Professor of Systematic Divinity in the Episcopal Seminary of Virginia*. Philadelphia: J. Hammond, 1876.

Whitefield, George. *Journals*. Edinburgh: Banner of Truth, 1960.

Williams, Charles R. *Life of Rutherford Berchard Hayes, Nineteenth President of the United States*. Vol. 1. Boston and New York, 1914.

Williams, Charles R., ed. *Diary and Letters of R. B. Hayes: Nineteenth President of the United States*. Vol. 1. *1834–1860*. Columbus: Ohio State Archaeological and Historical Society, 1922.

Wilmer, Richard H. *The Recent Past from a Southern Standpoint: Reminiscences of a Grandfather*. New York: T. Whittaker, 1887.

Wilson, Beirce. *Memoirs of the Life of the Rt. Rev. William White, D.D., Bishop of the Protestant Episcopal Church in the State of Pennsylvania*. Philadelphia: Kay and Brother, 1839.

Secondary Sources

Books and Articles

Abiding Values of Evangelicalism: Papers and Addresses Read at the Seventy-fifth Anniversary of the Evangelical Education Society of the Protestant Episcopal Church. Philadelphia: John C. Winston, 1938.

Addison, James T. *The Episcopal Church in the United States, 1789–1931*. New York: Charles Scribner's Sons, 1951.

Agnew, Christopher M. "The Reverend Charles Wharton, Bishop William White and the Proposed Book of Common Prayer, 1785." *Anglican and Episcopal History* 58 (1989): 510–525.

Ahlstrom, Sydney. *A Religious History of the American People*. New Haven and London: Yale University Press, 1972.

——. *Theology in America: The Major Voices from Puritanism to Neo-Orthodoxy*. Indianapolis: Bobbs-Merrill, 1967.

Albright, Raymond W. *A History of the Protestant Episcopal Church*. New York: Macmillan, 1964.

Allison, C. FitzSimmons. *The Rise of Moralism; The Proclamation of the Gospel from Hooker to Baxter*. Wilton, Conn.: Morehouse Barlow, 1966.

Andrew, John A. *Rebuilding the Christian Commonwealth: New England Congregationalists and Foreign Missions, 1800–1830*. Lexington: University Press of Kentucky, 1976.

Anstey, Roger. *The Atlantic Slave Trade and British Abolition 1760–1820*. London: Macmillan, 1975.

Anstice, Henry. *History of St. George's Church in the City of New York, 1752–1811–1911*. New York: Harper and Bros., 1911.

Applegate, Stephen H. "The Rise and Fall of the Thirty-Nine Articles: An Inquiry into the Identity of the Protestant Episcopal Church in the United States." *Historical Magazine of the Protestant Episcopal Church* 50 (1981): 409–421.

Baker, Frank. *John Wesley and the Church of England*. Nashville and New York: Abington, 1970.

Balda, Wesley D. "Ecclesiastics and Enthusiasts: The Evangelical Emergence in England, 1760–1800." *Historical Magazine of the Protestant Episcopal Church* 49 (1980): 221–231.

——. "Simeon's Protestant Papists: A Sampling of Moderate Evangelicalism Within the Church of England, 1839–1865." *Fides et Historia* (1983): 55–67.

Balleine, G. R. *A History of the Evangelical Party in the Church of England*. London: Longmans, Green, 1908.

Balmer, Randall. "The Princetonians and Scripture: A Reconsideration," *Westminster Theological Journal* 44 (1982): 352–365.

Banner, Lois W. "Religious Benevolence as Social Control: A Critique of an Interpretation," *Journal of American History* 60 (1973): 23–41.

Barnes, C. Rankin. *The General Convention Offices and Officers 1785–1950*. Philadelphia: Church Historical Society, 1951.

Barnhart, John D. *Valley of Democracy: The Frontier vs. the Plantation in the Ohio Valley, 1775–1818*. Bloomington: Indiana University Press, 1953.

Barratt, Norris Stanley. *Outline of the History of Old St. Paul's Church, Philadelphia, Pennsylvania*. Lancaster, Pa.: Colonial Society of Pennsylvania, 1917.

Bass, Clarence B. *Backgrounds to Dispensationalism: Its Historical Genesis and Ecclesiastical Implications*. Grand Rapids, Mich.: Eerdmans, 1960.

Bebbington, David W. *Evangelicalism in Modern Britain: A History from the 1730s to the 1980s*. London: Unwin Hyman, 1989.

Bilhartz, Terry. *Urban Religion and the Second Great Awakening: Church and Society in Early National Baltimore*. Rutherford, N.J.: Fairleigh Dickenson University Press, 1986.

Billington, Ray A. *The Protestant Crusade, 1800–1860: A Study of the Origins of American Nativism*. New York: Rinehart, 1952.

Blue, Frederick J. *Salmon P. Chase: A Life in Politics*. Kent, Ohio: Kent State University Press, 1987.

Bodine, William B. *The Kenyon Book*. Columbus, 1890.

Bodo, John R. *The Protestant Clergy and Public Issues, 1812–1848*. Princeton: Princeton University Press, 1954.

Bonomi, Patricia U. *Under the Cope of Heaven: Religion, Society, and Politics in Colonial America*. Oxford and New York: Oxford University Press, 1986.

Boylan, Anne M. *Sunday School: The Formation of an American Institution, 1790–1880*. New Haven and London: Yale University Press, 1988.

Bowden, Henry Warner. *Church History in an Age of Science: Historiographical Patterns in the United States, 1876–1918*. Chapel Hill: University of North Carolina Press, 1971.

Bozeman, T. D. *Protestants in an Age of Science: The Baconian Ideal and Antebellum American Religious Thought*. Chapel Hill: University of North Carolina Press, 1977.

Bradley, Ian. *The Call to Seriousness: The Evangelical Impact on the Victorians*. New York: Macmillan, 1976.

Bragg, George F. *A History of the Afro-American Group of the Episcopal Church*. Baltimore: 1922. Reprint. New York: Johnson, 1968.

Bridenbaugh, Carl. *Mitre and Sceptre: Transatlantic Faiths, Ideas, Personalities and Politics, 1689–1775*. New York: Oxford University Press, 1962.

Brilioth, Yngve. *The Anglican Revival: Studies in the Oxford Movement*. London: Longmans, Green, 1925.

Brown, Arthur Judson. *One Hundred Years: A History of the Foreign Missionary Work of the Presbyterian Church, U.S.A.*, with an introduction by Charles R. Erdman, 2nd ed. New York: Revell, 1936.

Brown, Bruce T. "Grace Church, Galesburg, Illinois, 1864–1866: The Supposed Neutrality of the Episcopal Church During the Years of the Civil War." *Historical Magazine of the Protestant Episcopal Church* 46 (1977): 187–208.

Brown, Ford K. *Fathers of the Victorians: The Age of Wilberforce*. Cambridge: Cambridge University Press, 1961.

Brown, Jerry W. *The Rise of Biblical Criticism in America, 1800–1870: The New England Scholars*. Middletown, Conn.: Wesleyan, 1969.

Brown, Lawrence L. "Documentary History of the American Church. Views of the Bishops of Ohio and Louisiana upon the Secession of the Southern States and Its Effects upon the Ecclesiastical Allegiance of the Dioceses." *Historical Magazine of the Protestant Episcopal Church* 31 (1963): 288–302.

——. "Richard Channing Moore and the Revival of the Southern Church." *Historical Magazine of the Protestant Episcopal Church* 35 (1966): 3–63.

Bryden, G. MacLaren. "The Origins of the Rights of the Laity in the American Episcopal Church." *Historical Magazine of the Protestant Episcopal Church* 12 (1943): 313–338.

Bucke, Emory S., ed. *The History of American Methodism.* 3 vols. New York: Abington, 1964.

Burr, Nelson R. *The Anglican Church in New Jersey.* Philadelphia: Church History Society, 1954.

Butler, Jon. *Awash in a Sea of Faith: Christianizing the American People.* Cambridge: Harvard University Press, 1990.

——. "Enthusiasm Described and Decried: The Great Awakening as Interpretative Fiction." *Journal of American History* 69 (1982): 305–325.

Campbell, Ted A. *The Religion of the Heart: A Study of European Religious Life in the Seventeenth and Eighteenth Centuries.* Charleston: University of South Carolina Press, 1991.

Carter, Paul A. *The Spiritual Crisis of the Gilded Age.* DeKalb: Northern Illinois University Press, 1971.

Carwardine, Richard. *Transatlantic Revivalism: Popular Evangelicalism in Britain and America, 1790–1865.* Westport, Conn.: Greenwood, 1978.

Cashdollar, C. *The Transformation of Theology.* Princeton: Princeton University Press, 1989.

Caskey, Marie. *Chariot of Fire: Religion and the Beecher Family.* New Haven: Yale University Press, 1978.

Cayton, Andrew R. L. *The Frontier Republic: Ideology and Politics in the Ohio Country 1780–1825.* Kent, Ohio: Kent State University Press, 1986.

——, and Peter S. Onuf. *The Midwest and the Nation: Rethinking the History of an American Region.* Bloomington: Indiana University Press, 1990.

Chadwick, Owen. *From Bossuet to Newman: The Idea of Doctrinal Development.* Cambridge: Cambridge University Press, 1957.

——. *The Mind of the Oxford Movement.* London: A. & C. Black, 1960.

——. *The Victorian Church: An Ecclesiastical History of England.* Vols. 1–2. New York: Oxford University Press, 1966–1970.

Chorley, E. Clowes. "Benjamin Treadwell Onderdonk, Fourth Bishop of New York." *Historical Magazine of the Protestant Episcopal Church* 9 (1940): 1–51.

——. *Men and Movements in the American Episcopal Church.* New York: Charles Scribner's Sons, 1946.

——. "The Oxford Movement in the General Theological Seminary." *Historical Magazine of the Protestant Episcopal Church* 5 (1936): 177–201.

Cole, Charles, Jr. *The Social Ideas of the Northern Evangelists, 1826–1860.* New York: Columbia University Press, 1954.

Conser, Walter H., Jr. *Church and Confession: Conservative Theologians in Germany, England, and America, 1815–1866.* Macon, Ga.: Mercer University Press, 1984.

Cragg, G. R. *From Puritanism to the Age of Reason, 1660–1700.* Cambridge: Cambridge University Press, 1950.

Crewdson, Robert L. "Bishop Polk and the Crisis in the Church: Separation or Unity?" *Historical Magazine of the Protestant Episcopal Church* 52 (1983): 43–51.

Cross, Arthur Lyon. *The Anglican Episcopate and the American Colonies.* Cambridge: Harvard University Press, 1902.

Cross, Whitney. *The Burned-Over District: The Social and Intellectual History of Enthusiastic Religion in Western New York, 1800–1850*. Ithaca, N.Y.: Cornell University Press, 1950.

Cummins, Evelyn A. "The Beginnings of the Church in Ohio and Kenyon College," *Historical Magazine of the Protestant Episcopal Church* 6 (1937): 276–298.

Curtis, William R. *The Lambeth Conferences: The Solution for Pan-Anglican Organization*. New York: Columbia University Press, 1942.

Dallimore, Arnold. *George Whitefield: The Life and Times of the Great Evangelist of the Eighteenth-Century Revival*. 2 vols. Edinburgh: Banner of Truth, 1970.

Daniels, Louis E. "The Diocese of Ohio, 1874–1937." *Historical Magazine of the Protestant Episcopal Church* 6 (1937): 316–336.

Davies, Horton W. *Worship and Theology in England*. Vols. 2–3. Princeton: Princeton University Press, 1961–1962.

Davis, David Brion, ed. *Ante-Bellum Reform*. New York: Harper and Row, 1967.

Dawley, Powell Mills. *The Story of the General Theological Seminary. A Sesquicentennial History, 1817–1967*. New York: Oxford University Press, 1969.

DeMille, George. *The Catholic Movement in the American Episcopal Church*, 2nd ed. Philadelphia: Church History Society, 1950.

Denison, S. D. *A History of the Foreign Missionary Work of the Protestant Episcopal Church*. 2 vols. New York: Foreign Committee of the Board of Foreign Missions, 1871.

Doan, Ruth Alden. *The Miller Heresy: Millennialism and American Culture*. Philadelphia: Temple University Press, 1987.

Donald, James M. "Bishop Hopkins and the Reunification of the Church." *Historical Magazine of the Protestant Episcopal Church* 47 (1978): 73–91.

Douglas, Ann. *The Feminization of American Culture*. New York: Knopf, 1978.

Dunham, Chester Forrester. *The Attitude of the Northern Clergy Toward the South, 1860–1865*. Toledo, Ohio: Gray, 1942.

Elliot-Binns, L. E. *The Early Evangelicals: A Religious and Social Study*. London: Lutterworth, 1953.

Ellis, Ieuan. *Seven Against Christ: A Study of "Essays and Reviews"*. London: Brill, 1980.

Emery, Julia C. *A Century of Endeavor, 1821–1921. A Record of the First One Hundred Years of the Domestic and Foreign Missionary Society of the Protestant Episcopal Church in the U.S.A*. New York: Department of Missions, 1921.

Epstein, Barbara Leslie. *The Politics of Domesticity: Women, Evangelicalism and Temperance in Nineteenth Century America*. Middletown, Conn.: Wesleyan University Press, 1981.

Fellman, Michall. "Rehearsal for the Civil War: Antislavery and Proslavery at the Fighting Point in Kansas, 1854–1856." In *Antislavery Reconsidered*, edited by Lewis Perry and Michall Fellman, 287–307. Baton Rouge and London: Louisiana State University Press, 1979.

Filler, Louis. *Crusade Against Slavery: Friends, Foes and Reforms, 1820–1869*. 2nd ed. Algonac, Mich.: Reference Publications, 1986.

Fiering, Norman. *Moral Philosophy at Seventeenth-Century Harvard: A Discipline in Transition*. Chapel Hill: University of North Carolina Press, 1981.

Foner, Eric. *Free Soil, Free Labor, Free Men: The Ideology of the Republican Party Before the Civil War*. New York: Oxford University Press, 1970.

——. *Politics and Ideology in the Age of the Civil War*. New York and Oxford: Oxford University Press, 1980.

Foote, Henry Wilder. *Three Centuries of American Hymnody*. Cambridge: Harvard University Press, 1940.

Foster, Charles I. *An Errand of Mercy: The Evangelical United Front, 1770–1837*. Chapel Hill: University of North Carolina Press, 1960.

Fox, Early Lee. *The American Colonization Society, 1817–1840*. Baltimore: Johns Hopkins Press, 1919.

Francis, Russell E. "The Religious Revival of 1858 in Philadelphia." *Pennsylvania Magazine of History and Biography* 70 (1946): 52–77.

Frankeil, Sandra Sizer. *Gospel Hymns and Social Religion: The Rhetoric of Nineteenth Century Revivalism*. Philadelphia: Temple University Press, 1978.

Franklin, J. H., and A. A. Moss, Jr. *From Slavery to Freedom: A History of Negro Americans*, 6th ed. New York: Knopf, 1988.

Furniss, Norman. *The Fundamentalist Controversy, 1918–1931*. Hamden, Conn.: Archon, 1963.

Gaustad, Edwin S., ed. *A Documentary History of Religion in America Since 1865*. Grand Rapids, Mich.: Eerdmans, 1983.

——. *The Rise of Adventism: Religion and Society in Mid-Nineteenth Century America*. New York: Harper and Row, 1974.

Genovese, Eugene D. *The Political Economy of Slavery: Studies in the Economy and Society of the Slave South*. New York: Pantheon, 1965.

Gerlach, Luther, and Virginia Hine. *People, Power, Change: Movements of Social Transformation*. Indianapolis: Bobbs-Merrill, 1970.

Goen, C. C. *Broken Churches, Broken Nation: Denominational Schisms and the Coming of the American Civil War*. Macon, Ga.: Mercer University Press, 1985.

Goodwin, Gerald J. "The Anglican Reaction to the Great Awakening." *Historical Magazine of the Protestant Episcopal Church* 35 (1966): 343–371.

Goodwin, W. A. R. *History of the Theological Seminary in Virginia and Its Historical Background*. 2 vols. New York: Gorham, 1923.

Goodykoontz, Colin Brummit. *Home Missions on the American Frontier, with Particular Reference to the American Home Missionary Society*. Caldwell, Idaho: Claxton Printers, 1939.

Griffin, Clifford S. *Their Brother's Keepers: Moral Stewardship in the United States, 1800–1865*. New Brunswick, N.J.: Rutgers University Press, 1960.

Guelzo, Allen. *Edwards on the Will: A Century of American Theological Debate*. Middleton, Conn.: Wesleyan, 1989.

Gunn, Julien. "Bishop Hobart's Emphasis on Confirmation." *Historical Magazine of the Protestant Episcopal Church* 24 (1955): 293–310.

Hall, Mark H. "Bishop McIlvaine, the Reluctant Frontiersman." *Historical Magazine of the Protestant Episcopal Church* 44 (1975): 81–96.

Hammond, John L. *The Politics of Benevolence: Revival Religion and American Voting Behavior*. Norwood, N.J.: Ablex, 1979.

Handy, Robert. *A Christian America: Protestant Hopes and Historical Realities*. New York: Oxford University Press, 1971.

Hardman, Keith J. *Charles Gandison Finney, 1792–1875, Revivalist and Reformer*. Syracuse, N.Y.: Syracuse University Press, 1987.

Hardy, E. R. "Evangelical Catholicism: W. A. Muhlenberg and the Memorial Movement." *Historical Magazine of the Protestant Episcopal Church* 13 (1944): 155–192.

Haroutunian, Joseph. *Piety Versus Moralism: The Passing of the New England Theology*. New York: Holt, 1932.

Hart, Albert Bushnell. *Salmon P. Chase*. [1899]. New York and London: Chelsea House, 1980.

Hatch, Nathan. *The Democratization of American Christianity*. New Haven and London: Yale University Press, 1989.

———. "Evangelicalism as a Democratic Movement." In *Evangelicalism in Modern America*, edited by George M. Marsden. Grand Rapids, Mich.: Eerdmans, 1984.

———. *The Sacred Cause of Liberty: Republican Thought and the Millennium in Revolutionary New England*. New Haven and London: Yale University Press, 1977.

———. "Sola Scriptura and Novus Ordo Seclorum." In *The Bible in America: Essays in Cultural History*, edited by Mark Noll and Nathan Hatch. New York: Oxford, 1983.

Hawks, Francis L. *Contributions to the Ecclesiastical History of the United States of America*. Vol. 2. *The Rise and Progress of the Protestant Episcopal Church in Maryland*. New York: Harper and Bros., 1836.

Heimert, Alan, and Perry Miller, eds. *The Great Awakening: Documents Illustrating the Crisis and Its Consequences*. Indianapolis: Bobbs-Merrill, 1967.

Heimert, Alan. *Religion and the American Mind from the Great Awakening to the Revolution*. Cambridge: Harvard University Press, 1966.

Henry, Stuart. *Unvanquished Puritan: A Portrait of Lyman Beecher*. Grand Rapids, Mich.: Eerdmans, 1973.

Herklots, H. G. G. *The Church of England and the American Episcopal Church. A Study in Relationships*. London: Mowbrays, 1966.

Hills, George Morgan. *History of the Church in Burlington, New Jersey*. 2nd ed. Trenton, N.J.: Sharp, 1885.

Hoffecker, W. Andrew. *Piety and the Princeton Theologians: Archibald Alexander, Charles Hodge, and Benjamin Warfield*. Phillipsburg, N.J.: Presbyterian and Reformed Publishing Co., 1981.

Holifield, E. Brooks. *The Gentlemen Theologians: American Theology in Southern Culture, 1795–1860*. Durham, N.C.: Duke University Press, 1978.

Holmes David L. "The Anglican Tradition and the Episcopal Church." In *Encyclopedia of the American Religious Experience*, 391–418. New York: Scribner, 1988.

———. "The Decline and Revival of the Church of Virginia." In *Up from Independence: The Episcopal Church in Virginia*, edited by Brewster S. Ford et al., 51–109. Orange, Va.: Green, 1976.

———. "Devereux Jarratt: A Letter and a Reevaluation." *Historical Magazine of the Protestant Episcopal Church* 47 (1978): 37–49.

———. "The Episcopal Church in the American Revolution." *Historical Magazine of the Protestant Episcopal Church* 47 (1978): 261–291.

———. "Restoration Ideology Among Early Episcopal Evangelicals." In *The American Quest for the Primitive Church*, edited by Richard T. Hughes, 153–170. Urbana and Chicago: University of Illinois Press, 1988.

———. "William Holland Wilmer: A Newly Discovered Memoir." *Maryland Historical Magazine* 81 (1986): 160–164.

Holmes, Urban T. "Education for Liturgy: An Unfinished Symphony in Four Movements." In *Worship Points the Way: A Celebration of the Life and Work of Massey Hamilton Shepherd, Jr.*, edited by Malcom C. Burson, 116–141. New York: Seabury, 1981.

Hopkins, Hugh Evan. *Charles Simeon of Cambridge*. Grand Rapids, Mich.: Eerdmans, 1977.

Hovenkamp, Herbert. *Science and Religion in America 1800–1860*. Philadelphia: University of Pennsylvania Press, 1978.

Howard, Victor B. *Conscience and Slavery: The Evangelistic Calvinist Domestic Missions, 1837–1861*. Kent, Ohio: Kent State University Press, 1990.

Howe, Daniel Walker. *The Political Culture of the American Whigs*. Chicago: University of Chicago Press, 1979.

———. *The Unitarian Conscience*. Middletown, Conn.: Wesleyan, 1988.

———, ed. *Victorian America*. Philadelphia: University of Pennsylvania Press, 1976.

Howse, E. M. *Saints in Politics: The Clapham Sect and the Growth of Freedom*. London: Allen and Unwin, 1953.

Hughes, Richard T., ed. *American Quest for the Primitive Church*. Urbana and Chicago: University of Illinois Press, 1988.

——, and Leonard Allen. *Illusions of Innocence: Protestant Primitivism in America, 1630–1875*. Chicago: University of Chicago Press, 1988.

Hutchison, William. *The Modernist Impulse in American Protestantism*. Cambridge,: Harvard University Press, 1976.

Hylson-Smith, Kenneth. *Evangelicals in the Church of England, 1734–1984*. Edinburgh: T and T Clark, 1989.

Isaac, Rhys. *The Transformation of Virginia, 1740–1790*. Chapel Hill: University of North Carolina Press, 1982.

Jay, Elisabeth. *The Religion of the Heart: Anglican Evangelicalism and the Nineteenth-Century Novel*. New York: Oxford University Press, 1979.

Johnson, Paul E. *A Shopkeeper's Millennium: Society and Revivals in Rochester, New York, 1815–1837*. New York: Hill and Wang, 1978.

Jones, Cheslyn, Geoffrey Wainwright, and Edward Yarnold, eds. *The Study of Liturgy*. New York: Oxford University Press, 1978.

Jones, Howard Mumford. *The Age of Energy: Varieties of American Experience, 1865–1915*. New York: Viking, 1973.

Jordan, Philip D. *The Evangelical Alliance for the United States of America, 1847–1900: Ecumenism, Identity and the Religion of the Republic*. New York: Edwin Mellen, 1982.

Kleppner, Paul. *The Cross of Culture: A Social Analysis of Midwestern Politics, 1850–1900*. New York: Free Press, 1970.

Kraus, C. Norman. *Dispensationalism in America: Its Rise and Development*. Richmond, Va.: John Knox Press, 1958.

Kuklick, Bruce. *Churchmen and Philosophers: From Jonathan Edwards to John Dewey*. New Haven: Yale University Press, 1985.

Lears, T. Jackson. *No Place of Grace: Antimodernism and the transformation of American Culture, 1880–1920*. New York: Pantheon, 1981.

Lewis, Donald M. *Lighten Their Darkness: The Evangelical Mission to Working Class London, 1828–1860*. Westport, Conn.: Greenwood, 1986.

Loetscher, Lefferts A. "The Problem of Christian Unity in Early Nineteenth Century America." *Church History* 32 (1963): 3–16.

Loveland, Clara O. *The Critical Years: The Reconstitution of the Anglican Church in the United States of America, 1780–1789*. Greenwich, Conn.: Seabury, 1956.

Maizlish, Stephen E. *The Triumph of Sectionalism: The Transformation of Ohio Politics: 1844–1856*. Kent, Ohio: Kent State University Press, 1983.

Manross, William W. "Episcopal Church and Reform." *Historical Magazine of the Protestant Episcopal Church* 12 (1943): 339–366.

——. *The Episcopal Church in the United States, 1800–1840*. New York: Columbia University Press, 1938.

——. *A History of the American Episcopal Church*. New York: Morehouse, 1935.

Marsden, George M. *The Evangelical Mind and the New School Presbyterian Experience*. New Haven: Yale University Press, 1970.

——. *Fundamentalism and American Culture: The Shaping of Twentieth-Century Evangelicalism, 1870–1925*. New York: Oxford University Press, 1980.

——. *Religion and American Culture*. San Diego and New York: Harcourt, Brace Jovanovich, 1990.

Marty, Martin. *Righteous Empire: The Protestant Experience in America*. New York: Dial, 1970.

Mathews, Donald. *Religion in the Old South*. Chicago: University of Chicago Press, 1977.

——. "The Second Great Awakening as an Organizing Process, 1780–1830: An Hypothesis," *American Quarterly* 21 (1969): 23–43.

May, Henry F. *The Enlightenment in America*. New York: Oxford University Press, 1976.

——. *Protestant Churches in Industrial America*. New York: Harper and Brothers, 1949.

McConnell, S. D. *History of the American Episcopal Church from the Planting of the Colonies to the End of the Civil War*. New York: Thomas Whittaker, 1899.

McDannell, Colleen. *The Christian Home in Victorian America, 1840–1900*. Bloomington, Ind.: Indiana University Press, 1986.

McLoughlin, William. *Modern Revivalism: Charles Grandison Finney to Billy Graham*. New York: Ronald Press, 1959.

——. *Revivals, Awakenings, and Reform*. Chicago: University of Chicago Press, 1978.

Mead, Sidney. *Nathaniel William Taylor, 1786–1858: A Connecticut Liberal*. Hamden, Conn.: Archon, 1967.

Meyer, D. H. *The Instructed Conscience: The Shaping of the American National Ethic*. Philadelphia: University of Pennsylvania Press, 1972.

Miller, Howard. *Revolutionary College: American Presbyterian Higher Education 1707–1837*. New York: New York University Press, 1976.

Miller, J. Barrett. "The Theology of William Sparrow." *Historical Magazine of the Protestant Episcopal Church* 43 (1977): 443–454.

Miller, Perry. *Errand into the Wilderness*. Cambridge, Mass.: Harvard, 1956.

——. *The Life of the Mind in America from the Revolution to the Civil War*. New York: Harcourt, Brace, 1965.

Mills, Frederick V., Sr. *Bishops by Ballot: An Eighteenth Century Esslesiastical Revolution*. New York: Oxford University Press, 1978.

——. "The Protestant Episcopal Churches in the United States, 1783–1789: Suspended Animation or Remarkable Recovery?" *Historical Magazine of the Protestant Episcopal Church* 46 (1977): 151–170.

Miyakawa, T. Scott. *Protestants and Pioneers: Individualism and Conformity on the American Frontier*. Chicago: University of Chicago Press, 1964.

Moorhead, James H. *American Apocalypse: Yankee Protestants and the Civil War, 1860–1869*. New Haven and London: Yale University Press, 1978.

——. "Between Progress and Apocalypse: A Reassessment of Millennialism in American Religious Thought, 1800–1880." *Journal of American History* 71 (1984): 524–542.

——. "Social Reform and the Divided Conscience of Antebellum Protestantism." *Church History* 48 (1979): 416–430.

More, Paul Elmer and Frank Leslie Cross, eds. *Anglicanism: The Thought and Practice of the Church of England, Illustrated from the Religious Literature of the Seventeenth Century*. London: S.P.C.K., 1935.

Morris, J. Wesley. *Christ Church, Cincinnati, 1817–1967*. Cincinnati: Cincinnati Lithographing Ohio Press, 1967.

Moulton, Elizabeth. *St. George's Church, New York*. New York: St. George's Church, 1964.

Muller, James A. *The Episcopal Theological School, 1867–1943*. Cambridge, Mass.: Episcopal Theological School, 1943.

——. "Philander Chase and the Frontier." *Historical Magazine of the Protestant Episcopal Church* 14 (1945): 168–184.

Mullin, Robert Bruce. "Biblical Critics and the Battle over Slavery." *Journal of Presbyterian History* 61 (1983): 210–226.

——. *Episcopal Vision/American Reality: High Church Theology and Social Thought in Evangelical America*. New Haven and London: Yale University Press, 1986.

——, ed. *Moneygripe's Apprentice: The Personal Narrative of Samuel Seabury III*. New Haven and London: Yale University Press, 1989.

——. "Ritualism, Anti-Romanism, and the Law in John Henry Hopkins," *Historical Magazine of the Protestant Episcopal Church* 50 (1981): 377–390.

Nagel, Paul C. *One Nation Indivisible: The Union in American Thought*. New York: Oxford University Press, 1964.

Nevins, Allen. *Ordeal of the Union: A House Dividing, 1852–1857*. New York: Scribner, 1947.

Newsome, David. "Justification and Sanctification: Newman and the Evangelicals." *Journal of Theological Studies* 15 (1964): 32–58.

——. *The Parting of Friends: The Wilberforces and Henry Manning*. London: John Murray, 1966.

Nichols, James H. *Romanticism in American Theology: Nevin and Schaff at Mercersburg*. Chicago: University of Chicago Press, 1961.

Noll, Mark A. *Between Faith and Criticism: Evangelicals, Scholarship and the Bible in America*. San Francisco: Harper and Row, 1986.

——, ed. *Charles Hodge: The Way of Life*. New York: Paulist Press, 1987.

——. "Commonsense Traditions and American Evangelical Thought." *American Quarterly* 37 (Summer 1985): 216–238.

——. "The Founding of Princeton Seminary." *Westminster Theological Journal* 42 (1979): 72–110.

——. *Princeton and the Republic, 1768–1822: The Search for a Christian Enlightenment in the Era of Samuel Stanhope Smith*. Princeton: Princeton University Press, 1989.

——, ed. *The Princeton Theology, 1812–1921*. Grand Rapids, Mich.: Baker, 1983.

——, and Nathan Hatch, eds. *The Bible in America: Essays in Cultural History*. New York and Oxford: Oxford University Press, 1983.

Norwood, Percy. "Bishop Whitehouse and the Church in Illinois." *Historical Magazine of the Protestant Episcopal Church* 16 (1947): 175–179.

Orr, J. Edwin. *The Fervent Prayer: The Worldwide Impact of the Great Awakening of 1858*. Chicago: Moody Press, 1974.

Parks, Joseph H. *General Leonidas Polk, CSA: The Fighting Bishop*. Baton Rouge: Louisiana State University Press, 1962.

Peck, Kenneth M. "The Oxford Controversy in America: 1839." *Historical Magazine of the Protestant Episcopal Church* 33 (1964): 49–63.

Pelikan, Jaroslav. *Christian Doctrine and Modern Culture (since 1700)*. Chicago: University of Chicago Press, 1989.

Perry, Lewis. *Intellectual Life in America: A History*. New York: F. Watts, 1984.

Perry, William Stevens. *The History of the American Episcopal Church*. Vol. 2. *The Origin and Progress of the American Church, 1783–1883*. Boston: James Osgood, 1885.

Phillips, Clifton J. *Protestant America and the Pagan World: The First Half-Century of the American Board of Commissioners for Foreign Missions*, 1810–1860. Cambridge: Harvard University Press, 1968.

Platt, Warren C. "The Reformed Episcopal Church: The Origins and Early Development of Its Ideological Expression." *Historical Magazine of the Protestant Episcopal Church* 52 (1983): 245–273.

Potter, David. *The Impending Crisis, 1848–1861*. New York: Harper, 1976.

Price, Annie Darling. *A History of the Formation and Growth of the Reformed Episcopal Church, 1873–1902*. Philadelphia: J. M. Armstrong, 1902.

Prichard, Robert W. *A History of the Protestant Episcopal Church*. Wilton, Conn.: Morehouse Barlow, 1991.

——. "Nineteenth Century Episcopal Attitudes on Predestination and Election." *Historical Magazine of the Protestant Episcopal Church* 51 (1982): 23–51.

Rasmussen, Jane. *Musical Taste as a Religious Question in Nineteenth Century America*. Lewiston, N.Y.: E. Mellen, 1986.

Reynolds, J. S. *The Evangelicals at Oxford, 1735–1871: A Record of an Unchronicled Movement*. Reprint. Appleford, Abington, and Oxford: Marcham Manor Press, 1975.

Rice, C. Duncan. *The Rise and Fall of Black Slavery*. New York: Harper and Row, 1975.

Rice, Edwin William. *The Sunday School Movement and the American Sunday School Union 1780–1927*. Philadelphia: Union Press, 1919.

Rightmeyer, Nelson W. "The Episcopate of Bishop Kemp of Maryland." *Historical Magazine of the Protestant Episcopal Church* 28 (1959): 66–84.

Rupp, Gordon. *Religion in England, 1688–1791*. Oxford: Oxford University Press, 1986.

Ryan, Edwin. "The Oxford Movement in the United States." *Catholic Historical Review* 19 (1933): 33–49.

Salomon, Richard G. "The Episcopate on the Carey Case: New Sources from the Chase Collection at Kenyon College." *Historical Magazine of the Protestant Episcopal Church* 18 (1949): 240–281.

Sandeen, Ernest R. *The Roots of Fundamentalism: British and American Millennarianism, 1800–1930*. Chicago: University of Chicago Press, 1970.

Saum, Lewis O. *The Popular Mood of Pre-Civil War America*. Westport, Conn.: Greenwood, 1980.

Schermerhorn, William E. *The History of Burlington, New Jersey*. Burlington, N.J.: Enterprise Publishing, 1927.

Schlesinger, Arthur M., Jr. *Age of Jackson*. Boston: Little, Brown, 1946.

Schmidt, Jay H. "Mission to Europe, 1861–62." *Michigan Alumni Quarterly Review* 62 (1956): 311–313.

Schmidt, Leigh Eric. *Holy Fairs: Scottish Communions and American Revivals in the Early Modern Period*. Princeton: Princeton University Press, 1989.

Shoemaker, Robert W. *The Origin and Meaning of the Name "Protestant Episcopal."* New York: American Church Publications, 1959.

Skardon, Alvin W. *Church Leader in the Cities: William Augustus Muhlenberg*. Philadelphia: Temple University Press, 1971.

Slattery, Charles Lewis. *Alexander Veits Griswold Allen, 1841–1908*. New York and London: Longmans, Green, 1911.

Smith, H. Shelton. *Changing Conceptions of Original Sin: A Study in American Theology Since 1750*. New York: Scribner, 1955.

——. *In His Image, But . . . Racism in Southern Religion, 1790–1910*. Durham, N.C.: Duke University Press, 1972.

——. Robert Handy, and Lefferts Leotscher. *American Christianity: An Historical Interpretation with Representative Documents*. Vol. 2. 1820–1960. New York: Scribner, 1963.

Smith, Laura Chase. *The Life of Philander Chase, First Bishop of Ohio and Illinois: Founder of Kenyon and Jubilee Colleges*. New York: Dutton, 1903.

Smith, Timothy. *Revivalism and Social Reform in Mid-Nineteenth Century America*. Nashville: Abington, 1957.

Smith, Timothy L. "The Ohio Valley: Testing Ground for America's Experiment in Religious Pluralism," *Church History* 60 (1991): 461–479.

Smith, Walter George and Helen Grace Smith. *Fidelis of the Cross: James Kent Stone*. New York and London: G.P. Putnam's Sons, 1926.

Smyth, C. E. H. *Simeon and Church Order: A Study of the Origins of the Evangelical Revivals in the 18th Century*. Cambridge: Cambridge University Press, 1940.

Smythe, George Franklin. *A History of the Diocese of Ohio Until the Year 1918*. Cleveland, Diocese of Ohio, 1931.

——. *Kenyon College: Its First Century*. New Haven: Yale University Press, 1924.

Spielmann, Richard M. *Bexley Hall: 150 Years, a Brief History*. Rochester, N.Y.: Colgate Rochester Divinity School, 1974.

Sprague, William B. *Annals of the American Pulpit*. Vol. 5. New York: Robert Carter, 1857.

Stambaugh, B. Z. "The McIlvaine Episcopate." *Historical Magazine of the Protestant Episcopal Church* 6 (1937): 299–307.

Stampp, Kenneth. *America at 1857*. New York: Oxford University Press, 1990.

Staudernraus, P. J. *The African Colonization Movement, 1816–1865*. New York: Columbia University Press, 1961.

Stephenson, Alan M. G. *The First Lambeth Conference, 1867*. London: SPCK, 1967.

Stout, Harry S. *The New England Soul: Preaching and Religious Culture in Colonial New England*. Oxford: Oxford University Press, 1986.

Stowe, Walter H. "A Turning Point: The General Convention of 1835." *Historical Magazine of the Protestant Episcopal Church* 4 (1935): 152–158.

Strong, William E. *The Story of the American Board*. New York: Pilgrim Press, 1910.

Sumner, David E. *The Episcopal Church's History, 1945–1985*. Wilton, Conn.: Morehouse Barlow, 1987.

Swatos, Jr. William H. *Into Denominationalism: The Anglican Metamorphosis*. Monograph Series #2. Storrs, Conn.: Society for the Scientific Study of Religion, 1979.

Sweet, Leonard I. *The Minister's Wife*. Philadelphia: Temple University Press, 1983.

——. " 'A Nation Born Again': The Union Prayer Meeting Revival and Cultural Revitalization." In *In the Great Tradition: In Honor of Winthop S. Hudson*, edited by Joseph D. Ban and Paul Dekar, 193–221. Valley Forge, Pa.: Judson Press, 1982.

Sweet, William W. *Circuit Riders Days Along the Ohio*. New York and Cincinnati: Methodist Book Concern, 1923.

——. *The Rise of Methodism in the West*. New York and Cincinnati: Methodist Book Concern, 1920.

Temple, Sydney A., Jr. *The Common Sense Theology of Bishop White*. New York: King's Crown, 1946.

Thistlewaite, Frank. *The Anglo-American Connection in the Early Nineteenth Century*. Philadelphia: University of Pennsylvania Press, 1959.

Thomas, George M. *Revivalism and Cultural Change: Christianity, Nation Building, and the Market in the Nineteenth-Century United States*. Chicago: University of Chicago Press, 1989.

Toon, Peter. *Evangelical Theology, 1833–1856: A Response to Tractarianism*. Atlanta: John Knox, 1979.

Tracy, Joseph. *The Great Awakening*. Boston, 1842. Reprint. Edinburgh: Banner of Truth, 1976.

Tuckerman, Bayard. *William Jay and the Constitutional Movement for the Abolition of Slavery*. [1893]. New York: Negro University Press, 1969.

Tuveson, Ernest Lee. *Redeemer Nation: The Idea of America's Millennial Role*. Chicago: University of Chicago Press, 1968.

Tyler, Alice Felt. *Freedom's Ferment: Phases of American Social History from the Colonial Period to the Outbreak of the Civil War*. New York: Harper and Row, 1962.

Venable, William H. *Beginnings of Literary Culture in the Ohio Valley*. Cincinnati: R. Clarke, 1891.

——. *A Centennial History of Christ Church, Cincinnati, 1817–1917*. Cincinnati: Stewart and Kidd, 1918.

Voll, Dieter. *Catholic Evangelicalism: The Acceptance of Evangelical Traditions by the Oxford Movement During the Second Half of the Nineteenth Century.* London: Faith Press, 1963.

Wacker, Grant. "The Holy Spirit and the Spirit of the Age in American Protestantism, 1880–1910." *Journal of American History* 72 (1985): 45–62.

Walsh, J. D. "Origins of the Evangelical Revival." In *Essays in Modern English Church History*, edited by G. V. Bennett and J. D. Walsh. London: Black, 1966.

Walworth, Clarence E. *The Oxford Movement in America.* New York, 1895. Reprint. New York: United States Catholic Historical Society, 1974.

Warnock, James. " 'This Year They More Nearly Approached Us Than Ever': A Response of the Protestant Episcopal Church to Jewish Immigration," *Fides et Historia* 22 (1990): 35–48.

Waters, Wilson. *The History of St. Luke's Church, Marietta, Ohio.* Marietta: n. p., 1884.

Weber, Timothy P. *Living in the Shadow of the Second Coming: American Premillennialism 1875–1925.* New York: Oxford University Press, 1979.

Weisberger, Bernard A. *They Gathered at the River: The Story of the Great Revivalists and Their Impact upon Religion in America.* Boston: Little, Brown, 1958.

Weisenberger, Francis P. *Ordeal of Faith: The Crisis of Church-Going America, 1865–1900.* New York: Philosophical Library, 1959.

Welch, Claude. *Protestant Thought in the Nineteenth Century.* Vol. 1. New Haven: Yale University Press, 1972.

Wells, David F., ed., *Reformed Theology in America.* Grand Rapids, Mich.: Eerdmans, 1985.

Welter, Barbara. "The Cult of True Womanhood: 1820–1860," *American Quarterly* 18:2 (1966): 151–174.

Wertenbaker, Thomas J. *Princeton, 1746–1896.* Princeton: Princeton University Press, 1946.

Williams, Peter. "Religion and the Old Northwest: A Bibliographical Essay." *Old Northwest* 5 (1979): 57–73.

Williams, William Henry. *The Garden of American Methodism: The Delmarva Peninsula, 1769–1820.* Wilmington, Del.: Scholarly Resources, 1984.

Wilson, Charles Reagan. *Baptized in Blood: The Religion of the Lost Cause, 1865–1920.* Athens, Ga.: University of Georgia Press, 1980.

Woodbridge, John. *Biblical Authority: A Critique of the Rogers/McKim Proposal.* Grand Rapids, Mich.: Zondervan, 1982.

Woolverton, John F. *Colonial Anglicanism in North America, 1607–1776.* Detroit: Wayne State University Press, 1984.

——. "John Williamson Nevin and the Episcopalians: The Debate on the Church Question, 1851–1874." *Historical Magazine of the Protestant Episcopal Church* 49 (1980): 361–387.

——. "Philadelphia's William White: Episcopalian Distinctiveness and Accommodation in the Post-Revolutionary Period." *Historical Magazine of the Protestant Episcopal Church* 43 (1974): 279–296.

——. "Whither Episcopalianism? A Century of Apologetic Interpretations of the Episcopal Church, 1835–1964." *Anglican Theological Review* Supplementary Series #1 (1973): 140–161.

Wyatt-Brown, Bertram. *Lewis Tappan and the Evangelical War Against Slavery.* Cleveland: Case Western Reserve University Press, 1969.

Zabriskie, Alexander C., "Rise and Major Characteristics of the Anglican Evangelical Movement." In *Anglican Evangelicalism*, Philadelphia: Church Historical Society, 1943.

Dissertations and Theses

Brickley, Charles, N. "The Episcopal Church in Protestant America, 1800–1860." Ph.D. diss., Clark University, 1950.

Clebsch, William A. "The Rev. Dr. William Holland Wilmer (1782–1827): His Life, Work, and Thought." S.T.M. thesis, Virginia Theological Seminary, 1951.

Davis, Edward Bradford. "Albert Barnes 1798–1870: An Exponent of New School Presbyterianism." Th.D. diss., Princeton Theological Seminary, 1961.

Francis, Russell. "Pentecost: 1858, a Study in Religious Revivalism." Ph.D. diss., University of Pennsylvania, 1948.

Gay, Ralph Gerald. "A Study of the American Liturgical Revival, 1825–1860." Ph.D. diss., Emory University, 1977.

Malone, Michael T. "Levi Silliman Ives: Priest, Bishop, Tractarian and Roman Catholic Convert." Ph.D. diss., Duke University, 1970.

McGraw, Marie Tyler. "The American Colonialization Society in Virginia, 1816–1832: A Case Study in Southern Liberalism." Ph.D. diss., George Washington University, 1980.

Prichard, Robert Walton. "Theological Consensus in the Episcopal Church, 1801–1873." Ph.D. diss., Emory University, 1983.

Pugh, Loren Dale. "Bishop Charles Pettit McIlvaine: The Faithful Evangel." Ph.D. diss., Duke University, 1985.

Slocum, Stephen E. "The American Tract Society: 1825–1975. An Evangelical Effort to Influence the Religious and Moral Life of the United States." Ph.D. diss., New York University, 1975.

Spicer, Carl L. "The Great Awakening of 1857 and 1858." Ph.D. diss., Ohio State University, 1935.

Stevens, Ann Heathcote. "The Unofficial Commission to England in 1861." M.A. thesis, Occidental College, 1937.

Trendel, Robert A. "William Jay: Churchman, Public Servant and Reformer." Ph.D. diss., Southern Illinois University, 1972.

Walsh, J. D. "The Yorkshire Evangelicals in the Eighteenth Century, with Special Reference to Methodism." Ph.D. diss., Cambridge University Press, 1956.

Index